Airframe Mechanic

2023 Test Guide

Study and prepare for your aviation mechanic FAA Knowledge Exam

AVIATION SUPPLIES & ACADEMICS, INC.
NEWCASTLE, WASHINGTON

The FAA Knowledge Exam Questions can change throughout the year. Stay current with test changes; sign up for ASA's free email update service at **asa2fly.com/testupdate**

Airframe Mechanic Test Guide
2023 Edition

Aviation Supplies & Academics, Inc.
7005 132nd Place SE
Newcastle, Washington 98059
asa@asa2fly.com | 425.235.1500 | asa2fly.com

Visit **asa2fly.com/AMA** for additional information and resources related to this book.

Cover photo: iStock.com/Ziviani

ASA-AMA-23
ISBN 978-1-64425-233-8

Additional format available:
eBook PDF ISBN 978-1-64425-234-5

Also sold as *Airframe Mechanic Test Guide Plus*, which includes this book plus Prepware software.
ASA-TPP-AMA-23, ISBN 978-1-64425-251-2

Printed in the United States of America
2023 2022 5 4 3 2 1

Aviation Supplies & Academics, Inc. (ASA) is an industry leader in the development and sale of aviation supplies and publications for pilots, flight instructors, aviation maintenance technicians, aircraft dispatchers, air traffic controllers, flight attendants, and drone operators. We manufacture and publish more than 1,000 products and have been providing trusted and reliable training materials to the aviation industry for over 80 years. Visit **asa2fly.com** to learn more.

Contents

Updates and Practice Tests

Free Test Updates for the One-Year Life Cycle of Test Guide Books

The FAA modifies tests as needed throughout the year. ASA keeps abreast of changes to the tests and posts free Test Updates on the ASA website. Before taking your test, be certain you have the most current information by visiting the ASA Test Updates webpage: **asa2fly.com/testupdate**. Additionally, sign up for free email notifications, which are sent when new Test Updates are available.

We Invite Your Feedback

After you take your FAA exam, let us know how you did. Were you prepared? Did ASA's products meet your needs and exceed your expectations? We want to continue to improve these products to ensure applicants are prepared and become safe aviators. Send your feedback to: **cfi@asa2fly.com**.

Introduction

Welcome to the Aviation Supplies & Academics, Inc., (ASA) Test Guide Series, based on the original Fast-Track series written by Dale Crane. This series has been helping aviation mechanics prepare for FAA Knowledge Exams with great success for more than 60 years. We are confident that with the proper use of this book you will score very well on your FAA Knowledge Exam. Additionally, the ASA Test Guides include typical oral test questions and practical projects to help you prepare for the final step in the Aviation Mechanic certification process.

Begin your studies with an instructor-led or home-study ground school course, which will involve reading a comprehensive textbook for aviation maintenance technicians (AMTs). Once complete, visit the Reader Resources for this Test Guide (**asa2fly.com/AMA**) and become familiar with the FAA guidance material available for this certification exam. Then use this Test Guide to prepare for your exam: Read the question, select your choice for the correct answer, and then read the explanation. Use the references that accompany the correct answer at the bottom of each page to identify additional resources for further study. Upon completion of your studies, take practice tests at **prepware.com** (see inside the front cover for your activation code).

Prior to taking an FAA Airman Knowledge Test, all applicants must establish an FAA Tracking Number (FTN) by creating a profile in the Integrated Airman Certification and Rating Application (IACRA) system at **iacra.faa.gov**. Then visit **faa.psiexams.com** to register for your exam and take FAA-created practice tests to become familiar with the computer testing platform.

The FAA exams are "closed tests" which means the exact database of questions is not available to the public. The question and answer choices in this book are based on our extensive history and experience with the FAA testing process as well as the FAA's publicly available information. You might see similarly worded questions on your official FAA exam and answer stems may be rearranged from the A, B, C order you see in this book. Therefore, be sure to fully understand the intent of each question and corresponding answer while studying, rather than memorizing the letter associated with the correct response. Studying and understanding the information in this book and the associated references will give you the tools to answer question variations with confidence.

If your study leads you to question an answer choice, we recommend you seek the assistance of a local instructor. We welcome your questions, recommendations or concerns—send them to:

Aviation Supplies & Academics, Inc.
7005 132nd Place SE
Newcastle, WA 98059-3153
Email: cfi@asa2fly.com
Voice: 425-235-1500
Fax: 425-235-0128
Website: asa2fly.com

The FAA appreciates testing experience feedback. Contact them at:

Federal Aviation Administration
AFS-630, Airman Testing Standards Branch
PO Box 25082
Oklahoma City, OK 73125
Email: afs630comments@faa.gov

Instructions

The general qualifications for an Aviation Mechanic certificate require you to have a combination of experience, knowledge, and skill. If you are pursuing an Aviation Mechanic certificate with Airframe and Powerplant ratings, you should review the appropriate sections of 14 CFR Part 65 for detailed information pertaining to eligibility requirements. Further information may be obtained from **faa.gov/mechanics**.

The table below lists the number of questions, allotted testing time, and required passing score for each aviation mechanic knowledge exam, as well as the Test Code you'll use to register for your test.

Test Code	Test Name	Number of Questions	Min. Age	Allotted Time (hrs)	Passing Score
AMA	Aviation Mechanic—Airframe	100	N/A	2.0	70
AMG	Aviation Mechanic—General	60	N/A	2.0	70
AMP	Aviation Mechanic—Powerplant	100	N/A	2.0	70

Description of the Knowledge Test

All test questions are objective multiple-choice and can be answered by the selection of a single response. Each test question is independent of other questions; therefore, a correct response to one does not depend upon, or influence, the correct response to another. Considerable effort is expended to write each question in a clear, precise manner. Make sure you read the instructions given with the test, as well as the statements in each test item. When taking a test, keep the following points in mind:

1. Answer each question in accordance with the latest regulations and guidance publications.
2. Read each question carefully before looking at the possible answers. You should clearly understand the problem before attempting to solve it.
3. After formulating an answer, determine which choice corresponds with that answer. The answer chosen should completely resolve the problem.
4. From the answers given, it may appear that there is more than one possible answer; however, there is only one answer that is correct and complete. The other answers are either incomplete, erroneous, or represent common misconceptions.
5. If a certain question is difficult for you, mark it for review and proceed to the next question. After you answer the less difficult questions, return to those you marked for review and answer them. The review marking procedure will be explained to you prior to starting the test. Although the computer should alert you to unanswered questions, make sure every question has an answer recorded. This procedure will enable you to use the available time to maximum advantage.
6. When solving a calculation problem, select the answer closest to your solution. The problem has been checked several times by various individuals; therefore, if you have solved it correctly, your answer will be closer to the correct answer than any of the other choices.

Your test will be graded immediately upon completion and your score will display on the computer screen.

Knowledge Test Eligibility Requirements

Before taking the certification knowledge and practical tests, you must meet the eligibility requirements for authorization. Applicants may present one or more of the following acceptable forms of authorization:

- Original FAA Form 8610-2, Airman Certificate and/or Rating Application. The proctor will verify that applicable blocks are marked (in upper left corner of form). Those not applicable will have a line drawn through them (identifying Airframe and/or Powerplant).
- Certificate of graduation or completion from an FAA-certificated Aviation Maintenance Technician School (AMTS).
- Military Certificate of Eligibility.

Learn more about the FAA's test authorization requirement by reviewing 14 CFR Parts 65 and 141 and the FAA Airman Knowledge Testing Authorization Requirements matrix posted in the reader resources at **asa2fly.com/AMA**.

Taking the Knowledge Test

The FAA testing provider authorizes hundreds of test center locations that offer a full range of airman knowledge tests. For information on authorized testing centers and to register for the knowledge test, visit **faa.psiexams.com**.

When you contact a knowledge testing center, be prepared to select a test date and make a payment. You may register for test(s) several weeks in advance online or with a telephone call, and you may cancel in accordance with the testing center's cancellation policy. Regardless of your registration method, you will need an FAA Tracking Number (FTN). This FTN will follow you throughout your aviation career. You will obtain your FTN by creating a profile in the Integrated Airman Certificate and Rating Application (IACRA) system at **iacra.faa.gov**. This FTN will be printed on your Airman Knowledge Test Report (AKTR).

For more information, contact:
PSI Services LLC
844-704-1487 or examschedule@psionline.com
faa.psiexams.com

On the day of the Airman Knowledge Test the applicant must provide the following information to be collected in order to complete the registration process at the testing center prior to the test proctor administering the Airman Knowledge Test: name, FAA Tracking Number (FTN), physical address, date of birth, email address, photo identification, phone number, test authorization (credentials of the individual such as an instructor endorsement), and previous number of test attempts. The **faa.psiexams.com** website, your instructor, or local FAA office can assist you with what documentation to take to the testing facility. Testing center personnel will not begin the test until your identification is verified. Acceptable forms of authorization are:

- FAA Form 8610-2.
- A graduation certificate or certificate of completion from an affiliated testing center.
- A failed, passing, or expired AKTR.

Upon completion of your test, you will receive your AKTR which will state your score. Visit **faa.psiexams.com** to request a duplicate or replacement Airman Test Report due to loss or destruction. The AKTR must be presented to the examiner prior to taking the Oral and Practical Exam. During the oral portion of the test, the examiner is required to evaluate the noted areas of deficiency.

Retesting Procedure

Retests do not require a 30-day waiting period if the applicant presents a signed statement from an airman holding the certificate and rating sought by the applicant. This statement must certify that the airman has given the applicant additional instruction in each of the subjects failed, and that the airman considers the applicant ready for retesting. A 30-day waiting period is required for retesting if the applicant presents a failed airman knowledge test report, but no authorized instructor endorsement.

Applicants taking retests ***after failure*** are required to submit the applicable test report indicating failure to the testing center prior to retesting. The original failed test report shall be retained by the proctor and attached to the applicable sign-in/out log. The latest test taken will reflect the official score.

Applicants retesting ***in an attempt to achieve a higher passing score*** may retake the same test for a better grade after 30 days. The latest test taken will reflect the official score. Applicants are required to submit the ***original*** applicable test report indicating previous passing score to the testing center prior to testing. Testing center personnel must collect and destroy this report prior to issuing the new test report.

Use of Test Aids and Materials

Airman knowledge tests require applicants to analyze the relationship between variables needed to solve aviation problems, in addition to testing for accuracy of a mathematical calculation. The intent is that all applicants are tested on concepts rather than rote calculation ability. It is permissible to use certain calculating devices when taking airman knowledge tests, provided they are used within the following guidelines. The term "calculating devices" is interchangeable with such items as calculators, computers, or any similar devices designed for aviation-related activities.

1. Guidelines for use of test aids and materials. The applicant may use test aids and materials within the guidelines listed below, if actual test questions or answers are not revealed.
    a. Applicants may use test aids, such as a calculating device that is directly related to the test. In addition, applicants may use any test materials provided with the test.
    b. The test proctor may provide a calculating device to applicants and deny them use of their personal calculating device if the applicant's device does not have a screen that indicates all memory has been erased. The test proctor must be able to determine the calculating device's erasure capability. The use of calculating devices incorporating permanent or continuous type memory circuits without erasure capability is prohibited.
    c. The use of magnetic cards, magnetic tapes, modules, computer chips, or any other device upon which prewritten programs or information related to the test can be stored and retrieved is prohibited. Printouts of data will be surrendered at the completion of the test if the calculating device used incorporates this design feature.
    d. The use of any booklet or manual containing instructions related to the use of the applicant's calculating device is not permitted.
    e. Dictionaries are not allowed in the testing area.
    f. The test proctor makes the final determination relating to test materials and personal possessions that the applicant may take into the testing area.
2. Guidelines for applicant's with learning or reading disabilities. An applicant with a learning or reading disability may request approval from the local Flight Standards Office to take an airman knowledge test using one of the following options listed in preferential order:

    (1) The applicant may request up to 1½ times the standard time allotted to complete the knowledge test.

    (2) The applicant may use a self-contained electronic device which pronounces and displays typed-in words (e.g., the Franklin Speaking Wordmaster®) to facilitate the testing process. The applicant must provide his or her own device, with approval of the device to be determined by the administrator. Note: The device should consist of an electronic thesaurus that audibly pronounces typed-in words and presents them on a display screen. The device should also have a built-in headphone jack for private listening in order to avoid disturbing others during testing.

Cheating or Other Unauthorized Conduct

Computer testing centers are required to follow strict security procedures to avoid test compromise. These procedures are established by the FAA and are covered in FAA Order 8080.6, Conduct of Airman Knowledge Tests. The FAA has directed testing centers to terminate a test at any time a test proctor suspects a cheating incident has occurred. An FAA investigation will then be conducted. If the investigation determines that cheating or other unauthorized conduct has occurred, then any airman certificate or rating that you hold may be revoked, and you will be prohibited for 1 year from applying for or taking any test for a certificate or rating under 14 CFR Part 65.

Validity of Airman Test Reports

Airman Knowledge Test Reports are valid for the 24-calendar month period preceding the month you complete the practical test. If the Airman Test Report expires before completion of the practical test, you must retake the knowledge test.

Learning Statement Codes

The expression *learning statement* refers to measurable statements about the knowledge a student should be able to demonstrate following a certain segment of training.

Your AKTR will list the Learning Statement Codes (LSCs) for questions you have answered incorrectly. Match the codes given on your test report to the ones listed below. Your instructor can provide instruction on each of the areas of deficiency listed on your AKTR to help you prepare for your Oral and Practical Exam. The AKTR must be presented to the examiner conducting your Oral and Practical Exam. During the oral portion of the test, the examiner will evaluate the noted areas of deficiency.

Learning Statement Codes are prefixed with a letter-identifier (for example, AMA031). For the purposes of reference within this ASA Test Guide, the letter prefix is omitted; therefore throughout this book, LSCs are referred to by their number-identifiers only, in parentheses.

LSC	Subject area
AMA001	Recall aerodynamic fundamentals
AMA002	Recall air conditioning system —components/operating principles/characteristics
AMA003	Recall aircraft component markings
AMA004	Recall aircraft components material—flame resistant
AMA005	Recall aircraft cooling system —charging/leaking/oil/ pressure / water
AMA006	Recall aircraft cooling system —components/operating principles/characteristics
AMA007	Recall aircraft corrosion —principles/control/prevention
AMA008	Recall aircraft engines—indicating system
AMA009	Recall aircraft exterior lighting—systems/components
AMA010	Recall aircraft flight indicator system
AMA011	Recall aircraft hardware—bolts/nuts/fasteners/fittings/valves
AMA012	Recall aircraft heating system—exhaust jacket inspection
AMA013	Recall aircraft instruments—install/inspect/adjust/repair/markings
AMA014	Recall aircraft instruments—types/components/operating principles/characteristics
AMA015	Recall aircraft lighting—install/inspect/repair/service
AMA016	Recall aircraft metals—inspect/test/repair/identify
AMA017	Recall aircraft metals —types/tools/fasteners
AMA018	Recall aircraft warning systems —navigation/stall/takeoff
AMA019	Recall airframe—inspections
AMA020	Recall airframe—repair/component installation
AMA021	Recall airframe design—structures/components
AMA022	Recall alternators—components/operating principles/characteristics
AMA023	Recall antenna system—install/inspect/repair/service
AMA024	Recall anti-icing/deicing—methods/systems
AMA025	Recall autopilot—components/operating principles/characteristics
AMA026	Recall autopilot—install/inspect/repair/service
AMA027	Recall avionics—components/operating principles/characteristics
AMA028	Recall avionics—install/inspect/repair/service
AMA029	Recall basic hand tools/torque values
AMA030	Recall batteries—capacity/charging/types/storage/rating/precautions
AMA031	Recall brake system—components/operating principles/characteristics
AMA032	Recall brake system—install/inspect/repair/service
AMA033	Recall carburetor—icing/anti-icing

LSC	Subject area
AMA034	Recall chemical rain repellant
AMA035	Recall combustion heaters—components/operating principles/characteristics
AMA036	Recall compass—components/operating principles/characteristics
AMA037	Recall composite materials—types/repairs/techniques/processes
AMA038	Recall control cables—install/inspect/repair/service
AMA039	Recall DC electric motors—components/operating principles/characteristics
AMA040	Recall dope and fabric—materials/techniques/hazards
AMA041	Recall electrical system—components/operating principles/characteristics/symbols
AMA042	Recall electrical system—install/inspect/repair/service
AMA043	Recall electronic test equipment
AMA044	Recall Emergency Locator Transmitter (ELT)—operation/battery/testing
AMA045	Recall fiberglass—install/troubleshoot/service/repair
AMA046	Recall fire detection system—types/components/operating principles/characteristics
AMA047	Recall fire detection systems—install/inspect/repair/service
AMA048	Recall fire extinguishing systems—components/operating principles/characteristics
AMA049	Recall flap overload valve
AMA050	Recall flight characteristics—longitudinal stability/instability
AMA051	Recall fluid lines—material/coding
AMA052	Recall fuel—types/characteristics/contamination/fueling/defueling/dumping
AMA053	Recall fuel/oil—anti-icing/deicing
AMA054	Recall fuel system—components/operating principles/characteristics
AMA055	Recall fuel system—install/troubleshoot/service/repair
AMA056	Recall fuel system—types
AMA057	Recall fuel/air mixture—idle rich mixture—RPM rise
AMA058	Recall fundamental material properties
AMA059	Recall fuselage stations
AMA060	Recall helicopter control system
AMA061	Recall helicopter control system—collective
AMA062	Recall helicopter drive system—free wheeling unit
AMA063	Recall hydraulic systems—components/operating principles/characteristics
AMA064	Recall hydraulic systems—fluids
AMA065	Recall hydraulic systems—install/inspect/repair/service
AMA066	Recall instrument panel installation—shock mounts
AMA067	Recall instruments—manifold pressure indicating system
AMA068	Recall landing gear system—components/operating principles/characteristics
AMA069	Recall landing gear system—install/inspect/repair/service
AMA070	Recall maintenance publications—service/parts/repair
AMA071	Recall navigation/communication systems—types/operational characteristics
AMA072	Recall oxygen system—components/operating principles/characteristics
AMA073	Recall oxygen system—install/inspect/repair/service/precautions
AMA074	Recall oxygen system—quality/types/contamination/cylinders/pressure
AMA075	Recall physics—work forces
AMA076	Recall pitot-static system—components/operating principles/characteristics
AMA077	Recall pitot-static system—install/inspect/repair/service

LSC	Subject area
AMA078	Recall plastic fundamentals—installation/cleaning/repair/characteristics
AMA079	Recall pneumatic system—components/operating principles/characteristics
AMA080	Recall pressurization system—components/operating principles/characteristics
AMA081	Recall primary flight controls—inspect/adjust/repair
AMA082	Recall primary flight controls—types/purpose/functionality
AMA083	Recall radar altimeter—indications
AMA084	Recall radar altimeter—signals
AMA085	Recall radio system—components/operating principles/characteristics
AMA086	Recall radio system—install/inspect/repair/service
AMA087	Recall radio system—license requirements/frequencies
AMA088	Recall regulations—airworthiness requirements/responsibilities
AMA089	Recall regulations—maintenance reports/records/entries
AMA090	Recall regulations—privileges/limitations of maintenance certificates/licenses
AMA091	Recall rotor system—components/operating principles/characteristics
AMA092	Recall secondary flight control system—inspect/adjust/repair
AMA093	Recall secondary flight control system—types/purpose/functionality
AMA094	Recall sheet metal fabrication—blueprints/shaping/construction
AMA095	Recall smoke detection systems—types/components/operating principles/characteristics
AMA096	Recall static pressure system—install/inspect/repair/service
AMA097	Recall tires—install/inspect/repair/service/storage
AMA098	Recall turbine engines—components/operational characteristics/associated instruments
AMA099	Recall type certificate data sheet (TCDS)/supplemental type certificate (STC)
AMA100	Recall weight and balance—equipment installation/CG/general principles
AMA101	Recall welding/soldering—types/techniques/equipment
AMA102	Recall wooden components—failures/decay/patching/gluing/substitutions

Knowledge Exam References

The FAA references the following documents to write the FAA Knowledge Exam questions. You should be familiar with all of these as part of your classroom studies, which you should complete before starting test preparation:

FAA-H-8083-30	*Aviation Maintenance Technician Handbook—General* (FAA)
FAA-H-8083-31, Vol. 1 & 2	*Aviation Maintenance Technician Handbook—Airframe* (FAA)
FAA-H-8083-32, Vol. 1 & 2	*Aviation Maintenance Technician Handbook—Powerplant* (FAA)
FAA-H-8083-3	*Airplane Flying Handbook* (FAA)
FAA-G-8082-11	*Inspection Authorization Test Guide* (FAA)

14 CFR Parts 1, 3, 21, 23, 39, 43, 45, 47, 65, 91, 147

Advisory Circulars (AC) 21-12, 23-21, 23.1309-1, 43.9-1, 43.13-1

Additional resources helpful for AMT studies:

AMT-G	*Aviation Mechanic Series: General* (ASA)
AMT-STRUC	*Aviation Mechanic Series: Airframe Structures* (ASA)
AMT-SYS	*Aviation Mechanic Series: Airframe Systems* (ASA)
AMT-P	*Aviation Mechanic Series: Powerplant* (ASA)
DAT	*Dictionary of Aeronautical Terms* (ASA)
AIM	*Aeronautical Information Manual* (FAA)

Acronyms

For reference, acronyms appearing in this book are defined below.

AC	alternating current
AD	Airworthiness Directive
AD (rivet)	aluminum alloy 2117 rivet
ADF	automatic direction finder
AFM	airplane flight manual
AGL	above ground level (altitude)
AMS	Aerospace Material Specification
AN	Army-Navy (specification standard)
ATC	air traffic control
AWG	American Wire Gauge
BTU	British thermal unit
CDS	copilot's display system
CG	center of gravity
CO_2	carbon dioxide
CRT	cathode-ray tube
CSD	constant speed drive
DC	direct current
DME	distance measuring equipment
DOT	Department of Transportation
DPST	double-pole, single-throw (switch)
EFIS	electronic flight instrument system
ELT	emergency locator transmitter
EMF	electromotive force
FCC	Federal Communications Commission
FMC	flight management computer
GCU	generator control unit
GPWS	ground proximity warning system
GTA	gas tungsten arc (welding)
HSI	horizontal situation indicator
HRD	high-rate discharge
IA	Inspection Authorization
IDG	integrated drive generator
ILS	instrument landing system
MEK	methyl ethyl ketone
mph	miles per hour
MS	military specification (standard)
MSL	mean sea level (altitude)
NO	normally open (switch)
PDS	pilot's display system
PMA	Parts Manufacturer Approval
psi	pounds per square inch
psig	pounds per square inch gauge (gauge pressure)
RPM	rotations per minute
SES	Society of Electrical Specifications
SG	symbol generator
SPDT	single-pole, double-throw (switch)
SPST	single-pole, single-throw
STC	Supplemental Type Certificate
TCAS	traffic collision avoidance system
TCDS	Type Certificate Data Sheet
TSO	Technical Standard Order
VD	voltage drop
VHF	Very High Frequency
VOR	Very-High-Frequency Omni Range
WX	weather radar

Airframe Test Questions, Explanations, Answers, and References

Answers are printed at the bottom of the page, with other coded items as explained below:

This is the question number.

The brackets enclose the letter answer selected by ASA's researchers. (For those questions for which none of the answer choices provide an accurate response, we have noted [X] as the Answer.)

8001 [B] (102) AMT-STRUC, 3

The parentheses enclose the appropriate Learning Statement Code (LSC)—refer to Pages x–xii. FAA Learning Statement Codes have letter-identifying prefixes, but for reference purposes in this book the letter prefix ("AMA") is omitted and only the number-identifying portion of the code is shown in parentheses.

The reference following the Learning Statement Code is the source from which the answer was derived. The meanings of these abbreviations are found on Page xiii. The number following the abbreviations is the specific chapter within that source to study for more information about the derived answer.

Wood Structures

8001. Laminated wood spars may be substituted for solid rectangular wood spars

A—only in certain instances where the primary load is shared by one or more other original structural member.
B—if the same quality wood is used in both.
C—only upon specific approval by the manufacturer or the FAA.

Laminated wood spars may be substituted for solid rectangular wood spars if the same quality of wood is used in both.

8002. The strength of a well-designed and properly prepared wood splice joint is provided by the

A—bearing surface of the wood fibers.
B—glue.
C—reinforcement plates.

The strength of a well-designed and properly prepared wood splice is provided completely by the glue.

No other type of load-carrying fastener is used in a glued joint.

8003. Where is information found concerning acceptable species substitutions for wood materials used in aircraft repair?

A—AC 43.13-1B.
B—Aircraft Specifications or Type Certificate Data Sheets.
C—Technical Standard Orders.

The list of acceptable species of wood materials used in aircraft structure is found in Table 1.1 of AC 43.13-1B.

8004. In cases of elongated bolt holes in a wood spar or cracks in the vicinity of boltholes,

A—it is permissible to ream the hole, plug with hardwood, and redrill.
B—the spar may be reinforced by using hardwood reinforcing plates.
C—a new section of spar should be spliced in or the spar replaced entirely.

The only repair that is approved for an elongated bolt hole in a wood aircraft wing spar is to cut out the section of the spar that contains the damage and splice in a new section.

8005. A faint line running across the grain of a wood spar generally indicates

A—compression failure.
B—shear failure.
C—decay.

A compression failure in a piece of wood is identified by a faint line running across the grain of the wood.

8005-1. Any wooden member that has been overstressed is subject to which type of failure?

A—Stretch.
B—Compression.
C—Torsion.

Compression failure of a wood structure can take place when that wood structure is overstressed.

8006. Which statement about wood decay is correct?

A—Decay that occurs before the wood is seasoned does not affect the strength of the finished piece.
B—A limited amount of certain kinds of decay is acceptable in aircraft woods since decay affects the binding between the fibers and not the fibers themselves.
C—Decay is not acceptable in any form or amount.

When inspecting a wooden aircraft structure, examine all stains and discolorations carefully to determine whether or not they are harmless or in a stage of preliminary or advanced decay. All pieces must be free from rot, dote, red heart, purple heart, and all other forms of decay.

8006-1. Which statement concerning wood decay is correct?

A—Decay that appears to be mineral streaks is acceptable.
B—A limited amount of decay along the beveled edges of unrouted beams is acceptable.
C—Any form or amount of decay is not permitted.

When inspecting a wooden aircraft structure, examine all stains and discolorations carefully to determine whether or not they are harmless or in a stage of preliminary or advanced decay. All pieces must be free from rot, dote, red heart, purple heart, and all other forms of decay.

Note: All Learning Statement Codes (in parentheses) are preceded by "AMA." See explanation on Page 1.

Answers *Note: AMT-STRUC references are given for the pertinent chapter numbers in that book.*

8001 [B] (102) AMT-STRUC, 3	8002 [B] (102) AC 43.13-1	8003 [A] (102) AC 43.13-1	8004 [C] (102) AC 43.13-1
8005 [A] (102) AC 43.13-1	8005-1 [B] (102) AC 43.13-1	8006 [C] (102) AC 43.13-1	8006-1 [C] (102) AC 43.13-1

8007. Which of the following conditions will determine acceptance of wood with mineral streaks?

A—Careful inspection fails to reveal any decay.
B—They produce only a small effect on grain direction.
C—Local irregularities do not exceed limitations specified for spiral and diagonal grain.

Wood having mineral streaks is acceptable for aircraft structure, provided careful inspection does not reveal any decay.

Mineral streaks have no effect on the direction of the grain in the wood.

8008. The I-beam wooden spar is routed to

A—increase strength.
B—obtain uniform strength.
C—reduce weight.

A wooden I-beam wing spar is routed to reduce its weight.

The material removed is in the web of the spar, and there is very little strength lost by removing this material.

8009. Pin knot clusters are permitted in wood aircraft structure provided

A—they produce a small effect on grain direction.
B—they have no mineral streaks.
C—no pitch pockets are within 12 inches.

Pin knot clusters in a piece of aircraft structural wood are permitted if they are small clusters and produce only a small effect on grain direction.

8010. The cantilever wing uses

A—external struts or wire bracing.
B—no external bracing.
C—the skin to carry most of the load to the wing butt.

A cantilever wing has all its strength inside its structure. The wing spars are built in such a way that they carry all the bending and torsional loads.

A cantilever wing uses no external bracing.

8011. Laminated wood is sometimes used in the construction of highly stressed aircraft components. This wood can be identified by its

A—parallel grain construction.
B—similarity to standard plywood construction.
C—perpendicular grain construction.

Laminated wood is made up of a number of pieces of wood glued together with the grain of all the pieces running in the same direction (parallel to each other).

Plywood is also made up of layers of wood, but the grain of each alternate layer runs at an angle to the ones next to it.

8012. When patching a plywood skin, abrupt changes in cross-sectional areas which will develop dangerous stress concentration should be avoided by using

A—circular or elliptical patches.
B—square patches.
C—doublers with any desired shaped patches.

Circular or elliptical patches are used when patching aircraft plywood skin to prevent abrupt changes in the cross-sectional area of the skin.

If a rectangular or triangular patch is used, the corners must have ample radii.

8013. Glue deterioration in wood aircraft structure is indicated

A—when a joint has separated and the glue surface shows only the imprint of the wood with no wood fibers clinging to the glue.
B—when a joint has separated and the glue surface shows pieces of wood and/or wood fibers clinging to the glue.
C—by any joint separation.

A satisfactory glue joint has the strength of the wood. When a glue joint fails, the wood fibers should separate before the glue fails.

If the joint separates with no wood fibers clinging to the glue, the glue has deteriorated.

8014. Compression failures in wood aircraft structures are characterized by buckling of the fibers that appear as streaks on the surface

A—at right angles to the growth rings.
B—parallel to the grain.
C—at right angles to the grain.

Compression failure in aircraft structural wood is characterized by a streak on the surface of the wood at right angles to the grain.

Answers

8007 [A] (102) AC 43.13-1	8008 [C] (021) AMT-STRUC, 3	8009 [A] (102) AC 43.13-1	8010 [B] (021) AMT-STRUC
8011 [A] (102) AMT-STRUC, 3	8012 [A] (102) AMT-STRUC, 3	8013 [A] (102) AMT-STRUC, 3	8014 [C] (102) AC 43.13-1

Aircraft Covering

8015. When and how is finishing tape applied on a fabric-covered aircraft?

A—Sewed or laced on before dope is applied.
B—Doped on immediately prior to the finish coat.
C—Doped on after the first or second coat of dope.

Finishing tape (surface tape) is applied to the wing surface with dope and is usually stuck down after the first or the second coat of dope has been applied.

8016. The determining factor(s) for the selection of the correct weight of textile fabric to be used in covering any type of aircraft is the

A—maximum wing loading.
B—speed of the aircraft.
C—speed of the aircraft and the maximum wing loading.

The weight of the fabric approved for use on an aircraft structure is determined by the never-exceed speed of the aircraft and by its maximum wing loading.

8017. How many fabric thicknesses will be found in a French-fell seam?

A—Five.
B—Three.
C—Four.

In a French-fell, machine-sewed seam used to join aircraft fabric, the edges of the fabric are folded over each other so the threads of the double row of stitches passes through four thicknesses of fabric.

8018. Finishing tape (surface tape) is used for what purpose?

A—To help prevent "ripple formation" in covering fabric.
B—To provide additional wear resistance over the edges of fabric forming structures.
C—To provide additional anti-tear resistance under reinforcement tape.

Surface tape, or finishing tape, should be placed over all lacing, seams, (both machine- and hand-sewn), corners, edges, and places where wear is likely to occur.

8019. Moisture, mildew, chemicals, and acids have no effect on

A—glass fabric.
B—cotton fabric.
C—polyester fabric.

Glass cloth used as an aircraft structural material is not affected by moisture, mildew, chemicals, or acids. It is also fire resistant.

8019-1. Fungicide and mildewicide additives are important for fabric covered aircraft, such as

A—cotton and dacron.
B—cotton and linen.
C—glass and linen.

Since cotton and linen are both natural fibers they are susceptible to mildew and fungal growth. To prevent the fabric from being weakened or destroyed, a fungicide must be mixed with the first coat of fabric dope. This mixture must completely saturate the fabric so all the fibers are completely encapsulated.

8020. The best method of repair for a fabric-covered surface which has an L-shaped tear, each leg of which is approximately 14 inches long, is to

A—re-cover the entire bay in which the tear is located.
B—sew from the end of each leg to the center of the tear with a baseball stitch and then dope on a patch.
C—sew with a baseball stitch from the center of the tear out toward the extremity of each leg and then dope on a patch.

When making a repair to an L-shaped tear in aircraft fabric, use a curved needle and well-waxed thread.

Start at the apex (center) of the tear and make baseball stitches every quarter inch to the end of the tear.

After both sides of the tear have been stitched, remove the colored and silver dopes by softening them with dope thinner or acetone.

Dope on a patch that extends at least 1-1/2 inches beyond all edges of the tear.

8021. The strength classification of fabrics used in aircraft covering is based on

A—bearing strength.
B—shear strength.
C—tensile strength.

The strength of aircraft covering fabric is based on its tensile strength.

Answers

8015 [C] (040) AC 43.13-1	8016 [C] (040) AMT-STRUC, 3	8017 [C] (040) AC 43.13-1	8018 [B] (040) AMT-STRUC, 3
8019 [A] (040) AMT-STRUC, 3	8019-1 [B] (040) AMT-STRUC, 3	8020 [C] (040) AMT-STRUC, 3	8021 [C] (040) AMT-STRUC, 3

8022. Fabric rejuvenator is used to

A—restore the condition of dope coatings.
B—restore fabric strength and tautness to at least the minimum acceptable level.
C—penetrate the fabric and restore fungicidal resistance.

Rejuvenator is a dopelike finishing material that has powerful solvents and plasticizers.

When a doped surface has aged and cracked, its resilience can be restored with rejuvenator. Rejuvenation does nothing to restore strength to deteriorated fabric.

8023. Machine-sewn seams in aircraft covering fabrics may be which of the following types?

A—Folded-fell or plain lapped.
B—Folded-fell, French-fell, or plain lapped.
C—French-fell or plain lapped.

Machine-sewn seams in aircraft coverings may be of the folded-fell or French-fell type.

A plain lapped seam is satisfactory where selvage edges or pinked edges are joined.

8024. When testing the strength of Grade A cotton fabric covering an aircraft that requires only intermediate grade, the minimum acceptable strength the fabric must have is

A—70 percent of its original strength.
B—70 percent of the original strength for intermediate fabric.
C—56 pounds per inch warp and fill.

Aircraft fabric is allowed to deteriorate to 70 percent of its required strength. When an airplane requiring intermediate fabric, whose new tensile strength is 65 pounds per inch, is covered with Grade A fabric whose new strength is 80 pounds per inch, the fabric can deteriorate to 70 percent of the strength of new intermediate fabric, or 46 pounds per inch, before it must be replaced.

8025. When dope-proofing the parts of the aircraft structure that come in contact with doped fabric, which of the following provide an acceptable protective coating?

A—Resin impregnated cloth tape and cellulose tape.
B—Aluminum foil and resin impregnated cloth tape.
C—Aluminum foil and cellulose tape.

Dope proofing a structure is done by covering all the parts that will come in contact with doped fabric with a protective coating such as aluminum foil or cellulose tape.

Aircraft Finishes

8026. If registration numbers are to be applied to an aircraft with a letter height of 12 inches, what is the minimum space required for the registration mark N1683C?

Note:
2/3 × height = character width.
1/6 × height = width for 1.
1/4 × 2/3 height = spacing.
1/6 × height = stroke or line width.

A—52 inches.
B—48 inches.
C—57 inches.

Registration numbers and letters that are 12 inches tall are 8 inches wide. The number 1 is 2 inches wide. The spaces between the characters are 2 inches. The minimum space required for the number N1683C is 52 inches.

8027. If masking tape is applied to an aircraft, such as for trim spraying, and is left on for several days and/or exposed to heat, it is likely that the tape will

A—not seal out the finishing material if the delay or heating occurs before spraying.
B—be weakened in its ability to adhere to the surface.
C—cure to the finish and be very difficult to remove.

Masking tape should be removed from a surface as soon as the finish has dried to the extent that it is no longer tacky. If the tape is left on the surface too long, it will cure to the finish and be extremely difficult to remove.

8028. What is used to slow the drying time of some finishes and to prevent blush?

A—Reducer.
B—Retarder.
C—Rejuvenator.

Retarder is a special type of thinner that dries slowly. It is used in dope and lacquer to slow its drying time. The slower drying time prevents blushing and provides a smoother finish.

Answers

8022 [A] (040) AMT-STRUC, 3	8023 [B] (040) AMT-STRUC, 3	8024 [B] (040) AC 43.13-1	8025 [C] (040) AC 43.13-1
8026 [A] (088) AMT-STRUC, 3	8027 [C] (088) AMT-STRUC, 3	8028 [B] (040) DAT	

8029. Which type of coating typically includes phosphoric acid as one of its components at the time of application?

A—Wash primer.
B—Epoxy primer.
C—Zinc chromate primer.

Wash primer is a two-part primer that contains phosphoric acid to etch the surface of the metal to improve the bond between the surface and the topcoats.

8030. Which properly applied finish topcoat is the most durable and chemical resistant?

A—Synthetic enamel.
B—Acrylic lacquer.
C—Polyurethane.

Polyurethane is the most durable of all of the finishes that are used for modern aircraft. It is noted for its chemical resistance and for its famous "wet look" that is caused by its slow flow-out time.

8031. Aluminum pigment in dope is used primarily to

A—provide a silver color.
B—aid in sealing out moisture from the fabric.
C—reflect ultraviolet from the fabric.

Aluminum-pigmented dope contains tiny flakes of aluminum metal that spread out to form a solid, lightproof film over the coats of clear dope. The aluminum dope prevents the ultraviolet rays from the sun damaging the fabric and the coats of clear dope.

8032. A correct use for acetone is to

A—thin zinc chromate primer.
B—remove grease from fabric.
C—thin dope.

Acetone is a fast-evaporating dope solvent that is suitable for removing grease from fabric prior to doping. It is also used for cleaning paint spray guns and as an ingredient in paint and varnish removers.

8033. Which of the following is a hazard associated with sanding on fabric covered surfaces during the finishing process?

A—Overheating of the fabric/finish, especially with the use of power tools.
B—Static electricity buildup.
C—Embedding of particles in the finish.

When dry-sanding a fabric-covered surface, be sure to electrically ground it to a cold water pipe or some other good electrical ground. Rubbing the sandpaper over the surface will generate enough static electricity that a spark could be caused to jump and ignite the highly flammable fumes inside the structure.

8034. When the humidity is low, what is likely to occur if unhydrated wash primer is applied to unpainted aluminum and then, about 30 to 40 minutes later, a finish topcoat is applied?

A—Corrosion.
B—A glossy, blush-free finish.
C—A dull finish due to the topcoat "sinking in" to primer that is still too soft.

Wash primer requires moisture to convert the phosphoric acid into a protective film on the surface of the metal. If unhydrated primer, primer without enough water to effect the cure, is applied, and within 30 to 40 minutes it is covered with a dense film of a finish such as a polyurethane, there is a good probability that filiform corrosion will form under the polyurethane.

8035. Fungicidal dopes are used in aircraft finishing as the

A—first, full-bodied, brushed-on coat to prevent fungus damage.
B—first coat to prevent fabric rotting and are applied thin enough to saturate the fabric.
C—final, full-bodied, brushed-on coat to reduce blushing.

Fungicidal dope is used for the first coat applied to cotton or linen aircraft fabric. It is thinned enough to allow it to thoroughly saturate both sides of the fabric.

The purpose of fungicidal dope is to retard the formation of fungus and mold, which would cause the fabric to rot.

8036. Before applying a protective coating to any unpainted clean aluminum, you should

A—wipe the surface with methyl ethyl ketone (MEK).
B—remove any contaminants from the surface with a paper towel.
C—avoid touching the surface with bare hands.

It is important when preparing a bare metal surface for painting that, after it has been cleaned, you do not touch it with your bare hands. There is enough oil on the surface of your skin that it can contaminate the surface enough that the finish will not adhere.

Answers

8029 [A] (040) AMT-STRUC, 3	8030 [C] (040) AMT-STRUC, 3	8031 [C] (040) AMT-STRUC, 3	8032 [B] (040) AMT-STRUC, 3
8033 [B] (040) AMT-STRUC, 3	8034 [A] (040) AMT-STRUC, 3	8035 [B] (040) AC 43.13-1	8036 [C] (040) AMT-STRUC, 3

8037. When humidity is low, what is likely to occur if hydrated wash primer is applied to unpainted aluminum and then, 30 to 40 minutes later, a finish top coat is applied?

A—Corrosion.
B—A glossy, blush-free finish.
C—A dull finish due to the topcoat "sinking in" to primer that is still too soft.

Hydrated wash primer is a wash primer that has enough water added to properly convert the phosphoric acid to a phosphate film on the metal. When this primer is applied to the surface, it is ready for a topcoat after it has been allowed to cure for at least 30 minutes. It should produce a glossy, blush-free finish.

8038. What is the usual cause of runs and sags in aircraft finishes?

A—Too much material applied in one coat.
B—Material is being applied too fast.
C—Low atmospheric humidity.

Runs and sags in the surface of paint that has been sprayed are normally caused by applying too much material in one coat.

8039. Which defect in aircraft finishes may be caused by adverse humidity, drafts, or sudden changes in temperature?

A—Orange peel.
B—Blushing.
C—Pinholes.

Blushing is a condition in dope or lacquer finishes in which moisture from the atmosphere condenses on the surface and causes some of the cellulose to precipitate from the finish. Blushing leaves a porous, dull, and weak finish.

Blushing may be caused by the temperature being too low, the humidity being too high, or by drafts or sudden changes in temperature.

8040. Which statement is true regarding paint system compatibility?

A—Old-type zinc chromate primer may not be used directly for touchup of bare metal surfaces.
B—Acrylic nitrocellulose lacquers may be used over old nitrocellulose finishes.
C—Old wash primer coats may be overcoated directly with epoxy finishes.

Old wash primer coats may be overcoated directly with epoxy finishes.

A second coat of wash primer, however, must be applied to the surface if an acrylic finish is to be applied.

Sheet Metal and Non-Metallic Structures

8041. A well-designed rivet joint will subject the rivets to

A—compressive loads.
B—shear loads.
C—tension loads.

A properly designed rivet joint has the major part of the load in the rivets as a shear load.

8042. A main difference between Lockbolt/Huckbolt tension and shear fasteners (other than their application) is in the

A—number of locking collar grooves.
B—shape of the head.
C—method of installation.

A lockbolt has locking grooves in its pin into which the collar is swaged. A shear lockbolt has two locking grooves, and the tension lockbolt has five grooves.

8043. Alloy 2117 rivets are heat treated

A—by the manufacturer and do not require heat treatment before being driven.
B—by the manufacturer but require reheat treatment before being driven.
C—to a temperature of 910 to 930°F and quenched in cold water.

Alloy 2117 rivets, which are called AD rivets, are heat-treated by the manufacturer. They do not require any further heat treatment before they are driven.

Answers

8037 [B] (040) AMT-STRUC, 3	8038 [A] (040) AMT-STRUC, 3	8039 [B] (040) AMT-STRUC, 3	8040 [C] (040) AMT-STRUC, 3
8041 [B] (011) AMT-STRUC, 2	8042 [A] (011) AMT-STRUC, 2	8043 [A] (017) AMT-G Ch 7	

8044. The general rule for finding the proper rivet diameter is

A—three times the thickness of the materials to be joined.
B—two times the rivet length.
C—three times the thickness of the thickest sheet.

A rule of thumb for determining the rivet diameter to be used for repairing aircraft sheet metal is to use a rivet whose diameter is approximately three times the thickness of the thickest sheet being joined.

8045. The shop head of a rivet should be

A—one and one-half times the diameter of the rivet shank.
B—one-half times the diameter of the rivet shank.
C—one and one-half times the diameter of the manufactured head of the rivet.

The shop, or bucked, head of a rivet should have a diameter of 1-1/2 times the rivet shank diameter and a thickness of 1/2 of the shank diameter.

8046. One of the main advantages of HI-LOK type fasteners over earlier generations is that

A—they can be removed and reused again.
B—the squeezed on collar installation provides a more secure, tighter fit.
C—they can be installed with ordinary hand tools.

HI-LOK fasteners are a new form of Hi-Shear fastener that can be installed with ordinary hand tools rather than requiring the special riveting tools. The pin is installed in an interference-fit hole and the collar screwed down over the threaded end. The pin is held with an Allen wrench and the collar is screwed down, using an open-end wrench until the proper torque is reached. At this point, the hex shear-nut portion of the collar will break off.

8046-1. Which of the following is one advantage of HI-LOK fasteners?

A—Shorter transition area between the shank and thread.
B—External counterbore at the base to accommodate material thickness.
C—Inability to be over-torqued.

The advantages of a HI-LOK two-piece fastener include its light weight, high fatigue resistance, high strength, and its inability to be over-torqued.

8047. The markings on the head of a Dzus fastener identify the

A—body diameter, type of head, and length of the fastener.
B—body type, head diameter, and type of material.
C—manufacturer and type of material.

Dzus fasteners are identified by marks on the head of the stud. A letter identifies the type of head, a number identifies the body diameter in 1/16-inch increments, and another number identifies the stud length in hundredths of an inch.

8048. The Dzus turnlock fastener consists of a stud, grommet, and receptacle. The stud length is measured in

A—hundredths of an inch.
B—tenths of an inch.
C—sixteenths of an inch.

The stud length of a Dzus fastener is measured in 1/100-inch increments.

8049. The Dzus turnlock fastener consists of a stud, grommet, and receptacle. The stud diameter is measured in

A—tenths of an inch.
B—hundredths of an inch.
C—sixteenths of an inch.

The diameter of the stud of a Dzus fastener is measured in 1/16-inch increments.

8050. Threaded rivets (Rivnuts) are commonly used to

A—join two or more pieces of sheet metal where shear strength is desired.
B—attach parts or components with screws to sheet metal.
C—join two or more pieces of sheet metal where bearing strength is desired.

Rivnuts are a special type of blind rivet whose shank has internal threads. When the Rivnut is upset in a piece of thin sheet metal, the threaded shank acts as a nut to receive a machine screw.

Rivnuts were originally designed to attach deicer boots to thin sheet metal wing and empennage leading edges.

Answers

8044 [C] (017) AMT-STRUC, 2	8045 [A] (017) AMT-STRUC, 2	8046 [C] (011) AMT-STRUC, 2	8046-1 [C] (011) FAA-H-8083-31
8047 [A] (011) AMT-G Ch 7	8048 [A] (011) AMT-G Ch 7	8049 [C] (011) AMT-G Ch 7	8050 [B] (011) AMT-STRUC, 2

8051. The installation of CherryMAX and Olympic-Lok rivets is accomplished by utilizing

A—rivet gun, special rivet set, and bucking bar.
B—a pulling tool.
C—ordinary hand tools.

CherryMAX and Olympic-Lok rivets are types of blind rivets that are installed by inserting them into the hole and pulling the stem with a special pulling tool. When the stem is pulled, a taper swells the end of the shank and upsets it. Continued pulling breaks the stem off and leaves part of it in the hollow shank to reinforce it.

8052. Hole filling fasteners (for example, MS20470 rivets) should not be used in composite structures primarily because of the

A—possibility of causing delamination.
B—increased possibility of fretting corrosion in the fastener.
C—difficulty in forming a proper shop head.

Hole filling fasteners such as conventional rivets should not be used in composite structures because of the probability of causing delamination. When a conventional rivet is driven, its shank expands to completely fill the hole. The force applied by the expanded shank will cause the material to delaminate around the edges of the hole.

8053. Metal fasteners used with carbon/graphite composite structures

A—may be constructed of any of the metals commonly used in aircraft fasteners.
B—must be constructed of material such as titanium or corrosion resistant steel.
C—must be constructed of high strength aluminum-lithium alloy.

One of the problems with carbon/graphite as a structural material is the fact that aluminum alloys in contact with it will corrode. For this reason fasteners used with carbon/graphite must be made of a corrosion-resistant material such as titanium or corrosion-resistant steel.

8054. Sandwich panels made of honeycomb construction are used on aircraft because this type of construction

A—has a high tensile strength and is non-flammable.
B—has a low weight and is corrosion resistant.
C—saves weight while not compromising strength.

Sandwich panels of metal honeycomb construction are used in modern aircraft because of their high strength-to-weight ratio.

8056. Which of these methods may be used to inspect fiberglass/honeycomb structures for entrapped water?

A—Backlighting and acoustic emission monitoring.
B—X-ray and acoustic emission monitoring.
C—X-ray and backlighting.

Fiberglass honeycomb structure can be inspected for entrapped water by either the X-ray or backlighting method.

The backlighting method of inspection is done by removing all of the paint from the surface and shining a strong light on one side of the panel and examining from the other side for any dark areas that would indicate entrapped water.

8057. When balsa wood is used to replace a damaged honeycomb core, the plug should be cut so that

A—the grain is parallel to the skin.
B—it is about 1/8 inch undersize to allow sufficient bonding material to be applied.
C—the grain is perpendicular to the skin.

A plug of balsa wood can be used to replace a section of damaged honeycomb core.

When using balsa for repair, cut the plug so that its grain is perpendicular to the skin.

8058. When repairing puncture-type damage to a metal-faced laminated honeycomb panel, the edges of the doubler should be tapered to

A—two times the thickness of the metal.
B—100 times the thickness of the metal.
C—whatever is desired for a neat, clean appearance.

When repairing puncture-type damage to a metal-faced laminated honeycomb panel, cut a piece of aluminum alloy the same thickness or thicker than the original face.

Taper the edges of this patch back to a ratio of about 100 to one.

8059. One of the best ways to assure that a properly prepared batch of matrix resin has been achieved is to

A—perform a chemical composition analysis.
B—have mixed enough for a test sample.
C—test the viscosity of the resin immediately after mixing.

One of the best ways of being sure that the matrix resin for a composite repair has been properly mixed is to mix enough extra resin of each batch to make an identical lay-up. Use the same cure time, pressure, and temperature as is used on the actual repair. The test sample should have the same finished characteristics as the repair.

Answers

8051 [B] (029) AMT-STRUC, 2	8052 [A] (017) AMT-STRUC, 3	8053 [B] (017) AMT-STRUC, 3	8054 [C] (037) AMT-STRUC, 3
8056 [C] (037) AMT-STRUC, 3	8057 [C] (037) AMT-STRUC, 3	8058 [B] (037) AMT-STRUC, 3	8059 [B] (037) AMT-STRUC, 3

8060. How does acoustic emission testing detect defects in composite materials?

A—By picking up the "noise" of any deterioration that may be present.
B—By analyzing ultrasonic signals transmitted into the parts being inspected.
C—By creating sonogram pictures of the areas being inspected.

Acoustic emission monitoring is a method of inspecting composite materials for the presence of active corrosion. A sensitive microphone and amplifier are used with the microphone held against the surface being inspected. If corrosion is present, the noise caused by the bubbles generated by the corrosion activity will be heard as a hissing sound. When the panel is heated to about 150°F the noise caused by disbonding of the adhesive will be heard as a crackling sound.

8060-1. When conducting a tap test on a composite panel, which of the following sounds would indicate delamination?

A—Sharp ringing.
B—Dull thud.
C—Sharp thud.

Tap testing is a common technique used for the detection of delamination and/or disbond. The method is accomplished by tapping the inspection area with a solid round disk or lightweight hammer-like device and listening to the response of the structure to the hammer. A clear, sharp ringing sound is indicative of a well-bonded solid structure, while a dull or thud-like sound indicates a discrepant area.

8061. What precaution, if any, should be taken to prevent corrosion inside a repaired metal honeycomb structure?

A—Prime the repair with a corrosion inhibitor and seal from the atmosphere.
B—Paint the outside area with several coats of exterior paint.
C—None. Honeycomb is usually made from a manmade or fibrous material which is not susceptible to corrosion.

When a repair to a metal honeycomb structure is made, the repair should be primed with a corrosion-inhibiting primer and should be sealed so no moisture or air can get to the inside of the repair.

8062. One method of inspecting a laminated fiberglass structure that has been subjected to damage is to

A—strip the damaged area of all paint and shine a strong light through the structure.
B—use dye-penetrant inspection procedures, exposing the entire damaged area to the penetrant solution.
C—use an eddy current probe on both sides of the damaged area.

One method of inspecting a laminated fiberglass structure for internal damage is to strip all the paint from the damaged area. Then shine a bright light through the structure to visually check for damage.

8063. When inspecting a composite panel using the ring test/tapping method, a dull thud may indicate

A—less than full strength curing of the matrix.
B—separation of the laminates.
C—an area of too much matrix between fiber layers.

When using the ring test/tapping method of inspecting a composite panel, a solid ringing sound usually indicates a sound material, but a dull thud may indicate a separation of the laminates, and the material should be examined more closely.

8064. Which of the following are benefits of using microballoons when making repairs to laminated honeycomb panels?

A—Improved strength-to-weight ratio, less density, and lower stress concentrations.
B—Greater concentrations of resin in edges and corners.
C—Less density and improved strength-to-weight ratio.

Phenolic microballoons are used to improve the strength-to-weight ratio of a repair, to decrease the density of the repair, and to give greater flexibility, thus lowering the stress concentrations in the repair area.

8065. The length of time that a catalyzed resin will remain in a workable state is called the

A—pot life.
B—work life.
C—plyable life.

The length of time a catalyzed resin will remain in a workable state is called its pot life.

Answers

8060 [A] (037) AMT-STRUC, 3	8060-1 [B] (037) FAA-H-8083-31	8061 [A] (037) AMT-STRUC, 3	8062 [A] (037) AMT-STRUC, 3
8063 [B] (037) AMT-STRUC, 3	8064 [A] (037) AC 43.13-1	8065 [A] (037) AMT-STRUC, 3	

8066. A category of plastic material that is capable of softening or flowing when reheated is described as a

A—thermoplastic.
B—thermocure.
C—thermoset.

A thermoplastic resin is one that may be softened by heat. When it cools, it returns to its hard condition.

8067. The classification for high tensile strength fiberglass used in aircraft structures is

A—E-glass.
B—S-glass.
C—G-glass.

There are two types of glass fibers used in aircraft composite structure: E-glass and S-glass.

E, or electrical glass, has a high dielectric strength and is designed primarily for electrical insulation. S, or structural glass, has a high tensile strength and is used for structural applications.

8068. Which is an identifying characteristic of acrylic plastics?

A—Zinc chloride will have no effect.
B—Acrylic has a yellowish tint when viewed from the edge.
C—Acetone will not soften plastic, but will change its color.

A quick and easy way to distinguish between cellulose acetate plastic and acrylic plastic is to put a drop of zinc chloride on them.

Zinc chloride has no effect on acrylic plastic, but it causes cellulose acetate plastic to turn milky.

8069. Superficial scars, scratches, surface abrasion, or rain erosion on fiberglass laminates can generally be repaired by applying

A—a piece of resin-impregnated glass fabric facing.
B—one or more coats of suitable resin (room-temperature catalyzed) to the surface.
C—a sheet of polyethylene over the abraded surface and one or more coats of resin cured with infrared heat lamps.

Superficial scars, scratches, surface abrasions, or rain erosion can generally be repaired by applying one or more coats of a suitable resin, catalyzed to cure at room temperature, to the abraded surface.

8070. The classification for fiberglass reinforcement material that has high resistivity and is the most common is

A—E-glass.
B—S-glass.
C—G-glass.

There are two types of glass fibers used in aircraft composite structure: E-glass and S-glass.

E, or electrical glass, has a high resistivity and is designed primarily for electrical insulation. Its low cost makes it the more widely used type of glass where high strength is not required

S, or structural glass, has a high tensile strength and is used for critical structural applications.

8071. A potted compound repair on honeycomb can usually be made on damages less than

A—4 inches in diameter.
B—2 inches in diameter.
C—1 inch in diameter.

A potted compound repair to a honeycomb structure can be used if the damage is less than one inch in diameter.

8072. Composite fabric material is considered to be the strongest in what direction?

A—Fill.
B—Warp.
C—Bias.

The threads that run the length of a piece of fabric are called the warp threads and they are generally stronger than the woof, weft, or fill threads that run across the material. For this reason, a piece of composite fabric is strongest in its warp direction.

8073. What reference tool is used to determine how the fiber is to be oriented for a particular ply of fabric?

A—Fill clock (or compass).
B—Bias clock (or compass).
C—Warp clock (or compass).

A warp clock, or warp compass, is a template with eight arms 45° apart that allows you to orient the warp threads in the various plies of a laid up repair in the direction specified by the aircraft structural repair manual.

Answers

8066 [A] (058) AMT-STRUC, 3	8067 [B] (058) AMT-STRUC, 3	8068 [A] (058) AMT-STRUC, 3	8069 [B] (058) AC 43.13-1
8070 [A] (037) AMT-STRUC, 3	8071 [C] (037) AMT-STRUC, 3	8072 [B] (037) AMT-STRUC, 3	8073 [C] (037) AMT-STRUC, 3

8074. The strength and stiffness of a properly constructed composite buildup depends primarily on

A—a 60 percent matrix to 40 percent fiber ratio.
B—the orientation of the plies to the load direction.
C—the ability of the fibers to transfer stress to the matrix.

The strength and stiffness of a properly constructed composite buildup depends primarily on the orientation of the plies to the load direction.

8075. Which fiber to resin (percent) ratio for advanced composite wet lay-ups is generally considered the best for strength?

A—40:60.
B—50:50.
C—60:40.

It is the fibers that carry the strength in a composite structure, and a 60:40 fiber to resin ratio provides the best strength.

8076. What is the material layer used within the vacuum bag pressure system to absorb excess resin during curing called?

A—Bleeder.
B—Breather.
C—Release.

The bleeder is the absorbent material which is used to absorb the excess resin that is squeezed from the plies that are being cured by the vacuum bag process.

8077. Proper prepreg composite lay-up curing is generally accomplished by

A—adding a catalyst or curing agent to the resin.
B—applying external heat and pressure.
C—room temperature exposure and applying pressure.

Preimpregnated materials, or prepregs, are fabrics that are uniformly impregnated with the matrix resins. They are rolled up and stored in a refrigerator to prevent their curing until they are to be used. One side of the material is covered with a plastic backing to prevent its sticking together while it is stored.

To make a prepreg composite lay-up, cut the plies to size, remove the plastic backing, lay the plies up observing the correct ply orientation, and apply pressure and external heat.

8078. When repairing large, flat surfaces with polyester resins, warping of the surface is likely to occur. One method of reducing the amount of warpage is to

A—add an extra amount of catalyst to the resin.
B—use short strips of fiberglass in the bonded repair.
C—use less catalyst than normal so the repair will be more flexible.

Using a long strip of glass fiber and resin to attach a hinge to a large flat surface will cause the surface to warp, but if short strips of fiberglass are used to bond the fasteners to the panel, the warpage will be minimized.

8079. When making repairs to fiberglass, cleaning of the area to be repaired is essential for a good bond. The final cleaning should be made using

A—MEK (methyl ethyl ketone).
B—soap, water, and a scrub brush.
C—a thixotropic agent.

MEK is used for cleaning an area of a fiberglass structure to be repaired by bonding.

8080. When necessary, what type of cutting fluid is usually acceptable for machining composite laminates?

A—Water soluble oil.
B—Water displacing oil.
C—Water only.

An improper cutting fluid used for machining composite materials would contaminate the material and prevent subsequent bonding. For this reason, water is the only fluid normally approved for use in machining composite materials.

8081. Fiberglass laminate damage not exceeding the first layer or ply can be repaired by

A—filling with a putty consisting of a compatible resin and clean, short glass fibers.
B—sanding the damaged area until aerodynamic smoothness is obtained.
C—trimming the rough edges and sealing with paint.

Fiberglass damage that does not exceed the first layer, or ply, can be repaired by filling it with a putty made of a compatible resin and clean, short glass fibers.

The mixture is used to fill in the damage. After it has cured, it is sanded smooth.

Answers

8074 [B] (037) AMT-STRUC, 3	8075 [C] (037) AMT-STRUC, 3	8076 [A] (037) AMT-STRUC, 3	8077 [B] (037) AMT-STRUC, 3
8078 [B] (045) AMT-STRUC, 3	8079 [A] (045) AMT-STRUC, 3	8080 [C] (045) AMT-STRUC, 3	8081 [A] (045) AC 43.13-1

8082. Fiberglass damage that extends completely through a laminated sandwich structure

A—may be repaired.
B—must be filled with resin to eliminate dangerous stress concentrations.
C—may be filled with putty which is compatible with resin.

According to AC 43.13-1B, fiberglass damage that goes completely through a laminate sandwich structure may be repaired by using either a stepped-joint or a scarfed-joint repair.

Both types of repair are described in AC 43.13-1B.

8083. Fiberglass laminate damage that extends completely through one facing and into the core

A—cannot be repaired.
B—requires the replacement of the damaged core and facing.
C—can be repaired by using a typical metal facing patch.

According to AC 43.13-1B, fiberglass damage that extends completely through one facing and into the core requires the replacement of the damaged core and facing.

8084. Repairing advanced composites using materials and techniques traditionally used for fiberglass repairs is likely to result in

A—restored strength and flexibility.
B—slightly stronger strength to weight ratio.
C—an unairworthy repair.

Modern composite materials use materials, procedures, and special precautions that are different from those used with conventional aircraft fiberglass. To use fiberglass practices on advanced composite structure will likely result in an unairworthy repair.

8085. The preferred way to make permanent repairs on composites is by

A—bonding on metal or cured composite patches.
B—riveting on metal or cured composite patches.
C—laminating on new repair plies.

The preferred way of making a permanent repair to a composite structure is to remove the damaged area and lay in new repair plies, observing the choice of materials, the overlap dimensions, ply orientation, and curing procedures.

8086. Which of the following, when added to wet resins, provide strength for the repair of damaged fastener holes in composite panels?

A—Flox and chopped fibers.
B—Microballoons.
C—Microballons and flox.

Chopped fibers may be any type of fiber cut to a length of 1/4 to 1/2 inch. Flox is the fuzzy fibers taken from the strands of fabric. Microballoons are tiny spheres of glass or phenolic resin.

When repairing damaged fastener holes in composite panels, chopped fibers or flox can be added to the wet resin to strengthen the repair. Microballoons do not add any strength.

8087. The part of a replacement honeycomb core that must line up with the adjacent original is the

A—cell side.
B—ribbon direction.
C—cell edge.

The ribbon direction of a honeycomb core is the direction of the strips of material that were used to form the honeycomb cells. Honeycomb core material has strength parallel to the ribbon direction, but not perpendicular to the ribbon. When replacing honeycomb core material, the ribbon direction of the insert must be the same as the ribbon direction of the original core.

8088. Which of the following are generally characteristic of aramid fiber (Kevlar) composites?

A—High tensile strength and flexibility.
B—High tensile strength and stiffness.
C—Corrosive effect in contact with aluminum and ability to conduct electricity.

Kevlar is an aramid fiber that is noted for its flexibility and high tensile strength. It does not conduct electricity and does not cause aluminum to corrode when it is held in contact with it.

8089. Which of the following are generally characteristic of carbon/graphite fiber composites?

A—Flexibility, high compressive strength, and corrosive effect in contact with aluminum.
B—Stiffness, high compressive strength, and corrosive effect in contact with aluminum.
C—Ability to conduct electricity.

Carbon/graphite fiber composites are noted for their stiffness and high compressive strength. One of their drawbacks is the fact that they will cause aluminum alloy to corrode when it is bonded to the carbon/graphite.

Answers

8082 [A] (037) AC 43.13-1	8083 [B] (037) AC 43.13-1	8084 [C] (037) AMT-STRUC, 3	8085 [C] (037) AMT-STRUC, 3
8086 [A] (037) AMT-STRUC, 3	8087 [B] (037) AMT-STRUC, 3	8088 [A] (037) AMT-STRUC, 3	8089 [B] (037) AMT-STRUC, 3

8090. If an aircraft's transparent plastic enclosures exhibit fine cracks which may extend in a network over or under the surface or through the plastic, the plastic is said to be

A—hazing.
B—brinelling.
C—crazing.

Crazing is the formation of a network of tiny cracks in the surface of the plastic material.

Crazing makes the transparent material difficult to see through and destroys its strength.

8091. When installing transparent plastic enclosures which are retained by bolts extending through the plastic material and self-locking nuts, the nuts should be

A—tightened to a firm fit, plus one full turn.
B—tightened to a firm fit, then backed off one full turn.
C—tightened to a firm fit.

When bolts and self-locking nuts are used to hold transparent plastic enclosures in place, the nut should be tightened to a firm fit, then backed off one full turn.

This installation procedure allows the plastic material to expand and contract without placing it under stress.

8092. If a new safety belt is to be installed in an aircraft, the belt must conform to the strength requirements in which document?

A—STC 1282.
B—14 CFR Part 39.
C—TSO C22.

Safety belts approved for installation in aircraft may be identified by the marking TSO C22 on the belt or by the military designation number for the belt.

Military belts are approved for installation, because their requirements meet or exceed those of TSO C22.

8093. Which is considered good practice concerning the installation of acrylic plastics?

A—When nuts and bolts are used, the plastic should be installed hot and tightened to a firm fit before the plastic cools.
B—When rivets are used, adequate spacer or other satisfactory means to prevent excessive tightening of the frame to the plastic should be provided.
C—When rivets or nuts and bolts are used, slotted holes are not recommended.

If rivets are used to install a transparent plastic panel or a windshield, spacers should be used to prevent the rivets from excessively tightening the frame on the plastic.

8094. The coefficient of expansion of most plastic enclosure materials is

A—greater than both steel and aluminum.
B—greater than steel but less than aluminum.
C—less than either steel or aluminum.

Plastics expand and contract considerably more than the steel or aluminum channels in which they are mounted.

Because of this high coefficient of expansion, provision must be made to allow for the material to change its dimensions without putting the plastic material under stress.

8095. If no scratches are visible after transparent plastic enclosure materials have been cleaned, their surfaces should be

A—polished with rubbing compound applied with a damp cloth.
B—buffed with a clean, soft, dry cloth.
C—covered with a thin coat of wax.

If, after all the dirt and grease are removed from a piece of transparent plastic material, no great amount of scratching is visible, the plastic material may be coated with a good grade of commercial wax.

Apply the wax in a thin, even coat and bring it to a high polish by rubbing it lightly with a soft cloth.

8096. Cabin upholstery materials installed in current standard category airplanes must

A—be fireproof.
B—be at least flame resistant.
C—meet the requirements prescribed in Part 43.

14 CFR §23.2325 requires that upholstery materials used for each compartment to be used by the crew or passengers must be at least flame resistant.

8097. What is the most common method of cementing transparent plastics?

A—Heat method.
B—Soak method.
C—Bevel method.

The most common method of cementing transparent plastic material is the soak method.

The edges of the pieces of plastic material to be joined are soaked in a solvent until they are softened and a cushion is formed.

The two softened edges are pressed together and allowed to remain under pressure until the softened areas diffuse and form a single piece of material.

Answers

8090 [C] (078) AMT-STRUC, 3	8091 [B] (078) AC 43.13-1	8092 [C] (078) AMT-STRUC	8093 [B] (078) AMT-STRUC, 3
8094 [A] (078) AMT-STRUC, 3	8095 [C] (078) AMT-STRUC, 3	8096 [B] (004) §23.2325	8097 [B] (078) AMT-STRUC, 3

8098. What type of bit should be used to drill holes in Plexiglas?

A—A standard twist drill.
B—A specially modified twist drill.
C—A dulled twist drill.

When holes are to be drilled completely through Plexiglas, the standard twist drill should be modified to a 60° tip angle, the cutting edge ground to a zero rake angle, and the back lip clearance angle increased to 12° to 15°.

8098-1. Which of the following drill bit types work best when drilling an aramid fiber (Kevlar) composite laminate?

A—Tool steel with standard grind.
B—Diamond dust coated.
C—Carbide W-point.

A carbide W-point bit (better known as a brad-point bit) is used to drill holes in aramid fiber (Kevlar) composite laminate to keep the hole free of the fuzzy fibers that other drilling methods leave behind in the hole.

8099. What is the purpose of a gusset or gusset plate used in the construction and repair of aircraft structures?

A—To hold structural members in position temporarily until the permanent attachment has been completed.
B—To provide access for inspection of structural attachments.
C—To join and reinforce intersecting structural members.

Gussets or gusset plates are used in an aircraft structure to join and reinforce intersecting structural members.

Gussets are used to carry stresses from one member into another at the point the members join each other.

8100. Select the alternative which best describes the function of the flute section of a twist drill.

A—Provides a method for cooling oil to be delivered to the cutting surface.
B—Forms the area where the drill bit attaches to the drill motor.
C—Forms the cutting edges of the drill point.

One of the functions of the flutes cut into the shank of a twist drill is to form the cutting edges of the drill point.

8101. How many MS20470 AD-4-6 rivets will be required to attach a 10" x 5" plate, using a single row of rivets, minimum edge distance, and 4D spacing?

A—56.
B—54.
C—52.

The plate is 10 inches long and 5 inches wide. The rivets have a diameter of 1/8 inch and there is an edge distance of two rivet diameters.

This requires two rows of rivets 9-1/2 inches long and two rows that are 4-1/2 inches long. The total length of the rivet seams is 28 inches.

If the rivets are spaced every 1/2 inch (4D spacing), 56 rivets are needed.

8102. On a semi-monocoque fuselage, the skin is reinforced by longitudinal structural members called

A—beams and struts.
B—longerons and stringers.
C—formers and bulkheads.

The longitudinal structural members of a semi-monocoque fuselage are called longerons and stringers.

8103. Shallow scratches in sheet metal may be repaired by

A—burnishing.
B—buffing.
C—stop drilling.

Shallow scratches in sheet metal may be repaired by burnishing.

Burnishing is a process in which a smooth tool is used to force the raised material back into the scratch.

8104. What should be the included angle of a twist drill for soft metals?

A—118°.
B—90°.
C—65°.

For drilling soft metals, an included angle of about 90° (45° either side of center) is suitable.

For normal metals, an angle of 118° (59° on either side of center) is considered the standard lip angle.

Answers

8098 [B] (078) AMT-STRUC, 3	8098-1 [C] (020) AMT-STRUC, 3	8099 [C] (016) AMT-STRUC	8100 [C] (016) AMT-G Ch 14
8101 [A] (017) AC 43.13-1	8102 [B] (021) AMT-STRUC, 2	8103 [A] (016) AMT-STRUC	8104 [B] (029) AMT-G Ch 14

8105. When comparing the machining techniques for stainless steel sheet material to those for aluminum alloy sheet, it is normally considered good practice to drill the stainless steel at a

A—higher speed with less pressure applied to the drill.
B—lower speed with more pressure applied to the drill.
C—lower speed with less pressure applied to the drill.

When drilling stainless steel, you should use a drill with a larger included angle. Use a lower speed and more pressure than you would use for aluminum alloy.

8106. A single-lap sheet splice is to be used to repair a section of damaged aluminum skin. If a double row of 1/8-inch rivets is used, the minimum allowable overlap will be

A—1/2 inch.
B—3/4 inch.
C—13/16 inch.

The minimum row distance is 2-1/2 D. (D = diameter)

4 D + 2-1/2 D = Total overlap.

6-1/2 D = 13/2 D

Given the rivet diameter (D) specified in this question:

13/2 (1/8") = 13/16 inches total overlap.

8106-1. What is the minimum edge distance allowed for aluminum alloy single lap sheet splices containing a single row of rivets as compared to a joint with multiple rows, all rivets being equal in diameter?

A—The minimum edge distance for the single row is greater than that for the multiple row.
B—The minimum edge distance for the single row is less than that for the multiple row.
C—The minimum edge distance for the single row is equal to that for the multiple row.

The minimum edge distance allowed for an aluminum alloy single lap sheet splice is the same whether a single row of rivets or if a multiple row of rivets is used. This distance is two times the diameter of the rivet being used.

8107. Which statement is true regarding the inspection of a stressed skin metal wing assembly known to have been critically loaded?

A—If rivets show no visible distortion, further investigation is unnecessary.
B—If bearing failure has occurred, the rivet shanks will be joggled.
C—If genuine rivet tipping has occurred, groups of consecutive rivet heads will be tipped in the same direction.

If the structure has actually been damaged, this would be indicated by groups of consecutive rivet heads being tipped in the same direction caused by a major deflection of the skin under load.

8108. What is the minimum edge distance for aircraft rivets?

A—Two times the diameter of the rivet shank.
B—Two times the diameter of the rivet head.
C—Three times the diameter of the rivet shank.

The minimum edge distance for aircraft rivets (the distance between the center of the rivet hole and the edge of the sheet) is twice the diameter of the rivet shank.

8109. When drilling stainless steel, the drill used should have an included angle of

A—90° and turn at a low speed.
B—118° and turn at a high speed.
C—140° and turn at a low speed.

The drill used for drilling stainless steel should have a much flatter angle than a drill used for soft material. An included angle of approximately 140° is good for stainless steel.
When drilling stainless steel, the drill should turn at a slow speed.

8110. What is the minimum spacing for a single row of aircraft rivets?

A—Two times the diameter of the rivet shank.
B—Three times the length of the rivet shank.
C—Three times the diameter of the rivet shank.

Rivets in a single row should be spaced no closer than three times the diameter of the rivet shank (3D).

Answers

8105 [B] (094) AMT-STRUC	8106 [C] (004) 8083-31V1, Ch 4	8106-1 [C] (004) AC 43.13-1	8107 [C] (094) AMT-STRUC, 2
8108 [A] (094) AC 43.13-1	8109 [C] (016) AMT-STRUC	8110 [C] (016) AMT-STRUC, 2	

8111. (Refer to Figure 1.) Which of the rivets shown will accurately fit the conical depression made by a 100° countersink?

A—1.
B—2.
C—3.

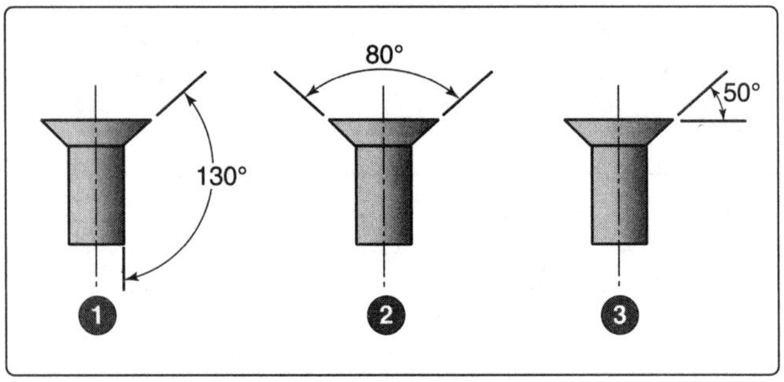

Figure 1. Rivets

The angle between the head and the shank of rivet 1 is 130° on each side (260° on both sides).

The angle formed by the rivet head is 100° (360° – 260°), which is the standard angle for the cutter in an aircraft rivet countersink.

8112. Which is correct concerning the use of a file?

A—Apply pressure on the forward stroke, only, except when filing very soft metals such as lead or aluminum.
B—A smoother finish can be obtained by using a double-cut file than by using a single-cut file.
C—The terms "double-cut" and "second-cut" have the same meaning in reference to files.

To prevent undue wear on the file, when filing any metal other than lead or soft aluminum, apply pressure only during the forward stroke. Relieve the pressure during the return stroke.

8113. What is one of the determining factors which permits machine countersinking when flush riveting?

A—Thickness of the material and rivet diameter are the same.
B—Thickness of the material is less than the thickness of the rivet head.
C—Thickness of the material is greater than the thickness of the rivet head.

To use machine countersinking for installing a countersunk rivet, the thickness of the material must be greater than the thickness of the rivet head.

8114. When repairing a small hole on a metal stressed skin, the major consideration in the design of the patch should be

A—the shear strength of the riveted joint.
B—to use rivet spacing similar to a seam in the skin.
C—that the bond between the patch and the skin is sufficient to prevent dissimilar metal corrosion.

When repairing a small hole in a metal stressed skin, the rivets should take all the stress from the skin and carry it into the patch. On the opposite side of the damage, this stress is carried back into the skin.

The shear strength of the riveted joints should be slightly less than the bearing strength of the skin. If a failure should occur, it will be a shear failure of the rivets, rather than a bearing failure of the skin.

8115. Which procedure is correct when using a reamer to finish a drilled hole to the correct size?

A—Turn the reamer in the cutting direction when enlarging the hole and in the opposite direction to remove from the hole.
B—Turn the reamer only in the cutting direction.
C—Apply considerable pressure on the reamer when starting the cut and reduce the pressure when finishing the cut.

When using a reamer to enlarge a hole, always turn the reamer in the direction of cutting.

If the direction of reamer motion is reversed, the reamer will be seriously dulled.

8116. Repairs or splices involving stringers on the lower surface of stressed skin metal wings are usually

A—not permitted.
B—permitted only if the damage does not exceed 6 inches in any direction.
C—permitted but are normally more critical in reference to strength in tension than similar repairs to the upper surface.

Repairs or splices to the stringers on the lower surface of a stressed skin metal wing are permitted, but since the lower surface of the wing is under a tensile load in flight, these repairs are more critical with regard to tensile strength than repairs to the upper surface.

Answers

8111 [A] (020) AC 43.13-1	8112 [A] (029) AMT-G Ch 14	8113 [C] (017) AMT-STRUC, 2	8114 [A] (016) AMT-STRUC, 2
8115 [B] (029) AMT-G Ch 14	8116 [C] (016) AC 43.13-1		

8117. When straightening members made of 2024-T4, you should

A—straighten cold and reinforce.
B—straighten cold and anneal to remove stress.
C—apply heat to the inside of the bend.

If a structural member made of 2024-T4 aluminum alloy is bent, it should be straightened cold and then reinforced.

8118. Clad aluminum alloys are used in aircraft because they

A—are naturally corrosion resistant, so they do not require corrosion resistant materials for protection.
B—have surface layers of pure aluminum or aluminum alloy bonded to the core material to inhibit corrosion.
C—are highly corrosion resistant because an oxide film forms on their surfaces upon contact with air.

Clad aluminum alloys are used in aircraft construction because they are less subject to corrosion than uncoated aluminum alloys.

Pure aluminum which is not susceptible to corrosion is used to coat a sheet of high-strength aluminum alloy to protect it from corrosion.

8119. Which statement is true regarding a cantilever wing?

A—It has nonadjustable lift struts.
B—No external bracing is needed.
C—It requires only one lift strut on each side.

A cantilever wing does not require any external bracing or struts. All the strength is within the wing itself.

8120. Aircraft structural units, such as spars, engine supports, etc., which have been built up from sheet metal, are normally

A—repairable, using approved methods.
B—repairable, except when subjected to compressive loads.
C—not repairable, but must be replaced when damaged or deteriorated.

Aircraft structural units which are built up from sheet metal are normally repairable, using procedures recommended by the manufacturer of the airframe and approved by the FAA.

8121. A factor which determines the minimum space between rivets is the

A—length of the rivets being used.
B—diameter of the rivets being used.
C—thickness of the material being riveted.

Rivet spacing is based on the diameter of the rivet shank. It is expressed in terms of rivet diameters.

8122. What should be the included angle of a twist drill for hard metal?

A—118°.
B—100°.
C—90°.

For most drilling, including that for hard metal, the cutting angle of a twist drill is ground to an included angle of 118° (59° on either side of center).

8123. Parts fabricated from Alclad 2024-T3 aluminum sheet stock must have all

A—bends made with a small radius to develop maximum strength.
B—bends 90° to the grain
C—scratches, kinks, tool marks, nicks, etc., held to a minimum.

When fabricating parts from Alclad 2024-T3 aluminum sheet stock, be sure that all damage such as scratches, kinks, tool marks, and nicks are held to a minimum to prevent exposing the alloy core through the damaged pure aluminum surface coating.

8124. The monocoque fuselage relies largely on the strength of

A—longerons and formers.
B—skin or covering.
C—bulkheads and longerons.

The greatest amount of strength in a monocoque fuselage is derived from the skin or covering.

8125. Which parts of a semi-monocoque fuselage prevent tension and compression from bending the fuselage?

A—Ribs and formers.
B—Longerons and stringers.
C—Bulkheads and skin.

In a semi-monocoque fuselage, the primary bending loads are taken by the longerons, which usually extend across several points of support. The longerons are supplemented by other longitudinal members called stringers.

Answers

8117 [A] (016) AMT-STRUC, 2	8118 [B] (017) AMT-G Ch 7	8119 [B] (021) AMT-STRUC, 4	8120 [A] (016) AMT-STRUC, 2
8121 [B] (017) AMT-STRUC, 2	8122 [A] (016) AMT-G Ch 14	8123 [C] (016) AMT-STRUC, 7	8124 [B] (021) AMT-STRUC, 2
8125 [B] (021) AMT-STRUC, 2			

8126. Rivet gauge, or transverse pitch is the distance between the

A—centers of rivets in adjacent rows.
B—centers of adjacent rivets in the same row.
C—heads of rivets in the same row.

Rivet gauge, or transverse pitch, is the distance between the centers of rivets in adjacent rows.

8127. Rivet pitch is the distance between the

A—centers of rivets in adjacent rows.
B—centers of adjacent rivets in the same row.
C—heads of rivets in the same row.

Rivet pitch is the distance between the centers of adjacent rivets in the same row.

8128. (Refer to Figure 2.) Select the preferred drawing for proper countersinking.

A—All are acceptable.
B—2.
C—1.

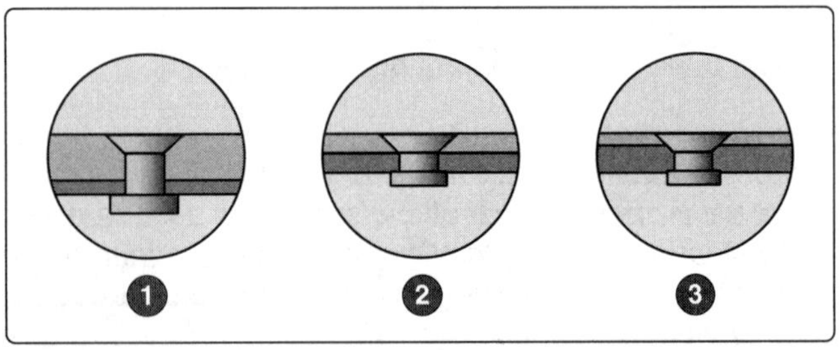

Figure 2. Countersinking

The type of countersinking shown in view 1 is preferred.

The type of countersinking shown in view 2 is acceptable.

The type of countersinking shown in view 3 is not acceptable.

8129. What is indicated by a black "smoky" residue streaming back from some of the rivets on an aircraft?

A—Filiform corrosion is occurring between the rivets and the skin.
B—Intergranular corrosion is occurring between the rivets and the skin.
C—Fretting corrosion is occurring between the rivets and the skin.

A smoky residue streaming back from some of the rivets in an aircraft structure is normally an indication of fretting corrosion.

An extremely small amount of relative movement between the rivet and the skin allows the oxide to be rubbed off the rivet and the surface of the rivet hole. It acts as an abrasive, wearing off more oxides. These loosened oxides work their way out between the skin and the rivet and resemble smoke streaming out from the rivet.

8130. The identifying marks on the heads of aluminum alloy rivets indicate the

A—degree of dimensional and process control observed during manufacture.
B—head shape, shank size, material used, and specifications adhered to during manufacture.
C—specific alloy used in the manufacture of the rivets.

The identifying mark on the head of an aluminum alloy rivet indicates the specific alloy used in the manufacture of the rivet.

8131. When an MS20470D rivet is installed, its full shear strength is obtained

A—only after a period of age hardening.
B—by the cold working of the rivet metal in forming a shop head.
C—by heat treating just prior to being driven.

An MS20470D rivet is an "icebox" rivet, and it must be heat-treated before it is driven. After it is removed from the quench bath, it is stored in a subfreezing refrigerator to keep it soft until it is ready to be driven. After it is driven, it age hardens. It regains approximately half of its strength in one hour and its full strength in four days.

8132. Which of the following need not be considered when determining minimum rivet spacing?

A—Rivet diameter.
B—Rivet length.
C—Type of material being riveted.

The length of the rivet does not enter into the determination of the minimum rivet spacing.

The rivet diameter and the type and thickness of the material do determine rivet spacing.

Answers

8126 [A] (016) AMT-STRUC, 2	8127 [B] (016) AMT-STRUC, 2	8128 [C] (016) AMT-STRUC, 2	8129 [C] (007) AMT-G Ch 7
8130 [C] (017) AMT-G Ch 7	8131 [A] (017) AMT-G Ch 7	8132 [B] (017) AC 43.13-1	

8133. What is the purpose of refrigerating 2017 and 2024 aluminum alloy rivets after heat treatment?

A—To accelerate age hardening.
B—To relieve internal stresses.
C—To retard age hardening.

2017 and 2024 aluminum alloy rivets must be heat treated before they are driven. Immediately after they are quenched, they should be stored in a subfreezing refrigerator.

Storing the rivets at the cold temperature retards their aging process and allows time to elapse between their heat treatment and their being driven.

8134. Under certain conditions, type A rivets are not used because of their

A—low strength characteristics.
B—unique design that causes crazing or cracking.
C—tendency toward embrittlement when subjected to vibration.

Type A rivets (commercially pure aluminum rivets) are not used for aircraft structural repair because of their low-strength characteristics.

8135. A rivet set used to drive MS20470 rivets should

A—have the same radius as the rivet head.
B—have a slightly greater radius than the rivet head.
C—be nearly flat on the end, with a slight radius on the edge to prevent damage to the sheet being riveted.

The rivet set used to drive AN470 or MS20470 universal head rivets should have a radius slightly larger than the radius of the rivet head.

This larger radius allows the hammering action of the rivet gun to be directly on the crown of the rivet.

8136. Heat-treated rivets in the D and DD series that are not driven within the prescribed time after heat treatment or removal from refrigeration

A—must be reheat treated before use.
B—must be discarded.
C—may be returned to refrigeration and used later without reheat treatment.

Heat-treated rivets of the D or DD series that are not driven within the prescribed time after heat treatment, or which have been removed from refrigeration, must be heat-treated again before they are used.

There is no specified number of times they may be reheat-treated.

8137. The dimensions of an MS20430AD-4-8 rivet are

A—1/8 inch in diameter and 1/4 inch long.
B—1/8 inch in diameter and 1/2 inch long.
C—4/16 inch in diameter and 8/32 inch long.

The first dash number in the rivet identification gives the rivet diameter in 1/32-inch increments. The second dash number gives the rivet length in 1/16-inch increments.

An MS20430AD-4-8 rivet is 4/32 inch (1/8 inch) in diameter and 8/16 inch (1/2 inch) long.

8138. The primary alloying agent of 2024-T3 is indicated by the number

A—2.
B—20.
C—24.

The primary alloying agent in 2024-T36 aluminum alloy is copper, which is identified by the first digit 2.

8138-1. Which part of 2017-T36 aluminum alloy indicates the temper designation?

A—T36.
B—2.
C—17.

To provide a visual means for identifying the various grades of aluminum and aluminum alloys, aluminum stock is usually marked with symbols such as a government specification number, the temper or condition furnished, or the commercial code marking. The commercial code marking consists of a number that identifies the particular composition of the alloy. Additionally, letter suffixes designate the basic temper designations and subdivisions of aluminum alloys.

8139. Which part of the 2017-T36 aluminum alloy designation indicates the primary alloying agent used in its manufacture?

A—2.
B—17.
C—20.

The primary alloying agent in 2017-T36 aluminum alloy is copper which is identified by the digit 2.

Answers

8133 [C] (017) AMT-STRUC, 2	8134 [A] (017) AMT-G Ch 7	8135 [B] (017) AC 43.13-1	8136 [A] (017) AMT-G Ch 7
8137 [B] (017) AMT-G Ch 7	8138 [A] (021) AMT-G Ch 7	8138-1 [A] (021) FAA-H-8083-31	8139 [A] (021) AMT-G Ch 7

8140. A sheet metal repair is to be made using two pieces of 0.040-inch aluminum riveted together. All rivet holes are drilled for 3/32-inch rivets. The length of the rivets to be used will be

A—1/8 inch.
B—1/4 inch.
C—5/16 inch.

This problem calls for joining two pieces of 0.040-inch material, using 3/32-inch rivets.

The total thickness of the material is 0.080 inch. The rivet should protrude through the material for 1-1/2 diameters, or 0.1406 inch (9/64 inch).

The total length of the rivet must be 0.080 + 0.1406, or 0.2206 inch. The nearest standard rivet to this length is 1/4 inch long (0.250 inch).

8141. Most rivets used in aircraft construction have

A—dimples.
B—smooth heads without markings.
C—a raised dot.

Most rivets used in aircraft construction and repair are made of aluminum alloy 2117.

2117 rivets are identified by a dimple in the center of the manufactured head.

8142. MS20426AD-6-5 indicates a countersunk rivet which has

A—a shank length of 5/16 inch (excluding head).
B—a shank length of 5/32 inch (excluding head).
C—an overall length of 5/16 inch.

An MS20426AD-6-5 rivet is a countersunk-head rivet made of 2117 aluminum alloy. It has a diameter of 6/32 inch (3/16 inch) and an overall length, including the head, of 5/16 inch.

8143. Which rivet may be used as received without further treatment?

A—2024-T4.
B—2117-T3.
C—2017-T3.

A 2117 rivet is known as an AD rivet. It may be driven as received, without further heat treatment.

8144. (Refer to Figure 3.) Which is the grip length of the flush rivet?

A—1.
B—2.
C—3.

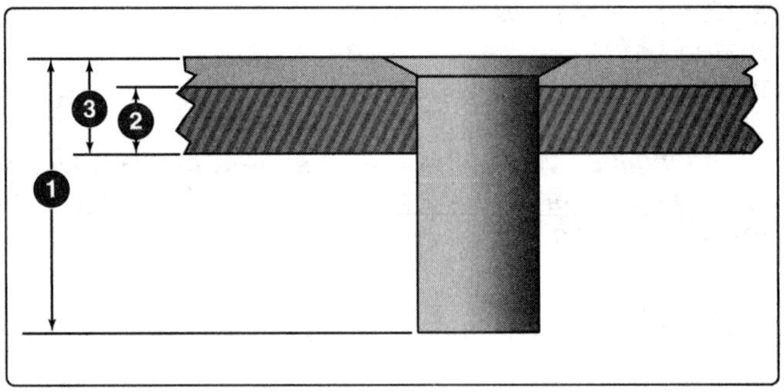

Figure 3. Grip length

The grip length of a rivet is the total thickness of the material held together by the rivet.

In this question, the grip length is dimension 3.

8145. Which rivets should be selected to join two sheets of .032-inch aluminum?

A—MS20425D-4-3.
B—MS20470AD-4-4.
C—MS20455DD-5-3.

The two pieces of material to be joined have a total thickness of 0.064 inch. The rivet used with this metal should have a diameter of about three times the thickness of the thickest sheet. This would cause us to choose a rivet with a diameter of 3 × 0.032 inch, or 0.096 inch. The closest rivet to this is one with a diameter of 1/8 inch (0.125 inch).

A 1/8-inch rivet should extend through the material for 3/16 inch, or 0.1875 inch.

The total length of the rivet must be 0.064 + 0.1875, or 0.2515 inch.

We would choose an MS20470AD-4-4 rivet. This is a universal head rivet, 1/8 inch in diameter and 1/4 inch long.

Answers

8140 [B] (017) AC 43.13-1	8141 [A] (017) AMT-G Ch 7	8142 [C] (017) AMT-G Ch 7	8143 [B] (017) AC 43.13-1
8144 [C] (017) AMT-STRUC, 2	8145 [B] (017) AMT-G Ch 7		

8146. A sheet metal repair is to be made using two pieces of 0.0625-inch aluminum riveted together. All rivet holes are drilled for 1/8-inch rivets. The length of the rivets to be used will be

A—5/32 inch.
B—3/16 inch.
C—5/16 inch.

Each of the two sheets of material to be riveted together has a thickness of 0.0625 inch.

The total thickness of the material is 0.125 inch, and the 1/8-inch rivets should extend through the material for 1-1/2 diameters, which is 0.1875 inch.

The total length of the rivet must be 0.3125 inch, which is 5/16 inch.

8147. Mild steel rivets are used for riveting

A—nickel-steel parts.
B—magnesium parts.
C—steel parts.

Mild steel rivets are used for joining steel parts.

8148. A DD rivet is heat treated before use to

A—harden and increase strength.
B—relieve internal stresses.
C—soften to facilitate riveting.

DD, or 2024-T, rivets are heat-treated before they are driven to soften them so they will not split when they are driven.

8149. When riveting dissimilar metals together, what precautions must be taken to prevent an electrolytic action?

A—Treat the surfaces to be riveted together with a process called anodic treatment.
B—Place a protective separator between areas of potential electrical difference.
C—Avoid the use of dissimilar metals by redesigning the unit according to the recommendations outlined in AC 43.13-1A.

One precaution to be observed when riveting together dissimilar metals is to place a nonconductive separator between the two surfaces. This separator prevents the migration of electrons between the areas of electrode potential difference.

8150. The length of a rivet to be used to join a sheet of .032-inch and .064-inch aluminum alloy should be equal to

A—two times the rivet diameter plus .064 inch.
B—one and one-half times the rivet diameter plus .096 inch.
C—three times the rivet diameter plus .096 inch.

The rivet length used to join two sheets of metal should be equal to the total thickness of the metal being joined, plus 1-1/2 times the diameter of the rivet.

The total thickness of the material being joined is 0.096 inch. The length of the rivet should be 1-1/2 times the rivet diameter plus 0.096 inch.

8151. What is generally the best procedure to use when removing a solid shank rivet?

A—Drill through the manufactured head and shank with a shank size drill and remove the rivet with a punch.
B—Drill to the base of the manufactured rivet head with a drill one size smaller than the rivet shank and remove the rivet with a punch.
C—Drill through the manufactured head and shank with a drill one size smaller than the rivet and remove the rivet with a punch.

When removing a solid shank rivet from a piece of aircraft structure, drill to the base of the manufactured head with a drill one size smaller than the rivet shank. Insert a pin punch into the hole and pry the head off, then use the pin punch to drive the rivet shank from the skin.

8152. Joggles in removed rivet shanks would indicate partial

A—bearing failure.
B—torsion failure.
C—shear failure.

A joggle (offset) in the shank of a rivet that has been removed from a damaged aircraft structure indicates that the rivet joint has failed in shear (shear failure).

8153. What type loads cause the most rivet failures?

A—Shear.
B—Bearing.
C—Head.

A shear load, which causes most rivet failures, is one that tries to cut a rivet by shearing it.

Rivets are designed to be used in joints loaded in shear only.

Answers

8146 [C] (016) AC 43.13-1	8147 [C] (017) AMT-G Ch 7	8148 [C] (017) AC 43.13-1	8149 [B] (017) AMT-G Ch 7
8150 [B] (017) AMT-STRUC, 2	8151 [B] (017) AMT-STRUC, 2	8152 [C] (016) AMT-STRUC, 2	8153 [A] (017) AMT-STRUC, 2

8154. Which rivet is used for riveting magnesium alloy structures?

A—Mild steel.
B—5056 aluminum.
C—Monel.

To prevent corrosion in a magnesium structure, 5056 aluminum alloy rivets should be used. Magnesium is the chief alloying agent in 5056 aluminum alloy.

8155. Which rivet is used for riveting nickel-steel alloys?

A—2024 aluminum.
B—Mild steel.
C—Monel.

Monel rivets are used for riveting nickel-steel alloys.

8156. The length of rivet to be chosen when making a structural repair that involves the joining of 0.032-inch and 0.064-inch aluminum sheet, drilled with a No. 30 drill, is

A—7/16 inch.
B—5/16 inch.
C—1/4 inch.

The two sheets of material to be riveted together have a total thickness of 0.096 inch.

The rivet installed in a No. 30 hole is a 1/8-inch rivet. It should extend through the material a distance of 0.1875 inch.

The total length of the rivet must be 0.096 + 0.1875 = 0.2835. The nearest standard rivet length to this is 5/16 inch (0.3125 inch).

8157. (Refer to Figure 4.) The length of flat A is

A—3.750 inches.
B—3.875 inches.
C—3.937 inches.

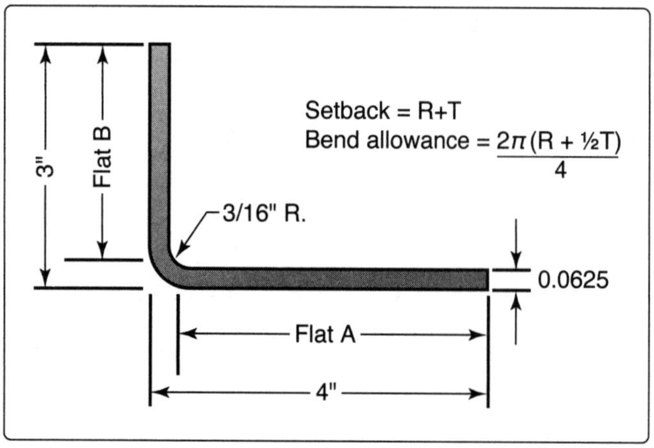

Figure 4. Bending sheet metal

The length of flat A is its mold-line length of 4.00 inches, minus the setback.

The setback is the metal thickness (0.0625 inch), plus the bend radius (0.1875 inch) or 0.250 inch.

The length of flat A is 4.00 – 0.250 = 3.750 inches.

8158. (Refer to Figure 4.) The amount of material required to make the 90° bend is

A—0.3436 inch.
B—0.3717 inch.
C—0.3925 inch.

Using the formula in Figure 4, we find the total amount of material needed to make the bend is 0.3434 inch.

$$BA = \frac{2\pi(R + 1/2T)}{4}$$

$$= \frac{6.28(0.1875 + 0.03125)}{4}$$

$$= \frac{1.3737}{4}$$

$$= 0.3434$$

8159. (Refer to Figure 5.) What is the length of flat A?

A—3.7 inches.
B—3.8 inches.
C—3.9 inches.

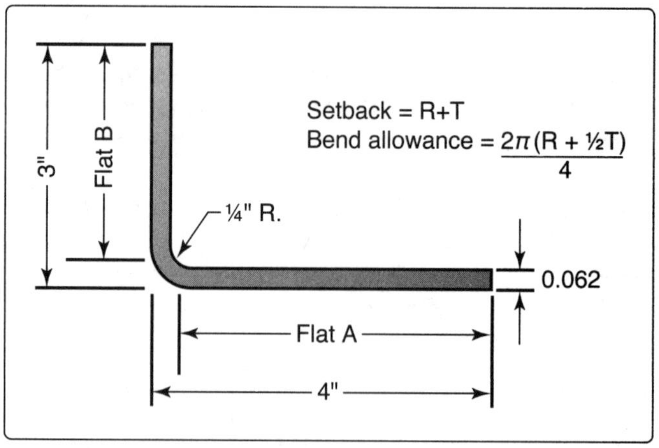

Figure 5. Sheet metal layout

The length of flat A is its mold-line length of 4.00 inches, minus the setback.

The setback is the metal thickness (0.062 inch), plus the bend radius (0.250 inch), or 0.312 inch.

The length of flat A is 4.00 – 0.312 = 3.688 inches.

Answers

8154 [B] (017) AMT-STRUC, 2	8155 [C] (020) AC 43.13-1	8156 [B] (017) AMT-STRUC, 2	8157 [A] (094) AMT-STRUC, 2
8158 [A] (094) AMT-STRUC, 2	8159 [A] (094) AMT-STRUC, 2		

8160. (Refer to Figure 5.) What is the flat layout dimension?

A—7.0 Inches.
B—6.8 inches.
C—6.6 inches.

The dimension of flat A is 3.688 inches.
The dimension of flat B is 2.688 inches.
Using the bend allowance formula, we find that 0.441 inch of material is used to make the bend.
The total layout dimension is 3.688 + 2.688 + 0.441 = 6.817 inches.

8161. If a streamline cover plate is to be hand formed using a form block, a piece of dead soft aluminum should first be placed over the hollow portion of the mold and securely fastened in place. The bumping operation should be

A—distributed evenly over the face of the aluminum at all times rather than being started at the edges or center.
B—started by tapping the aluminum lightly around the edges and gradually working down into the center.
C—started by tapping the aluminum in the center until it touches the bottom of the mold and then working out in all directions.

When using the bumping operation to form a compound curve in a piece of soft aluminum, use light blows of the mallet to work the material down gradually from the edges.
Remember that the object of the bumping process is to work the material into shape by stretching it, rather than by forcing it into the form with heavy blows.
Always start bumping near the edge of the form. Never start in the center.

8162. A piece of flat stock that is to be bent to a closed angle of 15° must be bent through an angle of

A—165°.
B—105°.
C—90°.

A closed angle is an angle that has been bent beyond 90°.
In order to form a closed angle of 15°, the sheet must be bent through an angle of 165° (180° – 15° = 165°).

8163. When a piece of aluminum alloy is to be bent using a minimum radius for the type and thickness of material,

A—the piece should be bent slowly to eliminate cracking.
B—the layout should be made so that the bend will be 90° to the grain of the sheet.
C—less pressure than usual should be applied with the movable (upper) clamping bar.

For the greatest strength in a bent piece of material, the layout should always be made so that the bend will be perpendicular to the grain of the sheet.

8164. The flat layout or blank length of a piece of metal from which a simple L-shaped bracket 3 inches by 1 inch is to be bent depends upon the radius of the desired bend. The bracket which will require the greatest amount of material is one which has a bend radius of

A—1/8 inch.
B—1/2 inch.
C—1/4 inch.

The larger the bend radius in this L-shaped bracket, the less material is needed.
If we assume a metal thickness of 0.063 inch, the bracket having a 1/8-inch bend radius will need 3.865 inches of material.
The bracket having a 1/2-inch radius will need only 3.704 inches of material.
The bracket having a 1/4-inch radius will need 3.811 inches of material.

8165. If it is necessary to compute a bend allowance problem and bend allowance tables are not available, the neutral axis of the bend can be

A—represented by the actual length of the required material for the bend.
B—found by adding approximately one-half of the stock thickness to the bend radius.
C—found by subtracting the stock thickness from the bend radius.

The neutral axis is not in the exact center of the thickness of the material (the stock). But for all practical purposes, the neutral axis of a bend can be considered to be the bend radius, plus one-half of the stock thickness.

Answers
8160 [B] (094) AMT-STRUC, 2
8161 [B] (094) AMT-STRUC, 2
8162 [A] (094) AMT-STRUC, 2
8163 [B] (094) AMT-STRUC, 2
8164 [A] (094) AMT-STRUC, 2
8165 [B] (094) AMT-STRUC, 2

8166. Unless otherwise specified, the radius of a bend is the

A—inside radius of the metal being formed.
B—inside radius plus one-half the thickness of the metal being formed.
C—radius of the neutral axis plus one-half the thickness of the metal being formed.

The bend radius of a piece of sheet metal is the radius of the inside of the bend.

8167. The sharpest bend that can be placed in a piece of metal without critically weakening the part is called the

A—bend allowance.
B—minimum radius of bend.
C—maximum radius of bend.

The minimum radius of bend, or as it is more commonly called, the minimum bend radius, is the sharpest bend that can be made in a piece of metal without critically weakening the part.

8168. The most important factors needed to make a flat pattern layout are

A—radius, thickness, and mold line.
B—radius, thickness, and degree of bend.
C—the lengths of the legs (flat sections).

When making a flat-pattern layout of a piece of formed sheet metal, there are four things we must consider:

1. *The radius of the bend*
2. *The thickness of the material being bent*
3. *The number of degrees in the bend, and*
4. *The lengths of all the flat portions of the part (the mold line dimension, minus the setback).*

8169. A piece of sheet metal is bent to a certain radius. The curvature of the bend is referred to as the

A—bend allowance.
B—neutral line.
C—bend radius.

When a piece of sheet metal is bent, the curvature of the inside of the bend is referred to as the bend radius.

8170. You can distinguish between aluminum and aluminum alloy by

A—filing the metal.
B—testing with an acetic acid solution.
C—testing with a 10 percent solution of caustic soda.

Aluminum alloys of the 2XXX series can be identified by using a 10 percent solution of caustic soda.

When this solution is applied to the material, it reacts with the copper in the alloy and forms a dark spot.

8171. The purpose of a joggle is to

A—allow clearance for a sheet or an extrusion.
B—increase obstruction for a sheet or an extrusion.
C—decrease the weight of the part and still retain the necessary strength.

A joggle is an offset bend in the end of a sheet or an extrusion made to allow clearance for another sheet or extrusion.

Joggles allow both the main portion of the material and the portion of the material over the sheet or the extrusion to lie flat.

8172. When bending metal, the material on the outside of the curve stretches while the material on the inside of the curve compresses. That part of the material which is not affected by either stress is the

A—mold line.
B—bend tangent line.
C—neutral line.

The material on the outside of a curve stretches, while the material on the inside of the curve compresses.

There is a location near the middle of the metal thickness that neither shrinks nor stretches. This is called the neutral line, or the neutral axis, of the material.

Answers

8166 [A] (094) AMT-STRUC, 2	8167 [B] (094) AMT-STRUC, 2	8168 [B] (094) AMT-STRUC, 2	8169 [C] (094) AMT-STRUC, 2
8170 [C] (016) AMT-G Ch 7	8171 [A] (094) AMT-STRUC, 2	8172 [C] (016) AMT-STRUC, 2	

8173. (Refer to Figure 6.) Determine the dimensions of A, B, and C in the flat layout.

Setback = .252
Bend allowance = .345

A—A = .748, B = 2.252, C = 2.004
B—A = .748, B = 1.496, C = 1.248
C—A = 1.252, B = 2.504, C = 1.752

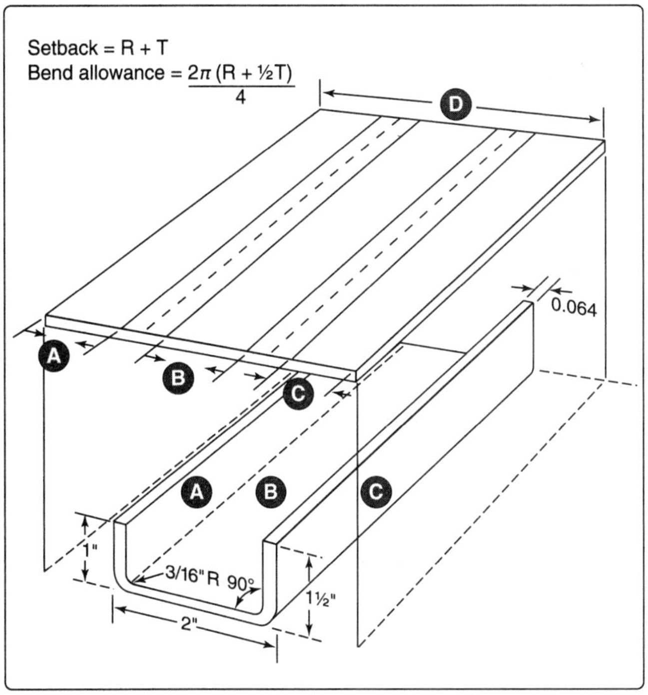

Figure 6. Sheet metal layout

Setback = R + T = 0.188 + 0.064 = 0.252 inch.

Dimension A is a mold line length of 1.00 inch, less one setback. This gives a length of 0.748 inch.

Dimension B is the mold line length of 2.00 inches, less two setbacks. This gives a length of 1.496 inches.

Dimension C is the mold line length of 1.50 inches, less one setback. This gives a length of 1.248 inches.

8174. (Refer to Figure 6.) What is dimension D?

Setback = .252
Bend allowance = .345

A—3.492.
B—4.182.
C—3.841.

Setback = 0.252 inch.

Bend allowance = 0.345 inch.

Dimension A is a mold line length of 1.00 inch, less one setback. This gives a length of 0.748 inch.

Dimension B is the mold line length of 2.00 inches, less two setbacks. This gives a length of 1.496 inches.

Dimension C is the mold line length of 1.50 inches, less one setback. This gives a length of 1.248 inches.

Dimension D is the sum of dimensions A, B, and C, plus two bend allowances.

Dimension D = 0.748 + 1.496 + 1.248 + 0.345 + 0.345 = 4.182 inches.

8175. The sight line on a sheet metal flat layout to be bent in a cornice or box brake is measured and marked

A—one-half radius from either bend tangent line.
B—one radius from either bend tangent line.
C—one radius from the bend tangent line that is placed under the brake.

When making a bend in a piece of sheet metal in a cornice or box brake, draw a sight line inside the bend allowance that is one bend radius from the bend tangent line that is placed under the brake.

Sight down vertically over the edge of the radius bar and place this sight line directly in line with the edge of the radius bar. In this position the bend tangent line is at the beginning of the radius.

Answers
8173 [B] (094) AMT-STRUC, 2
8174 [B] (094) AMT-STRUC, 2
8175 [C] (094) AMT-STRUC, 2

8176. (Refer to Figure 7.) What is dimension F?

Setback at D = .095
Setback at E = .068
Bend allowance at D = .150
Bend allowance at E = .112

A—4.836.
B—5.936.
C—5.738.

Flat A is 1.00 inch, minus setback D (0.095 inch) = 0.905 inch.

Flat B is 3.00 inches, minus setbacks D and E (0.095 + 0.068 = 0.163 inch) = 2.837 inches.

Flat C is 2.00 inches, minus setback E (0.068 inch) = 1.932 inches.

Add to the total length of the three flats the amount of material needed to make both of the bends (0.150 inch for bend D and 0.112 inch for bend E).

The total developed length (length F) is 0.905 + 2.837 + 1.932 + 0.150 + 0.112 = 5.936 inches.

8177. On a sheet metal fitting layout with a single bend, allow for stretching by

A—adding the setback to each leg.
B—subtracting the setback from one leg.
C—subtracting the setback from both legs.

When laying out a sheet metal fitting having a single bend, the setback must be subtracted from the mold line length of both of the legs.

8178. The aluminum alloys used in aircraft construction are usually hardened by which method?

A—Cold-working.
B—Aging.
C—Heat treatment.

Alloys used in aircraft sheet metal construction are hardened by heat treatment.

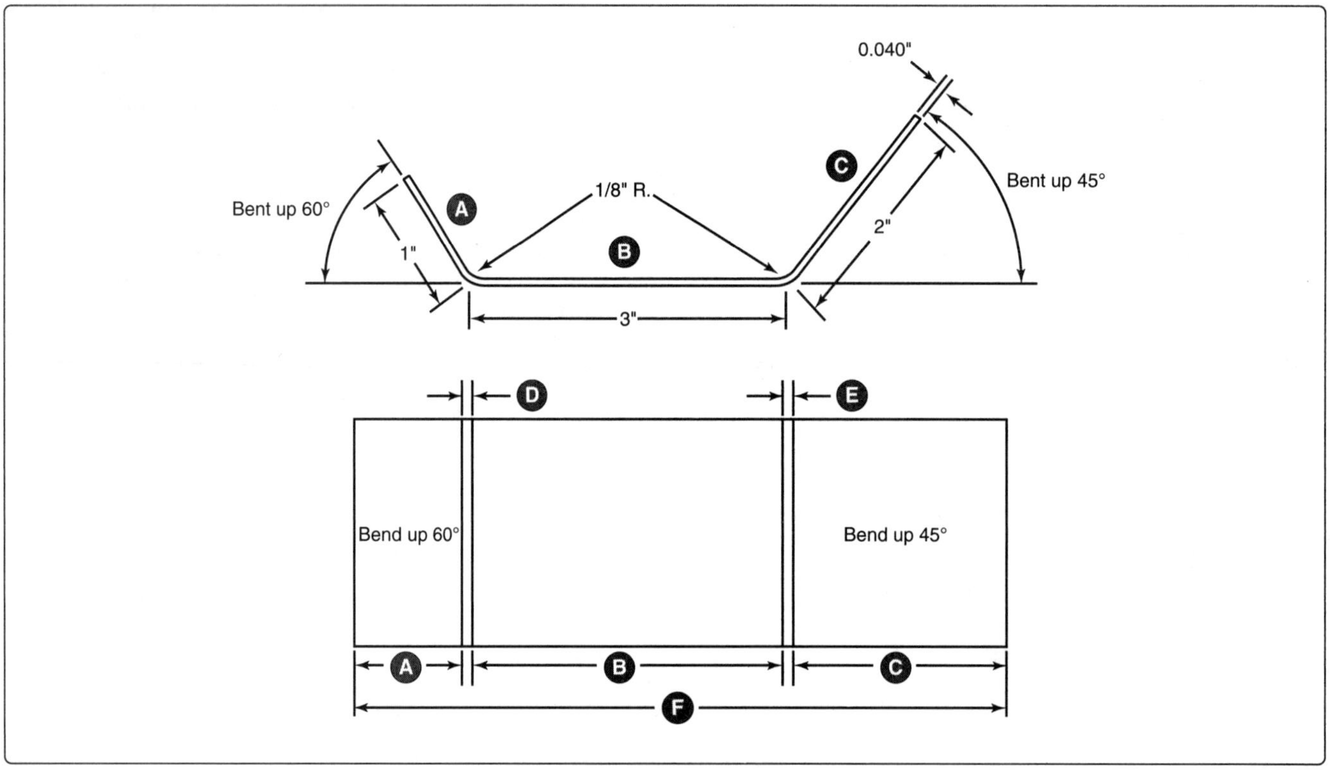

Figure 7. Sheet metal layout

Answers
8176 [B] (094) AMT-STRUC, 2
8177 [C] (094) AMT-STRUC, 2
8178 [C] (016) AMT-G Ch 7

Welding

8179. In Gas Tungsten Arc (GTA) welding, a stream of inert gas is used to

A—prevent the formation of oxides in the puddle.
B—concentrate the heat of the arc and prevent its dissipation.
C—lower the temperature required to properly fuse the metal.

A stream of helium or argon gas is used in GTA welding to keep oxygen away from the puddle of molten metal. This prevents the formation of oxides in the puddle.

8180. Which statement best describes magnesium welding?

A—Magnesium can be welded to other metals.
B—Filler rod should be nickel-steel.
C—Filler rod should be the same composition as base metal.

When welding magnesium, the filler rod must be of the same composition as the base metal and one prepared by the manufacturer to fuse with his alloy.

8180-1. Which statement best describes magnesium welding?

A—It has low thermal conductivity, so distortion and cracking rarely occur.
B—It is recommended to use larger welding beads and a slower welding speed than normal.
C—It can be welded successfully using the same type of joints that are used for aluminum.

Gas welding of magnesium is very similar to welding aluminum using the same equipment. Joint design also follows similar practice to aluminum welding.

8181. Which statement is true in regard to welding heat-treated magnesium?

A—The welded section does not have the strength of the original metal.
B—Flux should not be used because it is very difficult to remove and is likely to cause corrosion.
C—Magnesium cannot be repaired by fusion welding because of the high probability of igniting the metal.

A welded section of heat-treated magnesium cannot have the strength of the original metal until the entire part is again heat-treated.

8182. The oxyacetylene flame for silver soldering should be

A—oxidizing.
B—neutral.
C—carburizing.

A neutral oxyacetylene flame is normally used for silver soldering.

A flame having a slight excess of acetylene may sometimes be used, but it must be soft, not harsh.

8183. Why is it necessary to use flux in all silver soldering operations?

A—To chemically clean the base metal of oxide film.
B—To prevent overheating of the base metal.
C—To increase heat conductivity.

It is necessary to use flux in all silver soldering operations because the base metal must be chemically clean without the slightest film of oxide.

A film of oxide on the metal will prevent the silver solder from coming into intimate contact with the base metal.

8184. Engine mount members should preferably be repaired by using a

A—larger diameter tube with fishmouth and no rosette welds.
B—larger diameter tube with fishmouth and rosette welds.
C—smaller diameter tube with fishmouth and rosette welds.

The preferred repair to a welded steel tubular engine mount is one using a tube with a larger diameter, whose ends are cut with a fishmouth, slipped over the damaged tube.

Rosette welds are used to secure the outer tube to the inner tube.

8185. What method of repair is recommended for a steel tube longeron dented at a cluster?

A—Welded split sleeve.
B—Welded outer sleeve.
C—Welded patch plate.

A patch plate may be welded over a steel tube longeron that is dented at a cluster.

Answers

8179 [A] (101) AMT-STRUC, 2	8180 [C] (101) AMT-STRUC	8180-1 [C] (101) FAA-H-8083-31	8181 [A] (101) AMT-STRUC
8182 [B] (101) AMT-STRUC, 2	8183 [A] (101) AMT-STRUC, 2	8184 [B] (101) AMT-STRUC	8185 [C] (094) AC 43.13-1

8186. Welding over brazed or soldered joints is

A—not permitted.
B—permissible for mild steel.
C—permissible for most metals or alloys that are not heat treated.

Welding over a previously brazed or soldered joint is not permitted because the brazing and soldering materials will enter the pores of the metal. These materials will weaken the welded joint.

8187. Which statement concerning soldering is correct?

A—Joints in electric wire to be soldered should be mechanically secure prior to soldering.
B—Changeable shades of blue can be observed on the surface of a copper soldering tip when the proper temperature for soldering has been reached.
C—If the soldering temperature is too high, the solder will form in lumps and not produce a positive bond.

When soldering electrical wires, the joint must be mechanically secure before soldering. The solder provides a low-resistance connection, but it should not be depended upon for mechanical strength.

8188. A resurfaced soldering iron cannot be used effectively until after the working face has been

A—fluxed.
B—polished.
C—tinned.

When resurfacing a soldering iron, all of the pits are filed out and the tip shaped as desired. The iron is heated and immediately the entire surface is coated with solder to prevent the formation of oxides on the copper. This process is called tinning.

Oxides on the tip prevent the transfer of heat from the copper to the metal being soldered.

8189. Which of the following can normally be welded without adversely affecting strength?

A—Spring steel struts or aircraft bolts.
B—Most heat-treated steel/nickel alloy components.
C—SAE 4130 chrome/molybdenum tubing.

Of the materials listed, only chrome molybdenum tubing can be welded without adversely affecting its strength.

8190. In selecting a torch tip size to use in welding, the size of the tip opening determines the

A—amount of heat applied to the work.
B—temperature of the flame.
C—melting point of the filler metal.

The types of fuel gases used determine the temperature of the flame. The size of the orifice in the tip determines the amount of gas that is being burned and thus the amount of heat that is being put into the work.

8191. Why should a carburizing flame be avoided when welding steel?

A—It removes the carbon content.
B—It hardens the surface.
C—A cold weld will result.

A carburizing flame, a flame that has an excess of acetylene, adds carbon to the puddle so the weld is capable of being hardened more than the surrounding metal.

The metal surrounding the weld bead has less carbon in it than the weld itself.

8192. The most important consideration(s) when selecting welding rod is

A—current setting or flame temperature.
B—material compatibility.
C—ambient conditions.

The most important consideration when selecting a welding rod is its compatibility with the material being welded.

8192-1. When selecting a welding rod, one of the most important factors to consider is to ensure that

A—ferrous rods are used on aluminum.
B—the proper AMS number is used.
C—nonferrous rods are used on steel.

Use welding rods that are compatible with the materials to be welded. Welding rods for various applications have properties suitable for the application intended and will be identified by the AMS number.

8193. The oxyacetylene flame used for aluminum welding should

A—be neutral and soft.
B—be slightly oxidizing.
C—contain an excess of acetylene and leave the tip at a relatively low speed.

The flame used for welding aluminum should be neutral, soft, and slanted at an angle of approximately 45° to the metal.

Answers

8186 [A] (101) AC 43.13-1	8187 [A] (101) AMT-STRUC, 2	8188 [C] (101) AMT-STRUC, 2	8189 [C] (101) AMT-STRUC, 2
8190 [A] (101) AMT-STRUC, 2	8191 [B] (101) AMT-STRUC, 2	8192 [B] (101) AMT-STRUC, 2	8192-1 [B] (101) AC 43.13-1
			8193 [A] (101) AMT-STRUC, 2

8194. A very thin and pointed tip on a soldering copper is undesirable because it will

A—transfer too much heat to the work.
B—have a tendency to overheat and become brittle.
C—cool too rapidly.

A thin, pointed tip on a soldering copper is normally undesirable because it cools too rapidly and does not transfer enough heat into the metal being soldered.

8195. Filing or grinding a weld bead is considered to be

A—an acceptable means to achieve a smoother surface.
B—a way to bring about strength reduction in joint.
C—frequently necessary to avoid adding excessive weight to a weld joint.

Welds should never be filed or ground to present a smooth appearance, as the removal of the added filler material will reduce the strength of the joint.

8196. Acetylene at a line pressure above 15 psi is

A—dangerously unstable.
B—used when a reducing flame is necessary.
C—usually necessary when welding metal over 3/8-inch thick.

Under low pressure at normal temperatures, acetylene is a stable compound. But when it is compressed in a container to a pressure greater than 15 psi, it becomes dangerously unstable.

8197. Cylinders used to transport and store acetylene

A—are pressure tested to 3,000 psi.
B—are green in color.
C—contain acetone.

Cylinders used to transport and store acetylene contain acetone in which the acetylene gas is dissolved.

When acetylene gas is dissolved in acetone, it can safely be stored under pressure.

8198. A welding torch backfire may be caused by

A—a loose tip.
B—using too much acetylene.
C—a tip temperature that is too cool.

A welding torch backfire may be caused by touching the tip against the work, by overheating the tip, by operating the torch at other than recommended pressures, by a loose tip or head, or by dirt or slag in the end of the tip.

8199. Which statement concerning a welding process is true?

A—The inert-arc welding process uses an inert gas to protect the weld zone from the atmosphere.
B—In the metallic-arc welding process, filler material, if needed, is provided by a separate metal rod of the proper material held in the arc.
C—In the oxyacetylene welding process, the filler rod used for steel is covered with a thin coating of flux.

In the process of inert-gas arc welding, the molten metal is protected from the formation of oxides by flowing an inert gas, such as argon, over the surface being welded to exclude oxygen from the weld area.

8200. Where should the flux be applied when oxyacetylene welding aluminum?

A—Painted only on the surface to be welded.
B—Painted on the surface to be welded and applied to the welding rod.
C—Applied only to the welding rod.

The flux is painted directly on the top and the bottom of the joint, and if a filler rod is used, it is also coated with flux.

8201. What purpose does flux serve in welding aluminum?

A—Removes dirt, grease, and oil.
B—Minimizes or prevents oxidation.
C—Ensures proper distribution of the filler rod.

Flux minimizes or prevents oxidation in a weld. Flux removes the oxides that have formed and covers the weld so new oxides cannot form in the weld.

8202. Why are aluminum plates 1/4 inch or more thick usually preheated before welding?

A—Reduces internal stresses and assures more complete penetration.
B—Reduces welding time.
C—Prevents corrosion and ensures proper distribution of flux.

Thick aluminum plates are preheated to reduce the internal strains caused by the large amount of expansion when the thick plates are heated.

Answers

8194 [C] (101) AMT-STRUC, 2
8195 [B] (101) AMT-STRUC, 2
8196 [A] (101) AMT-STRUC, 2
8197 [C] (101) AMT-STRUC, 2
8198 [A] (101) AMT-STRUC, 2
8199 [A] (101) AMT-STRUC, 2
8200 [B] (101) AMT-STRUC, 2
8201 [B] (101) AMT-STRUC, 2
8202 [A] (101) AMT-STRUC, 2

8203. How should a welding torch flame be adjusted to weld stainless steel?

A—Slightly carburizing.
B—Slightly oxidizing.
C—Neutral.

A slightly carburizing flame (a flame with a slight excess of acetylene) is recommended for welding stainless steel.

The flame should be adjusted so a feather about 1/16 inch long, caused by the excess acetylene, forms around the inner cone.

Too much acetylene will add carbon to the metal and cause it to lose its resistance to corrosion.

8204. Oxides form very rapidly when alloys or metals are hot. It is important, therefore, when welding aluminum to use a

A—solvent.
B—filler.
C—flux.

Flux is used when welding aluminum to remove the oxides from the metal immediately ahead of the weld.

The flux then coats the metal and prevents oxygen from reaching its surface and re-forming the oxide.

8205. In gas welding, the amount of heat applied to the material being welded is controlled by the

A—oxygen-acetylene regulator.
B—size of the tip opening.
C—cutting oxygen valve lever.

The amount of heat put into a material being welded is determined by the size of the orifice in the welding tip.

8205-1. When welding or cutting, the acetylene pressure gauge should never be set higher than

A—15 psi.
B—20 psi.
C—25 psi.

The acetylene pressure gauge should never be set higher than 15 psi for welding or cutting.

8206. Oxygen and acetylene cylinders are made of

A—seamless aluminum.
B—steel.
C—bronze.

Both oxygen and acetylene cylinders are made of steel.

8206-2. High pressure cylinders used to transport and store acetylene must

A—be pressure tested to 3,000 psi.
B—be green in color.
C—contain acetone.

Acetylene is stable when stored under a pressure of less than 15 psi, but at pressures above this, it becomes dangerously unstable. Because of this instability, it is stored in steel cylinders filled with a porous material such as a mixture of asbestos and charcoal. The mixture is then saturated with acetone. The acetone absorbs approximately 25 times its own volume of acetylene, and allows the cylinder to be charged to a pressure of 250 psi without the acetylene becoming unstable.

8207. When a butt-welded joint is visually inspected for penetration, the penetration should be

A—50 percent of the thickness of the base metal.
B—100 percent of the thickness of the base metal.
C—75 percent of the thickness of the base metal.

The weld should penetrate 100 percent of the thickness of the base metal when making a butt weld.

8208. Annealing of aluminum

A—increases the tensile strength.
B—makes the material brittle.
C—removes stresses caused by forming.

Annealing removes stresses that have been put into aluminum by forming.

8209. Edge notching is generally recommended in butt welding above a certain thickness of aluminum because it

A—helps hold the metal in alignment during welding.
B—aids in the removal or penetration of oxides on the metal surface.
C—aids in getting full penetration of the metal and prevents local distortion.

Edge notching is recommended in welding thick aluminum sheets because it aids in getting full penetration and also prevents local distortion. All butt welds in materials over 0.125 inch thick are generally notched in some manner.

Answers

8203 [A] (101) AMT-STRUC, 2	8204 [C] (101) AMT-STRUC, 2	8205 [B] (101) AMT-STRUC, 2	8205-1 [A] (101) FAA-H-8083-31
8206 [B] (101) AMT-STRUC, 2	8206-2 [C] (101) AMT-STRUC	8207 [B] (101) AMT-STRUC, 2	8208 [C] (058) AC 43.13-1
			8209 [C] (101) AMT-STRUC, 2

8210. If too much acetylene is used in the welding of stainless steel,

A—a porous weld will result.
B—the metal will absorb carbon and lose its resistance to corrosion.
C—oxide will be formed on the base metal close to the weld.

A slightly carburizing flame is recommended for welding stainless steel. But too much acetylene will add carbon to the metal and cause it to lose its resistance to corrosion.

8211. The shielding gases generally used in the Gas Tungsten Arc (GTA) welding of aluminum consist of

A—a mixture of nitrogen and carbon dioxide.
B—nitrogen or hydrogen, or a mixture of nitrogen and hydrogen.
C—helium or argon, or a mixture of helium and argon.

The gases used as a shielding gas for GTA welding are normally argon or helium or a mixture of these two gases.

Assembly and Rigging

8212. The auxiliary (tail) rotor of a helicopter permits the pilot to compensate for and/or accomplish which of the following?

A—Altitude and pitch oscillation.
B—Airspeed and trimmed flight.
C—Torque and directional control.

The auxiliary rotor located on the tail of a single main rotor helicopter compensates for torque and provides for directional control.

8213. The vertical flight of a helicopter is controlled by

A—collective pitch changes.
B—cyclic pitch changes.
C—increasing or decreasing the RPM of the main rotor.

The amount of lift produced by a helicopter rotor system is determined by the collective pitch of the main rotor system.

Vertical flight of a helicopter is controlled by increasing or decreasing the collective pitch.

8214. A reduction in anti-torque thrust will cause the

A—tail to pivot in the opposite direction of torque rotation around the main rotor.
B—tail to pivot in the direction of torque rotation around the main rotor axis.
C—anti-torque system to become more efficient in the hover mode.

On a single-rotor helicopter with an antitorque tail rotor, the torque of the main rotor tends to rotate the fuselage in a clockwise direction as viewed from above. The tail rotor compensates for this by attempting to rotate the fuselage in a counterclockwise direction.

Decreasing the pitch of the tail rotor allows the torque of the main rotor to rotate the fuselage in a clockwise direction about the main-rotor axis.

8215. In rotorcraft external-loading, the ideal location of the cargo release is where the line of action passes

A—aft of the center of gravity at all times.
B—forward of the center of gravity at all times.
C—through the center of gravity at all times.

An ideal location for the cargo release would be one that allows the line of action to pass through the rotorcraft's center of gravity at all times.

8216. The acute angle formed by the chord line of a wing and the relative wind is known as the

A—longitudinal dihedral angle.
B—angle of incidence.
C—angle of attack.

The angle of attack is the acute angle formed between the chord line of a wing and the direction of the relative wind.

8217. A helicopter in forward flight, cruise configuration, changes direction by

A—varying the pitch of the main rotor blades.
B—changing rotor RPM.
C—tilting the main rotor disk in the desired direction.

A helicopter in forward-flight cruise configuration changes its direction by tilting the main rotor disk in the desired direction by using the cyclic pitch control.

The direction in which the fuselage rotates about the vertical axis is determined by the pitch of the tail rotor, but this does not change the direction of flight.

Answers

8210 [B] (101) AMT-STRUC, 2	8211 [C] (101) AMT-STRUC, 2	8212 [C] (091) AMT-STRUC, 4	8213 [A] (091) AMT-STRUC, 4
8214 [B] (091) AMT-STRUC, 4	8215 [C] (091) AC 43.13-2	8216 [C] (001) AMT-STRUC, 1	8217 [C] (091) AMT-STRUC, 4

8218. The purpose in checking main rotor blade tracking is to determine the

A—relative position of the blades during rotation.
B—flight path of the blades during rotation.
C—extent of an out of balance condition during rotation.

The purpose of blade tracking is to bring the tips of all blades into the same tip path throughout their entire cycle of rotation. Tracking shows only the relative position of the blades, not their path of flight.

8219. In a hovering helicopter equipped with a tail rotor, directional control is maintained by

A—changing the tail rotor RPM.
B—tilting the main rotor disk in the desired direction.
C—varying the pitch of the tail rotor blades.

The foot-operated pedals of a helicopter change the pitch of the tail rotor blades and thus the thrust they produce.

The thrust produced by the tail rotor maintains directional control of a hovering helicopter.

8220. If a single-rotor helicopter is in forward horizontal flight, the angle of attack of the advancing blade is

A—more than the retreating blade.
B—equal to the retreating blade.
C—less than the retreating blade.

The angle of attack of the advancing blade (the blade moving in the same direction the helicopter is traveling) is less than the angle of attack of the retreating blade.

The difference in the angle of attack between the two blades compensates in the difference in the airspeed of the two blades and provides uniform lift around the rotor disk. It prevents dissymmetry of lift.

8221. Main rotor blades that do not cone by the same amount during rotation are said to be out of

A—balance.
B—collective pitch.
C—track.

If the blades of a helicopter rotor do not cone in the same plane they are said to be out of track.

8222. One purpose of the freewheeling unit required between the engine and the helicopter transmission is to

A—automatically disengage the rotor from the engine in case of an engine failure.
B—disconnect the rotor from the engine to relieve the starter load.
C—permit practice of autorotation landings.

The freewheeling unit in a helicopter rotor system automatically disengages the rotor from the engine in the case of an engine failure.

The freewheeling unit allows the engine to drive the rotor, but if the rotor speed ever becomes greater than that of the engine, the freewheeling unit prevents the rotor driving the engine.

8223. Which statement is correct concerning torque effect on helicopters?

A—Torque direction is the same as rotor blade rotation.
B—As horsepower decreases, torque increases.
C—Torque direction is the opposite of rotor blade rotation.

The torque direction of a helicopter rotor system is opposite the direction of the rotor rotation.

8224. What is the purpose of the free-wheeling unit in a helicopter drive system?

A—It disengages the engine from the main rotor when engine RPM is less than rotor RPM.
B—It allows the engines to be started without any load from the transmission.
C—It allows the rotors to turn slowly as the engine RPM increases.

Since lift in a helicopter is provided by rotating airfoils, these airfoils must be free to rotate if the engine fails. The freewheeling unit automatically disengages the engine from the main rotor when engine RPM is less than main rotor RPM. This allows the main rotor and tail rotor to continue turning at normal in-flight speeds.

8225. Movement about the longitudinal axis (roll) in a helicopter is effected by movement of the

A—collective pitch control.
B—cyclic pitch control.
C—reduce lift.

Movement of a helicopter about its longitudinal (roll) axis is effected by moving the cyclic pitch control to the right or left.

8226. Movement about the lateral axis (pitch) in a helicopter is effected by movement of the

A—collective pitch control.
B—cyclic pitch control.
C—tail rotor pitch control.

Movement of a helicopter about its lateral (pitch) axis is effected by moving the cyclic pitch control fore and aft.

Answers

8218 [A] (091) AMT-STRUC, 4
8219 [C] (060) AMT-STRUC, 4
8220 [C] (091) AMT-STRUC, 4
8221 [C] (091) AMT-STRUC, 4
8222 [A] (091) 8083-21
8223 [C] (091) 8083-21
8224 [A] (091) FAA-H-8083-31
8225 [B] (091) AC 65-15A
8226 [B] (091) AMT-STRUC, 4

8227. Wing dihedral, a rigging consideration on most airplanes of conventional design, contributes most to stability of the airplane about its

A—longitudinal axis.
B—vertical axis.
C—lateral axis.

Lateral dihedral, which is the positive acute angle between the lateral axis of an aircraft and a line parallel to the center of a wing panel, contributes to the lateral stability of an aircraft.

Lateral stability (roll stability) is stability of an aircraft about its longitudinal axis.

8228. Other than the manufacturer maintenance manual what other document could be used to determine the primary flight control surface deflection for an imported aircraft that is reassembled after shipment?

A—Aircraft Type Certificate Data Sheet.
B—Import manual for the aircraft.
C—The certificate of airworthiness issued by the importing country.

The Type Certificate Data Sheet issued by the FAA for every aircraft that is FAA-certificated, regardless of its country of origin, includes the amount of deflection of the primary flight controls.

8229. If a pilot reports that an airplane flies left wing heavy, this condition may be corrected by

A—increasing the angle of incidence of the left wing, or decreasing the angle of incidence of the right wing, or both.
B—increasing the dihedral angle of the left wing, or decreasing the dihedral angle of the right wing, or both.
C—adjusting the dihedral angle of the left wing so that differential pressure between the upper and lower wing surfaces is increased.

A left-wing-heavy condition may be corrected by increasing the angle of incidence of (washing in) the left wing, decreasing the angle of incidence of (washing out) the right wing, or both.

A wing is washed-in by increasing its angle of incidence. Washing in a wing increases the lift it produces.

A wing is washed-out by decreasing its angle of incidence. Washing out a wing decreases the amount of lift it produces.

8230. If the vertical fin of a single-engine, propeller-driven airplane is rigged properly, it will generally be parallel to

A—the longitudinal axis but not the vertical axis.
B—the vertical axis but not the longitudinal axis.
C—both the longitudinal and vertical axes.

The vertical fin of a single-engine aircraft is offset to the left. Therefore, it is not parallel to the longitudinal axis of the aircraft. This offset provides directional stability.

The fin is parallel to the vertical axis; therefore, it is straight up and down.

8231. An airplane which has good longitudinal stability should have a minimum tendency to

A—roll.
B—pitch.
C—yaw.

Longitudinal stability is also called pitch stability.

An airplane that has good longitudinal stability has a minimum tendency to pitch.

8232. As the angle of attack of an airfoil increases, the center of pressure will

A—move toward the trailing edge.
B—remain stationary because both lift and drag components increase proportionally to increased angle of attack.
C—move toward the leading edge.

The center of pressure of an asymmetrical airfoil moves forward as the angle of attack increases and backwards as it decreases.

The center of pressure of a symmetrical airfoil does not move as the angle of attack changes.

8233. The angle of incidence is that acute angle formed by

A—the angular difference between the setting of the main airfoil and the auxiliary airfoil (horizontal stabilizer) in reference to the longitudinal axis of the aircraft.
B—a line parallel to the wing chord and a line parallel to the longitudinal axis of the aircraft.
C—a line parallel to the wing from root to tip and a line parallel to the lateral axis of the aircraft.

The angle of incidence is the acute angle formed between a line parallel to the wing chord and a line parallel to the longitudinal axis of the aircraft.

The British definition for angle of attack is the same as the American definition for angle of incidence.

Answers

8227 [A] (001) AMT-STRUC, 1	8228 [A] (099) AC 43.13-1	8229 [A] (081) AMT-STRUC, 4	8230 [B] (093) AMT-STRUC, 4
8231 [B] (050) AMT-STRUC, 1	8232 [C] (001) AMT-STRUC, 1	8233 [B] (001) AMT-STRUC, 4	

8234. An airplane's center of lift is usually located aft of its center of gravity

A—so that the airplane will have a tail-heavy tendency.
B—so that the airplane will have a nose-heavy tendency.
C—to improve stability about the longitudinal axis.

The center of lift is usually located slightly behind the CG of an airplane to improve longitudinal stability.

Locating the center of lift behind the CG produces a nose-heavy tendency that is balanced by the downward aerodynamic tail load.

When the nose pitches up, the aircraft slows down and the tail load decreases. Longitudinal stability causes the nose to drop back to the level flight attitude.

If the nose pitches down, the airspeed builds up and the tail load increases. The increased tail load brings the nose back to the level flight attitude.

8235. An airplane is controlled directionally about its vertical axis by the

A—rudder.
B—elevator(s).
C—ailerons.

An airplane is rotated about its vertical axis with the rudder, but directional flight is controlled by a combination of the ailerons and the rudder.

The ailerons tilt the lift produced by the airplane wings. This changes the direction of flight.

The rudder alone controls the rotation of the aircraft about its vertical axis.

8236. The elevators of a conventional airplane are used to provide rotation about the

A—longitudinal axis.
B—lateral axis.
C—vertical axis.

The elevators rotate an airplane about its lateral axis to produce pitch.

8237. Washing-in the left wing of a monoplane, for purposes of rigging corrections after flight test, will have what effect on the lift and drag of that wing?

A—Both drag and lift will decrease due to decreased angle of attack.
B—Both drag and lift will increase due to increased angle of attack.
C—The drag will decrease due to the effect of the lift increase.

When a wing is washed-in, its angle of incidence, and thus its angle of attack, is increased.

Increasing the angle of incidence increases both the lift and the drag for a given flight condition.

A wing is washed-in to correct a wing-heavy condition.

8238. What type of flap system increases the wing area and changes the wing camber?

A—Fowler flaps.
B—Slotted flaps.
C—Split flaps.

Fowler flaps slide out and downward from the trailing edge of the wing. When lowered, they increase the wing area as well as the wing camber.

8239. If the right wing of a monoplane is improperly rigged to a greater angle of incidence than designated in the manufacturer's specifications, it will cause the

A—airplane to be off balance both laterally and directionally.
B—airplane to pitch and roll about the lateral axis.
C—right wing to have both an increased lift and a decreased drag.

If the right wing of an airplane is rigged with a greater angle of incidence than is required, the right wing will have a greater amount of lift than the left wing.

This additional lift will cause the airplane to be unbalanced laterally and will cause the airplane to turn.

An improper angle of incidence on one wing will cause the airplane to be out of balance both laterally and directionally.

8240. The chord of a wing is measured from

A—wingtip to wingtip.
B—wing root to the wingtip.
C—leading edge to trailing edge.

The chord of a wing is the distance from the leading edge to the trailing edge.

8241. When the lift of an airfoil increases, the drag will

A—decrease.
B—also increase.
C—increase while the lift is changing but will return to its original value.

The lift produced by air flowing over an airfoil and the induced drag depend upon the same aerodynamic forces.

As the lift increases, the induced drag also increases.

Answers

8234 [B] (100) AMT-STRUC, 1	8235 [A] (001) AMT-STRUC, 1	8236 [B] (001) AMT-STRUC, 1	8237 [B] (001) AMT-STRUC, 4
8238 [A] (093) AMT-STRUC, 4	8239 [A] (081) AMT-STRUC, 4	8240 [C] (001) AMT-STRUC, 1	8241 [B] (001) AMT-STRUC, 1

8242. What physical factors are involved in the aspect ratio of airplane wings?

A—Thickness and chord.
B—Span and chord.
C—Dihedral and angle of attack.

The aspect ratio of a wing is the ratio of the span of the wing (length) to its chord (width).

8243. Improper rigging of the elevator trim tab system will affect the balance of the airplane about its

A—lateral axis.
B—longitudinal axis.
C—vertical axis.

The elevator trim tab adjusts the steady-state inflight balance of an aircraft about its lateral axis.
This is the longitudinal trim of the aircraft.

8244. An airplane that has a tendency to gradually increase a pitching moment that has been set into motion has

A—poor longitudinal stability.
B—good lateral stability.
C—poor lateral stability.

An aircraft with good (positive) static longitudinal stability automatically generates a restoring force anytime it pitches either nose up or nose down.
If the amount of pitching increases, the aircraft has dynamic longitudinal instability.
The aircraft in this question has poor longitudinal stability.

8245. The purpose of wing slats is to

A—reduce stalling speed.
B—decrease drag.
C—reduce lift.

A wing slat allows an aircraft to fly at a higher angle of attack before it stalls.
Allowing flight at a higher angle of attack reduces the stalling speed.

8246. The angle of incidence of an airplane at rest

A—affects the dihedral of the wings in flight.
B—is the same as the angle between the relative wind and the chord of the wing.
C—does not change when in flight.

The angle of incidence is a fixed angle between the chord line of the wing and the longitudinal axis of the airplane.
The angle of incidence does not change in flight.

8247. Buffeting is the intermittent application of forces to a part of an airplane. It is caused by

A—incorrect rigging of flaps.
B—an unsteady flow from turbulence.
C—incorrect rigging of ailerons.

Buffeting is an intermittent application of forces on aircraft surfaces caused by an unsteady flow of air from turbulence.

8248. Movement of an airplane along its lateral axis (roll) is also movement

A—around or about the longitudinal axis controlled by the elevator.
B—around or about the lateral axis controlled by the ailerons.
C—around or about the longitudinal axis controlled by the ailerons.

Movement of an aircraft along its lateral axis is also a movement around, or about, its longitudinal axis.
This movement is controlled by the ailerons.

8249. The primary purpose of stall strips is to

A—provide added lift at slow speeds.
B—stall the inboard portion of the wings first.
C—provide added lift at high angles of attack.

Stall strips are small triangular wedges fastened to the leading edge of the wing in the root area. Stall strips cause the wing root to stall before the tip. This allows the pilot to have aileron control during the stall.

8250. Rigging and alignment checks should not be undertaken in the open. However, if this cannot be avoided, the aircraft should be positioned with the

A—tail into the wind.
B—left wing into the wind.
C—nose into the wind.

Normally, rigging and alignment checks should not be undertaken in the open. If this cannot be avoided, the aircraft should be positioned with the nose pointed into the wind.

Answers

8242 [B] (001) AMT-STRUC, 1	8243 [A] (093) AMT-STRUC, 4	8244 [A] (050) AMT-STRUC, 1	8245 [A] (001) AMT-STRUC, 4
8246 [C] (001) AMT-STRUC, 1	8247 [B] (001) AMT-STRUC	8248 [C] (001) AMT-STRUC, 1	8249 [B] (001) AMT-STRUC, 1
8250 [C] (081) AMT-STRUC, 4			

8251. The correct dihedral angle can be determined by

A—measuring the angular setting of each wing at the rear spar with a bubble protractor.
B—placing a straightedge and bubble protractor across the spars while the airplane is in flying position.
C—using a dihedral board and bubble level along the front spar of each wing.

A dihedral board and a bubble level are used along the front spar of each wing to determine the correct amount of dihedral when rigging an airplane.

8252. The dihedral angle of a wing may be measured by placing a straightedge and level protractor on the

A—front spar.
B—wing root.
C—wing chord.

The dihedral angle of an aircraft wing is usually measured by placing a straightedge on the surface of the wing along its front spar and measuring the angle of the spar relative to the horizon, as is shown with a bubble protractor.

The rear spar is not used because if there is any twist in the wing, it would not give a true indication of the dihedral.

8253. Where would you find precise information to perform a symmetry alignment check for a particular aircraft?

A—Aircraft Specification or Type Certificate Data Sheet.
B—Manufacturer's service bulletins.
C—Aircraft service or maintenance manual.

The precise information needed to perform a symmetry-alignment check for a particular aircraft is in the service or maintenance manual for that aircraft.

8254. Where is the buttock line or buttline of an aircraft?

A—A height measurement left or right of, and perpendicular to, the horizontal centerline.
B—A width measurement left of, and perpendicular to, the vertical centerline.
C—A width measurement left or right of, and parallel to, the vertical centerline.

A buttock line on an aircraft is a width measurement to the left or right of, and parallel to, the vertical center line of an aircraft.

8255. Where is fuselage station No. 137 located?

A—137 centimeters aft of the nose or fixed reference line.
B—137 inches aft of the zero or fixed reference line.
C—Aft of the engine.

Fuselage station 137 is located 137 inches aft of fuselage station 0 (the datum line).

8256. Proper wing twist in a sheet metal constructed wing can usually be checked by utilizing a

A—plum bob, string, and straightedge.
B—bubble level and special fixtures described by the manufacturer.
C—straightedge, tape measure, and carpenter's square.

A bubble level and a special fixture may be used to determine the amount of twist that is put into a sheet-metal wing.

8257. The vast majority of aircraft control cables are terminated with swaged terminals, that must be

A—corrosion treated to show compliance with the manufacturer's requirements after the swaging operation.
B—pull tested to show compliance with the manufacturer's requirements after the swaging operation.
C—checked with a go-no-go gauge before and after, to show compliance with the manufacturer's requirements after the swaging operation.

The barrel of a swaged control cable terminal slips over the steel cable, and when the terminal is swaged, its inside diameter is reduced enough that the metal grips the cable tight enough that the swaged fitting provides 100 percent of the strength of the cable.

To ensure that the terminal is properly swaged, its diameter should be checked with go-no-go gauges before and after it is swaged.

8258. What nondestructive checking method is normally used to ensure that the correct amount of swaging has taken place when installing swaged-type terminals on aircraft control cable?

A—Check the surface of the swaged portion of the terminal for small cracks which indicate incomplete swaging.
B—Measure the finished length of the terminal barrel and compare with the beginning length.
C—Use a terminal gauge to check the diameter of the swaged portion of the terminal.

Answers

8251 [C] (081) AMT-STRUC, 4	8252 [A] (081) AMT-STRUC, 4	8253 [C] (081) AMT-STRUC, 4	8254 [C] (081) AMT-G Ch 5
8255 [B] (059) AMT-G Ch 6	8256 [B] (081) AMT-STRUC, 4	8257 [C] (038) AC 43.13-1	8258 [C] (038) AC 43.13-1

After a cable terminal has been swaged onto an aircraft control cable, the diameter of the terminal barrel should be checked with a go-no-go gauge. This gauge is referred to in this question as a "terminal" gauge.

The gauge mentioned here is a two-step go-no-go gauge. One step determines the correct diameter of the terminal before it is swaged, and the other step (the "after" step) determines the correct diameter after the terminal has been swaged.

8259. When inspecting a control cable turnbuckle for proper installation, determine that

A—no more than four threads are exposed on either side of the turnbuckle barrel.
B—the terminal end threads are visible through the safety hole in the barrel.
C—the safety wire ends are wrapped a minimum of four turns around the terminal end shanks.

When a turnbuckle is properly installed there should be no more than three threads exposed from either side of the turnbuckle barrel, and it should be safetied with at least four turns of the safety wire around the terminal-end shanks.

8260. If all instructions issued by the swaging tool manufacturer are followed when swaging a cable terminal, the resultant swaged terminal strength should be

A—the full rated strength of the cable.
B—80 percent of the full rated strength of the cable.
C—70 percent of the full rated strength of the cable.

Standard swaged cable terminals develop the full cable strength. They may be substituted for the original terminal wherever practical.

8261. Which is an acceptable safety device for a castle nut when installed on secondary structures?

A—Star washer.
B—Lockwasher.
C—Cotter pin.

The only safety device listed here that is suitable for a castle nut is a cotter pin.

When a castle nut is installed on a stud that is screwed into a casting, it should be safetied with safety wire.

8261-1. When installing a castle nut, start alignment with the cotter pin hole at the

A—minimum recommended torque without friction drag torque.
B—maximum recommended torque minus friction drag torque.
C—minimum recommended torque plus friction drag torque.

When installing a castle nut, start alignment with the cotter pin hole at the minimum recommended torque plus friction drag torque. Do not exceed the maximum torque plus the friction drag. If the hole and nut castellation do not align, change washer or nut and try again.

8262. When used in close proximity to magnetic compasses, cotter pins are made of what material?

A—Corrosion resisting steel.
B—Anodized aluminum alloy.
C—Cadmium-plated low carbon steel.

Any metal parts installed near a magnetic compass should be nonmagnetic.

The only nonmagnetic metal of which cotter pins are made that is listed among the alternatives is corrosion-resisting steel.

8263. When a fiber or nylon insert-type self-locking nut can be threaded on a bolt or stud through the insert with only the fingers, it should be

A—re-torqued frequently.
B—rejected.
C—reused only in a different location.

A fiber stop nut should be rejected if it can be screwed onto the bolt or stud through the fiber using only the fingers.

When the fiber is worn to this point, the nut can no longer be depended upon to hold against vibration.

8264. The purpose of the vertical fin is to provide

A—directional stability.
B—longitudinal stability.
C—lateral stability.

The vertical fin on an airplane is used to provide directional stability.

Answers

8259 [C] (038) AC 43.13-1
8260 [A] (038) AC 43.13-1
8261 [C] (011) AC 43.13-1
8261-1 [C] (011) AC 43.13-1
8262 [A] (011) AMT-G
8263 [B] (011) AC 43.13-1
8264 [A] (001) AMT-STRUC, 1

8265. How are changes in direction of a control cable accomplished?

A—Pulleys.
B—Bell cranks.
C—Fairleads.

Changes in the direction a control cable is run is accomplished by the use of pulleys.

8266. What is the smallest size cable that may be used in aircraft primary control systems?

A—1/4 inch.
B—5/16 inch.
C—1/8 inch.

According to 14 CFR §23.2250, no cable smaller than 1/8-inch diameter may be used in aircraft primary control systems.

8267. After repairing or re-covering a rudder, the surface should be rebalanced

A—to its spanwise axis.
B—in its normal flight position.
C—to manufacturer's specifications.

If the aircraft manufacturer requires it, any flight control surface that has been repaired or re-covered should be rebalanced to the manufacturer's specifications.

8268. Placing a piece of cloth around a stainless steel control cable and running it back and forth over the length of the cable is generally a satisfactory method of inspecting for

A—corrosion.
B—broken strands.
C—excessive wear.

Run a piece of cloth over the control cable to check for broken wires. If there are any broken wires in the cable, they will snag the cloth.

8269. The cable-operated control system of an all-metal aircraft, not incorporating a temperature compensating device, has been rigged to the correct tension in a heated hangar. If the aircraft is operated in very cold weather, the cable tension will

A—decrease when the aircraft structure and cables become cold.
B—increase when the aircraft structure and cables become cold.
C—be unaffected if stainless steel cable is installed.

An all-metal aircraft structure expands and contracts far more than steel control cables with changes in temperature. If the control cable tension is adjusted when the aircraft is warm, the tension will decrease when the aircraft and cables become cold.

Most large aircraft have cable tension regulators to maintain a constant cable tension with changes in temperature.

8270. Very often, repairs to a control surface require static rebalancing of the control surface. Generally, flight control balance condition may be determined by

A—checking for equal distribution of weight throughout the control surface.
B—the behavior of the trailing edge when the surface is suspended from its hinge points.
C—suspending the control surface from its leading edge in the stream line position and checking weight distribution.

The static balance of a control surface can be checked by suspending the surface from its hinge points and noting the movement of the trailing edge. If the trailing edge moves down, the surface is underbalanced. If the trailing edge moves upward, the surface is overbalanced.

8271. Excessive wear on both of the sides of a control cable pulley groove is evidence of

A—pulley misalignment.
B—cable misalignment.
C—excessive cable tension.

If a control pulley is misaligned, the cable will wear both sides of the groove in the pulley. If the cable is misaligned, it will wear only one side of the groove. If the cable is rigged with too much tension, the center of the groove will be worn deeply.

Answers

8265 [A] (038) AMT-STRUC, 4
8266 [C] (038) §23.2250
8267 [C] (081) AMT-STRUC, 4
8268 [B] (092) AMT-STRUC, 4
8269 [A] (038) AMT-STRUC, 4
8270 [B] (081) AMT-STRUC, 4
8271 [A] (038) AC 43.13-1

8272. Fairleads should never deflect the alignment of a cable more than

A—12°.
B—8°.
C—3°.

Fairleads should not cause a change in direction of a control cable of more than 3°.

8273. Where does the breakage of control cable wires occur most frequently?

A—Breakage usually occurs where cables pass over pulleys and through fairleads.
B—Breakage sites are unpredictable and usually occur randomly anywhere along the length of a cable.
C—Breakage usually occurs where cables are swaged to turnbuckle and ball terminals.

The wires in a control cable are most likely to break where the cable runs over, under, or around a pulley, sleeve, or through a fair-lead.

8274. With which system is differential control associated?

A—Trim.
B—Aileron.
C—Elevator.

Differential control is a term used to describe an aileron system in which the aileron moving upward deflects a greater number of degrees than the aileron moving downward.

8275. Which statement concerning the 100-hour inspection of an airplane equipped with a push-pull tube-type control system is true?

A—The threaded rod ends should not be adjusted in length for rigging purposes because the rod ends have been properly positioned and staked during manufacture.
B—The terminal end threads of the turnbuckles should be visible through the safety hole in the barrel.
C—The threaded rod ends should be checked for the amount of thread engagement by means of the inspection hole provided.

You can determine that the threaded rod ends are properly inserted into a push-pull control rod when the threads on the rod end extend beyond the inspection hole.

You should not be able to insert a piece of safety wire in the inspection hole, as it should be covered by the threaded rod end.

8276. If control cables are adjusted properly and the control surfaces tend to vibrate, the probable cause is

A—worn attachment fittings.
B—oil can effects on the control surfaces.
C—excessive cable tension.

If a control surface vibrates when all the cables are properly adjusted, there is a probability that the attachment fittings are worn.

8277. Aircraft flight control trim systems must be designed and installed so that the

A—pilot can determine the relative position of the trim tab from the cockpit.
B—operating control and the trim tab will always move in the same direction.
C—trim system will disengage or become inoperative if the primary flight control system fails.

An aircraft flight control trim system must provide a means to indicate to the pilot the position of the trim device with respect to the range of adjustment. This means must be visible to the pilot and must be located and designed to prevent confusion.

8278. Stability about the axis which runs parallel to the line of flight is referred to as

A—longitudinal stability.
B—lateral stability.
C—directional stability.

Stability about the axis of an aircraft that runs parallel to the line of flight (the longitudinal axis) is lateral, or roll stability.

8279. The purpose of spring tabs or servo tabs is to

A—assist the pilot in moving the control surfaces.
B—contribute to the static balance of the control surface.
C—make in-flight trim adjustments possible.

Spring tabs and servo tabs are both used to assist the pilot in moving the control surface.

A servo tab is moved by the cockpit control and it produces an aerodynamic force that moves the primary control on which it is mounted.

A spring tab does not move until the aerodynamic forces on the control surface are great enough to compress the spring in the system linkage. When this spring is compressed, the tab deflects and produces an aerodynamic force that aids the pilot in moving the control surface on which the tab is mounted.

Answers

8272 [C] (038) AC 43.13-1	8273 [A] (038) AC 43.13-1	8274 [B] (081) AMT-STRUC, 4	8275 [C] (038) AMT-STRUC, 4
8276 [A] (081) AMT-STRUC, 4	8277 [A] (093) §23.2300, 23.2600	8278 [B] (001) AMT-STRUC, 1	8279 [A] (093) AMT-STRUC, 4

8280. If the control stick of an aircraft with properly rigged flight controls is moved rearward and to the left, the right aileron will move

A—down and the elevator will move down.
B—up and the elevator will move down.
C—down and the elevator will move up.

When the control stick of a properly rigged airplane is moved rearward and to the left, the right aileron will move down and the elevators will move up.

When the controls move in this direction, the airplane will bank to the left and the nose will rotate upward.

8281. Movement of the cockpit control toward the nose-down position during a ground operational check of the elevator trim tab system will cause the trailing edge of the trim tab to move in which direction?

A—Downward regardless of elevator position.
B—Upward regardless of elevator position.
C—Downward if the elevator is in the UP position and upward if the elevator is in the DOWN position.

If the cockpit control for the elevator trim tab is rotated toward the nose-down position, the trailing edge of the trim tab will move upward, regardless of the position of the elevator.

When the trim tab moves upward, it produces an aerodynamic force that moves the elevators downward. This movement of the elevator rotates the airplane nose downward.

8282. If the control stick of an aircraft with properly rigged flight controls is moved forward and to the right, the left aileron will move

A—up and the elevator will move down.
B—down and the elevator will move up.
C—down and the elevator will move down.

When the control stick of a properly rigged airplane is moved forward and to the right, the left aileron will move down and the elevators will move down.

When the controls move in this direction, the airplane will bank to the right and the nose will rotate downward.

8283. If the travel of an airplane's controls is correct but the cables are rigged exceptionally tight, what probable effect will this have when flying the airplane?

A—The airplane will tend to fall off on one wing.
B—The airplane will be heavy on the controls.
C—The pilot will be unable to fly the airplane hands-off.

If the travel of the control surfaces is correct, but the cables are rigged too tight, the aircraft will be heavy on the controls.

The controls will be difficult to operate and there will be extreme wear in the control system.

8284. During inspection of the flight control system of an airplane equipped with differential-type aileron control, side-to-side movement of the control stick will cause

A—each aileron to have a greater up travel (from the streamlined position) than down travel.
B—each aileron to have greater down travel (from the streamlined position) than up travel.
C—the left aileron to move through a greater number of degrees (from full up to full down) than the right aileron.

Differential control of an aileron means that the aileron has a greater amount of travel upward than it has downward. This differential movement is used to minimize adverse yaw.

The aileron moving downward produces both additional lift and additional induced drag. To prevent the nose of the aircraft from starting to move in the direction opposite to the desired turn, additional parasite drag is generated by the aileron moving upward deflecting a greater number of degrees than the aileron moving downward.

8285. A universal propeller protractor used to measure the degrees of aileron travel should be zeroed

A—with the aileron in the NEUTRAL position.
B—with the aileron in the DOWN position.
C—when the aircraft is in a level flight attitude.

When measuring aileron travel with a universal propeller protractor, the aileron is placed in its neutral position and the protractor is zeroed.

With it zeroed in this position, the amount of aileron travel upward and downward from the neutral position can be measured.

8286. The universal propeller protractor can be used to measure

A—propeller track.
B—aspect ratio of a wing.
C—degrees of flap travel.

The universal propeller protractor is the type of protractor most generally used in aircraft maintenance shops for measuring the amount of control surface travel.

This includes the number of degrees of flap travel.

Answers

8280 [C] (082) AMT-STRUC, 4	8281 [B] (093) AMT-STRUC, 4	8282 [C] (082) AMT-STRUC, 4	8283 [B] (081) AMT-STRUC, 4
8284 [A] (082) AMT-STRUC, 4	8285 [A] (081) AMT-STRUC, 4	8286 [C] (081) AMT-STRUC, 4	

8287. (Refer to Figure 8.) Identify the cable that is used in primary control systems and in other places where operation over pulleys is frequent.

A—2.
B—1.
C—3.

The extra-flexible control cable shown in illustration 3 is used in aircraft primary control systems where operation over pulleys is frequent. This cable is called a 7 by 19 cable and is made up of seven strands of 19 wires each.

8288. A tension regulator in the flight control cable system of a large all-metal aircraft is used primarily to

A—increase the cable tension in cold weather.
B—provide a means of changing cable tension in flight.
C—retain a set tension.

Cable tension regulators are used in some flight control systems to compensate for the difference in the expansion of the aluminum aircraft structure and the steel control cables.

These cable tension regulators automatically maintain a given cable tension as the physical dimensions of the aircraft changes due to temperature changes.

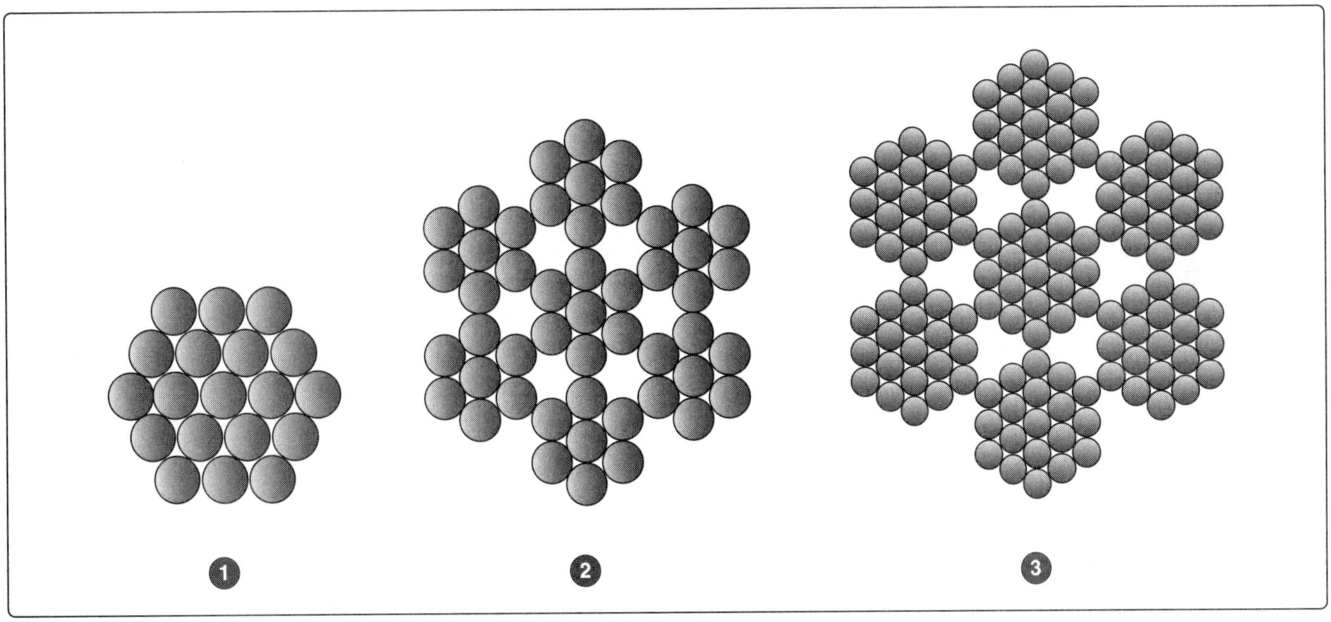

Figure 8. Control cable

Answers
8287 [C] (038) AMT-G Ch 7
8288 [C] (081) AMT-STRUC, 4

8289. (Refer to Figure 9.) When the outside air temperature is 80°F, select the acceptable 3/16 cable tension range.

A—130 pounds minimum, 140 pounds maximum.
B—117 pounds minimum, 143 pounds maximum.
C—120 pounds minimum, 140 pounds maximum.

Follow the vertical line for 80°F upward until it intersects the curve for 3/16-inch cable.

This intersection falls on the horizontal line for a nominal cable tension of 130 pounds.

The chart gives a tolerance of plus or minus 10 percent of the nominal reading. This gives a range between 117 pounds as a minimum value (130 pounds – 13 pounds) and 143 pounds (130 pounds + 13 pounds) as the maximum value.

8290. Differential control on an aileron system means that

A—the down travel is more than the up travel.
B—the up travel is more than the down travel.
C—one aileron on one wing travels further up than the aileron on the opposite wing to adjust for wash-in and wash-out.

Differential control of an aileron causes the aileron moving upward to deflect a greater number of degrees than the one moving downward.

8291. Why is it generally necessary to jack an aircraft indoors for weighing?

A—So aircraft may be placed in a level position.
B—So that air currents do not destabilize the scales.
C—So weighing scales may be calibrated to 0 pounds.

An aircraft should be weighed indoors to prevent the possibility of air currents moving the aircraft and knocking it off the jacks or causing the scales to give an inaccurate reading.

8292. Which should be accomplished before jacking an aircraft?

A—Install critical stress panels or plates.
B—Determine that the fuel tanks are empty.
C—Make sure the aircraft is leveled laterally.

Before some aircraft are jacked, stress panels or plates must be installed to distribute the weight of the aircraft over the jack pad.

When any aircraft is jacked, the recommendations of the aircraft manufacturer must be followed in detail.

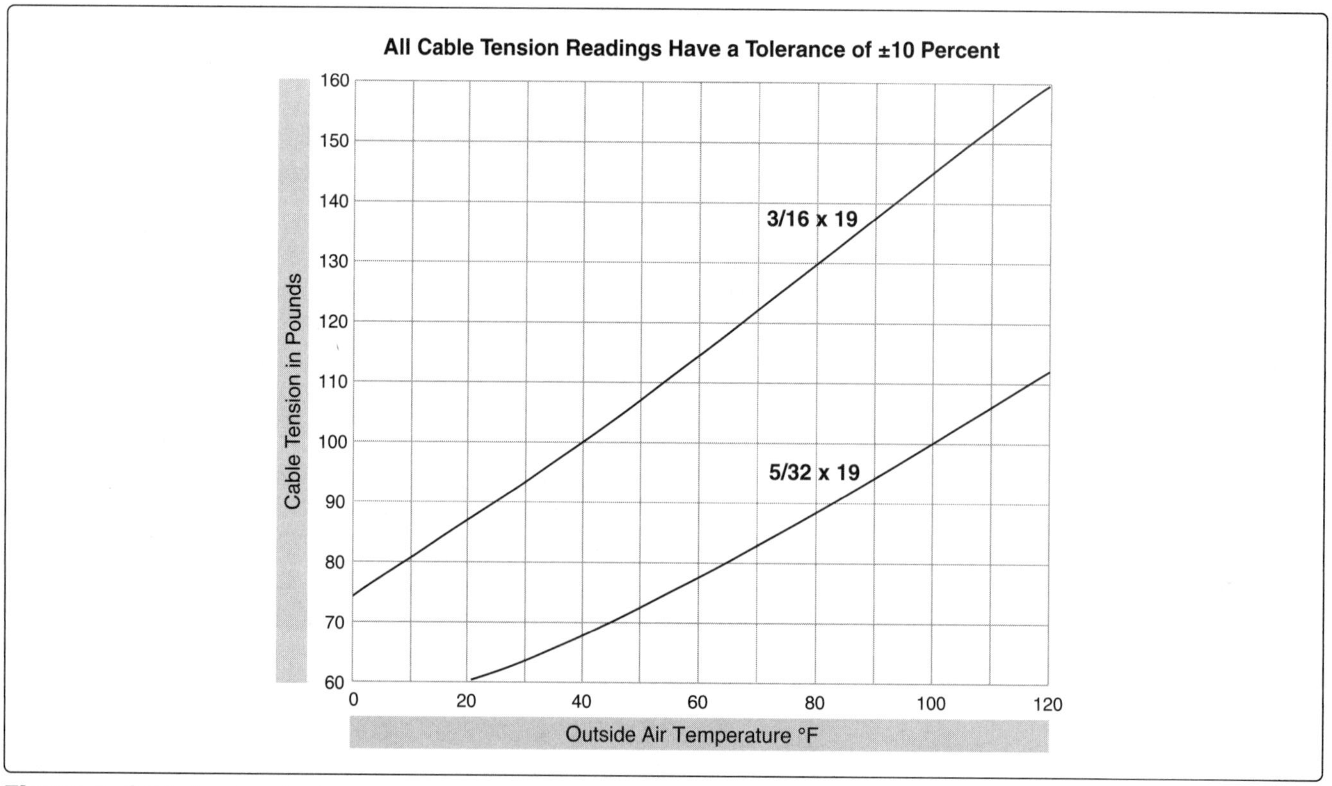

Figure 9. Cable tension chart

Answers
8289 [B] (038) AMT-STRUC, 4
8290 [B] (081) AMT-STRUC, 4
8291 [B] (100) AMT-G Ch 6
8292 [A] (100) AMT-G Ch 6

Airframe Inspection

8293. Which statement about Airworthiness Directives (ADs) is true?

A—ADs are information alert bulletins issued by the airframe, powerplant, or component manufacturer.
B—Compliance with an AD is not mandatory unless the aircraft affected is for hire.
C—Compliance with an applicable AD is mandatory and must be recorded in the maintenance records.

Compliance with all applicable ADs is mandatory. The fact of their compliance and the date and method of their compliance must be recorded in the aircraft's permanent maintenance records.

8293-1. Airworthiness Directives (ADs) are designed to notify

A—mechanics of an approved alternate method to perform a maintenance task other than specified in the aircraft maintenance manual.
B—aircraft owners and operators of methods, techniques, and acceptable practices for inspection and alterations of aircraft.
C—aircraft owners and other interested persons of unsafe conditions and prescribes the condition under which the product may continue to be operated.

ADs are published by the FAA as amendments to 14 CFR §39.13 and apply to the following products: aircraft, engines, propellers, and appliances. The FAA issues ADs when an unsafe condition exists in a product and is likely to exist or develop in other products of the same type design.

8294. When overhauling electrical equipment, all necessary information should be obtained from

A—the aircraft maintenance manual.
B—maintenance instructions published by the aircraft and/or equipment manufacturer.
C—illustrated parts manual for the aircraft.

The necessary information for overhauling electrical equipment is provided in the maintenance instructions published by the aircraft or the equipment manufacturer.

8295. Which statement is correct regarding an aircraft that is found to be unairworthy after an annual inspection, due to an item requiring a major repair (assuming approved data is used to accomplish the repair)?

A—An appropriately rated mechanic may accomplish the repair, and an IA may approve the aircraft for return to service.
B—An appropriately rated mechanic or repair station may repair the defect and approve the aircraft for return to service.
C—Only the person who performed the annual inspection may approve the aircraft for return to service, after the major repair.

If an aircraft is found unairworthy after an annual inspection because of a discrepancy that requires a major repair, the repair can be made by an appropriately rated mechanic. However, the aircraft can be approved for return to service only by a mechanic holding an IA.

8296. Radio equipment installations made in accordance with Supplemental Type Certificate data require approval for return to service

A—by a field approval from the FAA.
B—by an airframe and powerplant mechanic.
C—by the holder of an inspection authorization.

A radio equipment installation made in accordance with an STC can be approved for return to service by the holder of an inspection authorization.

The information included with an STC is considered to be approved data for this alteration.

8297. An aircraft may be flown beyond the 100-hour inspection requirement to reach a place where the inspection can be accomplished, provided it

A—does not exceed 10 flight hours.
B—has a special flight permit.
C—does not exceed 15 flight hours.

An aircraft that is due for a 100-hour inspection can be flown to a place at which the inspection can be done. A maximum of 10 hours beyond the 100-hour period is allowed for this purpose, and the time flown beyond the 100 hours must be subtracted from the time the next inspection is due.

Answers

8293 [C] (088) AMT-G Ch 11	8293-1 [C] (088) FAA-H-8083-31	8294 [B] (088) AMT-G Ch 11	8295 [A] (090) §43.7
8296 [C] (099) 14 CFR 43	8297 [A] (088) §91.409		

8298. Where would you find the recommended statement for recording the approval or disapproval for return to service of an aircraft after a 100-hour or annual inspection?

A—14 CFR Part 65.
B—14 CFR Part 43.
C—14 CFR Part 91.

The recommended statement for approving or disapproving an aircraft for return to service after a 100-hour or annual inspection is found in 14 CFR §43.11.

8299. The maximum time a 100-hour inspection may be extended is

A—10 hours.
B—10 hours with a special flight permit.
C—12 hours with a special flight permit.

A 100-hour inspection time may be extended for up to 10 hours, but these extended hours must be subtracted from the next inspection period.

8300. Which statement is correct when an aircraft has not been approved for return to service after an annual inspection because of several items requiring minor repair?

A—Only the person who performed the annual inspection may approve the aircraft for return to service.
B—An appropriately rated mechanic may repair the defects and approve the aircraft for return to service.
C—An appropriately rated mechanic may repair the defects, but an IA must approve the aircraft for return to service.

If an aircraft has failed an annual inspection because of several items that require minor repairs, the repairs can be made and the aircraft approved for return to service by an appropriately rated mechanic.

The mechanic approving the aircraft for return to service does not need to hold an IA.

8301. An aircraft that is due an annual inspection may be flown

A—if a special permit has been issued for the aircraft.
B—for the purpose of performing maintenance.
C—for a period of time not to exceed 10 hours.

An aircraft due for an annual inspection may be operated if the FAA grants a special flight permit.

A special flight permit is usually issued for such purposes as moving the aircraft to a point where the annual inspection can be performed.

8302. For an individual (not a repair station) to conduct a complete 100-hour inspection on an aircraft and approve it for return to service requires a mechanic certificate with

A—an airframe rating only.
B—airframe and powerplant ratings.
C—airframe and powerplant ratings with an inspection authorization.

A person must hold a mechanic certificate with both airframe and powerplant ratings to be authorized to conduct a complete 100-hour inspection on an aircraft and approve it for return to service.

8303. Where would you find the operating conditions that make a 100-hour inspection mandatory?

A—14 CFR Part 91.
B—14 CFR Part 43.
C—AC 43.13-2A.

The operating conditions that make a 100-hour inspection mandatory are found in 14 CFR §91.409(b).

8304. Large airplanes and turbine-powered multiengine airplanes operated under 14 CFR Part 91, General Operating and Flight Rules, must be inspected

A—in accordance with an inspection program authorized under 14 CFR Part 91, Subpart E.
B—in accordance with a continuous airworthiness maintenance program (camp program) authorized under 14 CFR Part 91, Subpart E.
C—in accordance with the progressive inspection requirements of 14 CFR §91.409(d).

Large airplanes and turbine-powered multiengine aircraft operated under 14 CFR Part 91 must be inspected in accordance with one of the inspection programs authorized under Subpart E of 14 CFR §91.409(e) and (f).

The inspection programs specified in 14 CFR §91.409(e) and (f) are not the progressive inspection covered in 14 CFR §91.409(d).

Answers

8298 [B] (089) §43.11	8299 [A] (088) §91.409	8300 [B] (090) §43.7	8301 [A] (090) §91.409
8302 [B] (090) 14 CFR 65	8303 [A] (019) §91.409	8304 [A] (088) §91.409	

Aircraft Landing Gear Systems

8305. Exposure to and/or storage near which of the following is considered harmful to aircraft tires?

A—Helium, fuel, oil, and low humidity.
B—Low humidity, helium, and ozone.
C—Fuel, oil, ozone, electrical equipment, hydraulic fluid, and solvents.

Aircraft tires can be damaged if they are exposed to or stored near fuel, oil, ozone, electrical equipment, hydraulic fluid, or solvents.

8306. What would be the effect if the piston return spring broke in a brake master cylinder?

A—The brakes would become spongy.
B—The brake travel would become excessive.
C—The brakes would drag.

If the piston return spring in a brake master cylinder were to break, the brakes would not release properly and they would drag.

8307. In brake service work, the term "bleeding brakes" is the process of

A—withdrawing air only from the system.
B—withdrawing fluid from the system for the purpose of removing air that has entered the system.
C—replacing small amounts of fluid in reservoir.

Bleeding the brakes means removing any fluid from the system that has air trapped in it.

8308. To prevent a very rapid extension of an oleo shock strut after initial compression resulting from landing impact,

A—various types of valves or orifices are used which restrict the reverse fluid flow.
B—the metering pin gradually reduces the size of the orifice as the shock strut extends.
C—the air is forced through a restricted orifice in the reverse direction.

Various types of valves and orifices are used inside an oleo strut to prevent a rapid extension of the strut after the initial landing impact has been absorbed.

8309. A pilot reports the right brake on an aircraft is spongy when the brake pedal is depressed in a normal manner. The probable cause is

A—the hydraulic master cylinder piston is sticking.
B—air in the brake hydraulic system.
C—the hydraulic master cylinder piston return spring is weak.

Brakes that have a spongy feel when the pedal is depressed have air in the brake system.

Hydraulic fluid is noncompressible and gives the brakes a solid feel, but if there is any air in the system, it will compress and cause the brakes to feel spongy.

8310. Aside from an external leak in the line, what will cause parking brakes to continually bleed off pressure?

A—An internal leak in the master cylinder.
B—Insufficient hydraulic fluid in the reservoir.
C—Glazed brake linings.

An internal leak in a brake master cylinder will cause the brakes to creep to the OFF position after the parking brake has been set.

8311. Why do most aircraft tire manufacturers recommend that the tubes in newly installed tires be first inflated, fully deflated, and then reinflated to the correct pressure?

A—To allow the tube to position itself correctly inside the tire.
B—To eliminate all the air between the tube and the inside of the tire.
C—To test the entire assembly for leaks.

When a tube-type tire is mounted, the tube should be fully inflated, deflated, and then re-inflated.

This procedure allows the tube to position itself inside the tire and to relieve all the stresses in the tube.

8312. The metering pins in oleo shock struts serve to

A—lock the struts in the DOWN position.
B—retard the flow of oil as the struts are compressed.
C—meter the proper amount of air in the struts.

The metering pin in an oleo shock strut retards the flow of oil as the strut is compressed. This retarded flow causes a more even absorption of shock.

Answers

8305 [C] (097) AMT-STRUC, 6	8306 [C] (063) AMT-STRUC, 6	8307 [B] (032) AMT-STRUC, 6	8308 [A] (032) AMT-STRUC, 6
8309 [B] (032) AMT-STRUC, 6	8310 [A] (068) AMT-STRUC, 7	8311 [A] (068) AC 43.13-1	8312 [B] (068) AMT-STRUC, 6

8313. What action should be taken whenever maintenance is performed that will affect the landing gear system performance?

A—A test flight should be performed to conduct an operational check.
B—A technician with an inspection authorization should perform a visual inspection.
C—The aircraft should be placed on jacks and a retraction test should be performed.

Any maintenance done to an aircraft landing gear that could affect its ability to retract and extend should be followed by a retraction test with the aircraft on jacks.

8314. When working with high pressure, high performance tires, why is it recommended to deflate the tires when removing wheels from the axle?

A—To relieve the strain on the wheel retaining nut and axle threads.
B—To ensure safety in case of a defective wheel or broken tie bolts.
C—To reduce the size of the tire for ease of removal.

If an aircraft tire is deflated before the axle nut is loosened, the wheel halves will not spread apart in case some of the wheel bolts are damaged or weakened.

8315. The braking action of a Cleveland disk brake is accomplished by compressing a rotating brake disk between two opposite brake linings. How is equal pressure on both sides of the rotating disk assured?

A—By allowing the brake rotor to float to automatically equalize as pressure is applied to the rotor.
B—By allowing the caliper to float to automatically equalize as pressure is applied to the rotor.
C—By allowing the brake linings to automatically equalize as pressure is applied to the rotor.

The disk in Cleveland single-disk brakes is rigidly attached to the wheel and rotates between linings that are riveted to the backplate and the pressure plate in the caliper. The caliper is free to float laterally on two anchor bolts that ride in holes in the torque plate.

When the brakes are applied, the caliper moves out on the anchor bolts to provide equal pressure on both sides of the rotating disk.

8316. If it is determined that spongy brake action is not caused by air in the brake system, what is the next most likely cause?

A—Worn brake lining.
B—Internal leakage in the master cylinder.
C—Deteriorated flexible hoses.

Spongy brake action not caused by air in the system may be caused by deteriorated flexible hoses.

The hose may expand as the pressure is built up.

8317. Many brake types can be adapted to operate mechanically or hydraulically. Which type is not adaptable to mechanical operation?

A—Single-disk spot type.
B—Single-servo type.
C—Expander-tube type.

Expander-tube brakes cannot be adapted for mechanical operation. They depend upon fluid inside the tube for their application.

8318. A brake debooster valve is installed in systems where the high pressure of the hydraulic system (3,000 psi) is used to operate brakes

A—that are designed to work with lower pressure.
B—that are used in conjunction with an antiskid system.
C—that are used on aircraft having high landing speeds.

Brake deboosters are installed between the power brake control valve and the wheel cylinders of aircraft that are equipped with power brakes that use pressure supplied by the aircraft main hydraulic system.

System pressure is too high for smooth brake application, so the debooster decreases the pressure and increases the flow of fluid to the brakes so they will apply smoothly and release quickly.

8319. A stripe or mark applied to a wheel rim and extending onto the sidewall of a tube-type tire is a

A—slippage mark.
B—wheel-to-tire balance mark.
C—wheel weight reference mark.

The stripe or mark that extends across the edge of a wheel onto a tube-type tire is a slippage mark that shows whether the tire has slipped on the wheel.

If the slippage mark is broken, the tire should be removed from the wheel to inspect the tube for possible damage to the valve.

Answers

8313 [C] (069) AMT-STRUC, 6
8314 [B] (097) AMT-STRUC, 6
8315 [B] (097) AMT-STRUC, 6
8316 [C] (032) AMT-STRUC, 6
8317 [C] (031) AMT-STRUC, 6
8318 [A] (031) AMT-STRUC, 6
8319 [A] (097) AC 43.13-1

8320. When bleeding aircraft brakes, one of the indications that the air has been purged from the system is

A—partial brake pedal travel.
B—full brake pedal travel.
C—firm brake pedals.

Brakes are bled to remove all air from the fluid. When all of the air has been removed, the pedal will have a firm, rather than spongy, feel.

8321. Overinflated aircraft tires may cause damage to the

A—brake linings.
B—wheel hub.
C—wheel flange.

Overinflated tires may cause damage to the wheel flange on a hard landing.

8322. Debooster valves are used in brake systems primarily to

A—ensure rapid application and release of the brakes.
B—reduce brake pressure and maintain static pressure.
C—reduce the pressure and release the brakes rapidly.

A debooster valve reduces the pressure applied to the brake by the power brake control valve.

When the brake pedal is released, pressure is removed from the inlet port. Then, the piston return spring moves the piston rapidly back to the top of the debooster. The rapid movement of the piston causes a suction in the line to the brake assembly that results in a fast release of the brakes.

8323. The repair for an out-of-tolerance toe-in condition of main landing gear wheels determined not to be the result of bent or twisted components consists of

A—shimming the axle in the oleo trunnion.
B—inserting, removing, or changing the location of washers or spacers at the center pivotal point of the scissor torque links.
C—placing shims or spacers behind the bearing of the out-of-tolerance wheel or wheels.

Toe-in on an aircraft equipped with an oleo landing gear may be adjusted by inserting, removing, or changing washers or spacers at the center pivot point of the scissors torque links.

8324. On an air valve core stem, what indicates high-pressure type?

A—An embossed letter "NP."
B—An embossed letter "HP."
C—An embossed letter "H."

The raised, or embossed, H on the stem of an air-valve core denotes that this is a high-pressure valve core used in an air-oil shock strut or in an accumulator, rather than in a tire or a tube.

8325. The primary purpose for balancing aircraft wheel assemblies is to

A—prevent heavy spots and reduce vibration.
B—distribute the aircraft weight properly.
C—reduce excessive wear and turbulence.

Aircraft tires and wheels are balanced to prevent localized heavy spots and to reduce vibrations.

If there is a heavy spot, it will hit the ground first and get the most wear.

8326. Power boost brake systems are used on aircraft that have

A—high landing speeds.
B—low normal hydraulic system pressure.
C—more than one brake assembly per axle.

As a general rule, power boost brake systems are used on aircraft that are too heavy or land too fast to employ independent brake systems, but are too light in weight to require a power brake system.

8327. On all aircraft equipped with retractable landing gear, some means must be provided to

A—retract and extend the landing gear if the normal operating mechanism fails.
B—extend the landing gear if the normal operating mechanism fails.
C—prevent the throttle from being reduced below a safe power setting while the landing gear is retracted.

All aircraft equipped with retractable landing gear must incorporate some means by which the gear may be extended if the normal operating mechanism fails.

Answers

8320 [C] (032) AMT-STRUC, 6	8321 [C] (097) AMT-STRUC, 6	8322 [C] (031) AMT-STRUC, 6	8323 [B] (068) AMT-STRUC, 6
8324 [C] (069) AMT-STRUC, 6	8325 [A] (097) AMT-STRUC, 6	8326 [A] (031) AMT-STRUC, 6	8327 [B] (068) AC 43.13-1

8328. An automatic damping action occurs at the steering damper if for any reason the flow of high-pressure fluid is removed from the

A—outlet of the steering damper.
B—inlet of the steering damper.
C—replenishing check valve.

A steering damper is a hydraulically operated device that accomplishes the functions of steering and eliminating shimmying.

The steering damper automatically reverts to damping when, for any reason, the flow of high-pressure fluid is removed from its inlet.

8329. What is the purpose of the torque links attached to the cylinder and piston of a landing gear oleo strut?

A—Limit compression stroke.
B—Hold the strut in place.
C—Maintain correct wheel alignment.

The torque links that attach the piston to the cylinder of a landing gear oleo strut maintain the correct wheel alignment.

8330. The removal, installation, and repair of landing gear tires by the holder of a private pilot certificate on an aircraft owned or operated is considered to be

A—a violation of the Federal Aviation Regulations.
B—a minor repair.
C—preventive maintenance.

According to 14 CFR Part 43, Appendix A, the removal, installation, and repair of landing gear tires by a private pilot, on an aircraft that is owned and operated by him or her, is considered to be preventive maintenance.

8331. Aircraft brakes requiring a large volume of fluid to operate the brakes generally

A—use independent master cylinder systems.
B—do not use brake system accumulators.
C—use power brake control valves.

Aircraft brakes that require a large volume of fluid normally use power brake control valves and fluid supplied by the aircraft's main hydraulic system.

8332. What is one effect a restricted compensator port of a master cylinder will have on a brake system?

A—The brakes will operate normally.
B—The reservoir will be filled by reverse flow.
C—The restriction will cause slow release of the brakes.

It is possible for a restricted compensator port in a brake master cylinder to cause slow release of the brakes.

With the port open when the brakes are released, there is an open passage between the master cylinder and the reservoir. But if the compensator port is clogged, some fluid can be trapped in the brake line, keeping the brake partially applied.

8333. When an air/oil type of landing gear shock strut is used, the initial shock of landing is cushioned by

A—compression of the air charge.
B—the fluid being forced through a metered opening.
C—compression of the fluid.

The initial landing impact is cushioned in an air-oil shock strut by the fluid being forced from one chamber to another through a metered opening.

8334. Internal leakage in a brake master cylinder unit can cause

A—fading brakes.
B—slow release of brakes.
C—the pedal to slowly creep down while pedal pressure is applied.

Internal leakage in the master cylinder of an aircraft brake system will cause the pedal to slowly creep down while pedal pressure is applied.

8335. A sleeve, spacer, or bumper ring is incorporated in a landing gear oleo shock strut to

A—limit the extension of the torque arm.
B—limit the extension stroke.
C—reduce the rebound effect.

A sleeve, spacer, or bumper ring is incorporated inside an air-oil shock strut to limit its extension stroke.

Answers

8328 [B] (021) AMT-STRUC, 6	8329 [C] (068) AMT-STRUC, 6	8330 [C] (069) §43.3 , App. A	8331 [C] (031) AMT-STRUC, 6
8332 [C] (031) AMT-STRUC, 6	8333 [B] (068) AMT-STRUC, 6	8334 [C] (031) AMT-STRUC, 6	8335 [B] (068) AMT-STRUC, 6

8336. The purpose of a sequence valve in a hydraulic retractable landing gear system is to

A—prevent heavy landing gear from falling too rapidly upon extension.
B—provide a means of disconnecting the normal source of hydraulic power and connecting the emergency source of power.
C—ensure operation of the landing gear and gear doors in the proper order.

A sequence valve is installed in a hydraulic landing gear system to ensure that the landing gear doors are fully open before the landing gear is either retracted or extended.

8337. The pressure source for power brakes is

A—the main hydraulic system.
B—the power brake reservoir.
C—a master cylinder.

The pressure source for aircraft power brakes is the main hydraulic system.

8338. Which statement is true with respect to an aircraft equipped with hydraulically operated multiple-disk type brake assemblies?

A—There are no minimum or maximum disk clearance checks required due to the use of self-compensating cylinder assemblies.
B—Do not set parking brake when brakes are hot.
C—No parking brake provisions are possible for this type of brake assembly.

Do not set the parking brakes on an aircraft equipped with multiple-disk brakes when the brakes are hot. Setting the parking brake on a hot brake will usually cause the brake disks to warp.

8339. What type of valve is used in the brake actuating line to isolate the emergency brake system from the normal power brake control valve system?

A—A bypass valve.
B—An orifice check valve.
C—A shuttle valve.

A shuttle valve is used in a brake system to isolate the emergency brake system from the normal power-brake control valve system.

8340. When servicing an air/oil shock strut with MIL-5606 the strut should be

A—collapsed and fluid added at the filler opening.
B—fully extended and fluid added at the filler opening.
C—partially extended and fluid added at the filler opening.

To service an air-oil shock strut, bleed all of the air out to collapse the strut, and remove the strut filler valve. Completely fill the collapsed strut with MIL-H-5606 fluid, and exercise the strut by moving the piston into and out of the cylinder to work all of the air out of the strut. Replace the filler valve and, with the weight of the aircraft on the wheel, fill the strut with compressed air or nitrogen until the strut extends to the correct height.

8341. Instructions concerning the type of fluid and amount of air pressure to be put in a shock strut are found

A—on the airplane data plate.
B—in the aircraft operations limitations.
C—in the aircraft manufacturer's service manual.

The type of fluid and the recommended air pressure to be used in an aircraft shock strut is found in the aircraft manufacturer's service manual.

8342. The purpose of a relief valve in a brake system is to

A—reduce pressure for brake application.
B—prevent the tire from skidding.
C—compensate for thermal expansion.

Some brake systems use a thermal relief valve to relieve pressure built up by thermal expansion of the fluid.

8343. Aircraft tire pressure should be checked

A—using only a push on stick-type gauge having one-pound increments.
B—at least once a week or more often.
C—as soon as possible after each flight.

Aircraft tire pressure should be checked at least once a week, or more often if the aircraft is flown a great deal.

Answers

8336 [C] (063) AMT-STRUC, 6	8337 [A] (063) AMT-STRUC, 6	8338 [B] (031) AMT-STRUC, 6	8339 [C] (031) AMT-STRUC, 6
8340 [A] (068) AMT-STRUC, 6	8341 [C] (068) AMT-STRUC, 6	8342 [C] (031) AMT-STRUC, 6	8343 [B] (097) AMT-STRUC, 6

8344. If the extended longitudinal axis of the main landing gear wheel assemblies intersects aft of the aircraft, the wheels can be termed as having

A—toe-out.
B—toe-in.
C—negative camber.

If lines drawn through the center of each of the wheels of an aircraft landing gear cross behind the wheels, the landing gear has toe-out.

The landing gear will tend to spread out as the aircraft rolls forward.

8345. What is the purpose of a compensating port or valve in a brake master cylinder of an independent brake system?

A—Permits the fluid to flow toward or away from the reservoir as temperature changes.
B—Assists in the master cylinder piston return.
C—Prevents fluid from flowing back to the reservoir.

A compensating port in a brake master cylinder is a passageway open between the reservoir and the master cylinder when the brake is completely released.

Fluid can flow from the reservoir into the master cylinder and from the master cylinder back into the reservoir as it expands or contracts because of temperature changes.

8346. If an aircraft shock strut (air/oil type) bottoms upon initial landing contact, but functions correctly during taxi, the most probable cause is

A—low fluid.
B—low air charge.
C—a restricted metering pin orifice.

If an aircraft shock absorber bottoms out on initial landing contact but functions properly during taxiing, the fluid supply is probably low but the air charge is proper.

8347. What is the function of a cam incorporated in a nose gear shock strut?

A—Provides an internal shimmy damper.
B—Straightens the nosewheel.
C—Provides steering of aircraft during ground operation.

Many retractable landing gears use a centering cam to center the nosewheel when all the weight is off of the shock strut.

The centering cam ensures that the wheel is positioned so it will fit into the wheel well properly when it is retracted.

8348. Extension of an oleo shock strut is measured to determine the

A—amount of oil in the strut.
B—physical condition of the strut itself.
C—proper operating position of the strut.

The amount of extension of an oleo strut is measured to determine the proper amount of air in the strut.

This is undoubtedly what is meant in this question by the proper "operating position" of the strut.

8349. Debooster cylinders are used in brake systems primarily to

A—reduce brake pressure and maintain static pressure.
B—relieve excessive fluid and ensure a positive release.
C—reduce the pressure to the brake and increase the volume of fluid flow.

Debooster cylinders are used in brake systems to reduce the pressure applied to the brake and to increase the volume of fluid flowing into the brake.

Brake deboosters are used only with brakes that have power brake control valves and get their fluid from the main aircraft hydraulic power system.

8350. If a shock strut bottoms after it has been properly serviced, the

A—strut should be disassembled and the metering pin orifice plate replaced.
B—air pressure should be increased.
C—strut should be removed, disassembled, and inspected.

If a shock strut bottoms after it has been properly serviced with both oil and air, it should be removed from the aircraft, disassembled, and inspected to find the problem.

8351. A high-speed aircraft tire with a sound cord body and bead may be recapped

A—a maximum of three times.
B—only by the tire manufacturer.
C—an indefinite number of times.

Quoting from AC 43.13-1A, Section 332, b, (1), dealing with retreading types VI and VII high-speed tires: "The wide variations in tire operating environments which may affect total carcass life and serviceability make it inadvisable to prescribe arbitrarily the maximum number of times a high-speed tire should be retreaded. This aspect, therefore, is controlled by a thorough inspection of the carcass before retreading."

Answers

8344 [A] (068) AMT-STRUC, 6	8345 [A] (031) AMT-STRUC, 6	8346 [A] (068) AMT-STRUC, 6	8347 [B] (068) AMT-STRUC, 6
8348 [C] (068) AMT-STRUC, 6	8349 [C] (031) AMT-STRUC, 6	8350 [C] (068) AMT-STRUC, 6	8351 [C] (097) AC 43.13-1

8352. If an airplane equipped with master cylinders and single-disk brakes has excessive brake pedal travel, but the brakes are hard and effective, the probable cause is

A—the master cylinder one-way cup is leaking.
B—worn brake linings.
C—worn brake disk causing excessive clearance between the notches on the perimeter of the disk and the splines or keys on the wheel.

Badly worn brake linings can cause excessive brake pedal travel, but the brakes will be hard and effective once the pressure is built up.

8353. The correct inflation pressure for an aircraft tire can be obtained from

A—tire manufacturer's specifications.
B—the aircraft service manual.
C—the information stamped on the aircraft wheel.

The aircraft service manual gives the proper inflation pressure for an aircraft tire.

The pressure recommended by the aircraft manufacturer is to be used, rather than the pressure specified by the tire manufacturer.

8354. What should be checked when a shock strut bottoms during a landing?

A—Air pressure.
B—Packing seals for correct installation.
C—Fluid level.

If a shock strut bottoms during landing, the fluid is probably low.

Transfer of the fluid from one chamber to another cushions the impact of landing, whereas the air pressure cushions the shocks produced when the aircraft is taxiing.

8355. How is it determined in a master cylinder brake system that all of the air has been purged from the system?

A—By operating a hydraulic unit and watching the system pressure gauge for smooth, full scale deflection.
B—By depressing the brake and noting that the brake is firm and not spongy.
C—By measuring the amount of fluid return to the master cylinder upon brake release.

If all the air has been purged from a master-cylinder brake system, the brake pedal will feel firm rather than spongy.

8356. The left brake is dragging excessively on an airplane on which no recent brake service work has been performed. The most probable cause is

A—foreign particles stuck in the master cylinder compensating port.
B—excessively worn brake linings.
C—low fluid supply in the brake system reservoir.

The compensating port in a brake master cylinder must be open to vent the fluid in the brake line to the reservoir.

If the port is plugged with a piece of foreign matter, the brake cannot release when pressure is removed from the pedal. The brake will drag.

8357. If a brake debooster is used in a hydraulic brake system, its position in the system will be

A—between the pressure manifold of the main hydraulic system and the power brake control valve.
B—between the brake control valve and the brake actuating cylinder.
C—in the brake pressure line between the brake pedal and the brake accumulator.

A brake debooster is located in the brake system between the power brake control valve and the brake actuator cylinder.

The debooster lowers the pressure of the fluid supplied by the power-brake control valve to the actuator.

8358. The hydraulic packing seals used in a landing gear shock strut are

A—generally designed to be compatible with more than one type of fluid.
B—kept from direct contact with fluid by teflon or nylon backup rings.
C—used only with a specific type of fluid.

The seals used in a landing gear shock strut are made of a material that is compatible only with the type of fluid that is used in the strut. When replacing the seals, use only the seal having the correct part number and a current cure date.

Answers

8352 [B] (032) AMT-STRUC, 6	8353 [B] (097) AMT-STRUC, 6	8354 [C] (068) AMT-STRUC, 6	8355 [B] (065) AMT-STRUC, 6
8356 [A] (032) AMT-STRUC, 6	8357 [B] (031) AMT-STRUC, 6	8358 [C] (068) AMT-STRUC, 6	

8359. Lockout deboosters are primarily pressure reducing valves that

A—allow full debooster piston travel without fluid from the high pressure side entering the low pressure chamber.
B—cannot allow full debooster piston travel without fluid from the high pressure side entering the low pressure chamber.
C—must be bled separately after brake bleeding has been completed.

A lockout debooster is different from an ordinary debooster as it also serves as a hydraulic fuse. It will lock out the system after a given amount of fluid passes through it.

In an ordinary debooster, when fluid is lost, the piston moves to the bottom of its stroke and the riser unseats the ball check valve, and fluid from the power control valve passes through the piston shaft to replace the lost fluid.

In a lockout debooster, when fluid is lost, the piston moves to the bottom of its stroke and the riser unseats the ball check valve, but the spring-loaded lockout valve prevents fluid entering the lower chamber until the reset handle is lifted.

8360. A close inspection of a fusible plug reveals the core has experienced some deformation. What is the appropriate maintenance procedure?

A—Replace all the fusible plugs.
B—Replace the affected fusible plugs.
C—Replace with new wheel assembly.

Fusible plugs or thermal plugs must be inspected visually. These threaded plugs have a core that melts at a lower temperature than the outer part of the plug. This is to release air from the tire should the temperature rise to a dangerous level. A close inspection should reveal whether any core has experienced deformation that might be due to high temperature. If detected, all thermal plugs in the wheel should be replaced with new plugs.

8361. Chines are used on some aircraft nose wheel tires to help

A—nose gear extension at higher air speeds.
B—reduce the possibility of hydroplaning.
C—deflect water away from the fuselage.

The nosewheel tires on aircraft with turbine engines mounted on the aft fuselage are often equipped with chines, or deflectors, molded into the outer sidewalls.

The chines deflect the water away from the fuselage and prevent it from getting into the engines.

8362. The best safeguards against heat buildup in aircraft tires are

A—proper tire inflation, minimum braking, and ground rolls into the wind.
B—short ground rolls, slow taxi speeds, minimum braking, and proper tire inflation.
C—minimum braking, proper tire inflation, and long ground rolls.

The best way to safeguard against a buildup of heat in an aircraft tire is short ground rolls, slow taxi speeds, and the minimum use of brakes.

Above all, proper tire inflation pressure must be maintained.

8363. The fusible plugs installed in some aircraft wheels will

A—indicate tire tread separation.
B—prevent overinflation.
C—melt at a specified elevated temperature.

Fusible plugs installed in an aircraft wheel will melt at a specified elevated temperature to relieve the air pressure and deflate the tire rather than allowing the tire to explode.

8364. What action, if any, should be taken when there is a difference of more than 5 pounds of air pressure in tires mounted as duals?

A—Replace both tires.
B—Correct the discrepancy and enter in the aircraft records.
C—Replace the tire with the lowest pressure.

If there is a difference of more than 5 psi pressure between tires mounted as duals on an aircraft, the discrepancy should be corrected and a note made of this in the aircraft records so the condition of these tires can be watched carefully.

8365. How long should you wait after a flight before checking tire pressure?

A—At least 2 hours (3 hours in hot weather).
B—At least 3 hours (4 hours in hot weather).
C—At least 4 hours (5 hours in hot weather).

Wait at least two hours—three hours in hot weather—after a flight, before checking the tire pressure.

Answers

8359 [A] (031) AMT-STRUC, 6	8360 [A] (097) FAA-H-8083-31	8361 [C] (097) AMT-STRUC, 6	8362 [B] (097) AMT-STRUC, 6
8363 [C] (097) AMT-STRUC, 6	8364 [B] (097) AMT-STRUC, 6	8365 [A] (097) AMT-STRUC, 6	

8365-1. What is the minimum amount of time to wait for tires to cool before checking tire pressure?

A—3 hours.
B—2 hours.
C—1 hour.

When checking tire pressure, allow three hours to elapse after a typical landing to ensure the tire has cooled to ambient temperature.

8366. Excessive wear in the shoulder area of an aircraft tire is an indication of

A—overinflation.
B—excessive toe-in.
C—underinflation.

Underinflation will cause the shoulders of a tire to wear more than the center of the tread.

8367. Excessive wear in the center of the tread of an aircraft tire is an indication of

A—misalignment.
B—underinflation.
C—overinflation.

Overinflation will cause the center of the tire tread to wear more than the shoulders.

8368. When servicing an empty shock strut with fluid, the strut should be completely compressed and extended several times to ensure

A—the piston rod and wiper are lubricated with hydraulic fluid.
B—all excess hydraulic fluid is forced out of the strut.
C—proper packing ring seating and removal of air bubbles.

When a shock strut has been filled with fluid, it should be extended and compressed at least twice to be sure that all the packing rings are properly seated and all the air is worked out of the fluid.

8369. In shock struts, chevron seals are used to

A—absorb bottoming effect.
B—prevent oil from escaping.
C—serve as a bearing surface.

The chevron seals installed in an oleo shock strut prevent oil from escaping from the strut.

8370. On most aircraft, the oil level of an air and oil shock strut is checked by

A—removing the oil filler plug and inserting a gauge.
B—measuring the length of the strut extension with a certain air pressure in the strut.
C—releasing the air and seeing that the oil is to the level of the filler plug.

The oil level in an oleo shock strut is checked by releasing the air from the strut and filling the strut with oil to the level of the filler plug.

8371. A pilot reports that the brake pedals have excessive travel. A probable cause is

A—weak return springs.
B—lack of fluid in the brake system.
C—oil or some foreign matter on the brake rotors and linings.

If there is a lack of fluid in the brake system, the pedals will have to be depressed more than normal to get enough fluid into the wheel cylinders to apply the brakes. Answers A and C have no effect on the amount of pedal travel.

8372. When will a continuous horn provide a warning in the cockpit?

A—When the throttle is retarded and gear is not down and locked.
B—When the throttle is advanced and gear is down and locked.
C—When the throttle is retarded and gear is down and locked.

A landing gear warning system will cause a warning horn in the cockpit to sound when the throttle is pulled back, as it would be for landing if the landing gears are not all down and locked.

8373. An electric motor used to raise and lower a landing gear would most likely be a

A—shunt field series-wound motor.
B—split field shunt-wound motor.
C—split field series-wound motor.

Aircraft landing gear that are retracted and lowered with an electric motor use a series-wound motor because of its high starting torque and a split-field motor to both raise and lower the gear.

Answers

8365-1 [A] (097) FAA-H-8083-31	8366 [C] (097) AMT-STRUC, 6	8367 [C] (097) AMT-STRUC, 6	8368 [C] (068) AMT-STRUC, 6
8369 [B] (068) AMT-STRUC, 6	8370 [C] (068) AMT-STRUC, 6	8371 [B] (068) AMT-STRUC, 6	8372 [A] (068) AMT-STRUC, 6
8373 [C] (068) AMT-G Ch 4			

8374. When installing a chevron-type seal in an aircraft hydraulic cylinder, the open side of the seal should face

A—opposite the direction of fluid pressure.
B—up or forward when the unit is installed in a horizontal position.
C—the direction of fluid pressure.

A chevron seal is installed in a hydraulic component in such a way that the open sides of the seal face in the direction of the fluid pressure.

When the seal is properly installed, the hydraulic pressure will force the seal tightly against the cylinder walls.

8375. Nose gear centering cams are used in many retractable landing gear systems. The primary purpose of the centering device is to

A—align the nosewheel prior to touchdown.
B—engage the nosewheel steering.
C—center the nosewheel before it enters the wheel well.

Many retractable nose gears use a centering cam to center the nosewheel when all the weight is off of the shock strut.

The centering cam ensures that the wheel is positioned so it will fit into the wheel well properly.

8376. What device in a hydraulic system with a constant-delivery pump allows circulation of the fluid when no demands are on the system?

A—Pressure relief valve.
B—Shuttle valve.
C—Pressure regulator.

A hydraulic system pressure regulator is also called an unloading valve. When the system pressure is high enough, the pressure regulator traps the fluid in the system, where it is held by the air pressure in the accumulator.

With the system pressure trapped, the pressure regulator directs the output of the pressure pump back into the reservoir. The fluid circulates with very little load on the pump.

As soon as fluid is demanded by the system, the pressure regulator directs the pump output back into the system.

8377. A fully charged hydraulic accumulator provides

A—air pressure to the various hydraulic components.
B—a source for additional hydraulic power when heavy demands are placed on the system.
C—positive fluid flow to the pump inlet.

The accumulator allows an incompressible fluid such as oil to be stored under pressure.

The fluid stored in the accumulator under pressure is available to supplement the pump as an additional source of hydraulic power when heavy demands are placed on the system.

8378. A hydraulic system referred to as a "power pack" system will

A—have an engine-driven pump for greater pressure.
B—have all hydraulic power components located in one unit.
C—have a pressurized reservoir.

A hydraulic power pack is a small, self-contained hydraulic system that includes the reservoir, pump, selector valves, and relief valves all in one easy-to-service unit.

8379. A flexible hydraulic hose identified as MIL-H-8788 will have a strip running the length of the hose. This stripe is

A—installed without excessive twisting.
B—for high pressure fluids with a flexing range.
C—suitable for a wide temperature range.

The stripe that runs the length of a hydraulic hose is called a twist stripe, or lay line.

The purpose of a twist stripe is to allow a technician to be sure that the hose is not twisted when it is being installed. The stripe should be straight down the hose, not spiraled around it.

8380. An O-ring intended for use in a hydraulic system using MIL-H-5606 (mineral base) fluid will be marked with

A—a blue stripe or dot.
B—one or more white dots.
C—a white and yellow stripe.

O-rings intended for use with MIL-H-5606 hydraulic fluid are identified by a blue stripe or a blue dot.

8381. What condition would most likely cause excessive fluctuation of the pressure gauge when the hydraulic pump is operating?

A—Accumulator air pressure low.
B—Inadequate supply of fluid.
C—System relief valve sticking closed.

The condition most likely to cause excessive fluctuation of the pressure gauge, when the pump is operating, is an inadequate supply of fluid.

When the pump alternately picks up fluid and then air, the pressure gauge fluctuates.

Answers

8374 [C] (069) AMT-STRUC, 5	8375 [C] (068) AMT-STRUC, 6	8376 [C] (063) AMT-STRUC, 5	8377 [B] (063) AMT-STRUC, 5
8378 [B] (063) AMT-STRUC, 5	8379 [A] (063) AMT-STRUC, 5	8380 [A] (063) AMT-STRUC, 5	8381 [B] (063) AMT-STRUC, 5

8382. A filter incorporating specially treated cellulose paper is identified as a

A—sediment trap.
B—CUNO filter.
C—Micronic filter.

A Micronic filter used in a hydraulic system has an element made of specially treated cellulose paper, formed in vertical convolutions, or pleats.

The Micronic element prevents the passage of solids greater than 10 microns (0.000394 inch) in size.

8383. The purpose of an orifice check valve is to

A—relieve pressure to a sensitive component.
B—restrict flow in one direction and allow free flow in the other.
C—relieve pressure in one direction and prevent flow in the other direction.

An orifice check valve is a component in a hydraulic system that allows a free flow of fluid in one direction, but restricts its flow in the opposite direction.

8384. (Refer to Figure 10.) The trunnion nut on an aircraft landing gear requires a torque of 320 inch-pounds. To reach the nut, a 2-inch straight adapter must be used on an 18-inch torque wrench. How many foot-pounds will be indicated on the torque wrench when the required torque of the nut is reached?

A—24.
B—28.8.
C—22.

To solve this problem, use the formula:

$$T_W = \frac{Ta \times L}{(L + A)}$$

$$= \frac{320 \times 18}{18 + 2}$$

$$= 288 \text{ inch-pounds}$$

288 inch-pounds is divided by 12 to get 24 foot-pounds.

8385. A special bolt in a landing gear attachment requires a torque value of 440 inch-pounds. How many foot-pounds are required?

A—36.8.
B—38.
C—36.6.

Inch-pounds can be converted into foot-pounds by dividing by 12.

440 inch-pounds is 36.6 foot-pounds.

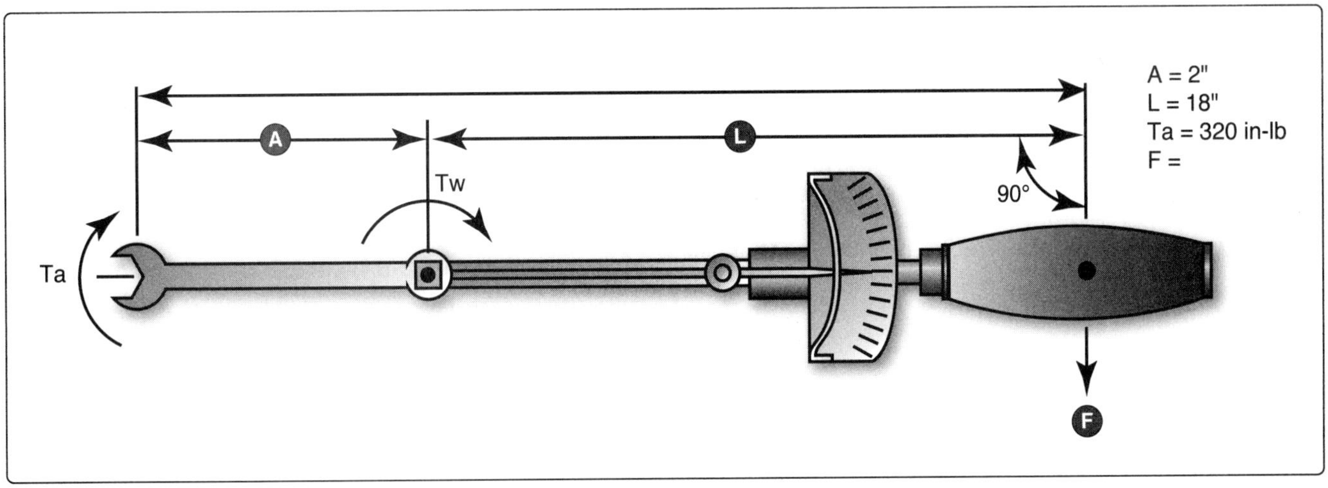

Figure 10. Torque value

Answers
8382 [C] (065) AMT-STRUC, 5
8383 [B] (031) AMT-STRUC, 5
8384 [A] (029) AMT-G Ch 7
8385 [C] (029) AMT-G Ch 7

Hydraulic and Pneumatic Power Systems

8386. To protect seals from damage when installed over a threaded section, the threaded section should be

A—coated with a heavy grease.
B—covered with tape.
C—covered with a suitable sleeve.

Packing rings or seals can be protected from damage when slipping them over the threads on an actuator by covering the threads with a suitable sleeve.

8387. Which of the following is the most commonly used seal to prevent internal and external leakage in both directions of a hydraulic unit?

A—O-ring.
B—V-ring.
C—U-ring.

The most commonly used type of seal for preventing both internal and external leakage in a hydraulic system component is an O-ring seal.

8388. Which of the following allows fluid to flow unimpeded in one direction but prevents fluid flow in the other direction?

A—Check valve.
B—Sequence valve.
C—Relief valve.

A check valve is a fluid power system component that allows a free flow of fluid in one direction, but it prevents any flow in the opposite direction.

8389. Select the valve used in a hydraulic system that directs pressurized fluid to one end of an actuating cylinder and simultaneously directs return fluid to the reservoir from the other end.

A—Sequence.
B—Shuttle.
C—Selector.

A selector valve is a fluid power system component that directs the flow of pressurized fluid to one end of an actuating cylinder, and simultaneously, directs return fluid to the reservoir from the other end of the cylinder.

8390. What function does the absolute pressure regulator perform in the pneumatic power system?

A—Regulates the compressor outlet air pressure to stabilize the system pressure.
B—Regulates the pneumatic system pressure to protect the moisture separator from internal explosion.
C—Regulates the compressor inlet air to provide a stabilized source of air for the compressor.

The absolute pressure regulator in an aircraft pneumatic system regulates the air pressure at the inlet to the compressor.

In doing this, it provides a stabilized source of air for the compressor.

8392. One of the distinguishing characteristics of an open-center selector valve used in a hydraulic system is that

A—fluid flows through the valve in the OFF position.
B—fluid flows in three directions in the ON position.
C—a limited amount of fluid flows in one direction and no fluid flows in the opposite direction.

In an open-center hydraulic selector valve, fluid flows through the valve when it is in the OFF position.

Open-center selector valves are installed in series with each other, while closed-center valves are installed in parallel with each other.

8393. What type of packings should be used in hydraulic components to be installed in a system containing Skydrol?

A—AN packings made of natural rubber.
B—Packing materials made for ester-base fluids.
C—AN packings made of neoprene.

Any packing used in a hydraulic system using Skydrol hydraulic fluid must be compatible with ester-base fluids, of which Skydrol is a type.

Only packings specifically called out by part number should be used in an aircraft hydraulic system.

Answers

8386 [C] (065) AC 43.13-1
8387 [A] (065) AMT-STRUC, 5
8388 [A] (063) AMT-STRUC, 5
8389 [C] (063) AMT-STRUC, 5
8390 [C] (063) AMT-STRUC, 5
8392 [A] (063) AMT-STRUC, 5
8393 [B] (065) AMT-STRUC, 5

8394. Relief valves are used in pneumatic systems

A—for one direction flow control.
B—to reduce the rate of airflow.
C—as damage-preventing units.

Relief valves in pneumatic systems are damage-preventing units that are preset and safetied.

They are installed to protect the system from excessive pressure buildup that can be caused by thermal expansion or by a compressor power system malfunction.

8395. An aircraft pneumatic system, which incorporates an engine-driven multistage reciprocating compressor, also requires

A—an oil separator.
B—a surge chamber.
C—a moisture separator.

A moisture separator must be used in an aircraft pneumatic system that incorporates engine-driven compressors. The moisture separator separates the moisture from the compressed air before the air is allowed to expand in the system.

If moisture were allowed to remain in the air, the temperature drop that occurs when the air expands would cause it to freeze and block the system.

8396. The removal of air from an aircraft hydraulic system is generally accomplished

A—through automatic bleed valves on individual components during system operation.
B—by operating the various hydraulic components through several cycles.
C—by allowing the system to remain inoperative for several hours.

Air is removed from most hydraulic systems by cycling the components through several operating cycles.

This operation will remove the fluid that contains air from double-acting hydraulic components.

Single-acting components, such as brakes, must be bled separately by bleeding some of the fluid from the system to remove the air.

8397. Pneumatic systems utilize

A—thermal valves.
B—relief valves.
C—shuttle valves.

The only components among the choices given with this question that are used in a pneumatic system are relief valves.

8398. The component in the hydraulic system that is used to direct the flow of fluid is the

A—check valve.
B—orifice check valve.
C—selector valve.

A selector valve is used in a hydraulic system to direct the flow of fluid.

8399. What type of selector valve is one of the most commonly used in hydraulic systems to provide for simultaneous flow of fluid into and out of a connected actuating unit?

A—Four-port, closed-center valve.
B—Three-port, four-way valve.
C—Two-port, open-center valve.

The most commonly used selector valve in an aircraft hydraulic system is a four-port, closed-center selector valve.

8400. What is the purpose of using backup rings with O-rings in hydraulic systems above 1,500 psi?

A—Prevent internal and external leakage of all moving parts within a hydraulic system.
B—Provide a seal between two parts of a unit which move in relation to each other.
C—Prevent high pressure from extruding the seal between the moving and stationary part.

A backup ring is used behind an O-ring in a high-pressure hydraulic system to prevent the high pressure from extruding the O-ring between the moving and the stationary parts.

8401. The purpose of the pressure regulator in a hydraulic system is to

A—maintain system operating pressure within a predetermined range and to unload the pump.
B—regulate the amount of fluid flow to the actuating cylinders within the system.
C—prevent failure of components or rupture of hydraulic lines under excessive pressure.

A hydraulic system pressure regulator maintains a system operating pressure within a predetermined range.
The regulator unloads the pump when the upper limit of this pressure is reached.

The pump remains unloaded, circulating the fluid through the system with no opposition until the lower limit of the pressure is reached, at which time the pump again forces fluid into the system.

Answers

8394 [C] (063) AMT-STRUC, 5	8395 [C] (079) AMT-STRUC, 5	8396 [B] (079) AMT-STRUC, 5	8397 [B] (079) AMT-STRUC, 5
8398 [C] (063) AMT-STRUC, 5	8399 [A] (063) AMT-STRUC, 5	8400 [C] (063) AMT-STRUC, 5	8401 [A] (063) AMT-STRUC, 5

8402. A flexible sealing element subject to motion is a

A—compound.
B—packing.
C—gasket.

A packing is a flexible sealing element that is subject to motion. A gasket is a flexible sealing element that is not subject to motion.

8403. Which characteristics apply to aircraft hydraulic systems?

A—About 80 percent operating efficiency (20 percent loss due to fluid friction).
B—Minimum maintenance requirements and simple to inspect.
C—Minimum maintenance requirements, lightweight, and simple to inspect.

Hydraulic systems have many advantages as a power source for operating various aircraft units. Hydraulic systems combine the advantages of light weight, ease of installation, simplicity of inspection, and minimum maintenance requirements. Hydraulic operations are also almost 100 percent efficient, with only a negligible loss due to fluid friction.

8404. If a rigid tube is too short for the flare to reach its seat before tightening, pulling it into place by tightening

A—is acceptable.
B—may distort the flare.
C—may distort the cone.

You must never pull a rigid tube into position by using the flare nut on the fitting.

This poor practice will distort the flare and could actually pull it off of the tube.

8405. The installation of a new metal hydraulic line should be made with

A—a straight tube to withstand the shocks and vibration to which it will be subjected.
B—a straight tube to permit proper alignment of the fitting and thereby reduce fluid loss through leakage.
C—enough bends to allow the tube to expand and contract with temperature changes and to absorb vibration.

All metal hydraulic lines should have enough bends in them to allow the tube to expand and contract with temperature and pressure changes and to absorb vibration.

8406. Extrusion of an O-ring seal is prevented in a high-pressure system by the use of a

A—backup ring on the side of the O-ring next to the pressure.
B—U-ring on the side of the O-ring away from the pressure.
C—backup ring on the side of the O-ring away from the pressure.

Extrusion of an O-ring seal is prevented in a high-pressure system by installing a backup ring in the groove with the O-ring, on the side of the O-ring away from the pressure.

The backup ring prevents the high-pressure fluid from forcing the O-ring into the space between the piston and cylinder wall.

8407. What is one advantage of piston-type hydraulic motors over electric motors?

A—They are considerably quieter in operation.
B—There is no fire hazard if the motor is stalled.
C—They work satisfactorily over a wider temperature range.

One of the main advantages of a piston-type hydraulic motor over an electric motor is the fact that there is no fire hazard when the hydraulic motor is stalled.

8408. Generally, the first step in removing an accumulator from an aircraft is to

A—relieve system pressure.
B—discharge the preload.
C—drain the reservoir.

Generally, the first step in removing an accumulator from an aircraft is to relieve all of the system pressure.

An accumulator can be removed from an aircraft with the air preload still in it, but the preload must be discharged before the accumulator is disassembled.

Answers

8402 [B] (063) AMT-STRUC, 5	8403 [C] (063) AMT-STRUC, 5	8404 [B] (065) AMT-G Ch 9	8405 [C] (063) AMT-G Ch 9
8406 [C] (063) AMT-STRUC, 5	8407 [B] (063) AMT-STRUC, 5	8408 [A] (065) AMT-STRUC, 5	

8409. (Refer to Figure 11.) The AN flared-tube fitting is referred to in which picture?

A—1.
B—2.
C—3.

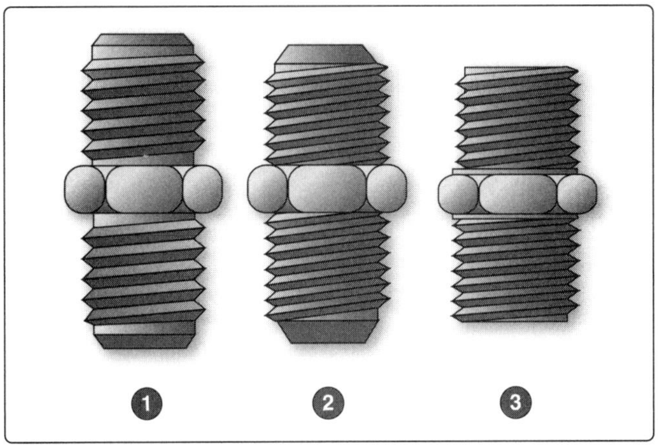

Figure 11. Fittings

An AN flared-tube fitting is shown as 1 in Figure 11. The AN fitting differs from the AC fitting shown as 2 because of the unthreaded portion of the fitting between the end of the threads and the flare cone.

8410. (Refer to Figure 12.) Which illustration(s) show(s) the correct spiral for teflon backup rings?

A—1 and 2.
B—3.
C—1 and 3.

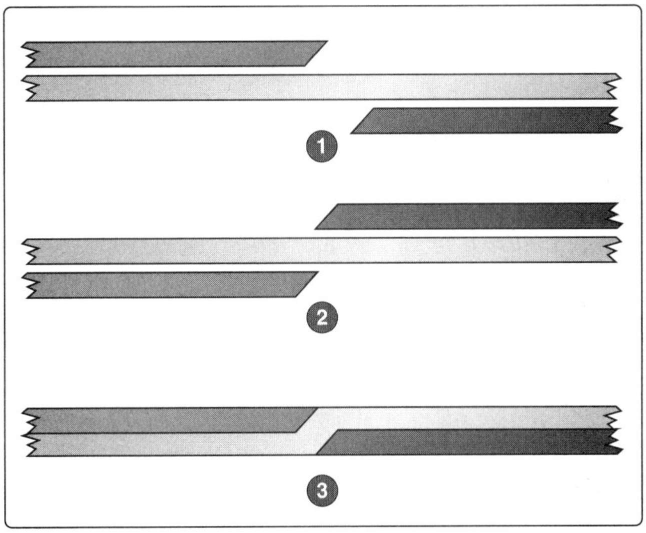

Figure 12. Backup rings

The correct spiral for a Teflon backup ring is shown in 1 and 3. View 1 shows the ring before pressure is applied. View 3 shows the way the ring shapes itself when pressure is applied.

8411. If a hydraulic brake system uses neoprene rubber packing materials, the correct hydraulic fluid to service the system is

A—mineral-base oil.
B—synthetic-base oil.
C—phosphate ester-base oil.

A hydraulic system that uses mineral-base fluid should use neoprene rubber packing materials. Systems using vegetable-base fluid should use natural rubber seals, and systems using phosphate ester-base fluid should use butyl seals.

8412. The internal resistance of a fluid which tends to prevent it from flowing is called

A—volatility.
B—viscosity.
C—stability.

The internal resistance of a fluid which tends to prevent its flowing is called the viscosity of the fluid.

8413. What is the viscosity of hydraulic fluid?

A—The increase in volume of a fluid due to temperature change.
B—The fluid's ability to resist oxidation and deterioration for long periods.
C—The internal resistance of a fluid which tends to prevent it from flowing.

The viscosity of a fluid is its internal resistance, which tends to prevent its flowing.

8414. Which is a characteristic of petroleum-base hydraulic fluid?

A—Flammable under normal conditions.
B—Compatible to natural rubber seals and packings.
C—Nonflammable under all conditions.

Petroleum-base hydraulic fluid is flammable under normal conditions.

Because of the flammability of mineral-base fluid, synthetic fluids have been developed.

Answers

8409 [A] (011) AMT-G Ch 9
8410 [C] (011) AMT-STRUC, 5
8411 [A] (065) AMT-STRUC, 5
8412 [B] (064) AMT-STRUC, 5
8413 [C] (064) AMT-STRUC, 5
8414 [A] (064) AMT-STRUC, 5

8415. When servicing aircraft hydraulic systems, use the type fluid specified in the

A—aircraft manufacturer's maintenance manual.
B—instruction plate affixed to the unit.
C—aircraft manufacturer's maintenance manual or instruction plate affixed to the unit.

When servicing aircraft hydraulic systems, be sure to use only the type of fluid specified in the aircraft manufacturer's maintenance manual or on the instruction plate attached to the reservoir or to the unit.

8416. Petroleum-base hydraulic fluid is which color?

A—Purple.
B—Blue.
C—Red.

MIL-H-5606 petroleum-base hydraulic fluid is dyed red.

8417. Which of the following is adversely affected by atmospheric humidity if left unprotected?

A—MIL-H-5606 and Skydrol hydraulic fluid.
B—MIL-H-5606 hydraulic fluid.
C—Skydrol hydraulic fluid.

Skydrol phosphate ester-base hydraulic fluid is susceptible to contamination from moisture in the atmosphere. Containers of Skydrol should be kept tightly closed to prevent this contamination.

8418. Which is a characteristic of synthetic-base hydraulic fluid?

A—Low moisture retention.
B—High flash point.
C—Low flash point.

One of the main advantages of the new synthetic-base hydraulic fluids over the older mineral-base hydraulic fluids is their higher flash point.

8419. Which statement about fluids is correct?

A—Any fluid will completely fill its container.
B—All fluids are considered to be highly compressible.
C—All fluids readily transmit pressure.

All fluids, whether gases or liquids, transmit pressure in a fluid power system.

A liquid is a noncompressible fluid and a gas, such as air, is a compressible fluid.

8420. Two types of hydraulic fluids currently being used in civil aircraft are

A—mineral base, and phosphate ester base.
B—mixed mineral base and phosphate ester base.
C—petroleum base and mixed mineral base.

Nearly all of the hydraulic fluid used in modern civilian aircraft is either mineral-base MIL-H-5606 (red oil), or phosphate ester-base fluid such as the various types of Skydrol.

8421. Which of the following lists only desirable properties of a good hydraulic fluid that has chemical stability?

A—High viscosity, low flash point, high fire point.
B—High flash point, low viscosity, low fire point.
C—Low viscosity, high flash point, high fire point.

A good hydraulic fluid must have a low viscosity so it is free to flow. It must be chemically stable and must have a high flash point and a high fire point.

8422. Characteristics of MIL-H-8446 hydraulic fluid are

A—blue color, phosphate ester base, fire resistant, butyl rubber seals.
B—light purple color, phosphate ester base, fire resistant, butyl rubber seals.
C—light green color, phosphate ester base, fire resistant, butyl rubber seals.

MIL-H-8446 hydraulic fluid is a light purple, phosphate ester-base, fire-resistant fluid.

Butyl rubber seals are used with MIL-H-8446 fluid.

8423. Where can information be obtained about the compatibility of fire-resistant hydraulic fluid with aircraft materials?

A—Fluid manufacturer's technical bulletins.
B—Aircraft manufacturer's specifications.
C—AC 43.13-1A.

Manufacturer's technical bulletins provide information on the compatibility of fire-resistant hydraulic fluids with aircraft materials.

Answers

8415 [C] (064) AMT-STRUC, 5	8416 [C] (064) AMT-STRUC, 5	8417 [C] (064) AMT-STRUC, 5	8418 [B] (064) AMT-STRUC, 5
8419 [C] (064) AMT-STRUC, 5	8420 [A] (064) AMT-STRUC, 5	8421 [C] (064) AMT-STRUC, 5	8422 [B] (064) AMT-STRUC, 5
			8423 [A] (064) AMT-STRUC, 5

8424. Characteristics of MIL-H-5606 hydraulic fluid are

A—light purple color, phosphate ester base, fire resistant, uses butyl rubber seals.
B—blue color, will burn, natural rubber seals.
C—red color, petroleum base, will burn, synthetic rubber seals.

MIL-H-5606 hydraulic fluid is a red, petroleum-base fluid. It will burn and should be used with components that have synthetic rubber seals.

8425. Characteristics of MIL-H-7644 hydraulic fluid are

A—red color, petroleum base, will burn, synthetic rubber seals.
B—light purple color, phosphate ester base, fire resistant, butyl rubber seals.
C—blue color, vegetable base, will burn, natural rubber seals.

MIL-H-7644 hydraulic fluid is a blue, vegetable-base fluid. It will burn and should be used with components that have natural rubber seals.

8426. If an aircraft hydraulic system requires mineral-base hydraulic fluid, but phosphate ester-base hydraulic fluid is used, what will be the effect on the system?

A—No effect.
B—System will be contaminated, fluids will not blend, and the seals will fail.
C—System will be contaminated, fluids will not blend, but there will be no seal problem.

If MIL-H-8446 fluid is used in a hydraulic system that is designed to use MIL-H-5606 fluid, the system will be contaminated. The seals are likely to fail.
These two fluids are not compatible.

8427. What is used to flush a system normally serviced with MIL-H-5606 hydraulic fluid?

A—Methyl ethyl ketone or kerosene.
B—Naphtha or varsol.
C—Lacquer thinner or trichlorethylene.

Naphtha or varsol can be used to flush a system that is normally serviced with MIL-H-5606 hydraulic fluid.

8428. Components containing phosphate ester-base hydraulic fluid may be cleaned with

A—Stoddard solvent.
B—Naphtha.
C—Carbon tetrachloride.

Systems using Skydrol fluid should be flushed with trichloroethylene. Components containing Skydrol fluid can be cleaned with Stoddard solvent, MEK, or isopropyl alcohol.

8429. How can the proper hydraulic fluid to be used in an airplane be determined?

A—By referring to the pilot operating handbook.
B—By consulting the aircraft's Type Certificate Data Sheet.
C—By consulting the aircraft manufacturer's service manual.

Aircraft service manuals specify the correct type of hydraulic fluid to be used in a particular aircraft.
The fluid specifications are also normally marked on the hydraulic reservoir.

8430. Phosphate ester-base hydraulic fluid is very susceptible to contamination from

A—rapid changes in temperature.
B—water in the atmosphere.
C—icing conditions.

Phosphate ester hydraulic fluid is susceptible to contamination from moisture in the atmosphere. For this reason, the fluid containers must always be tightly capped when not in use.

8431. Materials which are Skydrol compatible or resistant include

A—epoxy paints and most common aircraft metals.
B—polyurethane and epoxy paints.
C—common aircraft metals, polyurethane, and epoxy paints.

Skydrol does not appreciably affect common aircraft metals such as aluminum, silver, zinc, magnesium, cadmium, iron, stainless steel, bronze, chromium, and others—as long as the fluids are kept free from contaminants. Paints such as epoxies and polyurethanes are also Skydrol resistant.

Answers

8424 [C] (064) AMT-STRUC, 5	8425 [C] (064) AMT-STRUC, 5	8426 [B] (064) AMT-STRUC, 5	8427 [B] (065) AMT-STRUC, 5
8428 [A] (065) AMT-STRUC, 5	8429 [C] (064) AMT-STRUC, 5	8430 [B] (064) AMT-STRUC, 5	8431 [C] (064) AMT-STRUC, 5

8432. The hydraulic component that automatically directs fluid from either the normal source or an emergency source to an actuating cylinder is called a

A—bypass valve.
B—shuttle valve.
C—crossflow valve.

A shuttle valve is an automatic valve mounted on a landing-gear actuating cylinder or brake cylinder. It directs normal system fluid into the component for normal operation, but in an emergency it automatically shifts to allow fluid from the emergency system to enter the component.

8432-1. What is commonly used to connect an emergency source of power, and at the same time disconnect the normal hydraulic source from critical parts of a landing gear or wheel braking system for operation (usually when the normal source system fails)?

A—Selector valve.
B—Shuttle valve.
C—Sequence valve.

A shuttle valve is used in some systems to insure that if an emergency source of hydraulic power is needed, only the essential parts of the system are actuated.

8433. The primary purpose of a hydraulic actuating unit is to transform

A—fluid motion into mechanical pressure and back again.
B—fluid pressure into useful work.
C—energy from one form to another.

The primary purpose of any hydraulic actuating unit is to transform fluid pressure into useful work.

8434. The primary function of the flap overload valve is to

A—prevent the flaps from being lowered at airspeeds which would impose excessive structural loads.
B—cause the flap segments located on opposite sides of the aircraft centerline to extend and retract together so that the aircraft will not become aerodynamically unbalanced to the extent that it becomes uncontrollable.
C—boost normal system pressure to the flaps in order to overcome the air loads acting on the relatively large flap area.

A flap overload valve prevents the flaps from being lowered at an airspeed that would impose excessive structural loads on the aircraft.

8435. A unit which transforms hydraulic pressure into linear motion is called

A—an actuating cylinder.
B—an accumulator.
C—a hydraulic pump.

An actuating cylinder is a device that transforms hydraulic fluid pressure into linear motion.

8436. If it is necessary to adjust several pressure regulating valves in a hydraulic system, what particular sequence, if any, should be followed?

A—Units most distant from the hydraulic pump should be adjusted first.
B—Units with the highest pressure settings are adjusted first.
C—Units are independent of each other, and therefore, no particular sequence is necessary.

When adjusting several pressure regulating valves in a hydraulic system, always adjust the valve with the highest pressure setting first.

If a valve having a lower pressure setting is adjusted first, you will never be able to reach the pressure required for the higher setting.

8437. If an aircraft's constant-pressure hydraulic system cycles more frequently than usual and no fluid leakage can be detected, the most probable cause is

A—a too high relief valve setting.
B—pump volume output too high.
C—low accumulator air preload.

A hydraulic system cycling more frequently than it should is an indication that the accumulator air preload is low.

The accumulator is not holding the pressure on the system as long as it would if the preload pressure were correct.

Answers

8432 [B] (063) AMT-STRUC, 5
8432-1 [B] (063) FAA-H-8083-31
8433 [B] (063) AMT-STRUC, 5
8434 [A] (063) AMT-STRUC, 5
8435 [A] (063) AMT-STRUC, 5
8436 [B] (065) AMT-STRUC, 5
8437 [C] (065) AMT-STRUC, 5

8438. Unloading valves are used with many engine-driven hydraulic pumps to

A—dampen out pressure surges.
B—relieve the pump pressure.
C—relieve system pressure.

An unloading valve is another name for a system pressure regulator.

When the system pressure reaches the regulating range, a check valve in the unloading valve traps pressure in the system where it is held by the accumulator.

A valve then opens to allow fluid from the pump to circulate back to the reservoir with very little opposition.

The fluid flows with the pump unloaded until the system pressure drops to the kick-in pressure of the unloading valve. When the kick-in pressure is reached, the output of the pump is again directed into the system.

8439. What safety device is usually located between the driving unit and hydraulic pump drive shaft?

A—Thermal relief valve.
B—Pump motor safety switch.
C—Pump drive coupling shear section.

Almost all engine-driven hydraulic pumps have a shear section in their drive coupling. If all of the pressure relief devices should fail, or if the pump should seize, the shaft will shear and prevent the pump being further damaged.

8440. Which valve installed in a hydraulic system will have the highest pressure setting?

A—Pressure regulator valve.
B—Main relief valve.
C—Thermal relief valve.

A thermal relief valve would be adjusted to a higher pop-off pressure than any of the other valves in a hydraulic system.

Thermal relief valves are installed in portions of a hydraulic system that normally hold fluid trapped by a selector valve. They relieve the pressure that is built up in the lines as the fluid is heated by the surrounding air.

Thermal relief valves are set to relieve a pressure higher than any of the other valves, so they will not interfere with normal system operation or protection.

8441. Excluding lines, which components are required to make up a simple hydraulic system?

A—Actuator, pressure reservoir, accumulator, and selector valve.
B—Pump, reservoir, selector valve, and actuator.
C—Pump, reservoir, relief valve, and shuttle valve.

A simple hydraulic system includes a reservoir, a pump, a selector valve, and an actuator.

All of the other components in the system are used to make the system more efficient and more effective.

8442. Most variable displacement aircraft hydraulic pumps in use

A—must be driven at a nearly constant speed in order to be practical for use.
B—are not practical for use with a closed-center hydraulic system.
C—contain a built-in means of system pressure regulation.

Most modern variable-displacement hydraulic pumps have a built-in means of system pressure regulation. They require no separate system pressure regulator.

8443. In a gear-type hydraulic pump, a mechanical safety device incorporated to protect the pump from overload is the

A—bypass valve.
B—check valve.
C—shear pin.

A shear pin or a shear section of the drive shaft is used with a constant-displacement, engine-driven, gear-type hydraulic pump to protect the pump from damage in case of an overload.

If all the regulating and relief valves fail, the shaft will shear and keep the pump from being more seriously damaged.

8444. After installation of a rebuilt hydraulic hand pump, it is found that the handle cannot be moved in the pumping direction (pressure stroke). The most likely cause is an incorrectly installed

A—hand pump inport check valve.
B—inport/outport orifice check valve.
C—hand pump outport check valve.

If the handle of a rebuilt hydraulic hand pump cannot be moved in the normal pumping direction, the most likely cause would be that the pump outport check valve is incorrectly installed.

Answers

8438 [B] (065) AMT-STRUC, 5	8439 [C] (063) AMT-STRUC, 5	8440 [C] (063) AMT-STRUC, 5	8441 [B] (063) AMT-STRUC, 5
8442 [C] (065) AMT-STRUC, 5	8443 [C] (063) AMT-STRUC, 5	8444 [C] (063) AMT-STRUC, 5	

8445. Pressure is a term used to indicate the force per unit area. Pressure is usually expressed in

A—pounds per square inch.
B—pounds per inch.
C—pounds per cubic inch.

Pressure is a measure of force-per-unit area, and it is normally expressed in such terms as pounds per square inch (psi).

8446. If two actuating cylinders which have the same cross-sectional area but different lengths of stroke are connected to the same source of hydraulic pressure, they will exert

A—different amounts of force but will move at the same rate of speed.
B—equal amounts of force but will move at different rates of speed.
C—equal amounts of force and will move at the same rate of speed.

If two actuating cylinders with pistons having the same cross-sectional area but different lengths of stroke, are connected to the same source of hydraulic pressure, they will exert equal amounts of force and they will move at the same rate of speed. But it will take them different lengths of time to reach the end of their stroke.

8447. Using a hand pump, pressure of 100 psi has been built up in a hydraulic system. The hand pump piston is 1 inch in diameter. A 1/2-inch line connects the hand pump to an actuating cylinder 2 inches in diameter. What is the pressure in the line between the hand pump and the actuator?

A—100 psi.
B—150 psi.
C—200 psi.

According to Pascal's law, pressure is the same in all parts of an enclosed system. If the hand pump builds up a pressure of 100 psi, this same pressure will exist in the one-half-inch-diameter line as well as in the two-inch-diameter actuating cylinder.

8448. Heat exchanger cooling units are required in some aircraft hydraulic systems because of

A—fluid flammability.
B—high pressures and high rates of fluid flow.
C—the high heat generated from braking.

Some aircraft hydraulic systems have such a high fluid pressure and high rate of fluid flow that the fluid becomes too hot for efficient operation. These systems cool the fluid with heat exchangers that are similar to engine oil coolers.

8449. Which is true regarding the ground check of a flap operating mechanism which has just been installed?

A—If the time required to operate the mechanism increases with successive operations, it indicates the air is being worked out of the system.
B—If the time required to operate the mechanism decreases with successive operations, it indicates the air is being worked out of the system.
C—All hydraulic lines and components should be checked for leaks by applying soapy water to all connections.

It is a normal procedure for a double-acting system such as the flap operating mechanism to have air in it when it is first installed.

To remove this air, the system is cycled through its operation a number of times.

As the air is expelled from the system, the operating time will decrease because of the loss of the compressible fluid in the system.

8450. A hydraulic system operational check during ground runup of an aircraft indicates that the wing flaps cannot be lowered using the main hydraulic system, but can be lowered by using the emergency hand pump. Which is the most likely cause?

A—The flap selector valve has a severe internal leak.
B—The pressure accumulator is not supplying pressure to the system.
C—The fluid level in the reservoir is low.

If the level of the fluid in the reservoir is below the outlet that feeds the engine-driven pump, portions of the system can be actuated by the emergency hand pump, but not by the engine-driven pump.

8451. Many hydraulic reservoirs contain a small quantity of fluid which is not available to the main system pump. This fluid is retained to

A—prime the main system.
B—supply fluid to the auxiliary pump.
C—supply fluid to the pressure accumulator.

The outlet from the hydraulic reservoir to the main engine-driven hydraulic pump is above the outlet that goes to the hand pump.

If a line breaks and the engine-driven pump forces all the fluid to which it has access overboard, there is still fluid left in the reservoir. There is enough fluid available to the auxiliary hand pump for such critical operations as landing gear extension.

Answers

8445 [A] (063) AMT-G Ch 3
8446 [C] (063) AMT-G Ch 3
8447 [A] (063) AMT-G Ch 3
8448 [B] (063) AMT-STRUC, 5
8449 [B] (065) AMT-STRUC, 5
8450 [C] (065) AMT-STRUC, 5
8451 [B] (064) AMT-STRUC, 5

8452. The unit in a hydraulic system that requires a certain action to be completed before another action can begin is called a

A—check valve.
B—sequence valve.
C—snubber valve.

Sequence valves allows one hydraulic operation to follow another in a definite order, or sequence.

8453. The purpose of a hydraulic pressure regulator is to

A—prevent the system pressure from rising above a predetermined amount due to thermal expansion.
B—boost the pressure in portions of the system.
C—relieve the pump of its load when no actuating units are being operated.

A hydraulic system pressure regulator, or unloading valve, relieves the pump of its load when no units are being actuated. The accumulator holds the system pressure at the desired level while the pump is unloaded.

8454. Severe kickback of the emergency hydraulic hand pump handle during the normal intake stroke will indicate which of the following?

A—The hand pump inlet check valve is sticking open.
B—The main system relief valve is set too high.
C—The hand pump outlet check valve is sticking open.

If the hand pump kicks back during the normal intake stroke, it is an indication that the outlet check valve is stuck open, allowing system pressure stored in the accumulator to push back on the piston.

This pressure should have been stopped by the check valve.

8455. What type of valve in an aircraft hydraulic system permits fluid to flow freely in one direction, but restricts the rate at which fluid is allowed to flow in the other direction?

A—Check valve.
B—Orifice restrictor.
C—Orifice check valve.

An orifice check valve permits fluid to flow freely in one direction, but restricts the rate of flow in the opposite direction.

8456. The main system pressure relief valve in a simple hydraulic system equipped with a power control valve should be adjusted

A—with the power control valve held in the CLOSED position.
B—while one or more actuating units are in operation.
C—with the power control valve in the OPEN position.

A hydraulic power control valve is a hand-operated shutoff valve with an automatic turn-on feature. It must be closed manually, but it opens automatically.

When the unit is OPEN, it permits free circulation of fluid from the engine-driven pump to the reservoir. In this way, it relieves the pump of its load.

In order to adjust the system pressure relief valve, the power control valve must be pushed in to its CLOSED position and held until the system pressure builds up high enough to adjust the system pressure relief valve.

8456-1. Which of the following safeguards ensures proper system operation and mitigates damage to non-metallic components of the hydraulic system?

A—The manual bleed valve should be closed prior to servicing hydraulic fluid to prevent fluid loss as the cap is being removed.
B—Before assembly of any hydraulic components, seals and gaskets should be inspected and replaced only if they show signs of wear or leakage.
C—When adding fluid to a system, use the type specified in the aircraft manufacturer's maintenance manual or on the instruction plate affixed to the reservoir or unit being serviced.

To assure proper system operation and to avoid damage to nonmetallic components of the hydraulic system, the correct fluid must be used. When adding fluid to a system, use the type specified in the aircraft manufacturer's maintenance manual or on the instruction plate affixed to the reservoir or unit being serviced.

8457. A hydraulic accumulator is charged with an air preload of 1,000 psi. When a hydraulic system pressure of 3,000 psi is developed, the pressure on the air side of the accumulator will be

A—1,000 psi.
B—3,000 psi.
C—4,000 psi.

When hydraulic fluid flows into an accumulator, it compresses the air charge. The pressure of the air will be the same as the pressure of the hydraulic fluid.

When the hydraulic system pressure is 3,000 psi, the pressure of the air in the accumulator will also be 3,000 psi.

Answers

8452 [B] (063) AMT-STRUC, 5	8453 [C] (063) AMT-STRUC, 5	8454 [C] (063) AMT-STRUC, 5	8455 [C] (063) AMT-STRUC, 5
8456 [A] (065) AMT-STRUC, 5	8456-1 [C] (064) FAA-H-8083-31	8457 [B] (063) AMT-STRUC, 5	

8458. How is the air in a hydraulic accumulator prevented from entering the fluid system?

A—By forcing the oil/air mixture through a centrifugal separating chamber that prevents the air from leaving the accumulator.
B—By physically separating the air chamber from the oil chamber with a flexible or movable separator.
C—By including a valve that automatically closes when the fluid level lowers to a preset amount.

Air in the accumulator is kept out of the fluid portion of the hydraulic system by the two chambers of the accumulator being separated by a diaphragm, a bladder, or a movable piston.

8459. After a hydraulic accumulator has been installed and air chamber charged, the main system hydraulic pressure gauge will not show a hydraulic pressure reading until

A—at least one selector valve has been actuated to allow fluid to flow into the fluid side of the accumulator.
B—the air pressure has become equal to the fluid pressure.
C—the fluid side of the accumulator has been charged.

Even though a hydraulic accumulator has been charged with air, no system pressure will show on the main system gauge until fluid has been pumped into the fluid side of the accumulator.

8460. Which must be done before adjusting the relief valve of a main hydraulic system incorporating a pressure regulator?

A—Eliminate the action of the unloading valve.
B—Adjust all other system relief valves which have a lower pressure setting.
C—Manually unseat all system check valves to allow unrestricted flow in both directions.

Before any pressure relief valves in a hydraulic system can be adjusted, the pressure regulator, which is also known as the unloading valve, must be temporarily set to a pressure above that of the relief valve being set, or its action must be eliminated in some other way.

If the operation of the unloading valve is not eliminated, the pressure will never rise high enough to adjust the relief valve.

8461. Which seals are used with petroleum-base hydraulic fluids?

A—Polyester.
B—Butyl rubber.
C—Buna-N.

Seals used in hydraulic systems using petroleum-base fluids are made of neoprene or Buna-N. Butyl rubber seals are used with phosphate ester-base fluids.

8461-2. Seals used with a mineral-base hydraulic fluid are identified by which color code?

A—Green dash.
B—Blue dot or stripe.
C—Yellow dot or stripe.

The material of which the seal is made, its age, and its hardness are all important when making the proper replacement. Mineral-base hydraulic fluid (MIL-H-5606) should use a seal with a blue dot or stripe.

8462. The air that is expended and no longer needed when an actuating unit is operated in a pneumatic system is

A—exhausted or dumped, usually overboard.
B—returned to the compressor.
C—charged or pressurized for use during the next operating cycle.

After a pneumatic component has been actuated, the compressed air is dumped overboard.

8463. Some hydraulic systems incorporate a device which is designed to remain open to allow a normal fluid flow in the line, but closed if the fluid flow increases above an established rate. This device is generally referred to as a

A—hydraulic fuse.
B—flow regulator.
C—metering check valve.

A hydraulic fuse may shut off the flow of fluid when either an excessive rate of flow occurs or when an excessive amount of flow has occurred.

Under normal operation, a fuse acts as an open line.

Answers

8458 [B] (063) AMT-STRUC, 5	8459 [C] (065) AMT-STRUC, 5	8460 [A] (065) AMT-STRUC, 5	8461 [C] (063) AMT-STRUC, 5
8461-2 [B] (063) AMT-STRUC	8462 [A] (063) AMT-STRUC, 5	8463 [A] (063) AMT-STRUC, 5	

8464. When hydraulic system pressure control and relief units fail to function properly, how are most systems protected against overpressure?

A—A shear section on the main hydraulic pump drive shaft.
B—One or more hydraulic fuses installed in the pressure and return lines.
C—A shuttle valve interconnecting the main and emergency systems.

If the system pressure regulator and all of the system pressure relief valves fail, a shear section in the main hydraulic pump shaft will break.

This will protect the system against overpressure.

8465. A worn hydraulic pump shaft seal can normally be detected by

A—hydraulic fluid flowing from the pump drain line.
B—evidence of hydraulic fluid combined in the engine oil.
C—the presence of hydraulic fluid around the pump mounting pad.

Hydraulic pumps have a shaft seal vented into a compartment in the pump and drain overboard. If the pump shaft seal leaks, hydraulic fluid will drip out of the overboard drain line.

8466. If an engine-driven hydraulic pump of the correct capacity fails to maintain normal system pressure during the operation of a cowl flap actuating unit, the probable cause is

A—mechanical interference to the movement of the cowl flap.
B—a partial restriction in the inport of the selector valve.
C—restriction in the pump outlet.

If there is a restriction in the pump outlet or between the pump outlet and the system pressure regulator, the system pressure will drop when some unit is actuated.

8467. Before removing the filler cap of a pressurized hydraulic reservoir, in order to service the system, you must

A—relieve the hydraulic system pressure.
B—pressurize all components in the system.
C—relieve the air pressure.

Some hydraulic reservoirs are pressurized with bleed air from the engine compressor or from a venturi-tee.

All of the air pressure must be relieved before a pressurized reservoir is opened.

8468. What happens to the output of a constant-displacement hydraulic pump when the hydraulic system pressure regulator diverts the fluid from the system to the reservoir?

A—The output pressure remains the same, but the volume reduces.
B—The output pressure reduces, but the volume remains the same.
C—The output pressure and volume remain the same.

When the system pressure regulator opens to unload the pump, the fluid passes from the reservoir through the pump to the pressure regulator, back into the reservoir, with almost no opposition.

The volume remains the same, but the pump output pressure drops to almost zero.

The system pressure regulator traps the pressure in the system where it is held by the accumulator.

8469. Hydraulic system accumulators serve which of the following functions?

A—Dampen pressure surges.
B—Dampen pressure surges and ensure a continuous supply of fluid to the pump.
C—Supplement the system pump when demand is beyond the pump's capacity and store power for limited operation of components if the pump is not operating.

An accumulator in a hydraulic system is basically a chamber to store hydraulic fluid under pressure.

It dampens the pressure surges and aids, or supplements, the power pump when the demand is beyond the pump's capacity. It also stores power for limited operation of components when the pump is not operating.

8470. Chattering of the hydraulic pump during operation is an indication

A—of low accumulator preload.
B—that the main system relief valve is sticking open.
C—that air is entering the pump.

An air leak at the inlet side of a hydraulic pump will cause it to chatter as it alternately gets air and then hydraulic fluid.

Answers

8464 [A] (063) AMT-STRUC, 5	8465 [A] (063) AMT-STRUC, 5	8466 [C] (065) AMT-STRUC, 5	8467 [C] (065) AMT-STRUC, 5
8468 [B] (063) AMT-STRUC, 5	8469 [C] (063) AMT-STRUC, 5	8470 [C] (063) AMT-STRUC, 5	

8471. Quick-disconnect couplings in hydraulic systems provide a means of

A—easily replacing hydraulic lines in areas where leaks are common.
B—quickly connecting and disconnecting hydraulic lines and eliminate the possibility of contaminates entering the system.
C—quickly connecting and disconnecting hydraulic lines without loss of fluid or entrance of air into the system.

Hydraulic quick-disconnect fittings are normally found at the hydraulic pump.

They allow the lines to be quickly connected or disconnected without loss of fluid or entrance of air into the system.

8472. Which seal/material is used with phosphate ester-base hydraulic fluids?

A—Silicone rubber.
B—Butyl rubber.
C—Neoprene rubber.

Butyl rubber seals are used with phosphate ester-base hydraulic fluid.

8473. A hydraulic pump is a constant-displacement type if it

A—produces an unregulated constant pressure.
B—produces a continuous positive pressure.
C—delivers a uniform rate of fluid flow.

A constant-displacement type of hydraulic pump delivers a uniform rate of fluid flow. It moves the same amount of fluid each time it rotates.

8474. A hydraulic motor converts fluid pressure to

A—linear motion.
B—rotary motion.
C—angular motion.

A hydraulic motor converts fluid pressure into rotary motion.

8475. A crossflow valve which is designed to bypass fluid from one side of an actuating cylinder to the other side, under certain conditions, may be found in some aircraft installed in the

A—flap overload system.
B—engine cowl flap system.
C—landing gear system.

The function of a crossflow valve is to bypass hydraulic fluid from the landing gear up line to the down line when the landing gear is being extended.

When the landing gear is released from its uplocks, its weight causes it to fall so rapidly that fluid cannot fill in behind the piston in the actuating cylinder, and excessive pressure builds up on the opposite side of the piston.

The crossflow valve permits fluid to flow from the up side of the piston to the down side and thus allows the gear to fall more easily and with an even motion.

8476. Hydraulic fluid filtering elements constructed of porous paper are normally

A—cleaned and reused.
B—discarded at regular intervals and replaced with new filtering elements.
C—not approved for use in certificated aircraft.

The porous paper elements used in some hydraulic filters are discarded at regular intervals, rather than being cleaned.

8477. A pilot reports that when the hydraulic pump is running, the pressure is normal. However, when the pump is stopped, no hydraulic pressure is available. This is an indication of a

A—leaking selector valve.
B—low accumulator fluid preload.
C—leaking accumulator air valve.

If the hydraulic pressure is normal when the pump is running, but drops to zero when the pump stops, there is a good probability that the accumulator has lost its air preload. A leaking accumulator air valve could cause this.

8478. If fluid is added to a reservoir in a constant pressure hydraulic system while the system is pressurized, what will result?

A—Fluid will spray violently out of the reservoir when the filler neck cap is removed.
B—The fluid level will increase when system pressure is reduced.
C—Air will be drawn into the system, when the filler neck cap is removed.

Fluid is drawn from the reservoir when pressure is built up in the system and the accumulator is charged.

If fluid is added to the reservoir while the system is pressurized, the fluid level will increase when the system pressure is reduced.

Answers

8471 [C] (063) AMT-STRUC, 5	8472 [B] (064) AMT-STRUC, 5	8473 [C] (065) AMT-STRUC, 5	8474 [B] (063) AMT-STRUC, 5
8475 [C] (063) AMT-STRUC, 5	8476 [B] (065) AMT-STRUC, 5	8477 [C] (063) AMT-STRUC, 5	8478 [B] (064) AMT-STRUC, 5

8479. In a hydraulic system that has a reservoir pressurized with turbine-engine compressor bleed air, which unit reduces the air pressure between the engine and reservoir?

A—Relief valve.
B—Air bleed relief valve.
C—Air pressure regulator.

Hydraulic system reservoirs that are pressurized by turbine bleed air require an air pressure regulator between the engine and the reservoir to reduce the pressure to the proper value.

8480. What is the main purpose of a pressurized reservoir in a hydraulic system?

A—Prevent tank collapse at altitude.
B—Prevent hydraulic pump cavitation.
C—Prevent hydraulic fluid from foaming.

Reservoirs for hydraulic systems used in aircraft that fly at extremely high altitudes are normally pressurized to produce a positive supply of fluid to the engine-driven pump. This prevents the pump cavitation.

8481. One of the main advantages of Skydrol is its

A—wide operating temperature.
B—high operating pressure.
C—inability to mix with water.

Skydrol is a phosphate ester-base hydraulic fluid that has the advantages over MIL-H-5606 fluid in its being fire resistant and its wide temperature operating range of -65°F to greater than 225°F.

8482. Hydraulic fluid reservoirs are sometimes designed with a standpipe in one of the outlet ports in order to assure emergency supply of fluid. The outlet port with the standpipe in it furnishes fluid to the

A—emergency pump when the fluid supply to the normal system has been depleted.
B—emergency pump at any time it is required.
C—normal system power pump.

The normal system power pump connects to the fluid outlet of the reservoir that is fed from the standpipe.

If the power pump forces all of the fluid available to it overboard through a broken line, there will still be fluid in the reservoir that can be used by the emergency hand pump.

8483. An emergency supply of fluid is often retained in the main hydraulic system reservoir by the use of a standpipe. The supply line is connected to the

A—inlet of the main hydraulic system.
B—inlet of the emergency pump.
C—outlet of the main system pump.

The supply line from the standpipe in a hydraulic reservoir is attached to the inlet of the main hydraulic system pump.

This standpipe ensures that there will be an supply of fluid available to the emergency pump if the main system pump should force overboard all of the fluid available to it.

8484. To check the air charge in a hydraulic accumulator,

A—reduce all hydraulic pressure, then observe the reading on the accumulator air gauge.
B—observe the first reading on the hydraulic system gauge while operating a component in the system.
C—read it directly from the auxiliary pressure gauge.

The modern practice is to measure the hydraulic system pressure on the nitrogen, or air, side of the accumulator.

When no engine is running and all hydraulic pressure is removed from the system, the accumulator gauge reads the amount of the accumulator air preload.

8485. How would the air pressure charge in the accumulator be determined if the engine is inoperative, but the system still has hydraulic pressure?

A—Read it directly from the main system pressure gauge with all actuators inoperative.
B—Build up system pressure with the emergency pump and then read the pressure on a gauge attached to the air side of the accumulator.
C—Operate a hydraulic unit slowly and note the pressure at which a rapid pressure drop begins as it goes toward zero.

The air pressure charge in an accumulator may be determined by slowly operating some hydraulic unit, such as the power brakes, to bleed the pressure off of the system.

Watch the system pressure gauge. The last pressure indicated on the gauge before it suddenly drops to zero is the pressure of the air in the accumulator.

8486. How many of these seals are used with petroleum-base hydraulic fluids?

A—Natural rubber, Ethylene-propylene.
B—Neoprene, Buna-N.
C—Natural rubber, Butyl rubber.

Seals used with petroleum-base hydraulic fluid are made of synthetic rubber. Neoprene and Buna-N are forms of synthetic rubber.

Answers

8479 [C] (063) AMT-STRUC, 5	8480 [B] (065) AMT-STRUC, 5	8481 [A] (064) AMT-STRUC, 5	8482 [C] (064) AMT-STRUC, 5
8483 [A] (063) AMT-STRUC, 5	8484 [A] (065) AMT-STRUC, 5	8485 [C] (065) AMT-STRUC, 5	8486 [B] (063) AMT-STRUC, 5

8487. Hydraulic system thermal relief valves are set to open at a

A—lower pressure than the system relief valve.
B—higher pressure than the system relief valve.
C—lower pressure than the system pressure regulator.

Hydraulic system thermal relief valves are set at a higher pressure than the system pressure relief valve.

8488. Chatter in a hydraulic system is caused by

A—excessive system pressure.
B—insufficient system pressure.
C—air in the system.

Chatter in a hydraulic system is usually caused by air in the fluid that is moving through the pump.

8489. If hydraulic fluid is released when the air valve core of the accumulator is depressed, it is evidence of

A—excessive accumulator air pressure.
B—a leaking check valve.
C—a ruptured diaphragm or leaking seals.

A ruptured diaphragm or leaking seal in an accumulator will allow hydraulic fluid to get into the air side of the accumulator and be released with the air when the air valve core is depressed.

8490. Although dents in the heel of a bend are not permissible, they are acceptable in the remainder of the hydraulic tube providing they are less than what percent of the tube diameter?

A—5 percent.
B—10 percent.
C—20 percent.

Dents in the heel of a bend in a piece of hydraulic tubing are not acceptable.

Dents in other parts of hydraulic tubing are acceptable if their depth is less than 20 percent of the tube diameter.

8491. If the hydraulic system pressure is normal while the engine-driven pump is running, but there is no pressure after the engine has been shut off, it indicates

A—the system relief valve setting is too high.
B—no air pressure in the accumulator.
C—the pressure regulator is set too high.

Air is required in an accumulator to hold pressure in the system after the engine is shut down. If the system does not hold pressure, there is no air pressure in the accumulator.

8492. The purpose of restrictors in hydraulic systems is to

A—control the rate of movement of hydraulically operated mechanisms.
B—allow the flow of fluid in one direction only.
C—lower the operating pressure of selected components.

Restrictors in a hydraulic system control the rate of movement of hydraulically operated mechanisms.

They control the rate of movement by restricting the flow of fluid into the mechanism.

8493. A common cause of slow actuation of hydraulic components is

A—cold fluid.
B—restricted orifices.
C—internal leakage in the actuating unit.

Internal leakage in an actuating unit is a common cause of slow actuation of a hydraulic component.

8494. A loud hammering noise in a hydraulic system that has an accumulator usually indicates

A—air in the fluid.
B—too much preload in the accumulator.
C—too low or no preload in the accumulator.

A loud hammering noise in a hydraulic system using an accumulator is often caused by a loss of accumulator air preload.

The pressure regulator puts the pump on the line. Since there is no compressible fluid in the system, the cutout pressure is immediately reached. This causes a shock on the system. As soon as the regulator directs the pump outlet to the return manifold, the system pressure drops below the cut-in pressure and the pump is again put on the line.

Answers

8487 [B] (063) AMT-STRUC, 5	8488 [C] (063) AMT-STRUC, 5	8489 [C] (065) AMT-STRUC, 5	8490 [C] (065) AMT-G Ch 9
8491 [B] (065) AMT-STRUC, 5	8492 [A] (063) AMT-STRUC, 5	8493 [C] (065) AMT-STRUC, 5	8494 [C] (065) AMT-STRUC, 5

8495. Teflon hose that has developed a permanent set from being exposed to high pressure or temperature should

A—not be straightened or bent further.
B—not be reinstalled once removed.
C—be immediately replaced.

When a Teflon hose that has developed a permanent set from exposure to high pressure or temperature is removed from an aircraft hydraulic system, its ends should be supported to prevent the hose from being straightened or further bent.

8496. In a typical high-pressure pneumatic system, if the moisture separator does not vent accumulated water when the compressor shuts down, a likely cause is a

A—saturated chemical dryer.
B—malfunctioning pressure transmitter.
C—malfunctioning solenoid dump valve.

When the pneumatic system pressure reaches the pump cutoff pressure of 3,150 psi, the pressure-sensing switch opens the circuit to the hydraulic selector valve and shuts off pressure to the hydraulic motor which drives the air compressor. At the same time, the dump-valve solenoid is de-energized and the dump valve opens, venting overboard any moisture that has accumulated in the moisture separator.

If the solenoid-operated dump valve should malfunction, the water accumulated in the moisture separator will not be vented overboard when the compressor shuts down.

Cabin Atmosphere Control Systems

8497. Which section of a turbine engine provides high pressure bleed air to an air cycle machine for pressurization and air conditioning?

A—Low or high pressure compressor.
B—Compressor inlet.
C—C-D inlet compressor duct.

The bleed air that is used to drive the air-cycle machine is taken from one of the lower pressure stages of the turbine engine compressor.

8498. At which component in an air-cycle cooling system does air undergo a pressure and temperature drop?

A—Expansion turbine.
B—Primary heat exchanger.
C—Refrigeration bypass valve.

The refrigeration process takes place in an air cycle cooling system as the compressed air expands through the turbine wheel of the air-expansion turbine.

Expansion of the air reduces both its temperature and its pressure.

8499. In a freon vapor-cycle cooling system, where is cooling air obtained for the condenser?

A—Turbine engine compressor.
B—Ambient air.
C—Pressurized cabin air.

The air that passes through the condenser coils is ambient, or outside, air and it removes the heat from the heated and pressurized refrigerant. The loss of this heat causes the refrigerant to condense from a vapor into a liquid.

8500. What is ventilating air used for on a combustion heater?

A—Provides combustion air for ground blower.
B—Carries heat to the places where needed.
C—Provides air required to support the flame.

Ventilating air that flows through a combustion heater picks up heat from the heater and carries it to places in the aircraft where it is needed.

8501. Turbine engine air used for air conditioning and pressurization is generally called

A—compressed air.
B—ram air.
C—bleed air.

The air taken from a turbine engine for air conditioning and pressurization is normally called compressor bleed air.

Answers

8495 [A] (003) AC 43.13-1	8496 [C] (079) AMT-STRUC, 5	8497 [A] (002) AMT-SYS Ch 3	8498 [A] (006) AMT-SYS Ch 3
8499 [B] (006) AMT-SYS Ch 3	8500 [B] (035) AMT-SYS Ch 3	8501 [C] (006) AMT-P Ch 10	

8502. In the combustion heater, combustion air system, what prevents too much air from entering the heaters as air pressure increases?

A—Either a combustion air relief valve or a differential pressure regulator.
B—Only a differential pressure regulator can be used.
C—Only a combustion air relief valve can be used.

Combustion air for each cabin heater is received through either the main air intake or a separate outside air scoop.

To prevent too much air from entering the heaters as the air pressure increases, either a combustion-air-relief valve or a differential-pressure regulator is provided.

The combustion-air relief valve is located in the line leading from the ram intake air duct and is spring-loaded to dump excess air into the cabin-heater exhaust-gas stream.

The differential pressure regulator is also located in the combustion-air intake line. However, it controls the amount of air reaching the combustion heater in a slightly different manner.

8503. How is the cabin pressure of an aircraft maintained in flight?

A—By controlling the rate of the air flowing into the cabin.
B—By inflating the door seals and recirculating the conditioned cabin air.
C—By controlling the rate of the air flowing out of the cabin.

Cabin pressure of an aircraft in flight is controlled by controlling the rate at which the air is allowed to leave the cabin. The pressurization air source supplies more air than is needed for the proper cabin pressure, and the cabin altitude controller controls the outflow valves that regulate the amount of air that leaves the cabin.

8504. What controls the operation of the cabin pressure regulator?

A—Cabin altitude.
B—Bleed air pressure.
C—Compression air pressure.

The operation of the cabin pressure regulator is determined by the cabin air pressure or, more accurately, by the cabin altitude.

8505. The basic air-cycle cooling system consists of

A—a source of compressed air, heat exchangers, and a turbine.
B—heaters, coolers, and compressors.
C—ram air source, compressors, and engine bleeds.

The basic air-cycle cooling system consists of a source of compressed air, a heat exchanger, and a turbine to extract energy from the compressed air and expand it to drop its temperature.

8506. The purpose of the dump valve in a pressurized aircraft is to relieve

A—all positive pressure from the cabin.
B—a negative pressure differential.
C—pressure in excess of the maximum differential.

The dump valve in a pressurized aircraft relieves all positive pressure from the cabin when the aircraft is on the ground.

8507. What component might possibly be damaged if liquid refrigerant is introduced into the low side of a vapor-cycle cooling system when the pressure is too high or the outside air temperature is too low?

A—Compressor.
B—Condenser.
C—Evaporator.

If liquid refrigerant is introduced into the low side of a vapor-cycle air cooling system, it will likely not change into a vapor before it gets into the compressor and cause the reed valves in the compressor to be damaged.

8508. How can it be determined that a vapor-cycle cooling system is charged with the proper amount of freon?

A—Air bubbles in the sight glass disappear.
B—The compressor loads up and RPM decreases.
C—Air bubbles appear in the sight glass.

A full charge of refrigerant in a vapor-cycle air cooling system is indicated by the absence of bubbles in the sight glass in the receiver-dryer.

8509. When charging a vapor-cycle cooling system after evacuation, the low-pressure gauge fails to come out of a vacuum. What is indicated?

A—Blockage in the system.
B—The expansion valve failed to close.
C—The compressor is not engaging.

When charging a vapor-cycle air cooling system after it has been evacuated, refrigerant is put into the high side of the system.

If the compound gauge, connected to the low side, fails to come out of a vacuum, there is a blockage in the system. The low side is not getting any refrigerant.

Answers

8502 [A] (012) AMT-SYS Ch 3	8503 [C] (080) AMT-SYS Ch 3	8504 [A] (080) AMT-SYS Ch 3	8505 [A] (006) AMT-SYS Ch 3
8506 [A] (080) AMT-SYS Ch 3	8507 [A] (005) AMT-SYS Ch 3	8508 [A] (005) AMT-SYS Ch 3	8509 [A] (005) AMT-SYS Ch 3

8510. What component in a vapor-cycle cooling system would most likely be at fault if a system would not take a freon charge?

A—Expansion valve.
B—Condenser.
C—Receiver-dryer.

If a vapor-cycle air cooling system does not take a charge of refrigerant, the most likely component to be at fault is the thermal expansion valve.

It takes only a tiny particle of dirt or other contaminant to stop the flow of refrigerant through the tiny orifice in this valve.

8511. Frost or ice buildup on a vapor-cycle cooling system evaporator would most likely be caused by

A—the mixing valve sticking closed.
B—moisture in the evaporator.
C—inadequate airflow through the evaporator.

If there is not enough airflow through the evaporator coils to add heat from the cabin to the refrigerant, ice or frost will build up on the outside of the evaporator.

8512. What test is used to determine the serviceability of an oxygen cylinder?

A—Pressure test with manometer.
B—Pressure test with nitrogen.
C—Pressure test with water.

High-pressure oxygen cylinders must be periodically hydrostatically tested. In this test, they are filled with water and pressurized to 5/3 of their working pressure.

8513. How often should standard weight high-pressure oxygen cylinders be hydrostatically tested?

A—Every 5 years.
B—Every 4 years.
C—Every 3 years.

Standard-weight oxygen cylinders must be hydrostatically tested every five years. Lightweight cylinders must be hydrostatically tested every three years.

8514. To be eligible for recharging, a DOT 3HT oxygen cylinder must have been hydrostatically tested every three years and be retired from service after

A—24 years or 4,380 filling cycles.
B—15 years or 10,000 filling cycles.
C—10 years or 5,000 filling cycles.

AC 43.13-1B states "The lightweight cylinders must be hydrostatic tested every 3 years, and must be retired from service after 24 years or 4,380 pressurizations, whichever occurs first. These cylinders carry an ICC or DOT 3HT 1850 classification and must be stamped with the approval after being inspected."

8515. Which oxygen system employs a regulator that operates only when the user inhales?

A—Continuous-flow system.
B—Emergency-flow system.
C—Demand-flow system.

When oxygen is delivered only as the user inhales, or on demand, it is known as a demand-flow system. During the hold and exhalation periods of breathing, the oxygen supply is stopped. Thus, the duration of the oxygen supply is prolonged as none is wasted. Demand-flow systems are used most frequently by the crew on high performance and air transport category aircraft.

8516. The component that determines the pressure level in the cabin is the cabin air pressure

A—shut-off valve.
B—safety valve.
C—outflow valve.

The selected cabin altitude is maintained in a pressurized aircraft by the altitude controller modulating (opening or closing as needed) the outflow valve.

The safety valve is open when the aircraft is on the ground and is closed in flight unless the cabin pressure exceeds a preset value.

8517. Hot compressor bleed air operates the conditioned air system on some turbine aircraft, cold air supplied by the

A—hot air mixing valve.
B—vapor cycle air conditioning.
C—air cycle air conditioning.

Cold air is supplied for the air conditioning system in some turbine-engine-powered aircraft by an air-cycle cooling system.

Hot compressor bleed air loses some of its heat energy as it flows through a primary heat exchanger. This slightly cooled air then flows into the air-cycle machine where it is compressed and its temperature and pressure are both increased. This heated air then passes through a secondary heat exchanger, where it gives up some of its heat energy, and then it flows into the air-cycle expansion turbine. Here it uses up a large amount of its heat energy in driving the compressor. The air expands as it leaves the turbine and becomes cold.

Answers

8510 [A] (005) AMT-SYS Ch 3	8511 [C] (006) AMT-SYS Ch 3	8512 [C] (074) AC 43.13-1	8513 [A] (073) AC 43.13-1
8514 [A] (073) AC 43.13-1	8515 [C] (074) AMT-SYS Ch 3	8516 [C] (080) AMT-SYS Ch 3	8517 [C] (002) AMT-SYS Ch 3

8518. For use in pressurized aircraft, which is generally the least complicated and requires the least maintenance?

A—Chemical oxygen generator systems.
B—High-pressure oxygen systems.
C—Low-pressure oxygen systems.

Chemical oxygen generator systems are used as emergency backup for pressurized aircraft because of their lack of complexity, efficient use of space and weight, and the small amount of maintenance they require.

8519. What is the main cause of contamination in a gaseous oxygen system?

A—Moisture.
B—Dust.
C—Nitrogen.

The main form of contamination of an oxygen system is moisture. Moisture in the system may be due to damp charging equipment and condensation of moisture in the system.

8520. Where does the last stage of cooling in an air-cycle air conditioning system occur?

A—Refrigeration unit compressor.
B—Secondary heat exchanger.
C—Expansion turbine.

In an air-cycle air conditioning system, hot compressor bleed air mixes with bleed air that has been cooled in the primary heat exchanger. The air leaving the mixer is held at a constant temperature of 300°F.

This 300°F air is compressed by the refrigeration unit compressor, then flows through the secondary heat exchanger for its initial cooling.

After giving up some of its heat in the secondary heat exchanger, it flows through the expansion turbine where it gives up more heat energy for its last stage of cooling. From the expansion turbine, the cold air is mixed with just enough 300°F air to maintain its temperature at the level called for by the cabin temperature regulator.

8521. The point at which freon flowing through a vapor-cycle cooling system gives up heat and changes from a gas to a liquid is the

A—condenser.
B—evaporator.
C—expansion valve.

Refrigerant in a vapor-cycle cooling system enters the expansion valve as a high-pressure liquid and sprays out into the evaporator coils as tiny droplets of low-pressure liquid refrigerant.

Heat from the cabin enters the refrigerant in the evaporator coils and changes the liquid refrigerant into refrigerant vapors.

The refrigerant vapors are compressed in the compressor where their temperature and pressure are both increased. The hot, high-pressure refrigerant gas leaves the compressor and flows into the condenser.

In the condenser, ambient air blowing over the coils absorbs heat from the refrigerant and it changes back into a liquid, ready to begin its trip through the system again to pick up more heat from the cabin.

8522. The point at which freon flowing through a vapor-cycle cooling system absorbs heat and changes from a liquid to a gas is the

A—condenser.
B—evaporator.
C—expansion valve.

Refrigerant in a vapor-cycle cooling system enters the expansion valve as a high-pressure liquid and sprays out into the evaporator coils as tiny droplets of liquid refrigerant.

Heat from the cabin enters the refrigerant in the evaporator coils and changes the liquid refrigerant into a gas.

The gaseous refrigerant is compressed in the compressor where its temperature and pressure are both increased. The hot refrigerant gas leaves the compressor and flows into the condenser.

In the condenser, ambient air blowing over the coils absorbs heat from the refrigerant and changes back into a liquid, ready to begin its trip through the system again to pick up more heat from the cabin.

8523. How is the cabin pressure of a pressurized aircraft usually controlled?

A—By a pressure-sensitive switch that causes the pressurization pump to turn on or off as required.
B—By an automatic outflow valve that dumps all the pressure in excess of the amount for which it is set.
C—By a pressure-sensitive valve that controls the output pressure of the pressurization pump.

Cabin pressurization is normally controlled by the cabin pressure regulator and an automatic outflow valve. The outflow valve dumps from the cabin all pressure in excess of that called for by the regulator.

Answers

8518 [A] (080) AMT-SYS Ch 3	8519 [A] (074) AMT-SYS Ch 3	8520 [C] (006) AMT-SYS Ch 3	8521 [A] (006) AMT-SYS Ch 3
8522 [B] (006) AMT-SYS Ch 3	8523 [B] (080) AMT-SYS Ch 3		

8524. Which is considered a good practice concerning the inspection of heating and exhaust systems of aircraft utilizing a jacket around the engine exhaust as a heat source?

A—Supplement physical inspections with periodic operational carbon monoxide detection tests.
B—All exhaust system components should be removed periodically, and their condition determined by the magnetic-particle inspection method.
C—All exhaust system components should be removed and replaced at each 100-hour inspection period.

It is a good operating practice, when using exhaust-type heat exchangers for cabin heat, to periodically check for the presence of carbon monoxide.

8525. On some cabin pressurization systems, pressurization on the ground is restricted by the

A—main landing gear operated switch.
B—cabin pressure regulator.
C—negative pressure-relief valve.

When a pressurized aircraft is on the ground with the cabin closed, the safety dump valve is held open by vacuum controlled by the dump solenoid, which is actuated through the landing gear safety, or squat, switch.

As soon as the aircraft is airborne and the weight is off of the landing gear, the squat switch allows the dump solenoid to close the safety dump valve, allowing the cabin to be pressurized.

8526. The cabin pressure control setting has a direct influence upon the

A—outflow valve opening.
B—pneumatic system pressure.
C—inflow valve opening.

The cabin-pressure controller controls the opening of the outflow valve.

8527. The function of the evaporator in a freon cooling system is to

A—liquefy freon in the line between the compressor and the condenser.
B—lower the temperature of the cabin air.
C—transfer heat from the freon gas to ambient air.

Cabin air is drawn through the evaporator where it gives up some of its heat and is cooled. Liquid freon in the evaporator absorbs the heat and changes into a vapor.

8528. What is the purpose of a mixing valve in a compressor bleed air air conditioning system?

A—Control the supply of hot, cool, and cold air.
B—Distribute conditioned air evenly to all parts of the cabin.
C—Combine ram air with conditioned air.

The mixing valve in an air-cycle air conditioning system mixes air from three sources to get cabin pressurizing air of the desired temperature.

The three sources of air are: hot air before it passes through the primary heat exchanger, cool air after it has passed through the secondary heat exchanger, and cold air after it has passed through the air-cycle machine.

By controlling the amount of air from each of these three sources, the desired temperature of pressurization air can be obtained.

8529. What component of a pressurization system prevents the cabin altitude from becoming higher than airplane altitude?

A—Cabin rate-of-descent control.
B—Negative pressure relief valve.
C—Positive pressure relief valve.

All pressurized aircraft require some form of negative-pressure relief valve. This valve may be incorporated into the outflow valve or it may be a separate unit.

The negative-pressure relief valve opens when the outside air pressure is greater than the cabin pressure. In this way, it prevents cabin altitude from ever becoming higher than the aircraft altitude.

8530. If the liquid level gauge in a vapor-cycle cooling system indicates a low freon charge, the system should

A—be operated and a pressure check performed.
B—be operated for a period of time to reach a stable condition and then the freon level rechecked.
C—not be operated until freon and oil have been added.

Bubbles in the sight glass of the receiver-dryer of a vapor-cycle air cooling system indicate that the charge of refrigerant is low.

When bubbles are seen, the system should be operated for a period of time to allow the system to stabilize. The sight glass should be rechecked to see if it still indicates that the refrigerant charge is low.

Answers

8524 [A] (012) AMT-SYS Ch 3	8525 [A] (068) AMT-SYS Ch 3	8526 [A] (080) AMT-SYS Ch 3	8527 [B] (006) AMT-SYS Ch 3
8528 [A] (002) AMT-SYS Ch 3	8529 [B] (080) AMT-SYS Ch 3	8530 [B] (005) AMT-SYS Ch 3	

8531. If the cabin rate of climb is too great, the control should be adjusted to cause the

A—outflow valve to close slower.
B—outflow valve to close faster.
C—cabin compressor speed to decrease.

If the cabin rate of climb is too great, the outflow valve should be made to close faster to prevent the cabin altitude from changing too rapidly.

8532. The position of the thermostatic expansion valve in a vapor-cycle cooling system is determined by temperature and pressure of the

A—freon entering the evaporator.
B—air in the outlet of the condenser.
C—freon in the outlet of the evaporator.

The position of the thermostatic expansion valve is controlled by the temperature of the refrigerant as it leaves the evaporator. This temperature is sensed by the sensing bulb of the expansion valve.

An externally equalized thermal expansion valve also senses the pressure at the outlet of the evaporator to compensate for the pressure drop across a large evaporator.

8533. The function of the condenser in a freon cooling system is to

A—transfer heat from the freon gas to ambient air.
B—change liquid freon into a gas before it enters the compressor.
C—transfer heat from the cabin air to the liquid freon.

The condenser in a freon cooling system transfers heat from the hot, high-pressure freon gas to the ambient air.

When the hot gas gives up its heat, it condenses into a high-pressure liquid. It is then ready to begin its refrigeration cycle over again.

8534. The function of an expansion valve in a freon cooling system is to act as a metering device and to

A—reduce the pressure of the gaseous freon.
B—increase the pressure of the liquid freon.
C—reduce the pressure of the liquid freon.

High-pressure liquid freon passes through the expansion valve, where it changes into low-pressure liquid freon before it enters the evaporator coils.

In the evaporator, the low-pressure liquid changes into a low-pressure vapor by absorbing heat from cabin air flowing across the evaporator coils.

8535. Which prevents a sudden loss of pressurization in the event that there is a loss of the pressurization source?

A—Firewall shutoff valve.
B—Cabin pressure outflow valve.
C—Delivery air duct check valve.

There is a delivery air duct check valve, or isolation valve, at the discharge side of the air turbine that prevents the sudden loss of pressurization in the event of loss of the pressurization air source.

8536. When servicing an air conditioning system that has lost all of its freon, it is necessary to

A—check oil and add as necessary, evacuate the system, relieve vacuum, and add freon.
B—check oil and add as necessary, evacuate the system, and add freon.
C—check oil and add as necessary, and add freon.

If an air conditioning system has lost its freon charge, the oil level should be checked and oil added if needed.

The system is then evacuated by subjecting it to an extremely low pressure (a high vacuum) for a period of time. Freon is then put into the system while it is under vacuum.

Answers

8531 [B] (080) AMT-SYS Ch 3	8532 [C] (006) AMT-SYS Ch 3	8533 [A] (006) AMT-SYS Ch 3	8534 [C] (006) AMT-SYS Ch 3
8535 [C] (080) AMT-SYS Ch 3	8536 [B] (005) AMT-SYS Ch 3		

8537. The primary function of the cabin pressurization system outflow valve is to

A—provide protection against overpressurization.
B—maintain the desired cabin pressure.
C—maintain the same cabin air pressure at all altitudes.

The function of the outflow valve in a pressurization system is to control the amount of air that flows out of the cabin to maintain the cabin pressure called for by the pressure controller.

8538. One purpose of a jet pump in a pressurization and air conditioning system is to

A—produce a high pressure for operation of the outflow valve.
B—provide for augmentation of airflow in some areas of the aircraft.
C—assist in the circulation of freon.

A jet pump is essentially a special venturi in a line carrying air from certain areas in an aircraft that need an augmented airflow through them. Jet pumps are often used in the lines that pull air through galleys and toilet areas.

A nozzle blows a stream of high-velocity compressor bleed air into the throat of the venturi. This increases the velocity of the air flowing through the venturi and produces a low pressure that pulls air from the compartment to which it is connected.

8539. After cleaning or replacing the filtering element in a combustion heater fuel system, the system should be pressurized and

A—all connections checked for leaks.
B—the fuel filter bypass valve reset to the filter position.
C—a sample of fuel taken downstream from the filter to ensure proper operation of the new filtering element.

After the filter elements in a combustion heater fuel system have been cleaned or replaced, the fuel system should be pressurized and all connections checked for leaks.

8540. The operation of an aircraft combustion heater is usually controlled by a thermostat circuit which

A—alternately turns the fuel on and off, a process known as cycling.
B—meters the amount of fuel continuously entering the heater and therefore regulates the heater's BTU output.
C—regulates the voltage applied to the heater's ignition transformer.

The temperature produced by an aircraft combustion heater is controlled by the thermostat which alternately turns on and off the fuel going to the burner.

This process is known as cycling.

8541. The air-cycle cooling system produces cold air by

A—extracting heat energy across a compressor.
B—passing air through cooling coils that contain a refrigerant.
C—extracting heat energy across an expansion turbine.

An air-cycle cooling system produces its cold air by extracting heat energy from compressed air.

This is done by using some of the energy in the compressed air to drive an expansion turbine. As the air passes through the expansion turbine, its pressure and temperature are both decreased.

Answers

8537 [B] (080) AMT-SYS Ch 3
8538 [B] (080) AMT-SYS Ch 3
8539 [A] (080) AMT-SYS Ch 3
8540 [A] (035) AMT-SYS Ch 3
8541 [C] (006) AMT-SYS Ch 3

8542. (Refer to Figure 13.) Determine what unit is located immediately downstream of the expansion valve in a freon refrigeration system.

A—Condenser.
B—Compressor.
C—Evaporator coils.

The refrigerant in this diagram flows in a clockwise direction.

Refrigerant leaves the compressor as a high-pressure vapor and passes through the condenser where it becomes a high-pressure liquid. It then passes through the receiver-dryer to the expansion valve where it becomes a low-pressure liquid. After leaving the expansion valve, it passes through the evaporator coils where it absorbs heat from the cabin and becomes a low-pressure vapor.

Heat picked up from the cabin air changes the refrigerant from a liquid to a vapor in the evaporator. The loss of this heat cools the cabin air.

After leaving the evaporator, the low-pressure vapor goes into the compressor where its pressure and temperature are both raised.

8543. What does a steady stream of bubbles indicate when servicing a vapor cycle air conditioning system?

A—The system is over charged.
B—The system is properly charged.
C—The system is under charged.

Bubbles in the sight glass in the receiver-dryer of a freon air cooling system indicate that the charge of freon is low.

8544. An aircraft pressurization cycle is normally considered to be

A— one complete series of events or operations that recur regularly.
B— one take off and one landing.
C— when the fuselage reaches its maximum pressure differential one time.

A cycle is one complete series of events or operations that recur regularly. An aircraft pressurization cycle consists of a takeoff, scheduled pressurization, scheduled decrease in pressure, and depressurization.

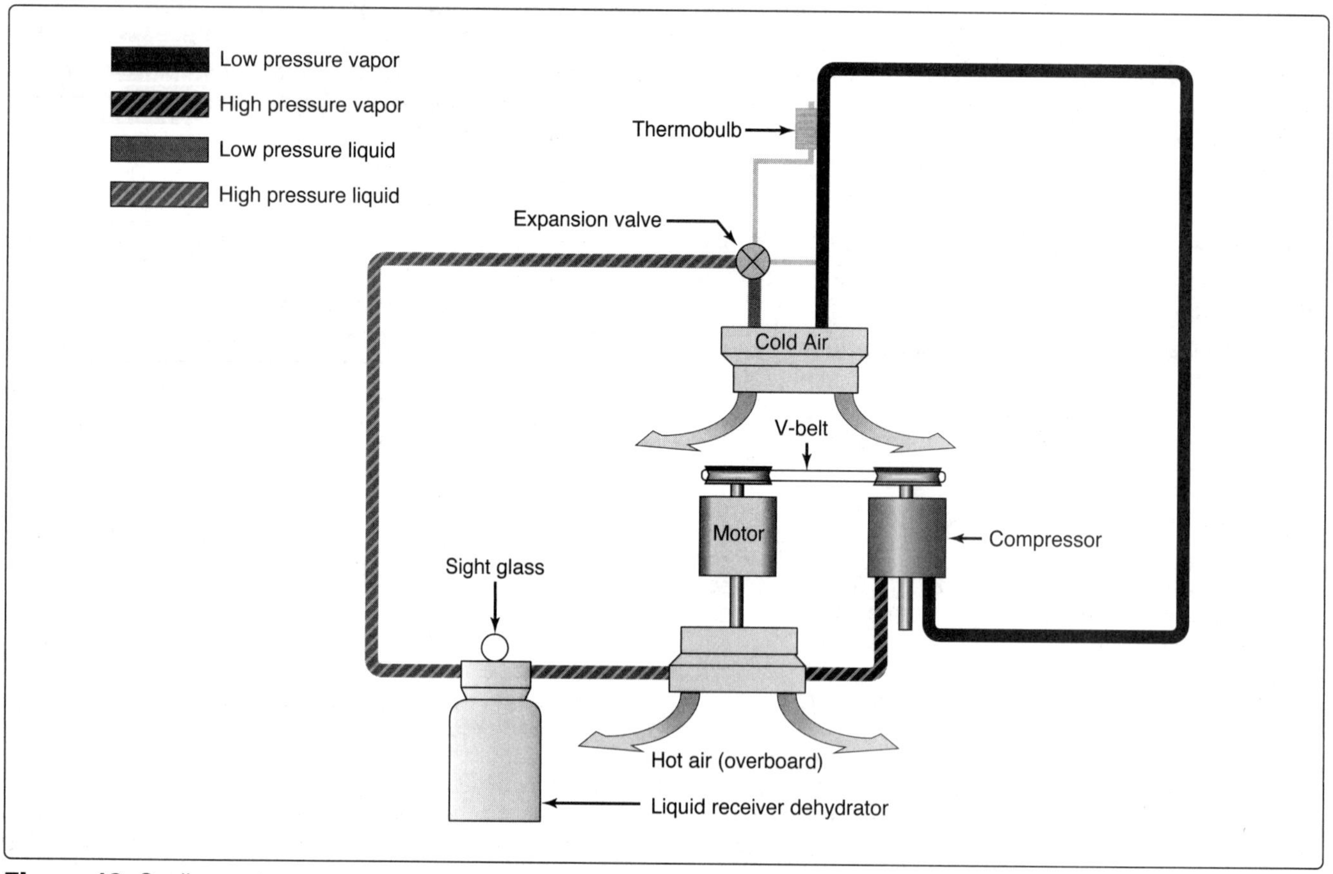

Figure 13. Cooling system

Answers
8542 [C] (002) AMT-SYS Ch 3
8543 [C] (002) AMT-SYS Ch 3
8544 [A] (080) DAT

8545. Which best describes cabin differential pressure?

A—Difference between cabin flight altitude pressure and mean sea level pressure.
B—Difference between the ambient and internal air pressure.
C—Difference between cabin pressure controller setting and actual cabin pressure.

Cabin differential pressure is the difference between the pressure inside the cabin and the pressure of the outside, or ambient, air.

8546. Composite oxygen bottles that conform to DOT-E-8162 have a service life of

A—5 years or 5,000 filling cycles whichever occurs first.
B—10 years or 5,000 filling cycles whichever occurs first.
C—15 years or 10,000 filling cycles whichever occurs first.

Composite oxygen cylinders which are made of an aluminum shell wrapped with Kevlar and conforming to DOT-E-8162 must be retired from service after 15 years or 10,000 filling cycles, whichever occurs first.

8547. The cabin pressurization modes of operation are

A—isobaric, differential, and maximum differential.
B—differential, unpressurized, and isobaric.
C—ambient, unpressurized, and isobaric.

The operating ranges (modes) in a pressurized aircraft are the unpressurized mode, the isobaric mode, and the differential mode.

In the isobaric mode, the pressure inside the cabin remains constant.

In the differential mode, a constant difference is maintained between the pressure inside the cabin and the pressure of the outside air.

8549. A pressurization controller uses

A—bleed air pressure, outside air temperature, and cabin rate of climb.
B—barometric pressure, cabin altitude, and cabin rate of change.
C—cabin rate of climb, bleed air volume, and cabin pressure.

A pressurization controller uses cabin altitude for the isobaric control and barometric pressure for the differential range of control.

A cabin rate of climb is used to control the rate of pressure change inside the cabin.

8550. What unit in a vapor-cycle cooling system serves as a reservoir for the refrigerant?

A—Receiver-dryer.
B—Evaporator.
C—Condenser.

The receiver-dryer serves as a reservoir for the refrigerant in a vapor-cycle air cooling system.

8551. What is the condition of the refrigerant as it enters the condenser of a vapor-cycle cooling system?

A—High-pressure liquid.
B—Low-pressure liquid.
C—High-pressure vapor.

The refrigerant in a vapor-cycle air cooling system is a hot, high-pressure vapor as it enters the condenser.

The refrigerant has absorbed heat from the cabin and it has had both its pressure and temperature raised by the compressor.

In the condenser, the hot vapor loses much of its heat and it becomes a high-pressure liquid.

8552. What is the condition of the refrigerant as it enters the evaporator of a vapor-cycle cooling system?

A—High-pressure liquid.
B—Low-pressure liquid.
C—High-pressure vapor.

The refrigerant in a vapor-cycle air cooling system leaves the receiver-dryer as a high-pressure liquid. Its pressure is dropped to that of a low-pressure liquid as it passes through the thermal expansion valve.

From the thermal expansion valve, the low-pressure liquid enters the evaporator coils.

As it passes through the evaporator, it absorbs heat from the cabin air flowing over the coils and changes into a low-pressure vapor.

8553. The evacuation of a vapor-cycle cooling system removes any water that may be present by

A—drawing out the liquid.
B—raising the boiling point of the water and drawing out the vapor.
C—lowering the boiling point of the water and drawing out the vapor.

A vapor-cycle cooling system is evacuated to remove any water that may be present. A vacuum pump is attached to the system and the pressure is lowered. This lowers the boiling point of any moisture, which then changes into a vapor and is removed by the vacuum pump.

Answers

8545 [B] (080) AMT-SYS Ch 3
8546 [C] (074) AMT-SYS Ch 3
8547 [B] (080) AMT-SYS Ch 3
8549 [B] (080) AMT-SYS Ch 3
8550 [A] (006) AMT-SYS Ch 3
8551 [C] (006) AMT-SYS Ch 3
8552 [B] (006) AMT-SYS Ch 3
8553 [C] (005) AMT-SYS Ch 3

8554. What is the condition of the refrigerant as it leaves the evaporator of a vapor-cycle cooling system?

A—Low-pressure liquid.
B—Low-pressure vapor.
C—High-pressure vapor.

The refrigerant in a vapor-cycle air cooling system leaves the evaporator as a low-pressure vapor. It has absorbed heat from the cabin as cabin air was blown over the evaporator coils.

8555. What is the condition of the refrigerant as it leaves the condenser of a vapor-cycle cooling system?

A—Low-pressure liquid.
B—High-pressure liquid.
C—High-pressure vapor.

The refrigerant in a vapor-cycle air cooling system leaves the condenser as a high-pressure liquid.

The compressor increased the pressure of the refrigerant vapor and raised its temperature higher than that of the outside air.

Outside air passing over the condenser coils removed some of the heat and caused the refrigerant to condense into a high-pressure liquid.

8556. In what position should the bottle be placed when adding liquid freon to a vapor-cycle cooling system?

A—Vertical with the outlet at the top.
B—Horizontal with the outlet to the side.
C—Vertical with the outlet at the bottom.

Liquid freon can be added to a vapor-cycle air cooling system by holding the bottle vertical with the outlet at the bottom.

Care must be used when adding liquid refrigerant. The outside air temperature must be high enough for all of the liquid to change into a vapor before it reaches the compressor.

8557. When purging a freon air conditioning system, it is important to release the charge at a slow rate. What is the reason for the slow-rate discharge?

A—Prevent the large amount of freon from contaminating the surrounding atmosphere.
B—Prevent excessive loss of refrigerant oil.
C—Prevent condensation from forming and contaminating the system.

When purging the refrigerant from a vapor-cycle air cooling system, the refrigerant should be released at a slow rate to prevent the loss of refrigeration oil.

The oil and refrigerant are sealed in the system. If the refrigerant is released too rapidly, it can blow some of the oil out with it.

8558. When a vapor-cycle cooling system is not in operation, what is an indication that the system is leaking freon?

A—Oil seepage.
B—Bubbles in the sight glass.
C—An ozone-like odor in the immediate area.

Lubricating oil is sealed in a vapor-cycle cooling system. If refrigerant leaks from the system, it is quite likely to carry some traces of oil with it.

Any trace of oil on the outside of hoses or components is a possible indication of the location of a refrigerant leak.

8559. In an operating vapor-cycle cooling system, if the two lines connected to the expansion valve are essentially the same temperature, what does this indicate?

A—The system is functioning normally.
B—The expansion valve is not metering freon properly.
C—The compressor is pumping too much refrigerant.

If the expansion valve is metering freon as it should, there will be an appreciable temperature difference between the lines connected to the expansion valve.

As freon passes through the expansion valve, it changes from a high-pressure liquid into a low-pressure liquid. The drop in pressure causes a drop in temperature. If the valve is not metering as it should, there will be no pressure drop and therefore, no temperature drop.

8560. The purpose of a subcooler in a vapor-cycle cooling system is to

A—augment the cooling capacity during periods of peak demand.
B—aid in quick cooling a hot aircraft interior.
C—cool the freon to prevent premature vaporization.

A subcooler is used in some vapor-cycle cooling systems to cool the refrigerant after it leaves the receiver. By cooling the refrigerant, premature vaporization (flash-off) is prevented.

Answers

8554 [B] (006) AMT-SYS Ch 3	8555 [B] (005) AMT-SYS Ch 3	8556 [C] (002) AMT-SYS Ch 3	8557 [B] (002) AMT-SYS Ch 3
8558 [A] (005) AMT-SYS Ch 3	8559 [B] (006) AMT-SYS Ch 3	8560 [C] (006) AMT-SYS Ch 3	

8561. A small amount of water in a vapor cycle cooling system can freeze

A—in the receiver-dryer and stop the entire system operation.
B—in the expansion valve and stop the entire system operation.
C—but the system is designed to continue operation.

A small amount of water in a vapor cycle cooling system can freeze and stop the entire system operation. Water vapor will freeze in the expansion valve, not in the receiver-dryer.

8562. When Refrigerant-12 is passed over an open flame, it

A—changes to methane gas.
B—is broken down into its basic chemical elements.
C—changes to phosgene gas.

Open-flame leak detectors should not be used on aircraft vapor-cycle cooling systems because of their fire hazard. Another reason for not using them is that any time Refrigerant-12 passes through an open flame, it produces phosgene, a deadly gas.

8563. What type of oil is suitable for use in vapor-cycle cooling system?

A—Low viscosity engine oil with the inability to absorb water.
B—Special high grade refrigeration oil.
C—Highly refined synthetic oil, free from impurities with special water absorbing additives.

The oil used in a vapor-cycle cooling system is a special high-grade refrigeration oil which is a highly refined mineral oil. It is specially treated to be free from water, sulfur, and wax.

Be sure to use only the oil recommended in the aircraft service manual.

8564. When an aircraft's oxygen system has developed a leak, the lines and fittings should be

A—removed and replaced.
B—inspected using a special oxygen system dye penetrant.
C—bubble tested with a special soap solution manufactured specifically for this purpose.

A leak in the plumbing of an oxygen system may be found by applying a solution of a special nonpetroleum-base soap to the suspected area. If a leak is present, bubbles will form.

8565. If oxygen bottle pressure is allowed to drop below a specified minimum, it may cause

A—the pressure reducer to fail.
B—the automatic altitude control valve to open.
C—moisture to collect in the bottle.

If an oxygen bottle is allowed to remain empty, it is possible for moisture to collect inside it and cause rust or corrosion.

For this reason, the pressure inside oxygen bottles should never be allowed to drop below approximately 50 psi.

8566. What controls the amount of oxygen delivered to a mask in a continuous-flow oxygen system?

A—Calibrated orifice.
B—Pressure reducing valve.
C—Pilot's regulator.

In the basic continuous-flow oxygen system, a calibrated orifice controls the amount of oxygen delivered to the mask.

However, a manual or automatic pressure regulator determines the pressure delivered to the orifice.

8567. When does the diluter-demand regulator operate?

A—When the user selects alternate oxygen.
B—When the user selects 100 percent oxygen.
C—When the user inhales.

With a diluter-demand oxygen regulator, the demand valve opens each time the wearer of the mask inhales.

8568. The primary difference between aviation breathing oxygen and other types of commercially available compressed oxygen is that

A—the other types are usually somewhat less than 99.5 percent pure oxygen.
B—aviation breathing oxygen has had all the water vapor removed.
C—aviation breathing oxygen has a higher percentage of water vapor to help prevent drying of a person's breathing passages and possible dehydration.

Aviator's breathing oxygen has all of the water vapor removed from it.

Answers

8561 [B] (005) AMT-SYS Ch 3	8562 [C] (002) AMT-SYS	8563 [B] (005) AMT-SYS Ch 3	8564 [C] (073) AMT-SYS Ch 3
8565 [C] (074) AMT-SYS Ch 3	8566 [A] (072) AMT-SYS Ch 3	8567 [C] (072) AMT-SYS Ch 3	8568 [B] (074) AMT-SYS Ch 3

8569. What is used in some oxygen systems to change high cylinder pressure to low system pressure?

A—Pressure reducer valve.
B—Calibrated fixed orifice.
C—Diluter demand regulator.

An oxygen pressure reducer valve may be used to change high cylinder pressure to low system pressure.

8570. In a high-pressure oxygen system, if the pressure reducer fails, what prevents high-pressure oxygen from entering the system downstream?

A—Check valve.
B—Pressure relief valve.
C—Manifold control valve.

If the pressure reducer valve in an installed, high-pressure oxygen system should fail, a pressure relief valve will prevent damage to the system.

8571. High-pressure cylinders containing oxygen for aviation use can be identified by their

A—green color and the words BREATHING OXYGEN stenciled in 1-inch white letters.
B—yellow color and the words AVIATOR'S BREATHING OXYGEN stenciled in 1-inch white letters.
C—green color and the words AVIATOR'S BREATHING OXYGEN stenciled in 1-inch white letters.

High-pressure oxygen cylinders used in aircraft should be painted green and should have the words AVIATOR'S BREATHING OXYGEN stenciled on them in 1-inch white letters.

8572. (Refer to Figure 14.) One hour after an oxygen system was charged for a leakage check, the oxygen pressure gauge read 460 psi at 63°F; 6 hours later the temperature was 51°F. (A 5 psi change is the maximum allowable in a 6-hour period.) What pressure gauge readings would be acceptable to remain within the allowable limits?

A—445 to 450 psi.
B—446 to 450 psi.
C—455 to 460 psi.

Pressure Temperature Correction Chart

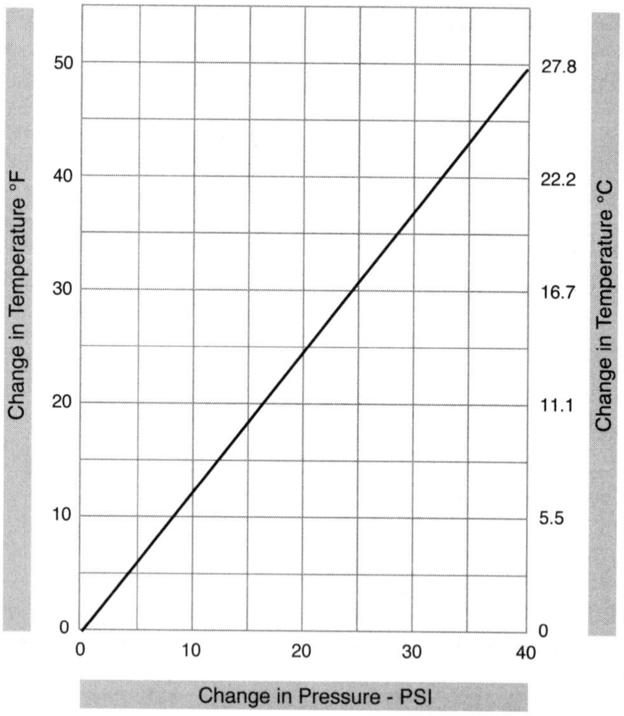

Correction of pressure during leakage test for change in temperature. Add pressure change if temperature rises. Subtract pressure change if temperature falls.

Figure 14. Pressure temperature correction chart

The pressure at the beginning of the leak test is 460 psi.

The temperature drops 12°F.

According to the curve, a 12° drop will cause a pressure change of 10 psi.

The pressure in the system with no leakage would be 450 psi.

The pressure is allowed to drop only 5 psi; therefore, the low pressure allowed in the system will be 445 psi.

8573. An aircraft oxygen bottle may be considered airworthy if it has been hydrostatically tested and identified

A—with the test date, DOT number, and serial number stamped on the cylinder near the neck.
B—with the DOT number, serial number, and manufacturer stamped on the cylinder near the neck.
C—with the DOT number and manufacturer stamped on the cylinder near the neck.

An aircraft oxygen bottle cannot be considered airworthy unless it is stamped on the cylinder, near the neck, with its DOT number, serial number, and the date of its last hydrostatic test.

Answers
8569 [A] (074) AMT-SYS Ch 3 8570 [B] (074) AMT-SYS Ch 3 8571 [C] (074) AMT-SYS Ch 3 8572 [A] (074) AMT-SYS Ch 3
8573 [A] (074) AMT-SYS Ch 3

8574. In a gaseous oxygen system, which of the following are vented to blow out plugs in the fuselage skin?

A—Pressure relief valves.
B—Filler shutoff valves.
C—Pressure reducer valves.

Pressure relief valves in a gaseous oxygen system are vented to blow-out plugs in the fuselage skin.

8575. What is the purpose of pressurizing the aircraft cabin?

A—To permit the aircraft to operate in thunderstorms.
B—To allow aircraft systems to operate properly.
C—To make human flight possible in the hostile environment of the upper atmosphere.

Pressurizing aircraft cabins creates the proper environment for prevention of hypoxia and permits operation at high altitude.

8576. Oxygen used in aircraft systems

A—is at least 99.5 percent pure and is practically water free.
B—is at least 99.5 percent pure and is the same as hospital-quality oxygen.
C—contains a higher level of water vapor than hospital-quality oxygen.

Oxygen used in aircraft systems is at least 99.5 percent pure and is practically water free while hospital-quality oxygen contains more water vapor than is allowed in aviator's breathing oxygen.

8577. Oxygen systems in unpressurized aircraft are generally of the

A—continuous-flow and pressure-demand types.
B—pressure-demand type only.
C—portable-bottle type only.

Oxygen systems in an unpressurized aircraft may use a continuous-flow system for the passengers and a diluter-demand or a pressure-demand system for the flight crew.

8578. The purpose of the airflow metering aneroid assembly found in oxygen diluter demand regulators is to

A—regulate airflow in relation to oxygen flow when operating in emergency or diluter demand positions.
B—regulate airflow in relation to cabin altitude when in diluter demand position.
C—automatically put the regulator in emergency position if the demand valve diaphragm ruptures.

The airflow metering aneroid in a diluter-demand oxygen regulator regulates the amount of cabin air that is allowed to flow through the regulator in relation to the cabin altitude, when the regulator is in the diluter-demand position.

8579. If a high-pressure oxygen cylinder is to be installed in an airplane, it must meet the specifications of the

A—aircraft manufacturer or the cylinder manufacturer.
B—Department of Transportation.
C—National Transportation Safety Board or the Standards of Compressed Gas Cylinders.

High-pressure oxygen cylinders installed in an aircraft must meet the specifications of the DOT.

8580. Before a high-pressure oxygen cylinder is serviced, it must be the correct type and have been

A—hydrostatically tested within the proper time interval.
B—approved by the National Transportation Safety Board.
C—inspected by a certificated airframe mechanic.

Before high-pressure oxygen cylinders can be serviced, it must be determined that they are of the correct type and that they have been hydrostatically checked for burst strength within the proper time interval.

DOT 3AA oxygen cylinders must be hydrostatically tested to 5/3 of their nominal working pressure every five years, and DOT 3HT cylinders must be tested in the same way every three years.

The date of the hydrostatic test must be stamped on the bottle near its neck.

8581. A contaminated oxygen system is normally purged with

A—oxygen.
B—compressed air.
C—nitrogen.

If an oxygen system has been opened, it is a good idea to purge it of any air that may be in the lines.

Plug masks into all of the outlets, and if diluter- or pressure-demand regulators are used, place them in the Emergency position.

Turn the oxygen supply on and allow oxygen to flow through the system for at least 10 minutes.

Answers

8574 [A] (072) AMT-SYS Ch 3	8575 [C] (080) AMT-SYS Ch 3	8576 [A] (074) AMT-SYS Ch 3	8577 [A] (074) AMT-SYS Ch 3
8578 [B] (072) AMT-SYS Ch 3	8579 [B] (074) AMT-SYS Ch 3	8580 [A] (074) AMT-SYS Ch 3	8581 [A] (073) AMT-SYS Ch 3

8582. How should you determine the amount of oxygen in a portable, high-pressure cylinder?

A—Weigh the cylinder and its contents.
B—Read the pressure gauge mounted on the cylinder.
C—Measure the pressure at the mask.

The amount of oxygen available in a portable high-pressure oxygen cylinder is indicated by the pressure shown on the pressure gauge mounted on the cylinder.

8583. What may be used as a lubricant on oxygen system tapered pipe thread connections?

A—Silicone dielectric compound.
B—Glycerine.
C—Teflon tape.

The only thread lubricant approved for use on tapered pipe thread connections in an aircraft oxygen system is MIL-T-5542 oxygen-compatible thread lubricant. Teflon tape applied to the male threads can be used in place of a thread lubricant.

8584. On transport category aircraft what might be an indication of an over pressure event of the aircraft oxygen system?

A—The green thermal expansion disk missing.
B—The green thermal expansion disk in the cockpit missing.
C—The green thermal expansion disk on the oxygen regulator missing.

If the pressure in an oxygen cylinder becomes too great, the safety disk ruptures and the oxygen is vented overboard through a discharge line which is covered with a green discharge indicator. This indicator is on the outside of the aircraft where it is visible on the preflight walk-around inspection.

8585. Which of the following are characteristic of a chemical or solid-state oxygen system?

A—A volume storage capacity about three times that of compressed oxygen and system generators that are inert below 400°F, even under severe impact.
B—An adjustable oxygen release rate and a volume storage capacity about three times that of compressed oxygen.
C—System generators are inert below 400°F, even under severe impact, and a distribution and regulating system similar to gaseous oxygen systems.

Once a chemical or solid-state oxygen system is initiated, it releases oxygen at a predetermined rate which is not adjustable according to demand.

On a volume basis, the storage capacity of oxygen in candles is about three times that of compressed gas.

The generators of a chemical oxygen system are inert below 400°F, even under severe impact.

The distribution and regulating system is self-contained. It consists of a stainless steel cylinder attached to manifolded hose nipples. The nipples contain orifices just small enough to ensure essentially equal flow to all masks.

Answers
8582 [B] (074) AOS
8583 [C] (073) AMT-SYS Ch 3
8584 [A] (073) AMT-SYS Ch 3
8585 [A] (072) AMT-SYS Ch 3

Aircraft Instrument Systems

8586. An aircraft magnetic compass is swung to update the compass correction card when

A—an annual inspection is accomplished on the aircraft.
B—the compass is serviced.
C—equipment is added that could effect compass deviation.

An aircraft compass is swung, or compensated, to correct for deviation error.

There is no time interval requirement for swinging a compass, but it normally is done when any equipment has been added to the aircraft that could affect the compass deviation.

8587. Which of the following operating mechanisms would be found in a hydraulic pressure gauge?

A—Bourdon tube.
B—Pressure diaphragm.
C—Evacuated bellows.

Most hydraulic pressure gauges use a Bourdon tube-type mechanism.

8588. What is the fixed line mark attached to the compass bowl of a magnetic compass called?

A—Reeder line.
B—Lubber line.
C—Reference line.

The reference marker on a magnetic compass is called the lubber line.

8590. Which of the following will cause inaccuracies in a magnetic compass that may be compensated for by an aircraft mechanic?

A—Deviation.
B—Current.
C—Variation.

When swinging a magnetic compass, the compensators adjust for the magnetic interference caused by localized magnetic fields in the aircraft structure. These magnetic disturbances within the aircraft are called deviations, and they deflect the compass needle from alignment with magnetic north.

8591. What will be the result if the instrument static pressure line becomes disconnected inside a pressurized cabin during cruising flight?

A—The altimeter and airspeed indicator will both read low.
B—The altimeter and airspeed indicator will both read high.
C—The altimeter will read low and the airspeed indicator will read high.

If an instrument static-pressure line becomes disconnected inside a pressurized cabin, the altimeter will indicate a lower altitude. The increased static pressure inside the airspeed indicator case will cause it to read low.

8592. The maximum deviation (during level flight) permitted in a compensated magnetic direction indicator installed on an aircraft certificated under 14 CFR Part 23 is

A—6°.
B—8°.
C—10°.

The compensated installation of a magnetic direction indicator may not have a deviation in level flight greater than 10° on any heading.

8593. Magnetic compass bowls are filled with a liquid to

A—retard precession of the float.
B—reduce deviation errors.
C—dampen the oscillation of the float.

Magnetic compass bowls are filled with liquid to dampen the oscillations of the float.

Answers
8586 [C] (036) AMT-SYS Ch 4
8587 [A] (063) AMT-SYS Ch 4
8588 [B] (036) AMT-SYS Ch 4
8590 [A] (036) AMT-SYS Ch 4
8591 [A] (096) AMT-SYS Ch 4
8592 [C] (014) 14 CFR Part 23
8593 [C] (036) AMT-SYS Ch 4

8594. Instrument static system leakage can be detected by observing the rate of change in indication of the

A—airspeed indicator after suction has been applied to the static system to cause a prescribed equivalent airspeed to be indicated.
B—altimeter after pressure has been applied to the static system to cause a prescribed equivalent altitude to be indicated.
C—altimeter after suction has been applied to the static system to cause a prescribed equivalent altitude to be indicated.

Instrument static system leakage can be detected by observing the rate of change in an altimeter indication.

A suction is applied to the static system that causes an equivalent altitude of 1,000 feet to be indicated on the altimeter. The system is sealed, and it must not leak more than 100 feet of altitude in one minute.

8595. The maximum altitude loss permitted during an unpressurized aircraft instrument static pressure system integrity check is

A—50 feet in 1 minute.
B—200 feet in 1 minute.
C—100 feet in 1 minute.

When a static pressure system integrity test is made, the pressure is allowed to leak a maximum of 100 feet in one minute.

8596. Which statement regarding an aircraft instrument vacuum system is true?

A—Dry-type vacuum pumps with carbon vanes are very susceptible to damage from solid airborne particles and must take in only filtered air.
B—Vacuum systems are generally more effective at high altitudes than positive pressure systems.
C—If the air inlet to each vacuum instrument is connected to a common atmospheric pressure manifold, the system generally will be equipped with individual instrument filters only.

Dry-type vacuum pumps do not require any lubrication, but their carbon vanes are highly susceptible to damage from solid particles in the air.

It is extremely important that only filtered air be allowed to flow through these pumps.

8597. When an aircraft altimeter is set at 29.92 "Hg on the ground, the altimeter will read

A—pressure altitude.
B—density altitude.
C—field elevation.

When the barometric scale on an aircraft altimeter is set to 29.92 inches of mercury, the altimeter reads pressure altitude, the altitude above standard sea level.

8598. Which of the following instrument discrepancies could be corrected by an aviation mechanic?

A—Case paint chipped, leaking at line B nut, mounting screws loose, or case leaking.
B—Red line missing, case leaking, glass cracked, or fogged.
C—Red line missing, mounting screws loose, case paint chipped, or leaking at line B nut.

A certificated aviation mechanic can correct any of these discrepancies: red line missing from an instrument, provided the red line is marked on the outside of the instrument glass; loose mounting screws; chipped paint on the outside of the instrument case; and leaking B-nut on the line connected to the instrument.

8599. Which of the following instrument discrepancies would require replacement of the instrument?

A—Case leaking, glass cracked, instrument will not zero out, or fogged.
B—Red line missing, case leaking, or glass cracked.
C—Instrument will not zero out, leaking at line B nut, or mounting screws loose.

Any of the following problems will require an instrument to be replaced: case leaking, glass cracked, the instrument will not zero out, or if the inside of an instrument case is fogged.

8600. Which instrument condition is acceptable and would not require correction?

A—Red line missing.
B—Case paint chipped.
C—Fogged.

Case paint chipped is the only one of these problems that would not require correction.

8601. A barometric altimeter indicates pressure altitude when the barometric scale is set at

A—29.92 "Hg.
B—14.7 "Hg.
C—field elevation.

Barometric altimeters indicate pressure altitude when the barometric scale is set to standard sea-level pressure of 29.92 inches of mercury.

Answers

8594 [C] (077) AMT-SYS Ch 4	8595 [C] (096) 14 CFR Part 23	8596 [A] (076) AMT-SYS Ch 4	8597 [A] (014) AMT-SYS Ch 4
8598 [C] (013) §65.81	8599 [A] (090) §65.81	8600 [B] (013) AMT-SYS Ch 4	8601 [A] (014) DAT

8601-1. At sea level, when the average atmospheric pressure is 14.7 psi, the barometric pressure is

A—29.92 "Hg.
B—29.92 Mb.
C—1013.25 "Hg.

In aviation, there is a commonly used pressure known as standard pressure which refers to an established or standard value that has been created for atmospheric pressure. This standard pressure value is 29.92 inches of mercury ("Hg), 1,013.2 hectopascals (hPa), or 14.7 psi.

8602. A Bourdon tube instrument may be used to indicate

A—pressure and temperature.
B—temperature and position.
C—position and pressure.

A Bourdon tube instrument is a pressure-measuring instrument. It can be used to measure temperature by connecting it to a temperature bulb containing a volatile liquid such as methyl chloride. The bulb and the Bourdon tube are connected with a small-diameter copper tube and are sealed as a unit. When the temperature surrounding the bulb changes, the pressure above the volatile liquid changes. The Bourdon tube instrument whose dial is calibrated in units of temperature measures this pressure change, which relates to the temperature change.

8603. A turn coordinator instrument indicates

A—the longitudinal attitude of the aircraft during climb and descent.
B—the need for corrections in pitch and bank.
C—both roll and yaw.

A turn coordinator uses a canted rate gyro as its sensing element and can therefore sense both roll and yaw.

8604. Aircraft temperature thermocouple leads may

A—not be altered and are designed for a specific installation.
B—be installed with either lead to either post of the indicator.
C—be repaired using solderless connectors.

Thermocouple leads must have a specific resistance. They are designed for a specific installation and should not be altered.

8605. A synchro transmitter is connected to a synchro receiver

A—mechanically through linkage.
B—electromagnetically without wires.
C—electrically with wires.

Synchro transmitters are connected to synchro receivers electrically with wires.

8606. The operation of an angle of attack indicating system is based on detection of differential pressure at a point where the airstream flows in a direction

A—not parallel to the true angle of attack of the aircraft.
B—parallel to the angle of attack of the aircraft.
C—parallel to the longitudinal axis of the aircraft.

The angle of attack system installed in some aircraft measures a differential pressure at the point the airstream flows in a direction not parallel to the true angle of attack of the aircraft.

8607. Turbine engine exhaust gas temperatures are measured by using

A—iron/constantan thermocouples.
B—chromel/alumel thermocouples.
C—ratiometer electrical resistance thermometers.

High temperatures, such as the exhaust-gas temperature of a turbine engine, are measured using chromel and alumel thermocouples.

8608. Fuel flow transmitters are designed to transmit data

A—mechanically.
B—electrically.
C—utilizing fluid power.

The fuel flow transmitters discussed in this examination transmit their data electrically.

8609. Which of the following causes of aircraft magnetic compass inaccuracies may be compensated for by mechanics?

A—Deviation.
B—Magnetic compass current.
C—Variation.

Deviation is a compass error caused by local magnetic fields in the aircraft.

Deviation can be corrected by an aircraft mechanic by swinging the compass. This is a procedure in which small magnets inside the compass are turned in such a way that their magnetic field cancels the effect of the offending magnetic fields.

Answers

8601-1 [A] (014) FAA-H-8083-31
8602 [A] (014) AMT-SYS Ch 4
8603 [C] (014) AMT-SYS Ch 4
8604 [A] (046) AMT-SYS Ch 4
8605 [C] (013) AMT-SYS Ch 4
8606 [A] (010) AMT-SYS Ch 4
8607 [B] (008) AMT-SYS Ch 4
8608 [B] (041) AMT-SYS Ch 2
8609 [A] (036) AMT-SYS Ch 4

8610. Who is authorized to repair an aircraft instrument?

A—A certified mechanic with an airframe rating.
B—A certificated airframe repair station.
C—A certificated repair station approved for that class instrument.

Only a certificated repair station approved for the specific class of instrument is authorized to repair an aircraft instrument.

8610-1. A certificated mechanic with at least an airframe rating may perform

A—minor internal repairs to aircraft instruments.
B—major repairs to aircraft instruments.
C—inspections and function checks on aircraft instruments.

Certificated airframe technicians and A&P technicians are charged with a wide variety of maintenance functions related to instruments and instrument systems. Installation, removal, inspection, troubleshooting, and functional checks are all performed in the field by certificated personnel. It is also a responsibility of the certificated technician holding an airframe rating to know what maintenance is required and to access the approved procedures for meeting those requirements.

8611. What does a reciprocating engine manifold pressure gauge indicate when the engine is not operating?

A—Zero pressure.
B—The differential between the manifold pressure and the atmospheric pressure.
C—The existing atmospheric pressure.

A manifold pressure gauge used with a reciprocating engine is an absolute pressure gauge.

When the engine is not operating, the manifold pressure gauge indicates the existing atmospheric pressure.

8612. The requirements for testing and inspection of instrument static pressure systems required by 14 CFR §91.411 are contained in

A—Type Certificate Data Sheets.
B—AC 43.13-1A.
C—Part 43, appendix E.

The minimum requirements for testing and inspection of instrument static pressure systems required by 14 CFR §91.411 are contained in Part 43, Appendix E.

8613. Which condition would be most likely to cause excessive vacuum in a vacuum system?

A—Vacuum pump overspeed.
B—Vacuum relief valve improperly adjusted.
C—Vacuum relief valve spring weak.

Excessive vacuum in a vacuum system could be caused by an improperly adjusted vacuum relief valve.

A vacuum relief valve is a spring-loaded, flat-disk valve that opens at a preset amount of vacuum to allow air to enter the system. If the spring is set with too much compression, the vacuum will have to be greater to allow the disk to offseat and allow air to enter the system.

8614. Data transmitted between components in an EFIS are converted into

A—digital signals.
B—analog signals.
C—carrier wave signals.

All of the data transmitted between the components in an EFIS are converted into digital signals and are transmitted via an avionics standard communication bus using a time-sharing basis.

8615. The function of a CRT in an EFIS is to

A—allow the pilot to select the appropriate system configuration for the current flight situation.
B—display alphanumeric data and representations of aircraft instruments.
C—receive and process input signals from aircraft and engine sensors and send the data to the appropriate display.

The CRT is the display unit used in an EFIS. It displays alphanumeric data and graphic displays that represent the aircraft instruments.

8616. The function of a symbol generator (SG) in an EFIS is to

A—display alphanumeric data and representations of aircraft instruments.
B—allow the pilot to select the appropriate system configuration for the current flight situation.
C—receive and process input signals from aircraft and engine sensors and send the data to the appropriate display.

Answers

8610 [C] (090) AMT-SYS Ch 4	8610-1 [C] (090) FAA-H-8083-31	8611 [C] (008) AMT-SYS Ch 4	8612 [C] (076) §91.411
8613 [B] (076) AMT-SYS Ch 4	8614 [A] (014) AMT-SYS Ch 5	8615 [B] (010) AMT-SYS Ch 5	8616 [C] (054) AMT-SYS Ch 5

The EFIS has three subsystems: the pilot's display system (PDS), the copilot's display system (CDS), and the weather radar (WX).

The PDS and CDS are identical and each contains two CRT displays, an SG, a display controller, and a source-select panel.

The SGs receive input signals from aircraft and engine sensors, process this information and send it to the appropriate display.

8617. The function of a display controller in an EFIS is to

A—display alphanumeric data and representations of aircraft instruments.
B—allow the pilot to select the appropriate system configuration for the current flight situation.
C—receive and process input signals from aircraft and engine sensors and send the data to the appropriate display.

In the EFIS, the pilot's display system (PDS) and the copilot's display system (CDS) are identical, and each contains two CRT displays, an SG, a display controller, and a source select panel.

The display controller allows the pilot to select the appropriate system configuration for the current flight situation.

8618. A radar altimeter determines altitude by

A—transmitting a signal and receiving back a reflected signal.
B—receiving signals transmitted from ground radar stations.
C—means of transponder interrogation.

A radar altimeter measures the height of the aircraft above the ground by transmitting a VHF signal vertically downward from the aircraft and receiving the reflected signal. A computer inside the instrument measures the time required for the signal to reach the ground and return, and converts this time into feet of radar altitude. This altitude is displayed on the radar altimeter indicator.

8619. A radar altimeter indicates

A—flight level (pressure) altitude.
B—altitude above sea level.
C—altitude above ground level.

A radar altimeter measures the actual altitude above the terrain over which the aircraft is flying. This is called above ground level or AGL altitude.

8620. Resistance-type temperature indicators using Wheatstone bridge or ratiometer circuits may be used to indicate the temperatures of which of the following?

A—Free air, carburetor air, oil temperature, and cylinder head temperature.
B—Free air, carburetor air, coolant (engine), and oil temperature.
C—Exhaust gas temperature and cylinder head temperature.

When temperatures below about 300°F are to be measured by an aircraft instrument, resistance-change instruments such as Wheatstone bridge or ratiometer instruments are normally used rather than thermocouples. Free air temperature, carburetor air temperature, engine coolant temperature, and oil temperature are all measured by resistance-change instruments.

8621. When flags such as NAV, HDG, or GS are displayed on an HSI, the indication is

A—that function is inoperative.
B—that function is operating.
C—to call attention to deviation from the desired setting, or flight path, or heading, etc.

Warning flags show in an HSI when the function identified by the flag is inoperative.

Warning flags are included in the navigation (NAV), the gyro (HDG), and the glide slope (GS) circuits.

8622. Instrument panel shock mounts absorb

A—high energy impact shocks caused by hard landings.
B—low-frequency, high-amplitude shocks.
C—high G shock loads imposed by turbulent air.

Instrument panels are usually shock-mounted to absorb low-frequency, high-amplitude shocks.

8623. Which procedure should you use if you find a vacuum-operated instrument glass loose?

A—Mark the case and glass with a slippage mark.
B—Replace the glass.
C—Install another instrument.

If the glass is found to be loose in any aircraft instrument, the instrument must be removed from the aircraft and the glass resealed by an instrument repair shop.

A mechanic is not allowed to make either major or minor repairs to any aircraft instrument.

Answers

8617 [B] (010) AMT-SYS Ch 5	8618 [A] (085) AMT-SYS Ch 5	8619 [C] (085) AMT-SYS Ch 5	8620 [B] (008) AMT-SYS Ch 4
8621 [A] (014) AMT-SYS Ch 5	8622 [B] (014) AMT-SYS Ch 5	8623 [C] (090) AMT-SYS Ch 4	

8624. Which instruments are connected to an aircraft's pitot-static system?

A—Cabin altimeter and cabin rate-of-change indicator.
B—Vertical speed indicator and altimeter.
C—Vertical speed indicator, altimeter, and airspeed indicator.

The vertical speed indicator, the altimeter and the airspeed indicator are connected to the aircraft pitot-static system.

8625. Which of the following instruments will normally have range markings?

A—Altimeter.
B—Cylinder head temperature gauge and airspeed indicator.
C—Altimeter and airspeed indicator.

Of the instruments listed here, only the airspeed indicator and the cylinder head temperature gauge have range markings.

8626. How would an airspeed indicator be marked to show the best rate-of-climb speed (one engine inoperative)?

A—A red radial line.
B—A blue radial line.
C—A green arc.

A blue radial line is used on an airspeed indicator to indicate single-engine, best rate-of-climb speed for a multiengine aircraft.

8627. The green arc on an aircraft temperature gauge indicates

A—the instrument is not calibrated.
B—the desirable temperature range.
C—a low, unsafe temperature range.

The green arc on an aircraft temperature gauge indicates the desirable temperature range of operation.

8628. What must be done to an instrument panel that is supported by shock mounts?

A—Bonding straps must be installed across the instrument mounts as a current path.
B—The instrument mounts must be grounded to the aircraft structure as a current path.
C—The instrument mounts must be tightened to the specified torque required by the maintenance manual.

When an aircraft instrument panel is supported in shock mounts, the mounts must have bonding straps across them to provide a path for electrical current to return from the instruments to the aircraft structure.

8629. What marking color is used to indicate if a cover glass has slipped?

A—Red.
B—White.
C—Yellow.

A white slip mark painted across the glass and the bezel of an aircraft instrument is used to indicate to the mechanic whether the cover glass has slipped.

Slip marks are used on instruments that have range marks on the glass rather than on the dial.

8630. Aircraft instruments should be marked and graduated in accordance with

A—the instrument manufacturer's specifications.
B—both the aircraft and engine manufacturers' specifications.
C—the specific aircraft maintenance or flight manual.

The markings to be used on an aircraft instrument are those specified by the aircraft manufacturer and listed in the maintenance or flight manual for the particular aircraft.

8631. Aircraft instrument panels are generally shock-mounted to absorb

A—all vibration.
B—low-frequency, high-amplitude shocks.
C—high-frequency, high-amplitude shocks.

Aircraft instrument shock mounts absorb low-frequency, high-amplitude shocks and vibration.

Answers

8624 [C] (076) AMT-SYS Ch 4	8625 [B] (013) AMT-SYS Ch 4	8626 [B] (014) §23.2610	8627 [B] (013) AMT-SYS Ch 4
8628 [A] (013) AMT-SYS Ch 4	8629 [B] (013) AMT-SYS Ch 4	8630 [C] (013) AMT-SYS Ch 4	8631 [B] (013) AMT-SYS Ch 5

8632. The method of mounting aircraft instruments in their respective panels depends on the

A—instrument manufacturer.
B—design of the instrument case.
C—design of the instrument panel.

The design of the instrument case determines the way the instrument is mounted in the instrument panel.

Some instruments are held in place with screws. Others are clamped in a special mounting ring.

8633. How is a flangeless instrument case mounted in an instrument panel?

A—By four machine screws which extend through the instrument panel.
B—By an expanding-type clamp secured to the back of the panel and tightened by a screw from the front of the instrument panel.
C—By a metal shelf separate from and located behind the instrument panel.

Flangeless instrument cases are mounted in an instrument panel by an expanding-type clamp secured to the back of the instrument panel.

A screw, accessible from the front of the panel, is loosened to release the instrument and tightened to clamp the instrument tightly in its mount.

8634. Cases for electrically operated instruments are made of

A—Aluminum or composite cases.
B—Iron or steel cases.
C—Bakelite or plastic cases.

Most electrical instruments are mounted in iron or steel cases to prevent interference from outside magnetic fields.

Lines of magnetic flux cannot cross iron or steel because the metal traps the lines of flux rather than allowing them to pass across it.

8635. When installing an instrument in an aircraft, who is responsible for making sure it is properly marked?

A—The aircraft owner or pilot.
B—The mechanic installing the instrument.
C—The manufacturer of the instrument.

When an instrument is installed in an aircraft instrument panel, it is the responsibility of the technician making the installation to be sure the instrument is properly marked for the aircraft in which it is being installed.

8636. Where may a person look for the information necessary to determine the required markings on an engine instrument?

A—Aircraft flight manual or aircraft maintenance manual.
B—Engine manufacturer's specifications.
C—Instrument manufacturer's specifications.

Engine instruments should be marked in accordance with the information found in the aircraft specifications or Type Certificate Data Sheets for the aircraft in which the instrument is installed. This information is also found in the aircraft maintenance manual or the aircraft flight manual.

8637. A certificated mechanic with airframe and powerplant ratings may

A—perform minor repairs to aircraft instruments.
B—perform minor repairs and minor alterations to aircraft instruments.
C—not perform repairs to aircraft instruments.

Aircraft instruments may be repaired only by a certificated repair station that has approval for the specific instrument.

A certificated mechanic with airframe and powerplant ratings may not perform any repairs or any alterations to aircraft instruments.

8638. The red radial lines on the face of an engine oil pressure gauge indicates

A—minimum engine safe RPM operating range.
B—minimum precautionary safe operating range.
C—minimum and/ or maximum safe operating limits.

A red radial line on an aircraft instrument dial indicates the maximum and/or minimum safe operating limit.

8639. A certificated mechanic may perform

A—minor repairs to instruments.
B—100-hour inspections of instruments.
C—instrument overhaul.

The only function among the alternatives given here that is allowed a certificated mechanic is that of performing a 100-hour inspection of instruments.

The other operations must be done by a certificated repair station with the appropriate approvals.

Answers

8632 [B] (013) AMT-SYS Ch 4	8633 [B] (013) AMT-SYS Ch 4	8634 [B] (013) AMT-SYS Ch 4	8635 [B] (090) AMT-SYS Ch 4
8636 [A] (013) AMT-SYS Ch 4	8637 [C] (090) §65.81	8638 [C] (013) AMT-SYS Ch 4	8639 [B] (090) §65.81(a)

8640. An aircraft instrument panel is electrically bonded to the aircraft structure to

A—act as a restraint strap.
B—provide current return paths.
C—aid in the panel installation.

An instrument panel is electrically bonded to the aircraft structure with flexible metal braid to carry return current from the instruments back to the aircraft battery.

8641. How many of the following are controlled by gyroscopes?

1. Attitude indicator.
2. Heading indicator.
3. Turn needle of the turn-and-slip indicator.

A—Three.
B—Two.
C—One.

An attitude indicator is controlled by an attitude gyro that senses aircraft rotation about the roll and pitch axes.

A heading indicator is controlled by an attitude gyro that senses aircraft rotation about the yaw axis.

The turn needle of a turn and slip indicator is controlled by a rate gyro that senses aircraft rotation about the yaw axis.

8642. The lubber line on a directional gyro is used to

A—represent the nose of the aircraft.
B—align the instrument glass in the case.
C—represent the wings of the aircraft.

The lubber line on a directional gyro is used as a reference to represent the nose of the aircraft. The number on the dial opposite the lubber line is the heading of the aircraft.

8643. Which instruments are connected to an aircraft's static pressure system only?

A—Vertical speed indicator and altimeter.
B—Cabin altimeter and rate-of-change indicator.
C—Vertical speed indicator, altiemeter, and airspeed indicator.

Only the vertical speed indicator and the altimeter are connected to the aircraft's static pressure system only. The cabin altimeter and cabin rate-of-change indicator sense their static pressure from inside the cabin. The airspeed indicator is connected to the aircraft's static pressure system and to the pitot system.

8644. When an unpressurized aircraft's static pressure system is leak checked to comply with the requirements of 14 CFR §91.411, what aircraft instrument may be used in lieu of a pitot-static system tester?

A—Airspeed indicator.
B—Vertical speed indicator.
C—Altimeter.

The static system on an unpressurized aircraft can be checked for leakage by placing a negative pressure of approximately one inch of mercury on the static system and sealing it off. This negative pressure will cause the altimeter to increase its indication by approximately 1,000 feet. Seal the system and watch the altimeter for one minute. If the system is not leaking, the altimeter will not change its indication by more than 100 feet.

8645. If a static pressure system check reveals excessive leakage, the leak(s) may be located by

A—pressurizing the system and adding leak detection dye.
B—isolating portions of the line and testing each portion systematically starting at the instrument connections.
C—removing and visually inspecting the line segments.

If, when checking the static system for leaks, a leak is indicated, isolate portions of the system and check each portion systematically. Begin at the connection nearest the instruments and check it. If this is good, reseal the connection and check the next portion, working your way out to the static ports until the leak is found.

8646. When performing the static system leakage check required by 14 CFR §91.411, the technician utilizes

A—static pressure.
B—positive pressure.
C—negative pressure.

The altimeter, airspeed indicator, and vertical speed indicator that are attached to an aircraft static air system all work on negative pressure. Static system leakage tests are performed using a negative pressure of approximately one inch of mercury.

Answers

8640 [B] (013) AMT-SYS Ch 4	8641 [A] (014) AMT-SYS Ch 4	8642 [A] (014) AMT-SYS Ch 4	8643 [A] (014) AMT-SYS Ch 4
8644 [C] (096) AMT-SYS Ch 4	8645 [B] (096) AMT-SYS Ch 4	8646 [C] (096) AMT-SYS Ch 4	

Communication and Navigation Systems

8647. What is the primary purpose of an autopilot?

A—To relieve the pilot of control of the aircraft during long periods of flight.
B—To allow for longer flights and more precise courses flown by the pilot.
C—To stabilize flight control in turbulent conditions.

The primary purpose of an automatic pilot is to relieve the human pilot of having to manually control the aircraft at all times.

8648. Which of the following provides manual maneuverability of the aircraft while the autopilot is engaged?

A—Servo-amplifier.
B—Directional gyro indicator.
C—Flight controller.

The flight controller allows the pilot to provide manual maneuverability to the aircraft when the autopilot is engaged.

The pilot can insert a command signal through the controller at any time.

8649. In an autopilot, which signal nullifies the input signal to the ailerons?

A—Displacement signal.
B—Course signal.
C—Follow-up signal.

The follow-up signal in an autopilot nulls out the input signals to the control surfaces when the correct amount of deflection is reached.

8650. In which control element of an autopilot system is an attitude indicator?

A—Command.
B—Sensing.
C—Input.

The attitude indicator, which senses deviation from a level flight attitude, is in the sensing system of an autopilot.

8651. What is the operating principle of the sensing device used in an autopilot system?

A—The reaction of the force 90° away from the applied force in the direction of gyro rotation.
B—The relative motion between a gyro and its supporting system.
C—The rate of change of motion between the gyro gimbal rings and the aircraft.

The gyro in a flight instrument remains rigid in space and the aircraft rotates about it.

The gyro is used as the reference device in an autopilot which senses the relative motion between the gyro and its supporting system.

8652. What will occur if an aircraft attitude is changed by its autopilot system in order to correct for an error and the involved control surfaces are returned to streamline by the time the aircraft has reached its correct position?

A—Overshoot and oscillation.
B—Undershoot and oscillation.
C—Normal operation.

A displacement follow-up in an autopilot system develops a signal proportional to the amount of error sensed. It stops the control surface movement as soon as sufficient displacement has been reached.

If the left wing drops, the gyro senses an error and sends a signal to the aileron servo that moves the left aileron down. When the aileron moves an amount proportional to the amount the wing has dropped, the followup system generates a signal equal in amplitude but opposite in polarity to the error signal and cancels it.

The left wing is still down and the aileron is deflected. Since the signals have canceled, the autopilot does not call for any more aileron deflection. As the aerodynamic forces bring the wing back to level flight attitude, an error signal opposite to the one that started the action is produced. This signal is gradually canceled. By the time the wing comes level, the aileron is in the streamlined position and there is no overshooting or oscillation.

8653. What component of an autopilot system applies torque to the control surfaces of an aircraft?

A—Servo.
B—Controller.
C—Gyro.

The servo is the component in an autopilot system that applies the force to actuate the control surface.

8654. What is the main purpose of a servo in an autopilot system?

A—Correct for displacement of the aircraft about its axis.
B—Change mechanical energy to electrical energy.
C—Move the control surface as commanded.

The servo in an autopilot system moves the control surface as commanded by the control units.

Answers

8647 [A] (025) AMT-SYS Ch 4	8648 [C] (025) AMT-SYS Ch 4	8649 [C] (025) AMT-SYS Ch 4	8650 [B] (025) AMT-SYS Ch 4
8651 [B] (025) AMT-SYS Ch 4	8652 [C] (025) AMT-SYS Ch 4	8653 [A] (025) AMT-SYS Ch 4	8654 [C] (025) AMT-SYS Ch 4

8655. Which channel of an autopilot detects changes in pitch attitude of an aircraft?

A—Elevator.
B—Aileron.
C—Rudder.

The autopilot detects changes in pitch attitude in the elevator control channel.

8656. The elevator channel of an autopilot controls the aircraft about which axis of rotation?

A—Roll.
B—Longitudinal.
C—Lateral.

The elevator channel of an autopilot controls the aircraft about its pitch axis (its lateral axis).

8657. What component is the sensing device in an electromechanical autopilot system?

A—Servo.
B—Gyro.
C—Controller.

Most electromechanical and electronic autopilots use gyros to sense movement of an aircraft about its pitch, roll, and yaw axes.

8658. A fully integrated autopilot controls the aircraft around how many axes?

A—Two.
B—Three.
C—Four.

A fully integrated autopilot controls an airplane about all three of its axes: roll, pitch, and yaw.

8659. Dutch roll, a combination yawing and rolling oscillation that affects many sweptwing aircraft, is counteracted with

A—a flight director system.
B—an aileron damper system.
C—a yaw damper system.

A yaw damper is installed in many swept wing airplanes to counteract Dutch roll.

Dutch roll is an undesirable, low-amplitude oscillation about both the yaw and roll axes. These oscillations are sensed by a rate gyro. Signals are sent to the rudder servo that provides the correct rudder movement to cancel these oscillations.

8660. When operationally checking an autopilot system on the ground, after the aircraft's main power has been switched on, the autopilot should be engaged

A—only after the gyros come up to speed and the amplifier warms up.
B—whenever the operator desires.
C—for only a few minutes at a time.

When operationally checking an autopilot system on the ground, the autopilot should not be engaged until the gyros are up to speed and the amplifier is properly warmed up.

8661. Installed radio equipment is protected from damage due to jolts and vibration by

A—shock mounts.
B—spring and/or viscous damper mounted racks.
C—rubber or foam cushioning material between circuit chassis and case.

Shock-mounted racks are used to protect radio equipment installed in an aircraft from vibration damage.

8662. Radio equipment is bonded to the aircraft in order to

A—provide a low-impedance ground.
B—minimize radio interference from static electrical charges.
C—provide a low-impedance ground and minimize radio interference from static electrical charges.

Radio equipment is bonded to the aircraft to provide a low-impedance ground and to minimize radio interference from static electrical charges.

8663. When must the radio station license be displayed in an aircraft equipped with a two-way radio?

A—When the aircraft is operated outside the United States.
B—When the aircraft is returned to service.
C—When the aircraft is certified for IFR flight.

A radio station license issued by the FCC was formerly required to be displayed in all operating aircraft equipped with a two-way radio. A recent change in the FCC regulations requires this license to be in the aircraft only when it is operated outside the United States.

Answers

8655 [A] (025) AMT-SYS Ch 4	8656 [C] (025) AMT-SYS Ch 4	8657 [B] (025) AMT-SYS Ch 4	8658 [B] (025) AMT-SYS Ch 4
8659 [C] (025) AMT-SYS Ch 4	8660 [A] (026) AMT-SYS Ch 4	8661 [A] (086) AMT-SYS Ch 5	8662 [C] (086) AC 43.13-2
			8663 [A] (087) AMT-SYS Ch 5

8664. When would a U.S. resident NOT be required to hold a Federal Communications Commission (FCC) Restricted Radio Telephone Operator Permit to operate two-way aircraft VHF radio equipment?

A—When flying to or communicating with destinations outside the United States.
B—When flying or communicating within the United States.
C—When the radio equipment is operated in aircraft certified for VFR flight only.

The FCC regulations require a restricted radio telephone operator permit only when the aircraft is operated outside the United States.

8665. Part of the ADF system used on aircraft includes

A—RMI indicator antenna.
B—marker beacon antenna.
C—sense and loop antennas.

The ADF system operates in the low- and medium-frequency (LF/MF) band, and the airborne equipment consists of a receiver, a loop (directional) antenna, a sense (nondirectional) antenna, an indicator, and a control unit.

8666. When installing coaxial cable, it should be secured firmly along its entire length

A—at one-foot intervals.
B—wherever the cable sags.
C—at two-foot intervals.

When installing a coaxial cable, secure the cable firmly along its entire length at intervals of approximately every two feet.

8667. When must the emergency locator transmitter (ELT) battery be replaced (other than reading the replacement date)?

A—When the transmitter has been in use for more than one cumulative hour.
B—Must be replaced annually or if the five-G switch has been activated.
C—When the transmitter has been tested more than ten times.

According to 14 CFR §91.207, the batteries of an ELT must be replaced or recharged (if they are rechargeable):

- *By the date marked on the outside of the transmitter.*
- *When the transmitter has been in use for more than one cumulative hour.*
- *When 50 percent of their useful life has expired.*

8668. An emergency locator transmitter (ELT) battery must be capable of furnishing power for signal transmission for at least

A—36 hours.
B—48 hours.
C—72 hours.

When activated, the battery installed in an ELT must be capable of furnishing power for signal transmission for at least 48 hours.

8669. The preferred location of an ELT is

A—as far forward as possible but aft of the firewall.
B—at the lowest point possible in the fuselage.
C—as far aft as possible but forward of the empennage.

An ELT must be installed in a location where it is least likely to be destroyed in a crash. This is normally as far aft as possible, but forward of the empennage.

8670. An emergency locator transmitter (ELT) is normally activated by an inertial switch or equivalent mechanism if subjected to a force of a prescribed intensity and duration. It must activate when the force is applied

A—parallel to the longitudinal axis of the aircraft.
B—parallel to the vertical axis of the aircraft.
C—in any direction relative to the aircraft axes.

An ELT is activated by an inertial switch that senses impact forces primarily parallel to the longitudinal axis to the aircraft.

8671. How may the battery replacement date be verified for an emergency locator transmitter (ELT)?

A—By removing the batteries and testing them under a measured load to determine if 50 percent of the useful life remains.
B—By observing the battery replacement date marked on the outside of the transmitter.
C—By activating the transmitter and measuring the signal strength.

According to 14 CFR §91.207, the batteries of an ELT must be replaced or recharged (if they are rechargeable):

- *By the date marked on the outside of the transmitter.*
- *When the transmitter has been in use for more than one cumulative hour.*
- *When 50 percent of their useful life has expired.*

Answers

8664 [B] (087) §91.203	8665 [C] (071) AMT-SYS Ch 5	8666 [C] (023) AMT-SYS Ch 5	8667 [A] (044) AMT-SYS Ch 5
8668 [B] (044) AMT-SYS Ch 5	8669 [C] (086) FAA-H-8083-31	8670 [A] (044) AC 91-44A	8671 [B] (044) AMT-SYS Ch 5

8672. How may the operation of an installed emergency locator transmitter (ELT) be verified during aircraft inspection?

A—By moving the deactivating switch from the DISARM position to the ARM position while monitoring the civil emergency frequency with a communications receiver at five minutes after the hour.
B—By activating the five-G switch and turning the unit on at five minutes after the hour.
C—By tuning a communications receiver to the civil emergency frequency and activating the ELT momentarily within five minutes after the hour.

Operation of an ELT is verified by tuning a communications receiver to 406 MHz and activating the transmitter for no more than three audible sweeps. The test must be conducted within the first five minutes after any hour. If the ELT must be operated outside of this time frame, you should contact the control tower before conducting this test.

8673. Static dischargers help eliminate radio interference by dissipating static electricity into the atmosphere at

A—low current levels.
B—high voltage level.
C—high current levels.

Static dischargers are mounted on the trailing edges of aircraft control surfaces to conduct charges of static electricity into the atmosphere before they build up enough voltage to cause a high current to flow and cause radio interference. By the proper design and location of these dischargers, the static charges will be dissipated while its current level is low.

8675. Aircraft antennae must be grounded to the

A—airframe.
B—wing spar.
C—bus bar.

When an aircraft radio antenna installation is required to be grounded, it is grounded to the airframe structure.

8676. VHF radio signals are commonly used in

A—ATC communications.
B—VOR navigation.
C—both VOR navigation and ATC communications.

VHF radio transmissions operate in the 118.000 to 135.975 MHz range. This frequency range is used for ATC communications and VOR navigation.

8677. On modern large aircraft, what electronic device typically monitors flight parameters and performs autopilot functions?

A—Flight management computer.
B—Transponder.
C—Control/display unit.

Large aircraft have many sophisticated electronic control devices. The FMC monitors flight parameters and performs autopilot functions. It regulates the movement of the control surface actuators which control the stabilizers, elevators, rudders, speed brakes, and spoilers.

8678. In the landing configuration GPWS typically monitors the radio (radar) altimeter, air data computer, instrument landing system, and

A—aileron, rudder, and elevator positions.
B—landing gear and flap positions.
C—spoiler, slat, and stabilizer positions.

The GPWS senses the nearness of the ground and warns the pilot if the aircraft has gotten too near the ground when it is not in a configuration for landing. It does this by monitoring the radar altimeter to determine the actual height above the ground.

It also monitors the air data computer, instrument landing system, and landing gear and flap position to determine if the aircraft is properly configured for its distance from the ground. If it is too near the ground for its location or configuration, the system will warn the pilot.

8679. In general, the purpose of an aircraft transponder is to

A—continually transmit heading, speed, and rate of climb/descent, etc., information to ATC.
B—monitor aircraft speed, heading, altitude, and attitude whenever the autopilot system is engaged.
C—receive an interrogation signal from a ground station and automatically send a reply back.

An ATC transponder is a special radio transceiver that receives an interrogation signal from an ATC radar and automatically replies with a coded signal. The coded response to the ground station interrogation allows the controller to identify the aircraft.

Answers

8672 [C] (044) AMT-SYS Ch 5	8673 [A] (071) AMT-SYS Ch 5	8675 [A] (023) AMT-SYS Ch 5	8676 [C] (071) AMT-SYS Ch 5
8677 [A] (071) AMT-SYS Ch 5	8678 [B] (018) AMT-SYS Ch 5	8679 [C] (071) AMT-SYS Ch 5	

8680. When an antenna is installed, it should be fastened

A—to the primary structure at the approximate intersection of the three aircraft axes.
B—with a reinforcing doubler on each side of the aircraft skin.
C—so that loads imposed are transmitted to the aircraft structure.

An antenna must be installed on an aircraft in such a way that the loads imposed are transmitted into the aircraft structure.

8681. After an automatic direction finding antenna has been installed, the

A—antenna must be grounded.
B—loop must be calibrated.
C—transceiver must be compensated.

When an automatic direction finder is installed on a particular type of aircraft for the first time, it is important that the loop antenna be checked for quadrantal error.

Quadrantal error is the error caused by the metal in the aircraft structure distorting the electromagnetic field of the received signal.

Quadrantal error causes azimuth inaccuracies, which are greatest between the four cardinal points with respect to the center line of the aircraft.

8682. Doublers are used when antennas are installed to

A—eliminate antenna vibration.
B—prevent oil canning of the skin.
C—reinstate the structural strength of the aircraft skin.

A doubler is used under an antenna when it is installed on an aircraft skin to replace the strength in the structure that was lost when the hole was cut for mounting the antenna.

8683. One antenna can be used for the radio range and standard broadcast bands in light aircraft because the

A—two ranges are close together.
B—antenna is omnidirectional.
C—antenna length may be electronically adjusted.

One antenna can be used on light aircraft to receive both the low-frequency radio range and the standard broadcast bands.

The frequency range of these two types of radio transmissions are so close together that one antenna can effectively receive both signals.

8684. What characteristics of the installation of a rigid antenna on a vertical stabilizer should be evaluated?

A—Polarization and impedance.
B—Impedance and interference.
C—Flutter and vibration.

When any rigid antenna is mounted on a vertical stabilizer, the flutter and vibration characteristics must be carefully evaluated.

An antenna can change the resonant frequency of the vertical surface.

8685. A gasket or sealant is used between the antenna mast and fuselage skin

A—to prevent the entry of moisture.
B—for aircraft pressurization only.
C—to prevent abrasion between the antenna mast and fuselage skin.

A gasket or sealant is used between a radio antenna mast and the fuselage skin to prevent the entry of moisture into the fuselage.

8686. The preferred location of a VOR antenna on light aircraft is on

A—the bottom of the fuselage and as far forward as possible.
B—top of the cabin with the apex of the V pointing forward.
C—top of the vertical stabilizer.

The preferred location for a VOR antenna on a single-engine aircraft is on top of the cabin, with the apex of the V pointing forward.

8687. The purpose of a localizer is to

A—set the airplane on the proper approach angle to the runway.
B—indicate the distance the airplane is from the end of the runway.
C—align the airplane with the center of the runway.

The function of a localizer in an ILS is to align the aircraft with the center line of the instrument runway.

Answers

8680 [C] (023) AC 43.13-2	8681 [B] (023) AMT-SYS Ch 5	8682 [C] (023) AMT-SYS Ch 5	8683 [A] (023) AMT-SYS Ch 5
8684 [C] (023) AC 43.13-2	8685 [A] (023) AMT-SYS Ch 5	8686 [B] (023) AC 43.13-2	8687 [C] (085) AMT-SYS Ch 5

8688. (Refer to Figure 15.) What is the approximate drag load on an antenna with a frontal area of .125 square feet installed on an aircraft with a speed of 225 mph?

A—2.069 pounds.
B—2.073 pounds.
C—2.080 pounds.

$$D = .000327AV^2$$

Figure 15. Formula

This computation is described in AC 43.13-2.

The constant 0.000327 is multiplied by the frontal area of the antenna (in this case, 0.125 square foot). This quantity is multiplied by the square of the never-exceed speed of the aircraft which is 225 mph.

$$D = 0.000327 \times 0.125 \times 225^2$$
$$= 2.069 \text{ pounds}$$

8689. (Refer to Figure 15.) What is the approximate drag load on an antenna with a frontal area of .137 square feet installed on an aircraft with a speed of 275 mph?

A—3.387 pounds.
B—3.741 pounds.
C—3.592 pounds.

This computation is described in AC 43.13-2.

The constant 0.000327 is multiplied by the frontal area of the antenna (in this case, 0.137 square foot). This quantity is multiplied by the square of the never-exceed speed of the aircraft which is 275 mph.

$$D = 0.000327 \times 0.137 \times 275^2$$
$$= 3.3879 \text{ pounds}$$

8690. A DME antenna should be installed on the aircraft in a position that will

A—not be blanked out by the wing when the aircraft is banked.
B—not be blanked out by the vertical stabilizer.
C—facilitate cleaning, inspection, and maintenance.

To prevent an interruption in DME operation, the antenna must be located in a position that will not be blanked by the wing when the aircraft is banked.

8691. When bending coaxial cable, the bend radius should be at least

A—10 times the diameter of the cable.
B—15 times the diameter of the cable.
C—20 times the diameter of the cable.

Because it is essential that the center conductor of a coaxial cable remain in its exact center, coax should not be bent with a radius of less than 10 times its diameter.

8692. When installing a DME antenna, it should be aligned with the

A—VOR antenna.
B—chord line.
C—centerline on the airplane.

A DME antenna should be mounted on the center line of the belly of an airplane.

8693. (Refer to Figure 16.) Which of the antennas shown is a typical DME antenna?

A—1.
B—2.
C—4.

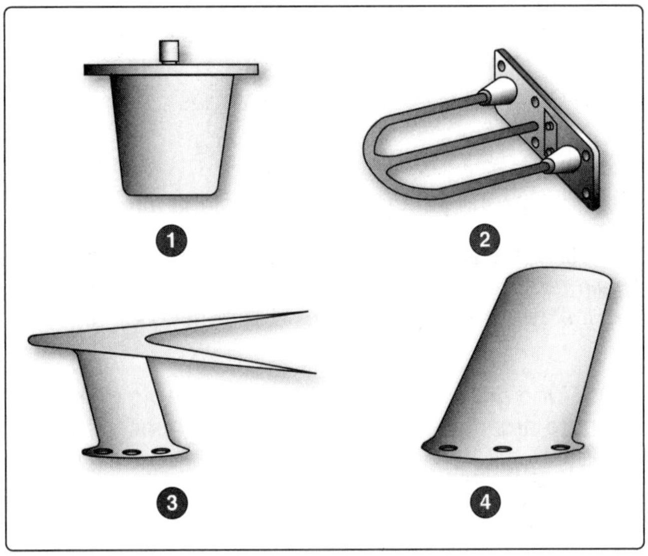

Figure 16. Antennas

The antenna shown in 1 is a DME or a radar beacon trans-ponder antenna.

The antenna shown in 2 is a glide slope antenna.

The antenna shown in 3 is a VOR and localizer antenna.

The antenna shown in 4 is a VHF communications antenna.

Answers
8688 [A] (023) AC 43.13-2
8689 [A] (023) AC 43.13-2
8690 [A] (085) AMT-SYS Ch 5
8691 [A] (023) AMT-SYS Ch 5
8692 [C] (023) AMT-SYS Ch 5
8693 [A] (023) AMT-SYS Ch 5

8694. (Refer to Figure 16.) Which of the antennas shown is a typical glideslope antenna?

A—2.
B—3.
C—4.

The antenna shown in 2 is a glide slope antenna.

8694-1. (Refer to Figure 22.) What kind of antenna is this?

A—This is a glide slope antenna.
B—This is a DME or a radar beacon transponder.
C—This is a loop and sense antenna.

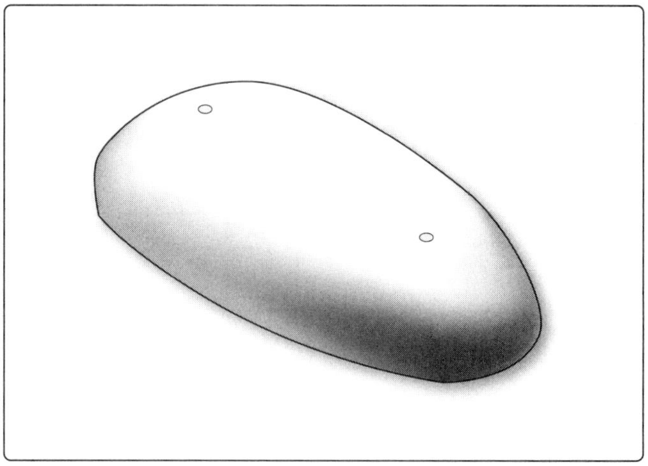

Figure 22. Antenna

The low-profile single antenna in Figure 22 is a loop and sense antenna, which is used for ADF navigation.

8694-2. (Refer to Figure 23.) What is this antenna used for?

A—This is an altitude encoder used with transponders.
B—This is a TCAS receiver used with monitoring and alerting systems.
C—This is an aircraft radar beacon transponder used for location identification.

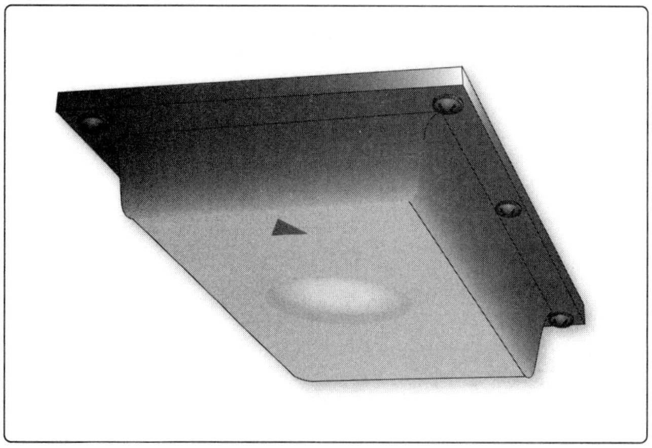

Figure 23. Antenna

The ceiling-mounted box in Figure 23 depicts an altitude encoder used to convert the aircraft's pressure altitude into a code sent by the transponder to ATC.

8694-3. (Refer to Figure 24.) What kind of antenna is this?

A—A dipole antenna.
B—A Marconi antenna.
C—A loop antenna.

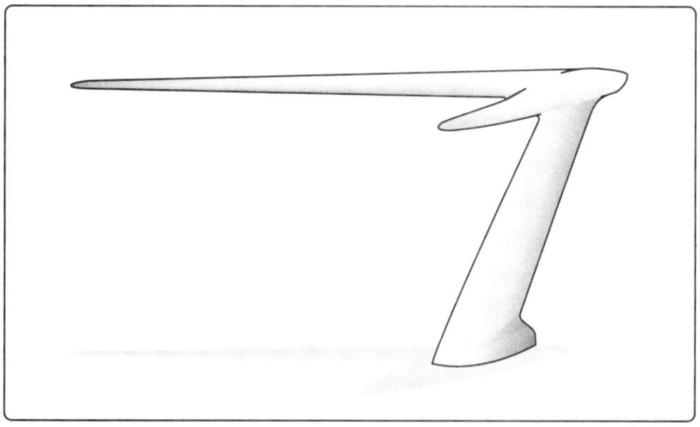

Figure 24. Antenna

Figure 24 depicts a V-shaped VOR navigation antenna, which is a common dipole antenna.

Answers
8694 [A] (023) AMT-SYS Ch 5   8694-1 [C] (023) AMT-SYS Ch 5   8694-2 [A] (023) AMT-SYS Ch 5   8694-3 [A] (023) AMT-SYS Ch 5

8694-4. (Refer to Figure 25.) What kind of antenna is this?

A—A dipole antenna.
B—A canted antenna.
C—A Marconi antenna.

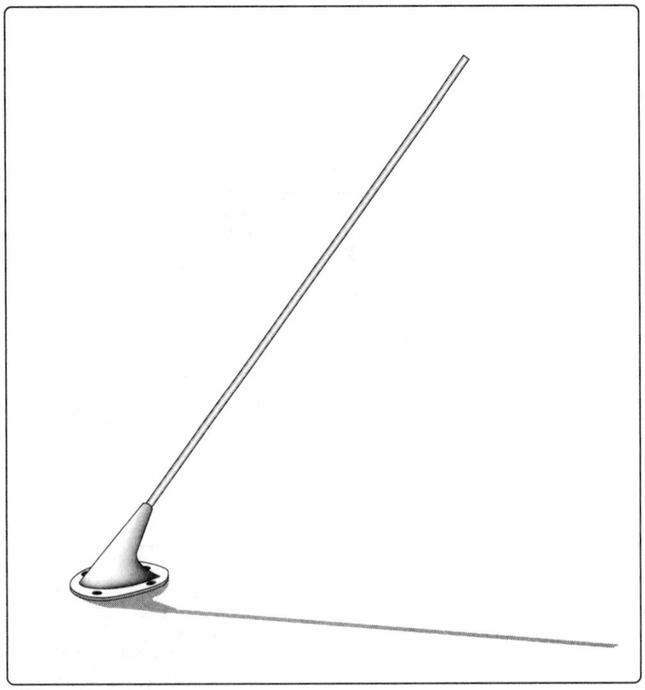

Figure 25. Antenna

Figure 25 depicts a canted antenna. Many antennas are canted (or slanted) for better reception.

8694-5. (Refer to Figure 26.) Where is the strongest signal for this antenna?

A—Below the antenna.
B—Above the antenna.
C—Ahead of the antenna.

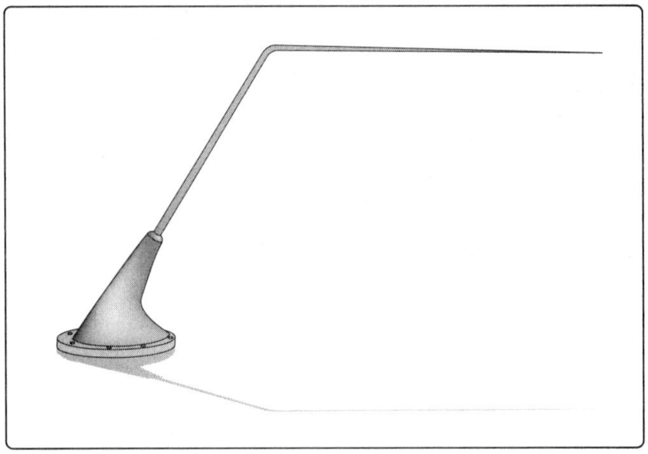

Figure 26. Antenna

The strongest signals come from, or are received at, 90° to the length of the antenna. There is no field generated off of the end of the antenna.

8694-6. (Refer to Figure 27.) What kind of antenna is this?

A—A glide slope antenna.
B—A VOR and localizer antenna.
C—A radar beacon transponder antenna.

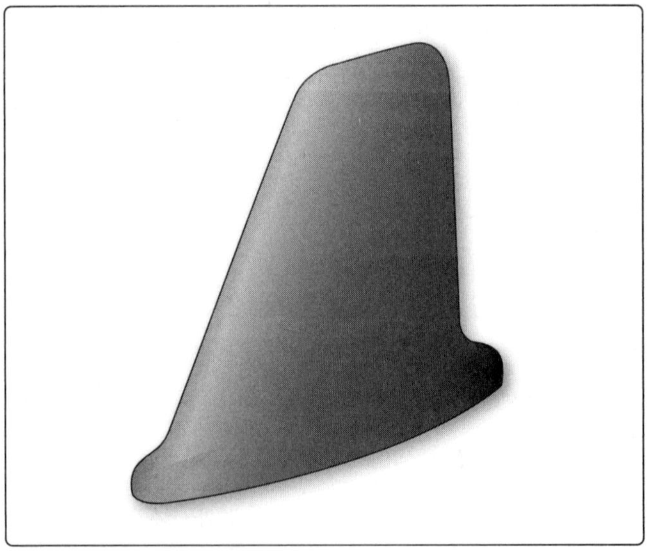

Figure 27. Antenna

Figure 27 depicts an aircraft radar beacon transponder antenna.

Answers
8694-4 [B] (023) AMT-SYS Ch 5   8694-5 [B] (023) AMT-SYS Ch 5   8694-6 [C] (023) AMT-SYS Ch 5

8694-7. (Refer to Figure 28.) What kind of antenna is this?

A—An ELT antenna.
B—A DME antenna.
C—A VHF communications antenna.

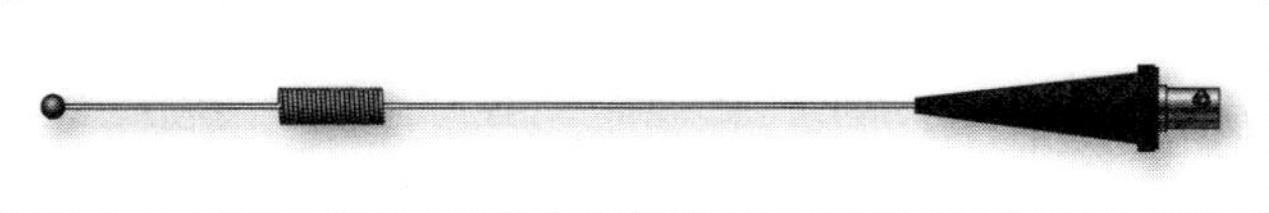

Figure 28. Antenna

Figure 28 depicts an ELT antenna.

8694-8. (Refer to Figure 29.) What kind of antenna is this?

A—A glide slope antenna.
B—A VOR and localizer antenna.
C—A radar beacon transponder antenna.

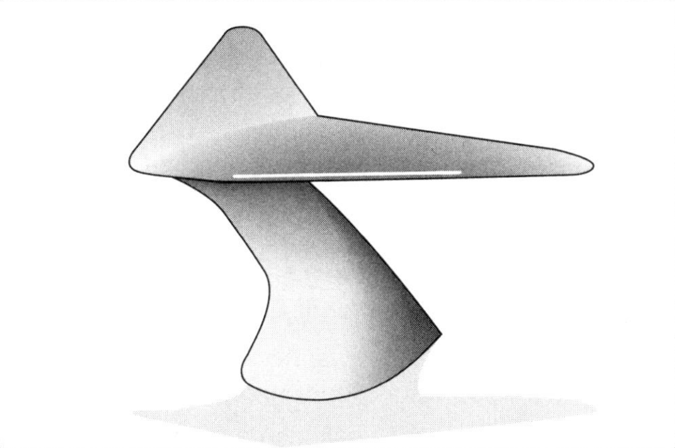

Figure 29. Antenna

Figure 29 depicts a VOR and localizer antenna.

8694-9. (Refer to Figure 30.) What kind of antenna is this?

A—A lightning detector system antenna.
B—A VOR and localizer antenna.
C—A satellite weather antenna.

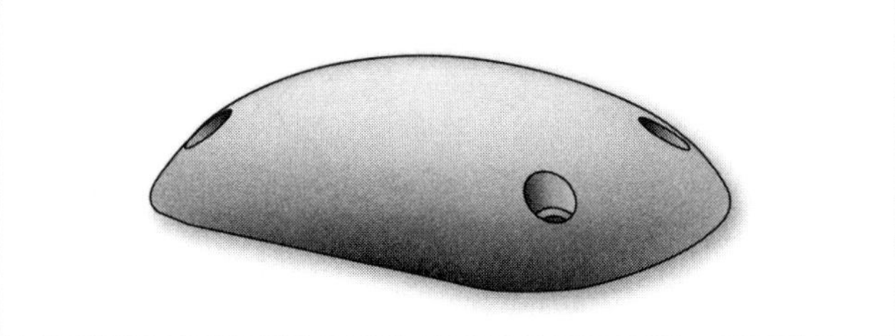

Figure 30. Antenna

Figure 30 depicts a lightning detector system antenna.

8694-10. (Refer to Figure 31.) What kind of antenna is this?

A—A lightning detector system antenna.
B—A marker beacon receiver antenna.
C—A satellite weather antenna.

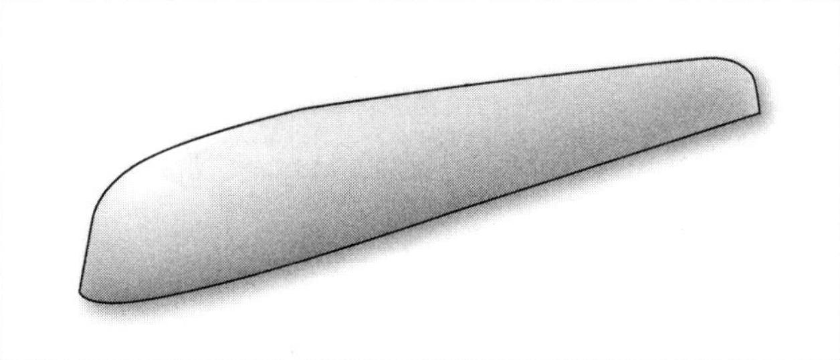

Figure 31. Antenna

Figure 31 depicts a marker beacon receiver antenna.

Answers

8694-7 [A] (023) AMT-SYS Ch 5
8694-8 [B] (023) AMT-SYS Ch 5
8694-9 [A] (023) AMT-SYS Ch 5
8694-10 [B] (023) AMT-SYS Ch 5

8694-11. (Refer to Figure 32.) What kind of antenna is this?

A—A lightning detector system antenna.
B—A marker beacon receiver antenna.
C—A radar beacon transponder antenna.

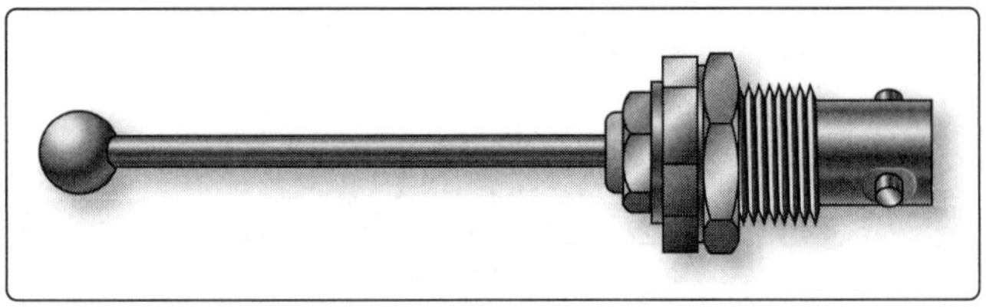

Figure 32. Antenna

Figure 32 depicts a radar beacon transponder antenna.

8694-12. (Refer to Figure 33.) What kind of antenna is this?

A—A VOR/glide slope antenna.
B—A marker beacon receiver antenna.
C—A radar beacon transponder antenna.

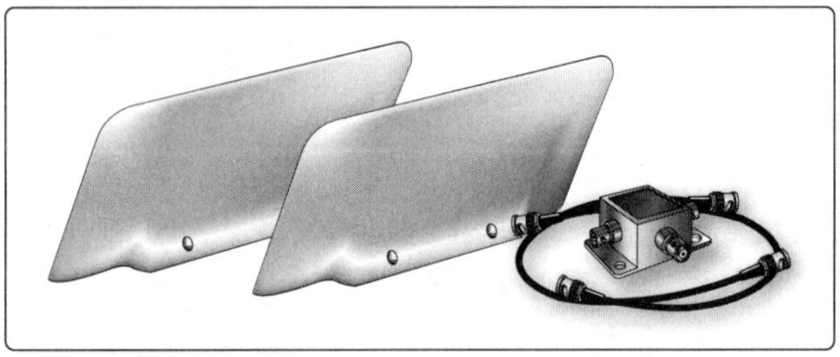

Figure 33. Antenna

Figure 33 depicts a VOR/glide slope antenna.

8694-13. (Refer to Figure 34.) What kind of antenna is this?

A—A VOR/glide slope antenna.
B—A marker beacon receiver antenna.
C—A radar beacon transponder antenna.

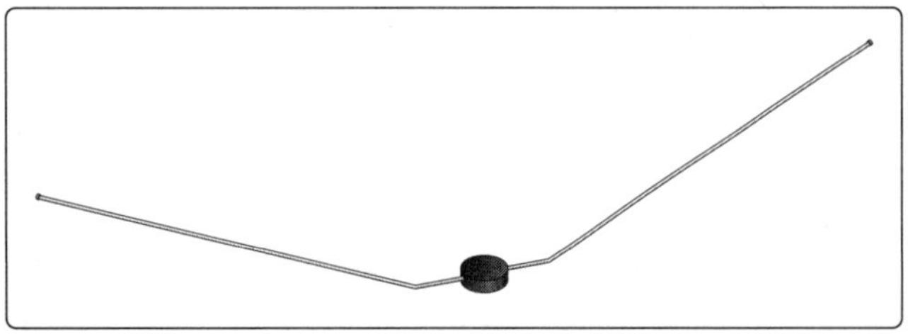

Figure 34. Antenna

Figure 34 depicts a VOR/glide slope antenna.

8695. The addition of avionics and associated antenna systems forward of the CG limit will affect

A—empty weight and useful load.
B—CG limits and useful load.
C—useful load and maximum gross weight.

The installation of avionics equipment and its associated antenna, ahead of the CG limit, will affect the empty weight of the aircraft, its CG, and its useful load.

When such equipment is installed, a new weight and balance record must be made showing the change in the empty weight and empty-weight CG of the aircraft. The addition of avionics equipment will decrease the useful load of the aircraft.

8696. How much clearance from the seat bottom is required when installing radio equipment under a seat?

A—3 inches with the seat unoccupied.
B—No set minimum as long as the equipment receives adequate cooling and damage protection.
C—1 inch with the seat occupied and subjected to maximum downward seat spring deflection.

When installing radio equipment under an aircraft seat, there must be one inch of clearance between the equipment and the bottom of the seat when it is occupied and subjected to a downward force of 1,122 pounds. This load is found by multiplying the 170-pound nominal weight of an occupant by a load factor of 6.6.

8697. The purpose of a glideslope system is to

A—provide for automatic altitude reporting to air traffic control.
B—indicate the distance the airplane is from the end of the runway.
C—assist the pilot in making a correct angle of descent to the runway.

The glide slope system is the part of an ILS that allows a pilot to make the correct angle of descent to the instrument runway during an approach.

Answers

8694-11 [C] (023) AMT-SYS Ch 5	8694-12 [A] (023) AMT-SYS Ch 5	8694-13 [A] (023) AMT-SYS Ch 5	8695 [A] (028) AMT-SYS Ch 5
8696 [C] (028) AC 43.13-2	8697 [C] (028) AMT-SYS Ch 5		

Aircraft Fuel Systems

8698. Fuel jettisoning is usually accomplished

A—through a common manifold and outlet in each wing.
B—by gravity flow into the outboard wing tanks and overboard through a common outlet in each wing.
C—through individual outlets for each tank.

Fuel jettisoning is usually accomplished by a fuel dump manifold, which connects the dumpable fuel tanks to the dump valves and to a fixed or extendable dump chute in each wing.

8699. The primary purpose of an aircraft's fuel jettison system is to quickly achieve a

A—lower landing weight.
B—balanced fuel load.
C—reduced fire hazard.

Some aircraft are allowed to have a higher takeoff weight than is allowed for landing. These aircraft must have a fuel jettison system that allows the pilot or flight engineer to safely dump, or jettison, enough fuel to reduce the aircraft weight to its allowable landing weight.

8700. The fuel jettison valve must be designed to allow flight personnel

A—to close the valve at any time and the fuel must discharge clear of the aircraft.
B—to discharge fuel clear of the aircraft.
C—to close the valve at anytime.

The fuel jettison valve must be designed to allow flight personnel to close the valve during any part of the jettisoning operation. During the fuel-jettisoning operation, the fuel must discharge clear of any part of the airplane.

8701. Which of the following is employed to maintain lateral stability when jettisoning fuel?

A—Two separate independent systems.
B—Crossfeed system.
C—Two interconnected systems.

Lateral stability during fuel jettisoning is maintained by having two separate and independent jettisoning systems. There is one system for each side of the aircraft.

8702. A fuel jettison system is required under certain conditions if the maximum takeoff weight exceeds the maximum landing weight. What regulations cover the requirements of fuel jettisoning?

A—14 CFR Parts 43 and 91.
B—14 CFR Parts 23 and 25 and CAM 4b.
C—14 CFR Parts 21 and 43 and CAM 8.

The regulations governing fuel jettisoning systems are covered in 14 CFR Parts 23 and 25, and in the Civil Air Regulations Part 04 for aircraft that were certificated by the Civil Aeronautics Administration before the formation of the FAA.

8703. Fuel is moved overboard in most fuel jettison systems by

A—boost pumps.
B—gravity.
C—gravity and engine-driven fuel pumps.

Fuel is moved overboard in a jettison system by boost pumps located in the fuel tanks.

8704. Fuel jettisoning past the limits prescribed by Federal Aviation Regulations is usually prevented by

A—closely monitoring the fuel quantity and turning off the fuel dump switch(es).
B—dump limit valves or a low-level circuit.
C—standpipes in the fuel tanks.

Fuel tanks whose fuel can be jettisoned are equipped with a dump limit switch that will shut off the flow to the dump chute if the pressure drops below that needed to supply the engine with adequate fuel, or when the tank level reaches a preset dump shutoff level.

8705. Which procedure must be followed when defueling aircraft with sweptback wings?

A—Defuel all the tanks at one time.
B—Defuel the inboard wing tanks first.
C—Defuel the outboard wing tanks first.

Unless the service manual specifies otherwise, the outboard fuel tanks on an aircraft with swept back wings should be defueled first.

This procedure minimizes the twisting effect on the wing caused by the fuel being located behind the wing attachment points on the fuselage.

Answers
8698 [A] (052) AMT-SYS Ch 2
8699 [A] (054) AMT-SYS Ch 2
8700 [A] (054) 14 CFR Part 23
8701 [A] (055) AMT-SYS
8702 [B] (052) 14 CFR Part 23, AMT-SYS
8703 [A] (054) AMT-SYS Ch 2
8704 [B] (054) AMT-SYS Ch 2
8705 [C] (052) AMT-SYS

8706. (Refer to Figure 17.) What is the purpose of the pump crossfeed valve?

A—Balance the fuel in the tanks.
B—Allow operation of engines from one tank.
C—Allow operation of the left engine when the right fuel-boost pump is inoperative.

The pump crossfeed valve shown here allows both engines to operate from either of the two tanks.

8707. Normal fuel crossfeed system operation in multiengine aircraft

A—calls for jettisoning of fuel overboard to correct lateral instability.
B—reduces contamination and/or fire hazards during fueling or defueling operations.
C—provides a means to maintain a balanced fuel load condition.

Multi-engine aircraft normally have fuel tanks located in widely separated parts of the aircraft. A crossfeed fuel system allows fuel to be used from any tank by any of the engines. This allows a balanced fuel load to be maintained.

8707-2. How many vents, arranged so that they are not likely to become plugged at the same time, must be used in multiengine fuel systems?

A—Two.
B—Four.
C—Six.

If a single fuel tank (or series of fuel tanks interconnected to function as a single tank) is used on a multi-engine airplane, the tank must have at least two vents arranged to minimize the probability of both vents becoming obstructed simultaneously.

8708. What is the primary purpose of the crossfeed system?

A—It allows any tank to supply fuel to any engine.
B—It bypasses the engine shutoff valve if it fails.
C—It divides the fuel and sends it to the injectors.

A crossfeed system allows any engine on a multiengine aircraft to be fed from any tank.
This can be used to maintain a balanced fuel load.

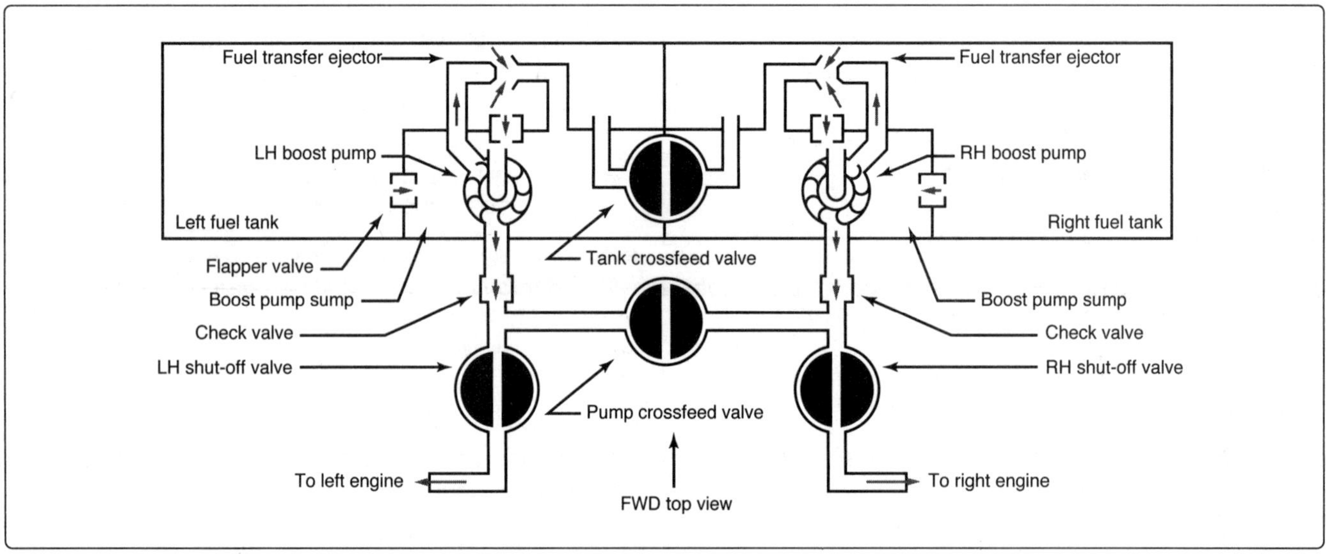

Figure 17. Fuel system

Answers
8706 [B] (054) AMT-SYS Ch 2 | 8707 [C] (056) AMT-SYS Ch 2 | 8707-2 [A] (054) AMT-SYS Ch 2 | 8708 [A] (056) AMT-SYS Ch 2

8709. Fuel system components must be bonded and grounded in order to

A—drain off static charges.
B—prevent stray currents.
C—retard galvanic corrosion.

Aircraft fuel system components must be bonded to the aircraft structure and must be grounded in order to prevent a buildup of static electricity.

Static electricity could cause a spark and a fire.

8709-2. How many engine driven fuel pumps per engine are required for engines requiring fuel pumps?

A—Two engines can share one fuel pump.
B—One fuel pump for each engine.
C—Two fuel pumps for each engine.

For reciprocating engine installations having fuel pumps to supply fuel to the engine, at least one pump for each engine must be directly driven by the engine and must meet 14 CFR Part 23. This pump is the main pump. There must be at least one main fuel pump for each turbine engine.

8710. A typical large transport aircraft fuel manifold system allows how many of the following?

1. All tanks can be serviced through a single connection.
2. Any engine can be fed from any tank.
3. All engines can be fed from all tanks simultaneously.
4. A damaged tank can be isolated from the rest of the fuel system.

A—1 and 2.
B—1, 2, and 3.
C—1, 2, 3, and 4.

In a large aircraft manifold fuel system, all tanks can be serviced through a single connection, any engine can be fed from any tank, all engines can be fed from all tanks simultaneously, and a damaged tank can be isolated from the rest of the fuel system.

8710-2. A fuel system must be designed to prevent fuel-vapor ignition caused by

A—over-heating.
B—back-fire.
C—lightning.

A fuel system must be designed to prevent fuel-vapor ignition caused by lightning.

8710-3. What is the minimum distance allowed between a fuel tank and the fire wall separating the engine?

A—One-half inch.
B—One inch.
C—Two inches.

There must be at least one-half inch of clearance between the fuel tank and the firewall.

8710-4. Fuel baffles are installed in tanks to prevent ______________ caused by changes in the attitude of the aircraft.

A—vapors
B—surging
C—starvation

Baffles are installed in aircraft fuel tanks to prevent the fuel sloshing or surging in the tank caused by changes in attitude of the aircraft.

8710-5. Many fuel tanks incorporate ______________ valves to prevent fuel from flowing away from the boost pump or tank outlet when the aircraft is in a high-G maneuver.

A—flapper
B—check
C—dump

Many fuel tanks incorporate flapper valves that prevent fuel in the tank from flowing away from the boost pump or tank outlet any time the aircraft is in a high-G maneuver. These valves are normally open, but if a maneuver causes the fuel to flow away from the pump or outlet, they flap shut until the force moving the fuel no longer exists, then they automatically open.

8710-6. Fuel heaters are used with fuel systems for turbine engines to prevent ______________ in the fuel from clogging system filters.

A—moisture
B—ice crystals
C—contamination

Turbine powered aircraft incorporate fuel heaters to prevent ice crystals from forming in the fuel and clogging the fuel system filters.

Answers

8709 [A] (055) AMT-SYS Ch 2	8709-2 [B] (054) AMT-SYS Ch 2	8710 [C] (055) AMT-SYS Ch 2	8710-2 [C] (054) AC 20-53
8710-3 [A] (054) 14 CFR Part 23	8710-4 [B] (054) AMT-SYS Ch 2	8710-5 [A] (054) AMT-SYS Ch 2	8710-6 [B] (054) AMT-SYS Ch 2

8710-7. A transducer in a fuel pressure system serves what function?

A—Transmits an electrical signal to the transmitter for fluid pressure.
B—Transmits electrical signal proportional to the fluid pressure.
C—Converts fluid pressure directly through a transmitter to the indicator.

A transducer is a device that changes energy from one form into another. A fuel pressure transducer converts fuel pressure into an electrical signal that is proportional to the fuel pressure. This signal is transmitted to the fuel pressure indicator.

8711. The use of turbine fuels in aircraft has resulted in some problems not normally associated with aviation gasolines. One of these problems is

A—increasing viscosity of fuel as fuel temperature lowers at altitude.
B—higher vapor pressure.
C—microbial contaminants.

Microbial contamination is a fuel system problem that is associated with the higher viscosity fuel used in turbine engine aircraft.

Turbine engine fuel holds water more readily than gasoline. Microorganisms live in this water and form a scum which clogs the fuel filters, lines, and fuel controls. The scum holds water against the fuel tank structure and causes tank corrosion.

8712. What is used in many aircraft to prevent bubbles in the fuel after it leaves the tank when atmospheric pressure is lower than fuel vapor pressure?

A—Air-fuel separators.
B—Anti-foaming additives.
C—Boost pumps.

Boost pumps installed in many aircraft fuel tanks have an agitator on their shaft along with the impeller. The agitator causes bubbles in the fuel to be released into the tank before the fuel is forced into the fuel lines. The boost pumps hold a pressure on the fuel in the lines to prevent additional vapors from forming.

8713. Which of the following precautions is most important during refueling operations?

A—All outside electrical sources must be disconnected from the aircraft.
B—Fuel to be used must be appropriately identified.
C—All electrical switches must be in OFF position.

It is extremely important when fueling an aircraft that the fuel be properly identified. The use of fuel with a lower than allowed octane or performance rating can cause detonation which can destroy an engine.

A number of airplanes have been destroyed by the inadvertent fueling of a reciprocating engine aircraft with turbine-engine fuel. Turbine-engine fuel will cause severe detonation when a reciprocating engine is operated at takeoff power.

8714. Before fueling an aircraft by using the pressure fueling method, what important precaution should be observed?

A—The truck pump pressure must be correct for that refueling system.
B—The truck pump pressure must be adjusted for minimum filter pressure.
C—The aircraft's electrical system must be on to indicate quantity gauge readings.

Before fueling an aircraft, it is important that the fuel truck pump pressure be correct for the refueling system.

Some systems, such as that used on the Boeing 727, require a maximum fuel delivery pressure of 50 psi. The delivery pressure varies with the different aircraft.

8715. What flight safety-related advantage does a pressure fueling system provide?

A—Keeps the aircraft within weight and balance limitations.
B—Reduces the chances for fuel contamination.
C—Reduces the time required for fueling.

Pressure fueling of an aircraft reduces the chances of fuel contamination, as well as reducing the danger of static electricity igniting fuel vapors.

8716. Aircraft pressure fueling systems instructional procedures are normally placarded on the

A—fuel control panel access door.
B—lower wing surface adjacent to the access door.
C—aircraft ground connection point.

Pressure fueling instructional procedures are normally placarded on the fuel control panel access door.

No one should fuel an aircraft with a fuel pressure fueling system unless he or she has been thoroughly checked out on the procedure.

Answers

8710-7 [C] (054) AMT-SYS Ch 2	8711 [C] (052) AC 43.13-1	8712 [C] (052) AMT-SYS Ch 2	8713 [B] (052) AMT-SYS Ch 2
8714 [A] (052) AMT-SYS Ch 2	8715 [B] (052) AMT-SYS Ch 2	8716 [A] (055) AMT-SYS Ch 2	

8717. Pressure fueling of aircraft is usually accomplished through

A—pressure connections on individual fuel tanks.
B—at least one single point connection.
C—individual fuel tank overwing and/or fuselage access points.

A manifold fuel system allows an aircraft to be fueled by the pressure fueling method. All of the tanks can be fueled at the same time through a single manifold connection. This reduces the fueling time, minimizes the chance of contamination, and minimizes the buildup of static electrical charges.

8718. Which of the following may be used for the repair of fuel leaks on most integral fuel tanks?

A—Welding and resealing.
B—Brazing and resealing.
C—Riveting and resealing.

Since an integral fuel tank is a part of the aircraft structure, it is repaired by riveting, and resealing the repaired area.

8719. How is the outlet fuel pressure regulated on a submerged, single-speed, centrifugal-type fuel pump?

A—By the engine-driven pump's design and internal clearance.
B—By the first check valve downstream from the pump.
C—By the pump's design and internal clearances.

The outlet fuel pressure produced by a submerged, single-speed, centrifugal-type fuel pump is determined by the pump's design and its internal clearances and characteristics.

8720. What is one purpose of a fuel tank vent?

A—To maintain atmospheric pressure.
B—To decrease fuel vapor pressure.
C—To decrease tank internal air pressure.

A fuel tank vent maintains atmospheric pressure on top of the fuel in the tank to provide for proper fuel flow from the tank to the engine.

8721. When inspecting a removable rigid fuel tank for leaks, what procedure should be followed?

A—pressurize the tank with air and brush with soapy water.
B—fill the tank with water and pressurize with air and brush with soapy water.
C—pressurize the tank with air and submerge in water to locate leaks.

After a removable rigid fuel tank has been repaired, it should be pressurized with no more than 1/2-psi air pressure, and all seams and the repaired area should be inspected by brushing on liquid soap or a soap bubble solution to check for any indication of leaks.

8722. If it is necessary to enter an aircraft's fuel tank, which procedure should be avoided?

A—Continue purging the tank during the entire work period.
B—Station an assistant outside the fuel tank access to perform rescue operations if required.
C—Conduct the defueling and tank purging operation in an air-conditioned building.

You are asked which procedure should be avoided.

All defueling and purging must be done outside, not in any building, air-conditioned or otherwise.

8723. What is the recommended practice for cleaning a fuel tank before welding?

A—Purge the tank with air.
B—Flush the inside of the tank with clean water.
C—Steam clean the tank interior.

Before a gasoline tank is welded, it should be washed out with hot water and a detergent. Then, live steam should be passed through the tank for about a half hour.

This treatment vaporizes and removes any residual fuel that may be left in the tank.

8724. An aircraft's integral fuel tank is

A—usually located in the bottom of the fuselage.
B—a part of the aircraft structure.
C—a self-sealing tank.

An aircraft integral fuel tank is actually a portion of the aircraft structure that is sealed off and is used as a fuel tank.

Answers

8717 [B] (052) AMT-SYS Ch 2	8718 [C] (055) AMT-SYS Ch 2	8719 [C] (054) AMT-SYS Ch 2	8720 [A] (054) AMT-SYS Ch 2
8721 [A] (055) §23.2430	8722 [C] (052) AMT-SYS Ch 2	8723 [C] (055) AMT-SYS Ch 2	8724 [B] (054) AMT-SYS Ch 2

8725. Which gas is used for purging an aircraft fuel tank?

A—Helium or argon.
B—Carbon dioxide.
C—Carbon monoxide.

Carbon dioxide can be used to purge an aircraft fuel tank of fuel vapors.

8726. Why is the main fuel strainer located at the lowest point in the fuel system?

A—It traps any small amount of water that may be present in the fuel system.
B—It is near the fuel tank heater to help prevent vapor lock in the system.
C—It filters and traps all micro-organisms that may be present in the fuel system.

One reason for having the main fuel strainer of an aircraft located at the lowest point in the fuel system is so it will trap and hold any small amount of water that is in the fuel system.

8727. The purpose of a diaphragm in a vane-type fuel pump is to

A—equalize fuel pressure at all speeds.
B—vary fuel pressure according to throttle setting.
C—compensate fuel pressures to altitude changes.

The diaphragm in a compensated vane-type fuel pump is used to compensate the fuel pressure for altitude changes.

It maintains the fuel pressure a constant amount above the pressure of the ambient air.

8728. When moving the mixture control on a normally operating engine into the idle cutoff position, engine RPM should

A—slightly increase before the engine starts to die.
B—slightly decrease and then drop rapidly.
C—remain the same until the cutoff is effected, then drop rapidly.

An engine normally uses an idling fuel-air mixture richer than that which produces the most efficient burning.

When the mixture control is moved into the IDLE CUTOFF position, the mixture passes through the ratio that produces the best burning. The RPM picks up a few RPMs before it drops off completely.

8729. Entrained water in aviation turbine fuel is a hazard because of its susceptibility to freezing as it passes through the filters. What are common methods of preventing this hazard?

A—Micromesh fuel strainers and fuel heater.
B—High-velocity fuel pumps and fuel heater.
C—Anti-icing fuel additives and fuel heater.

Turbine engine fuel may have moisture entrained in it that will condense out and freeze on the fuel filters. This ice will shut off the flow of fuel to the engines.

To eliminate this danger, anti-icing additives may be put in the turbine fuel to lower the freezing temperature of the water and prevent its freezing on the filters.

Most jet transport aircraft have fuel heaters, or heat exchangers, that use engine compressor bleed air or engine oil to raise the temperature of the fuel enough that it will not freeze on the filters.

8730. As a general rule, which statement is true regarding fuel leaks?

A—Stains, seeps, and heavy seeps are not flight hazards.
B—All fuel leaks regardless of location or severity are considered a hazard to flight.
C—Stains, seeps, and heavy seeps (in addition to running leaks), are considered flight hazards when located in unvented areas of the aircraft.

Any fuel leaking from an aircraft fuel tank can constitute a safety of flight situation under certain conditions.

A stain, seep, or even a heavy seep is not considered to be a flight hazard unless it is in an unvented area where the fumes can collect and cause a fire hazard. Any type of leak that allows fuel vapors to accumulate must be repaired before the aircraft can be released for flight.

8731. The presence of fuel stains around a fuel nozzle would indicate

A—too much fuel pressure.
B—excessive airflow across the venturi.
C—clogged fuel nozzle.

A clogged fuel-injection nozzle will allow the fuel to escape through the air bleed holes in the side of the nozzle.

There will be fuel stains on the cylinder head around the clogged nozzle.

Answers

8725 [B] (052) AC 43.13-1	8726 [A] (054) AMT-SYS Ch 2	8727 [C] (054) AMT-SYS Ch 2	8728 [A] (055) FMS
8729 [C] (053) AC 43.13-1	8730 [C] (055) AMT-SYS Ch 2	8731 [C] (052) AMT-P	

8732. What should be used to inert an integral fuel tank before attempting repairs?

A—CO_2.
B—Water.
C—Steam.

Before working inside an integral fuel tank, you should inert it (replace the gasoline fumes with an inert gas).

Integral fuel tanks can be inerted by filling them with CO_2.

8733. What should be used to remove flux from an aluminum tank after welded repairs?

A—Soft brush and warm water.
B—Five percent solution of nitric or sulfuric acid.
C—Mild solution of soap and warm water.

Promptly, upon completion of welding, wash the inside and outside of the tank with liberal quantities of hot water and then drain.

Next, immerse the tank in either a 5 percent nitric-acid or 5 percent sulfuric-acid solution.

8734. What method would be used to check for internal leakage of a fuel valve without removing the valve from the aircraft?

A—Place the valve in the OFF position, drain the strainer bowl, and with boost pump on, watch to see if fuel flows to the strainer bowl.
B—Remove fuel cap(s), turn boost pump(s) on, and watch for bubbling in the tanks.
C—Apply regulated air pressure on the downstream side of the fuel pump and listen for air passing through the valve.

Internal leakage in a fuel valve can be checked by placing the valve in the OFF position and then draining the fuel strainer bowl.

Turn the fuel tank boost pump on. If fuel flows into the empty strainer bowl, the valve has an internal leak.

8735. Why are jet fuels more susceptible to water contamination than aviation gasoline?

A—Jet fuel has a higher viscosity than gasoline.
B—Jet fuel is lighter than gasoline; therefore, water is more easily suspended.
C—Condensation is greater because of the higher volatility of jet fuels.

Jet fuels have a higher viscosity than aviation gasoline. Because of this higher viscosity, contaminants such as water remain suspended in the fuel and do not settle out into the fuel tank sumps.

8736. When installing a rigid fuel line, 1/2 inch in diameter, at what intervals should the line be supported?

A—24 inches.
B—12 inches.
C—16 inches.

Rigid fuel lines installed in an aircraft should be supported by clamps or brackets at the distances specified in AC 43.13-1B.

For a 1/2-inch line, the supports should be installed every 16 inches along the run of the line.

8737. The probe of a capacitance-type fuel level gauge is essentially a

A—float-actuated variable capacitor.
B—capacitor with fuel and air acting as one plate.
C—capacitor with fuel and air acting as a dielectric.

A capacitance-type, fuel quantity indicating system uses a capacitor (condenser) as a tank probe. Fuel and air are the dielectric between the plates of the probe.

8738. Which statement concerning an electronic capacitance-type fuel quantity indicating system is true?

A—It has no moving parts in the tank.
B—It has two tubes separated by an electronic field in the tank.
C—It utilizes a variable capacitor to indicate the fuel tank capacity.

The capacitance-type, fuel quantity indicating system uses probes with no moving parts inside the tank.

These probes are made of two concentric tubes that serve as the plates of a capacitor. Fuel and air act as the dielectric.

8739. What type of remote-reading fuel quantity indicating system has several probes installed in each fuel tank?

A—Electromechanical.
B—Electronic.
C—Direct reading.

The electronic (capacitance-type), remote-reading, fuel quantity indicating system has several probes installed in each fuel tank.

The total capacity of the probes accurately relates to the amount of fuel in the tank.

Answers

8732 [A] (055) AC 43.13-1
8733 [B] (055) AC 43.13-1
8734 [A] (055) AC 43.13-1
8735 [A] (052) AMT-SYS Ch 2
8736 [C] (055) AC 43.13-1
8737 [C] (054) AMT-SYS Ch 2
8738 [A] (054) AMT-SYS Ch 2
8739 [B] (054) AMT-SYS Ch 2

8740. Which aircraft fuel quantity indicating system incorporates a signal amplifier?

A—Electronic.
B—Sight glass.
C—Electrical.

An electronic (capacitance-type) fuel quantity indicating system incorporates a signal amplifier.

8741. A drip gauge may be used to measure

A—the amount of fuel in the tank.
B—system leakage with the system shut down.
C—fuel pump diaphragm leakage.

A drip gauge is used to measure the quantity of fuel in a fuel tank when the aircraft is on the ground.

The drip gauge is pulled down from the bottom of the tank until fuel begins to drip from its end. The quantity of fuel in the tank is indicated on the gauge by the amount the gauge is pulled from the tank before it begins to drip.

8742. The electronic-type fuel quantity indicating system consists of a bridge circuit,

A—an amplifier, an indicator, and a tank unit.
B—a tank, an amplifier, and an indicator.
C—a tank unit, a tank, and an amplifier.

An electronic (capacitance-type) fuel quantity indicating system contains the following parts:

- *Capacitor probes, mounted in the tanks.*
- *A bridge circuit to measure the capacity of the probes.*
- *An amplifier to increase the amplitude of the signal from the bridge circuit to a value high enough to drive the indicator.*
- *An indicator mounted in the instrument panel to show the amount of fuel in the tanks.*

8743. A probe or a series of probes is used in what kind of fuel quantity indicating system?

A—Selsyn.
B—Capacitor.
C—Synchro.

Probes, which are capacitors, are used as the fuel-quantity-sensing elements in a capacitor-type, fuel quantity indicating system.

8744. Why is the capacitance fluid quantity indicating system more accurate in measuring fuel level than a mechanical type?

A—Only one probe and one indicator are necessary for multiple tank configurations.
B—It measures in gallons and converts to pounds.
C—It measures by weight instead of volume.

The electronic (capacitance-type) fuel quantity indicating system is more accurate than other types of systems used for measuring fuel quantity.

These systems use several capacitor-type probes extending across each tank from top to bottom. When the attitude of the aircraft changes, fuel rises in some probes and lowers in others. The total capacitance of all probes remains constant as the aircraft attitude changes. This causes the fuel-level indication to remain constant as attitude changes.

The dielectric constant of the fuel changes with its density. Therefore, the system is able to determine the mass (weight) of the fuel rather than its volume.

8745. One advantage of electrical and electronic fuel quantity indicating systems is that

A—the indicators are calibrated in gallons; therefore, no conversion is necessary.
B—only one transmitter and one indicator are needed regardless of the number of tanks.
C—several fuel tank levels can be read on one indicator.

Two important advantages of the electronic and electrical fuel quantity indicating systems are that the indicator can be located any distance from the tanks and the fuel levels of several tanks can be read on one indicator.

8746. A fuel totalizer is a component which indicates the

A—total amount of fuel being consumed by all engines.
B—amount of fuel in any given tank.
C—amount of fuel in all tanks.

A fuel totalizer is a single instrument that gives an indication of the total quantity of the fuel remaining on board the aircraft.

The totalizer adds the quantities of the fuel in all of the tanks.

Answers

8740 [A] (054) AMT-SYS Ch 2	8741 [A] (054) AMT-SYS Ch 2	8742 [A] (054) AMT-SYS Ch 2	8743 [B] (054) AMT-SYS Ch 2
8744 [C] (054) AMT-SYS Ch 2	8745 [C] (041) AMT-SYS Ch 2	8746 [C] (041) AMT-SYS Ch 2	

8746-2. A digital fuel totalizer automatically indicates the amount of fuel used, fuel remaining, current rate of consumption, and fuel

A—weight aboard at takeoff.
B—remaining at the 45-minute IFR fuel reserve.
C—remaining, flight time at the current power setting.

A fuel totalizer is a fuel quantity indicator that gives the total amount of fuel remaining on board the aircraft on one instrument. The totalizer adds the quantities of fuel in all of the tanks and gives the pilot an indication of the total number of pounds of fuel remaining.

8747. What is the dielectric (nonconducting material) in a capacitance-type fuel quantity indicating system?

A—Outer shell of the capacitor.
B—Fuel in the tank.
C—Fuel and air in the tank.

The dielectric used in the tank probes of a capacitor-type fuel quantity indicating system is the fuel and the air in the tank above the fuel.

Fuel has a dielectric constant of approximately two. Air has a dielectric constant of one.

8748. A capacitance-type fuel quantity indicating system measures fuel in

A—pounds.
B—pounds per hour.
C—gallons.

A capacitance-type fuel quantity indicating system measures the density of the fuel (the dielectric constant of the fuel changes with its density). It indicates the quantity of fuel in pounds rather than in gallons.

8749. What are the four general types of fuel quantity gauges?

A—Sight glass, mechanical, electrical, and electronic.
B—Electrical, electronic, bourbon tube, and litmus indicator.
C—Electrical, direct reading static pressure type, sight glass, and litmus indicator.

The types of fuel quantity indicating systems used in aircraft are sight glasses, mechanical systems, electrical systems, and electronic systems.

8750. How does temperature affect fuel weight?

A—Cold fuel is heavier per gallon.
B—Warm fuel is heavier per gallon.
C—Temperature has no effect.

The density of aircraft fuel varies with its temperature. The colder the fuel, the more pounds of fuel there are in a gallon. Aircraft engines use fuel on the basis of its weight rather than its volume.

8751. One advantage of electrical and electronic fuel quantity indicating systems is that the indicator

A—can be located any distance from the tank(s).
B—has no movable devices.
C—always measures volume instead of mass.

Most modern aircraft use electrical or electronic fuel quantity indicating systems because of the ease with which the indicator can be located a distance from the fuel tanks.

8752. When fuel quantity is measured in pounds instead of gallons, the measurement will be more accurate because fuel volume

A—varies with temperature change.
B—increases when temperature decreases.
C—varies with changes in atmospheric pressure.

An indication of the weight of the fuel in an aircraft fuel tank is more important than a measure of its volume. The engine uses the fuel on the basis of its weight, and the volume of the fuel in the tanks changes as the temperature of the fuel changes.

8753. An electrical type fuel quantity indicating system consists of an indicator in the cockpit and a float

A—in the tank that moves a connecting arm to the wiper on a variable resistor in the tank.
B—attached to a rod that moves up or down in a calibrated cylinder.
C—in the tank that operates with alternating current and uses constant resistance in a circuit to drive a ratiometer-type indicator.

Electric fuel quantity indicators operate with DC and use variable resistance in a circuit to drive a ratiometer-type indicator. The movement of a float in the tank moves a connecting arm to the wiper on a variable resistor in the tank unit. This resistor is wired in series with one of the coils of the ratiometer-type fuel gauge in the instrument panel. Changes to the current flowing through the tank unit resistor change the current flowing through one of the coils in the indicator. This alters the magnetic field in which the indicating pointer pivots. The calibrated dial indicates the corresponding fuel quantity.

Answers

8746-2 [A] (055) AMT-SYS	8747 [C] (041) AMT-SYS Ch 2	8748 [A] (054) AMT-SYS Ch 2	8749 [A] (054) AMT-SYS Ch 2
8750 [A] (052) AMT-SYS Ch 2	8751 [A] (041) AMT-SYS Ch 2	8752 [A] (052) AMT-SYS Ch 2	8753 [A] (041) FAA-H-8083-31

8754. What is the purpose of a float-operated transmitter installed in a fuel tank?

A—It sends an electric signal to the fuel quantity indicator.
B—It senses the total amount of fuel density.
C—It senses the dielectric qualities of fuel and air in the tank.

A float-operated fuel quantity transmitter is normally a variable resistor whose resistance changes with the fuel level in the tank. Information on the fuel level is sent as an electrical signal to the fuel quantity indicator on the instrument panel.

8755. In an electronic-type fuel quantity indicating system, the tank sensing unit is a

A—capacitor.
B—variable resistor.
C—variable inductor.

The fuel tank transmitters in an electronic-type fuel quantity indicating system are capacitors.

A tank probe (transmitter) is made of two concentric metal tubes that act as the plates of a capacitor. The fuel in the tank and the air above the fuel act as the dielectric. The capacitance of the probe is determined by the relative amount of fuel and air between the plates.

8756. What must each fuel quantity indicator be calibrated to read during level flight when the quantity of fuel remaining is equal to the unusable fuel supply?

A—The total unusable fuel quantity.
B—Both the total unusable fuel quantity and the unusable fuel quantity in each tank.
C—Zero.

Each fuel quantity indicator must be calibrated to read "zero" during level flight when the quantity of the fuel remaining in the tank is equal to the unusable fuel supply.

8757. What unit would be adjusted to change the fuel pressure warning limits?

A—Fuel flowmeter bypass valve.
B—Pressure-sensitive mechanism.
C—Fuel pressure relief valve.

The contacts on the pressure-sensitive mechanism would be adjusted to change the pressure at which the fuel pressure warning unit actuates.

8758. Select one means of controlling the fuel temperature on turbine-powered aircraft.

A—Engine bleed air to the fuel filter.
B—Engine bleed air to the fuel tank.
C—Engine bleed air to a heat exchanger.

Ice is prevented from clogging the filter of a turbine-powered aircraft fuel system by routing warm compressor bleed air through an air-to-fuel heat exchanger.

All of the fuel that flows to the engine must pass through this heat exchanger.

8759. What is the purpose of flapper-type check valves in integral fuel tanks?

A—To allow defueling of the tanks by suction.
B—To prevent fuel from flowing away from the boost pumps.
C—To allow the engine-driven pumps to draw fuel directly from the tank if the boost pump fails.

Some integral fuel tanks have flapper-type check valves that allow fuel to flow to the booster pump, but prevent rough air or abrupt flight maneuvers from causing the fuel to flow away from the booster pump.

Some aircraft also have a pump-removal, flapper-type check valve that allows a booster pump to be removed from the tank without having to first drain the tank.

8760. What unit is generally used to actuate the fuel pressure warning system?

A—Fuel flowmeter.
B—Pressure-sensitive mechanism.
C—Fuel pressure gauge.

A pressure-sensitive mechanism (generally a bellows) is used to actuate the fuel pressure warning system.

8761. What method is used on turbine-powered aircraft to determine when the condition of the fuel is approaching the danger of forming ice crystals?

A—Fuel pressure warning.
B—Fuel pressure gauge.
C—Fuel temperature indicator.

Fuel temperature indicating systems are required in turbine aircraft to warn when there is danger of ice crystals forming in the fuel.

A fuel strainer differential pressure gauge gives an indication that ice crystals have already formed and are restricting the fuel filter. Ice crystals on the filter element cause an excessive pressure drop across the filter.

Answers

8754 [A] (054) AMT-SYS Ch 2	8755 [A] (054) AMT-SYS Ch 2	8756 [C] (054) 14 CFR Part 23	8757 [B] (055) AMT-SYS Ch 2
8758 [C] (055) AMT-SYS Ch 2	8759 [B] (054) AMT-SYS Ch 2	8760 [B] (054) AMT-SYS Ch 2	8761 [C] (054) AMT-SYS Ch 2

8762. Which of the following would give the first positive indication that a change-over from one fuel tank to another is needed?

A—Fuel pressure warning.
B—Fuel pressure gauge.
C—Fuel quantity indicator.

The fuel pressure warning system should give the first indication, by a loss of pressure, that a fuel tank is empty. This drop in pressure warns the pilot to switch to a full tank.

8763. A fuel pressure warning switch contacts close and warning light is turned on when

A—a measured quantity of fuel has passed through it.
B—the fuel flow stops.
C—the fuel pressure drops below specified limits.

The fuel pressure warning switch contacts close and a warning light turns on when the fuel pressure drops below a specified limit.

8764. A transmitter in a fuel pressure warning system serves what function?

A—Transmits an electrical signal to fluid pressure.
B—Converts fluid pressure to an electrical signal.
C—Transmits fluid pressure directly to the indicator.

The transmitter in a fuel pressure warning system converts the pressure of the fuel into an electrical signal that turns on a warning light or flashes a warning on an annunciator panel.

8765. Where is fuel pressure taken for the pressure warning signal on most aircraft engines?

A—Outlet side of the boost pump.
B—Fuel pressure line of the carburetor.
C—Between the fuel pump and the strainer.

The fuel pressure warning signal used with most aircraft engines is taken from the fuel-pressure line that goes to the fuel inlet of the carburetor.

8766. Which of the following is necessary to effectively troubleshoot a fuel pressure warning system?

A—The manufacturer's maintenance manuals.
B—AC 43.13-1B, Acceptable Methods, Techniques, and Practices—Aircraft Inspection and Repair.
C—A set of Federal Aviation Regulations.

The manufacturer's maintenance manuals give all the information needed to effectively troubleshoot a fuel pressure warning system.

8767. Which of the following would be most useful to locate and troubleshoot an internal fuel leak in an aircraft fuel system?

A—Structural repair manual.
B—Orthographic projection troubleshooting tree.
C—Maintenance manual diagrams and descriptions.

Close visual inspection is required whenever a leak or defect is suspected in a fuel system. Follow the aircraft manufacturer's instructions on the repair of fuel leaks and the requirements that need to be met for airworthiness.

8768. In some aircraft with several fuel tanks, the possible danger of allowing the fuel supply in one tank to become exhausted before the selector valve is switched to another tank is prevented by the installation of

A—a fuel pressure warning signal system.
B—a fuel pressure relief valve.
C—an engine fuel pump bypass valve.

Fuel pressure warning signal systems are installed in many large aircraft to warn the pilot or flight engineer that a tank has been emptied and a full tank should be selected.

8769. The function of a fuel heater is to

A—protect the engine fuel system from ice formation.
B—protect the fuel from freezing.
C—heat the fuel to combustion temperature.

The function of a fuel heater is to protect the engine fuel system from ice formation. It can also be used to thaw ice that has formed on the fuel screen.

8770. (1) Gas-turbine-engine fuel systems are very susceptible to the formation of ice in the fuel filters.

(2) A fuel heater operates as a heat exchanger to warm the fuel.

Regarding the above statements,

A—only 1 is true.
B—only 2 is true.
C—both 1 and No. 2 are true.

Statement 1 is true. Gas-turbine-engine fuel systems are very susceptible to the formation of ice on the fuel filters.

Statement 2 is also true. The fuel heater operates as a heat exchanger to warm the fuel. These heat exchangers may use engine compressor bleed air or warm engine oil to furnish the heat.

Answers

8762 [A] (055) AMT-SYS Ch 2
8763 [C] (054) AMT-SYS Ch 2
8764 [B] (054) AMT-SYS Ch 2
8765 [B] (054) AMT-SYS Ch 2
8766 [A] (055) AMT-SYS Ch 2
8767 [C] (055) FAA-H-8083-31
8768 [A] (055) AMT-SYS Ch 2
8769 [A] (053) AMT-P Ch 11
8770 [C] (053) AMT-P Ch 11

8771. (1) A fuel heater can use engine bleed air as a source of heat.

(2) A fuel heater can use engine lubricating oil as a source of heat.

Regarding the above statements,

A—only 1 is true.
B—both 1 and 2 are true.
C—neither 1 nor 2 is true.

Statement 1 is true. A fuel heater can use engine bleed air as a source of heat.

Statement 2 is also true. A fuel heater can use engine lubricating oil as a source of heat.

8772. (1) A fuel pressure gauge is a differential pressure indicator.

(2) A fuel pressure gauge indicates the pressure of the fuel entering the carburetor.

Regarding the above statements,

A—only 2 is true.
B—both 1 and 2 are true.
C—neither 1 nor 2 is true.

Statement 1 is true. Most fuel-pressure gauges are differential pressure gauges. They measure the difference in the pressure of the fuel and the pressure of some reference air. When a pressure carburetor is used, this reference air pressure is the carburetor upper-deck air pressure.

Statement 2 is also true. The pressure shown on the gauge is the pressure of the fuel as it enters the carburetor.

8773. A fuel pressure relief valve is required on an aircraft

A—positive-displacement fuel pump.
B—centrifugal boost fuel pump.
C—positive-displacement fuel pump and centrifugal boost fuel pump.

A pressure relief valve is required for a positive-displacement aircraft fuel pump. A pressure relief valve is not needed with a centrifugal fuel boost pump.

8774. The primary purpose of a fuel tank sump is to provide a

A—way to shut off fuel flow or to route the fuel to a desired location.
B—place for contaminants and water to settle, with a drain valve to remove the impurities.
C—way to manually operate valves on a fuel tank to isolate or direct fuel to a pump.

Fuel tanks are equipped with sumps (low points in the tank) in which water and dirt will accumulate to be collected and drained.

8775. Why are integral fuel tanks used in many large aircraft?

A—To reduce fire hazards.
B—To facilitate servicing.
C—To reduce weight.

Integral fuel tanks are used in large aircraft to reduce weight and to utilize as much of the space as possible for carrying fuel.

8776. When an aircraft is fueled from a truck or fuel farm that has not been contaminated, daily draining

A—is not required because fuel trucks and fuel farms may make use of laser contaminant identification technology.
B—of strainers and sumps is combined with periodic filter changes and inspection to ensure fuel is contaminant free.
C—is only required if the fuel truck or farm has not been in continuous service.

Even though an aircraft is fueled from an uncontaminated source, the fuel tank sumps and strainers must be periodically checked, as there is always the possibility of contamination from other sources.

8777. When defueling an aircraft, which of the following must be accomplished?

A—Defuel inside the hangar when fire suppression is available.
B—Defuel outside the hangar when possible.
C—Always defuel outside the hangar.

Both fueling and defueling operations should be conducted in the open air where there is good ventilation.

Answers

8771 [B] (053) AMT-P	8772 [B] (054) AMT-SYS Ch 2	8773 [A] (054) AMT-SYS Ch 2	8774 [B] (054) AMT-SYS Ch 2
8775 [C] (056) AMT-SYS Ch 2	8776 [B] (052) AMT-SYS Ch 2	8777 [C] (052) AC 43.13-2	

8778. Integral fuel tanks on transport aircraft are

A—easily removed for service or inspection.
B—constructed of plastic or fiberglass.
C—supported by the aircraft structure.

Integral fuel tanks are actually a part of the aircraft structure in which all of the seams and riveted joints are sealed with an appropriate sealant. The fuel is carried in the sealed-off aircraft structure.

8779. What precautions must be observed if a gravity-feed fuel system is permitted to supply fuel to an engine from more than one tank at a time?

A—The tank airspaces must be interconnected.
B—The fuel outlet ports of each tank must have the same cross-sectional area.
C—Each tank must have a valve in its outlet that automatically shuts off the line when the tank is empty.

If a gravity-feed fuel system is permitted to supply fuel to an engine from more than one tank at a time, the air space above the fuel in the tanks must be interconnected.

8780. The purpose of the baffle plate in a fuel tank is to

A—provide an expansion space for the fuel.
B—resist fuel surging within the fuel tank.
C—provide internal structural integrity.

Baffle plates in a fuel tank resist (prevent) the fuel from surging in the tank.

8781. What markings must be placed on or near each appropriate fuel filler cover on standard category aircraft?

A—The word "Avgas" and the minimum fuel grade, and the total fuel tank capacity.
B—The word "Avgas" and the minimum fuel grade or designation for the engines, and the usable fuel tank capacity.
C—The word "Avgas" and the minimum fuel grade.

The fuel filler openings must be marked at or near the filler cover with the word "Avgas" and the minimum fuel grade. If the airplane is turbine engine powered, the markings must include the words "Jet Fuel" and the permissible fuel designations or reference to the AFM for permissible fuel designations.

8782. What is one disadvantage of using aromatic aviation fuels?

A—A fuel intercooler is required.
B—Deteriorates rubber parts.
C—Results in low fuel volatility.

Aromatic additives in aviation gasoline increase its anti-detonation characteristics, but they also cause deterioration of rubber parts.

Any hose, seal, or diaphragm used with a fuel that contains aromatic additives must be specifically formulated to withstand these additives.

8783. Fuel-boost pumps are operated

A—to provide a positive flow of fuel to the engine.
B—primarily for fuel transfer.
C—automatically from fuel pressure.

Fuel boost pumps are used to provide a positive flow of fuel from the tank to the engine.

Boost pumps are used for engine starting, as a backup for takeoff and landing, and in many cases, to transfer fuel from one tank to another.

8784. Flapper valves are used in fuel tanks to

A—reduce pressure.
B—prevent a negative pressure.
C—act as check valves.

Flapper valves are used in fuel tanks to serve as check valves.

Flapper valves allow fuel to flow to the booster pump but prevent its flowing away from the pump during certain flight maneuvers.

8785. Why are centrifugal-type boost pumps used in fuel systems of aircraft operating at high altitude?

A—Because they are positive displacement pumps.
B—To supply fuel under pressure to engine-driven pumps.
C—To permit cooling air to circulate around the motor.

Centrifugal boost pumps are used in the fuel tanks of aircraft that operate at high altitude.

Boost pumps supply fuel under positive pressure to the inlet of the engine-driven fuel pumps under conditions where the ambient pressure is too low to ensure a positive supply.

Answers

8778 [C] (054) AMT-SYS Ch 2	8779 [A] (054) 14 CFR Part 23	8780 [B] (054) AMT-SYS Ch 2	8781 [C] (003) FAA-H-8083-31
8782 [B] (052) AMT-SYS Ch 2	8783 [A] (054) AMT-SYS Ch 2	8784 [C] (054) AMT-SYS Ch 2	8785 [B] (055) AMT-SYS Ch 2

8786. Why is it necessary to vent all aircraft fuel tanks?

A—To ensure a positive head pressure for a submerged boost pump.
B—To exhaust fuel vapors.
C—To limit pressure differential between the tank and atmosphere.

Fuel tanks must be vented with the vents having sufficient capacity to allow the rapid relief of excessive pressure between the interior and the exterior of the tank.

8787. According to Part 23, what minimum required markings must be placed at or near each appropriate fuel filler cover for reciprocating engine-powered airplanes?

A—The word "Avgas" and the minimum fuel grade.
B—The word "Fuel" and usable fuel capacity.
C—The word "Avgas" and the total fuel capacity.

Fuel filler openings for reciprocating engine-powered airplanes must be marked at or near the filler cover with the word "Avgas" and the minimum fuel grade.

8788. The location of leaks and defects within the internal portions of the fuel system can usually be determined by

A—visual inspection for evidence of wet spots and stains, and feeling for unusually warm components.
B—performing a fuel flow check.
C—observing the pressure gauge and operating the selector valves.

It is possible, by watching the fuel pressure gauge and operating the selector valves, to isolate a portion of a large-aircraft fuel system that has an internal leak.

8789. What type of fuel-booster pump requires a pressure relief valve?

A—Concentric.
B—Sliding vane.
C—Centrifugal.

A sliding vane fuel pump requires a pressure-relief valve because it is a constant-displacement pump.

8790. To prevent vapor lock in fuel lines at high altitude, some aircraft are equipped with

A—vapor separators.
B—direct-injection-type carburetors.
C—booster pumps.

Booster pumps are installed in the fuel tanks of some aircraft to prevent vapor lock in the fuel lines at high altitudes.

The booster pump holds a positive pressure on the fuel in the lines, between the tank and the engine-driven fuel pump.

8791. Some turbine-powered aircraft have a fuel temperature indicator located in the cockpit to

A—monitor the fuel flow in the event that ice crystals form in the fuel system.
B—monitor the fuel temperature during high altitude flight.
C—ascertain the amount of fuel onboard the aircraft when ice starts to form in the fuel tanks.

The fuel temperature indicator allows the crew to monitor the fuel temperature during high altitude flight in extremely frigid conditions.

8792. When inspecting a fuel system, you should check all valves located downstream of boost pumps with the pumps

A—at idle.
B—dormant.
C—operating.

In order to inspect a fuel system for leaks, you should inspect all of the valves located downstream of the booster pump, with the pumps operating and producing maximum pressure.

8793. The type of fuel-boost pump that separates air and vapor from the fuel before it enters the line to the carburetor is the

A—gear-type pump.
B—centrifugal-type pump.
C—sliding vane-type pump.

Centrifugal boost pumps normally have a small agitator (a small propeller) that spins when the pump impeller is turning to separate the vapor from the fuel before the fuel enters the lines to the carburetor.

Answers

8786 [C] (054) AMT-SYS Ch 2	8787 [A] (054) §23.2610	8788 [C] (055) AMT-SYS Ch 2	8789 [B] (054) AMT-SYS Ch 2
8790 [C] (054) AMT-SYS Ch 2	8791 [B] (052) FAA-H-8083-31	8792 [C] (055) AC 43.13-1	8793 [B] (054) AMT-SYS Ch 2

8794. On a large aircraft pressure refueling system, a pressure refueling receptacle and control panel will permit one person to

A—fuel or defuel any of the tanks on an aircraft.
B—fuel any of the tanks on an aircraft.
C—defuel any of the tanks on an aircraft.

Large aircraft pressure fueling systems consist of a refueling receptacle and a panel of controls and gauges that permit one person to fuel or defuel any or all fuel tanks of an aircraft.

8795. When routing a fuel line between two rigidly mounted fittings the line should

A—have at least one bend between such fittings.
B—be a straight length of tubing and clamped to the aircraft structure.
C—have a flexible line added between two metal lines to allow for ease of installation.

Never install a straight length of tubing between two rigidly mounted fittings. Always incorporate at least one bend between such fittings to absorb strain caused by vibration and temperature changes.

8796. Which of the following tests can determine an aviation gasoline's tendency to vapor lock?

A—Reid vapor pressure test.
B—Octane vapor pressure test.
C—True vapor pressure test.

The Reid vapor pressure of a fuel is a measure of the fuel's tendency to vapor lock.

8797. Microbial growth is produced by various forms of micro-organisms that live and multiply in the water interfaces of jet fuels. Which of the following could result if microbial growth exists in a jet fuel tank and is not corrected?

A—Interference with fuel flow, interference with fuel quantity indicators, and electrolytic corrosive action in a metal tank.
B—Interference with fuel quantity indicators, engine seizure, or a lower grade rating of the fuel.
C—Interference with fuel flow, lower grade rating of the fuel, aor electrolytic corrosive action in a rubber tank.

The buildup of microorganisms in the fuel tank of a jet aircraft can not only interfere with fuel flow and with the fuel quantity indicators, but more importantly, can start electrolytic corrosion in metal fuel tanks.

8798. The vapor pressure of aviation gasoline is

A—lower than the vapor pressure of automotive gasoline.
B—higher than the vapor pressure of automotive gasoline.
C—approximately 20 psi at 100°F.

The vapor pressure of aviation gasoline is limited to a maximum of 7 psi, which is lower than the vapor pressure of many grades of automobile gasoline.

8799. What can be done to eliminate or minimize the microbial growth problem in an aircraft jet fuel tank?

A—Use anti-icing and antibacterial additives.
B—Add CO_2 as a purgative.
C—Keep the fuel tank topped off.

An anti-icing and antibacterial additive is often used in jet aircraft fuel tanks to minimize the problems caused by microbial growth inside the fuel tanks.

8800. What is the maximum vapor pressure allowable for an aircraft fuel?

A—7 psi.
B—5 psi.
C—3 psi.

A Reid vapor pressure of 7 psi at 100°F is the maximum allowed for aviation gasoline.

8801. If a bladder-type fuel tank is to be left empty for an extended period of time, the inside of the tank should be coated with a film of

A—engine oil.
B—linseed oil.
C—ethylene glycol.

If a rubberized fabric bladder tank is to remain empty for an extended period of time, it should be cleaned out thoroughly and its interior covered with a film of clean engine oil.

8802. How may the antiknock characteristics of a fuel be improved?

A—By adding a knock inhibitor.
B—By adding a knock enhancer.
C—By adding a fungicide agent.

The antiknock characteristics of a fuel may be improved by adding a knock inhibitor such as tetraethyl lead to the fuel.

Answers

8794 [A] (054) AMT-SYS Ch 2	8795 [A] (055) AMT-SYS Ch 2	8796 [A] (052) AMT-SYS Ch 2	8797 [A] (052) AMT-SYS Ch 2
8798 [A] (052) AMT-SYS Ch 2	8799 [A] (052) AC 43.13-1	8800 [A] (052) AMT-SYS Ch 2	8801 [A] (055) AMT-SYS Ch 2
8802 [A] (052) AMT-SYS Ch 2			

Aircraft Electrical Systems

8803. Some electric motors have two sets of field windings wound in opposite directions so that the

A—speed of the motor can be more closely controlled.
B—power output of the motor can be more closely controlled.
C—motor can be operated in either direction.

Reversible DC motors have two sets of field windings wound in opposite directions.

By using two sets of windings, the direction of the armature rotation can be reversed by the action of a switch.

8804. One purpose of a growler test is to determine the presence of

A—an out-of-round commutator.
B—a broken field lead.
C—a shorted armature.

A growler test may be made of an armature to determine if any of the windings are shorted.

8805. Electric wire terminals for most aircraft applications must be what type?

A—Slotted.
B—Hook.
C—Ring.

Most aircraft electrical wiring is terminated with ring-type terminals rather than hook or slotted terminals. If the nut on the terminal stud should become loose, the ring-type terminal will remain on the stud whereas a hook or slotted terminal will slip off.

8806. What is the principal advantage of the series-wound DC motor?

A—High starting torque.
B—Suitable for constant speed use.
C—Low starting torque.

One of the chief characteristics, or advantages, of a series-wound DC motor is its high starting torque.

8807. If a generator is equipped with a vibrator-type voltage regulator, the actual time the voltage regulator points remain open

A—depends on the load carried by the generator.
B—is controlled by the reverse-current cutout relay point clearance.
C—is increased when the external load is greater than the generator output.

The actual time the voltage regulator points in a vibrator-type voltage regulator remain open is determined by the amount of load being carried by the generator.

When the load is great, the voltage drops and the points must remain closed longer to allow the voltage to rise.

When the load is light, the voltage is high and the points remain closed a very short time.

8808. What is a cause of generator brush arcing?

A—Seating brushes with No. 000 sandpaper.
B—Carbon dust particles.
C—Low spring tension.

Low spring tension on generator brushes could cause the brushes to bounce and arc.

8809. What is required when operating two aircraft AC generators in parallel?

A—Amperes and frequency must both be equal.
B—Frequency and voltage must both be equal.
C—Amperes and voltage must both be equal.

Before AC generators may be connected in parallel, it must be determined that the output voltage, the frequency, and the phase rotation of all the generators are the same.

8810. The starting current of a series-wound DC motor, in passing through both the field and armature windings, produces a

A—low starting torque.
B—speed slightly higher when unloaded.
C—high starting torque.

A series-wound DC motor has a very high starting torque because all of the current that passes through the armature also passes through the field.

Answers

8803 [C] (039) AMT-G Ch 4
8804 [C] (042) AMT-SYS
8805 [C] (041) AMT-SYS Ch 1
8806 [A] (039) AMT-G Ch 4
8807 [A] (041) AMT-SYS Ch 1
8808 [C] (054) AMT-G
8809 [B] (054) AMT-G
8810 [C] (041) AMT-G Ch 4

8811. Which motor would be most likely to have an armature brake?

A—Starter motor.
B—Landing light retraction motor.
C—Inverter drive motor.

A landing light retraction motor is the most likely of the motors listed here to have an armature brake.
The brake causes the armature to stop turning as soon as the switch is released.

8812. The method most often used in overcoming the effect of armature reaction is through the use of

A—interpoles.
B—shaded poles.
C—drum-wound armatures in combination with a negatively connected series field.

Interpoles are used in large compound-wound DC generators to overcome the effect of armature reaction.
If armature reaction is not corrected, it will cause the brushes to arc under certain load conditions.

8813. The only practical method of maintaining a constant voltage output from an aircraft generator under varying conditions of speed and load is to vary the

A—strength of the magnetic field.
B—number of conductors in the armature.
C—speed at which the armature rotates.

A constant generator output voltage is maintained under varying load and speed conditions by varying the strength of the magnetic field in the generator.

8814. The pole pieces or shoes used in a DC generator are a part of the

A—armature assembly.
B—field assembly.
C—brush assembly.

The pole pieces (pole shoes) in a DC generator are part of the field assembly. The pole pieces form a part of the magnetic circuit for the field.

8815. How many cycles of AC voltage are produced in a six-pole alternator of the revolving-field type for each revolution of the rotor?

A—Four.
B—Three.
C—Six.

Three cycles of alternating current are produced by a six-pole alternator for each revolution of the rotor. Each pair of poles produces one cycle of AC.

8816. If the reverse current cutout relay contact points fail to open after the generator output has dropped below battery potential, current will flow through the generator armature

A—in the normal direction and through the shunt field opposite the normal direction.
B—and the shunt field opposite the normal direction.
C—opposite the normal direction and through the shunt field in the normal direction.

If the reverse current cutout relay contacts fail to open when the generator output drops below the battery potential, current will flow from the battery through the armature in the direction opposite its normal flow.
Current will also flow through the shunt field but it will flow through the field coils in the normal direction of flow.

8817. How does the magnetic brake used to stop rotation of an electric motor armature operate?

A—Centrifugal force releases a rotating brake cog from a stationary notch when the armature reaches a certain speed and magnetic force re-engages the cog when the electrical power is turned off.
B—A friction brake is applied by a magnet and released by a spring.
C—A friction brake is applied by a spring and released by a magnet.

A magnetic brake used to stop rotation of an electric-motor armature is applied by spring force and is released by an electromagnet energized when the motor is turned on.
As soon as the motor is turned off, the spring applies the brake and stops the rotation of the armature.

Answers
8811 [B] (039) AMT-G
8812 [A] (041) AMT-P Ch 17
8813 [A] (041) AMT-P Ch 17
8814 [B] (054) AMT-P Ch 17
8815 [B] (022) AMT-P Ch 17
8816 [C] (054) AMT-P Ch 17
8817 [C] (039) AMT-G

8818. In a generator, what eliminates any possible sparking to the brush guides caused by the movement of the brushes within the holder?

A—The brush pigtail.
B—Brush spring tension.
C—Undercutting the mica on the commutator.

The brush pigtail eliminates any possible sparking between the brush and the brush guide.

All of the current is carried from the brush into the holder through the pigtail rather than through the sliding contact made between the brush and the brush guide.

8819. A series-wound DC electric motor will normally require

A—more current at high RPM than at low RPM.
B—approximately the same current throughout its operating range of speed.
C—more current at low RPM than at high RPM.

A series-wound DC motor produces an extremely high starting torque. It uses a large amount of current when it first starts to rotate and when it is operating at slow speeds. The current drops off as the armature speed and the counter EMF builds up.

8820. The type of electric wire terminals used for most aircraft applications, in addition to providing good current carrying capabilities, are designed primarily

A—to prevent circuit failure due to terminal disconnection.
B—for uncomplicated and rapid circuit connection and disconnection.
C—for permanent connection to the circuit.

Terminals used on aircraft electrical wires must safely carry all of the current the wire can carry. They must also be designed in such a way that they cannot cause a circuit failure by inadvertently disconnecting from the terminal on which they are installed.

8821. Aluminum wire must be stripped very carefully because

A—high resistance will develop in stripping nicks.
B—stripping nicks can cause short circuits.
C—individual strands will break easily after being nicked.

Aluminum wire must be stripped very carefully, because if a strand is nicked, it will quite likely break.

8822. The commutator of a generator

A—changes direct current produced in the armature into alternating current as it is taken from the armature.
B—changes alternating current produced in the armature into direct current as it is taken from the armature.
C—reverses the current in the field coils at the proper time in order to produce direct current.

The commutator and the brushes used on a DC generator acts as a mechanical rectifier that changes the AC produced in the armature coils into DC before it leaves the generator.

8823. An ammeter in a battery charging system is for the purpose of indicating the

A—amperage available for use.
B—total amperes being used in the airplane.
C—rate of current used to charge the battery.

An ammeter in a battery-charging circuit in an aircraft is used to indicate the rate of current that flows into or out of the battery.

8824. Which of the following is not one of the purposes of interpoles in a generator?

A—Reduce field strength.
B—Overcome armature reaction.
C—Reduce arcing at the brushes.

Interpoles are used in high-output compound-wound DC generators to counteract field distortion and to overcome armature reaction. Armature reaction causes arcing at the brushes.

Interpoles do not reduce the field strength, they increase it.

8825. To test generator or motor armature windings for opens,

A—place armature in a growler and connect a 110V test light on adjacent segments; light should light.
B—check adjacent segments on commutator with an ohmmeter on the high resistance scale.
C—use a 12/24V test light between the armature core segments and the shaft.

A generator armature may be checked for an open winding by placing it on a growler and using the built-in 110-volt test lamp to test for continuity between the individual segments.

The lamp will light if the coil between the segments being checked is good.

Answers

8818 [A] (054) AMT-P Ch 17	8819 [C] (039) AMT-G Ch 4	8820 [A] (041) AMT-SYS Ch 1	8821 [C] (041) AMT-SYS Ch 1
8822 [B] (041) AMT-G Ch 4	8823 [C] (041) AMT-G Ch 4	8824 [A] (054) AMT-G	8825 [A] (054) AMT-SYS

8826. What is the color and orientation of the position lights for navigation on civil airplanes?

A—Left side, green; right side, red; rear aft, white.
B—Left side, red; right side, green; rear aft, white.
C—Left side, white; right side, green; rear aft, red.

Position lights for navigation on an aircraft are located on the wing tips and the tail. There is a red light on the left wing, a green light on the right wing, and a white light on the tail that shines aft.

8827. To what depth is the mica insulation between the commutator bars of a DC generator undercut?

A—One-half the width of the mica.
B—Equal to twice the width of the mica.
C—Equal to the width of the mica.

When a DC generator is overhauled, the commutator is turned on a lathe until it is perfectly round and smooth.

After the commutator is turned, the mica separators between the commutator bars are undercut to approximately the width of the mica, or somewhere in the neighborhood of 0.02 inch.

8828. A voltage regulator controls generator output by

A—introducing a resistance in generator-to-battery lead in the event of overload.
B—shorting out field coil in the event of overload.
C—varying current flow to generator field coil.

A voltage regulator controls generator output voltage by varying the amount of current allowed to flow in the generator field coil.

8829. Which type of DC generator is not used as an airplane generator?

A—Externally grounded.
B—Series wound.
C—Compound wound.

Series-wound DC generators are not used in aircraft electrical systems because of the difficulty in regulating and controlling the output voltage.

8830. What is the most accurate type of frequency measuring instrument?

A—Integrated circuit chip having a clock circuit.
B—Electrodynamometers using electromagnetic fields.
C—Electromagnets using one permanent magnet.

The most accurate frequency measuring instruments in use today are digital instruments that contain integrated circuit chips and a clock circuit.

8831. During ground operation, aircraft generator cooling is usually accomplished by

A—auxiliary air cooled through an air/fuel heat exchanger.
B—an integral fan.
C—an external motor-driven fan.

When an aircraft is operating on the ground, the generator is cooled by air pulled through its windings by an integral fan (a fan that is mounted on the armature shaft).

8832. What does a rectifier do?

A—Changes direct current into alternating current.
B—Changes alternating current into direct current.
C—Reduces voltage.

A rectifier is an electrical device or circuit that allows electrons to pass in one direction but blocks them when they try to flow in the opposite direction.

A rectifier changes alternating current into direct current.

8833. What type of instrument is used for measuring very high values of resistance?

A—Megohmmeter.
B—Shunt-type ohmmeter.
C—Multimeter.

A megohmmeter is a special type of ohmmeter used to measure very high values of resistance.

Many megohmmeters have their own high-voltage power supply built into them.

Answers

8826 [B] (009) §23.2530
8827 [C] (054) AMT-G
8828 [C] (041) AMT-SYS Ch 1
8829 [B] (041) AMT-G Ch 4
8830 [A] (043) AMT-SYS
8831 [B] (041) AMT-SYS
8832 [B] (041) AMT-G Ch 4
8833 [A] (043) AMT-SYS

8834. When a diode is checked for an open circuit or a short circuit, it should be

A—in the circuit.
B—checked with a milliamp ammeter.
C—disconnected from the circuit.

When a semiconductor diode is checked for an open or short circuit, it is removed from the circuit and its resistance is checked with an ohmmeter.

The diode is good if it has a high resistance when checked in one direction and a low resistance when it is checked in the opposite direction.

The diode is shorted if both readings are low, and it is open if both readings are high.

8835. When handling a high voltage capacitor in an electrical circuit, be sure it

A—has a full charge before removing it from the circuit.
B—has at least a residual charge before removing it from the circuit.
C—is fully discharged before removing it from the circuit.

A high-voltage capacitor can store enough electrical charge to cause a dangerous shock when it is removed from the circuit. Before removing any high-voltage capacitor, short across its terminals with an insulated-handle screwdriver to fully discharge it.

8836. Which of the following is most likely to cause thermal runaway in a nickel-cadmium battery?

A—A high internal resistance condition.
B—Excessive current draw from the battery.
C—Constant current charging of the battery to more than 100 percent of its capacity.

Thermal runaway of a nickel-cadmium battery occurs when some of the cells become excessively hot. The heat lowers both the voltage and the resistance so the cells can accept a high rate of charging current. This high current produces more heat and the battery can destroy itself.

The temperature rise that triggers the thermal problems can come from heat generated by a fast discharge, from high ambient temperature, or from a breakdown of the separator material.

8837. How can it be determined if a transformer winding has some of its turns shorted together?

A—Measure the input voltage with an ohmmeter.
B—The output voltage will be high.
C—The transformer will get hot in normal operation.

If some of the windings in a transformer are shorted together, an excessive amount of current will flow in the windings and the transformer will get hot in normal operation.

8838. Which of the following are the major parts of a DC motor?

A—Armature assembly, field assembly, brush assembly, and end frame.
B—Field assembly, brush assembly, commutator, and pole piece.
C—Brush assembly, pole piece, rheostat, and end frame.

The major parts of a practical DC motor are the armature assembly, the field assembly, the brush assembly, and the end frame.

8839. (1) There are three basic types of DC motors; series, shunt, and compound.

(2) In the series motor, the field windings, consisting of relatively few turns of heavy wire, are connected in series with the armature winding.

Regarding the above statements,

A—only 1 is true.
B—only 2 is true.
C—both 1 and 2 are true.

Statement 1 is true. There are three basic types of DC motors: series motors, shunt motors, and compound motors.

Statement 2 is also true. In a series motor, the field windings, consisting of a relatively few turns of heavy wire, are connected in series with the armature winding.

8840. What is the appropriate method for installing pre-insulated terminal lugs and splices to electric wires?

A—Using a crimping tool to secure the terminal lug.
B—Soldering the terminal lug to the end of the wire.
C—Soldering the exposed wire prior to crimping on the terminal lug.

Crimped terminals on an aircraft electrical wire transmit the tension and vibration loads from the wire into the terminal gradually and do not cause stress concentrations, as is done with a soldered connection. Soldered terminals are not considered satisfactory for aircraft wiring because vibration will likely cause them to break off of the wire.

Answers

8834 [C] (043) AMT-SYS Ch 2	8835 [C] (041) AMT-SYS	8836 [B] (041) AMT-G Ch 4	8837 [C] (041) AMT-SYS
8838 [A] (039) AMT-G Ch 4	8839 [C] (039) AMT-G Ch 4	8840 [A] (041) AMT-SYS Ch 1	

8841. Which of the following factors must be taken into consideration when determining the wire size to use for an aircraft installation?

A—Allowable power loss, permissible voltage drop, current carrying capability of the conductor, type of load.
B—Mechanical strength, allowable power loss, resistance of current return path through the aircraft structure, type of load.
C—Allowable power loss, resistance of current path through the aircraft structure, type of load.

When selecting the size wire to use in an aircraft electrical system, you must consider the allowable power loss (the amount of electrical energy converted into heat), the permissible voltage drop, the current-carrying ability of the wire, and the type of load (continuous or intermittent) that is carried by the wire.

8842. When selecting hardware for attaching bonding connections to an aircraft structure, which of the following should be considered?

A—Mechanical strength, ease of installation, amount of current to be carried.
B—Permissible voltage drop, amount of current to be carried, type of load.
C—Mechanical strength, allowable power loss, ease of installation.

Hardware used for attaching bonding connections to an aircraft structure should be selected on the basis of mechanical strength, the amount of current to be carried, and the ease of installation.

8843. How should the splices be arranged if several are to be located in an electrical wire bundle?

A—Staggered along the length of the bundle.
B—Grouped together to facilitate inspection.
C—Splicing within wire bundles is not permitted.

Splices of the individual wires in a wire bundle should be staggered so the bundle does not become excessively enlarged.

8844. What is the minimum bend radius for an electrical wire bundle?

A—Ten times the outside diameter of the bundle.
B—Five times the outside diameter of the bundle.
C—Fifteen times the outside diameter of the bundle.

Wire bundles should not be bent with a bend radius of less than 10 times the outside diameter of the bundle.

8845. When approved, splices may be used to repair manufactured harnesses or installed wiring. The maximum number of splices permitted between any two connectors is

A—one.
B—two.
C—three.

There shall not be more than one splice in any one wire segment between any two connectors or other disconnect point unless it is specifically approved by the engineering department of the aircraft manufacturer.

8846. Electrical connectors used in aircraft assemblies should meet which of the following specifications?

A—Parts Manufacturer Approval (PMA).
B—Military Specifications (MS).
C—Society of Electrical Specifications (SES).

Electrical connectors are specifically designed to meet military specifications. Components that meet these specifications are almost all approved for use in FAA-certificated aircraft.

8847. The most common method of attaching a pin or socket to an individual wire in an MS electrical connector is by

A—crimping.
B—soldering.
C—crimping and soldering.

For years, wires were connected into AN or MS connectors by soldering them into pots on the end of the pin or socket.

A newer and far more common method of attachment to MS connectors is by crimping a tapered pin on the end of the wire and inserting this pin into a tapered hole in the back side of the pin or socket in the connector.

8848. The pin section of an AN/MS connector is normally installed on

A—the power supply side of a circuit.
B—the ground side of a circuit.
C—either side of a circuit (makes no difference).

The pin section of an AN/MS connector should be installed on the ground side of a circuit and the socket on the "hot" side. This arrangement minimizes the possibility of a short between a connector and ground when the connectors are separated.

Answers

8841 [A] (042) AMT-SYS Ch 1	8842 [A] (041) AMT-SYS Ch 1	8843 [A] (041) AC 43.13-1	8844 [A] (042) AC 43.13-1
8845 [A] (042) AC 43.13-1	8846 [B] (041) AMT-SYS Ch 1	8847 [A] (041) AMT-SYS Ch 1	8848 [B] (041) AMT-SYS Ch 1

8849. The voltage output of an alternator may be regulated by controlling the

A—speed of the alternator.
B—voltage output of the DC exciter.
C—resistance in the rotor windings.

The voltage output of an AC alternator is determined by the amount of current flowing in its exciter field.

The alternator output voltage may be controlled by varying the output voltage of the DC exciter.

8850. If several long lengths of electrical cable are to be installed in rigid conduit, the possibility of damage to the cable as it is pulled through the conduit will be reduced by

A—dusting the cable with powdered graphite.
B—dusting the cable with powdered soapstone.
C—applying a light coat of dielectric grease.

Long lengths of electrical cable may be lubricated as they are slid into either a rigid or a flexible conduit by dusting the cable and the inside of the conduit with powdered soapstone, tire talc, or regular talcum powder.

8851. Grounding is electrically connecting a conductive object to the primary structure. One purpose of grounding is to

A—prevent current return paths.
B—allow static charge accumulation.
C—prevent development of radio frequency potentials.

The most reasonable choice is that electrically grounding a conductive object prevents the development of radio-frequency potential that causes static in a radio. Grounding actually keeps all components at the same electrical potential, so there is no buildup of static charges.

Static charges cause sparks to jump and these sparks produce radio frequency energy.

8852. What is normally used to bond noncontinuous stainless steel aircraft components?

A—Stainless steel jumpers.
B—Copper jumpers.
C—Aluminum jumpers.

Electrolytic action may rapidly corrode a bonding connection if suitable precautions are not taken.

Copper jumpers may be safely used to bond together noncontinuous stainless steel components.

8853. Aircraft fuse capacity is rated in

A—volts.
B—ohms.
C—amperes.

Aircraft fuse capacity is rated in amperes.

8854. When adding a rheostat to a light circuit to control the light intensity, it should be connected in

A—parallel with the light.
B—series with the light.
C—series parallel with the light switch.

When installing a rheostat in a light circuit to control the light intensity, install it in series with the light.

8855. Circuits that must be operated only in an emergency or whose inadvertent activation could endanger a system frequently employ

A—guarded switches.
B—push-pull-type circuit breakers only (no switches).
C—spring-loaded to off toggle or rocker switches.

When it is important that an electrical switch not be inadvertently operated, it is normally installed with a guard over its operating handle. The guard requires a conscious effort to get to the switch to actuate it.

8856. If one switch is used to control all navigation lights, the lights are most likely connected

A—in series with each other and parallel to the switch.
B—in series with each other and in series with the switch.
C—parallel to each other and in series with the switch.

If navigation lights on an aircraft are controlled by one switch, the lights are connected in parallel with each other and in series with the switch.

8857. Oil canning of the sides of aluminum or steel electrical junction boxes is considered to be

A—normal operation in vibration prone areas.
B—a shorting hazard.
C—acceptable operation.

Oil canning is the condition of a piece of sheet metal that causes it to snap back and forth when it is distorted or vibrated. If the sides of an electrical junction box oil-can, there is a possibility of some of the wires becoming shorted.

Answers

8849 [B] (022) AMT-G Ch 4
8850 [B] (042) AMT-SYS Ch 1
8851 [C] (041) AMT-SYS Ch 1
8852 [B] (042) AMT-SYS Ch 1
8853 [C] (041) AMT-G Ch 4
8854 [B] (015) AMT-G
8855 [A] (041) AMT-SYS Ch 1
8856 [C] (015) AMT-G Ch 4
8857 [B] (042) AC 43.13-1

8858. Electric wiring installed in aircraft without special enclosing means (open wiring) offers the advantages of ease of installation, simple maintenance, and reduced weight. When bundling open wiring, the bundles should

A—be limited as to the number of cables to minimize damage from a single electrical fault.
B—include at least one shielded cable to provide good bonding of the bundle to the airframe.
C—be limited to a minimum bend radius of five times the bundle diameter to avoid excessive stresses on the cable insulation.

The number of wires run in a single bundle in an open wiring installation should be limited to minimize the damage that could result from a single electrical fault.

8859. During inspection of the terminal strips of an aircraft electrical system, it should be determined that

A—only locknuts have been used for terminal attachment to the studs.
B—the terminal studs are anchored against rotation.
C—only plain nuts and lockwashers have been used for terminal attachment to the studs.

Studs used in terminal strips must be anchored to prevent their rotation.

This anchoring is normally done by using a square end on the stud set into a square hole in the terminal strip.

8860. What protection to wires and cables does conduit provide when used in aircraft installations?

A—Electromagnetic.
B—Mechanical.
C—Structural.

Conduit is used to give mechanical protection to electrical wiring in an aircraft installation.

8861. Which of the following should be accomplished in the installation of aircraft wiring?

A—Support the bundle to structure and/ or solid fluid lines to prevent chafing damage.
B—Provide adequate slack in the wire bundle to compensate for large changes in temperature.
C—Locate the bundle above flammable fluid lines and securely clamp to structure.

Any time a wiring bundle is installed in an aircraft in such a way that it passes through a compartment parallel to a fluid line carrying flammable fluids, the bundle should be routed above the fluid line, and it should be clamped securely to the aircraft structure.

In no case should a wire be supported by a flammable fluid line.

8862. If the (+) terminal of a voltmeter is connected to the (–) terminal of the source voltage and the (–) terminal of the meter is connected to the (+) terminal of the source voltage, the voltmeter will read

A—correctly.
B—low voltage.
C—backwards.

If a voltmeter is connected into a circuit with the polarity reversed, the meter will read backwards.

8863. When using the voltage drop method of checking circuit resistance, the

A—input voltage must be maintained at a constant value.
B—output voltage must be maintained at a constant value.
C—input voltage must be varied.

When using the voltage-drop method to check circuit resistance, the input voltage must be maintained at a constant value.

8864. The nominal rating of electrical switches refers to continuous

A—current rating with the contacts open.
B—voltage rating with the contacts closed.
C—current rating with the contacts closed.

The nominal current rating of conventional aircraft switches is usually stamped on the switch housing.

This rating represents the continuous current rating of the switch with the contacts closed.

8865. Aircraft electrical junction boxes located in a fire zone are usually constructed of

A—aluminum sheets.
B—carbon steel.
C—stainless steel.

A stainless steel junction box is recommended for installation in a fire zone.

Answers

8858 [A] (041) AC 43.13-1	8859 [B] (042) AC 43.13-1	8860 [B] (042) AMT-SYS Ch 1	8861 [C] (041) AMT-SYS Ch 1
8862 [C] (043) AMT-G Ch 4	8863 [A] (042) AC 43.13-1	8864 [C] (041) AC 43.13-1	8865 [C] (041) AC 43.13-1

8866. To help minimize radio interference a capacitor will largely eliminate and provide a steady direct current if the capacitor is connected to the generator in

A—parallel.
B—series.
C—series/parallel.

The output of a DC generator normally has some AC hash, or noise, caused by brush arcing superimposed on it. This AC can cause radio interference, and it may be removed by connecting a capacitor between the armature and ground, in parallel with the armature windings. The AC passes to ground through the low impedance path provided by the capacitor.

8867. The primary considerations when selecting electric cable size are

A—current-carrying capacity and allowable voltage drop.
B—the voltage and amperage of the load it must carry.
C—the system voltage and cable length.

When selecting electrical cable size, you must consider both the current-carrying capacity of the wire and the allowable voltage drop.

8868. The navigation lights of some aircraft consist of a single circuit controlled by a single switch which has an ON position and an OFF position, with no additional positions possible. This switch is referred to as a

A—double-pole, single-throw (DPST), two-position switch.
B—single-pole, double-throw (SPDT), two-position switch.
C—single-pole, single-throw (SPST), two-position switch.

A switch that controls a single circuit and has only an OFF and an ON position is referred to as a single-pole, single-throw (SPST), two-position switch.

8869. Electric circuits are protected from overheating by

A—thermocouples.
B—AN/MS connectors.
C—fuses.

Electrical circuits are protected from overheating by means of fuses or circuit breakers.

8870. How should a coaxial cable be routed?

A—Parallel with stringers or ribs.
B—Perpendicular to stringers or ribs.
C—As directly as possible.

Generally speaking, coaxial cable, which must have as short a run as possible, is allowed to be routed directly rather than being run parallel to or at right angles to stringers and ribs.

8871. Which of the following copper electrical cable sizes should be selected to replace a No. 6 aluminum electrical cable?

A—No. 4.
B—No. 6.
C—No. 8.

The general rule of thumb for replacing aluminum electrical cable with copper is that copper of two wire gages smaller (larger number) may be used to replace aluminum. This rule does not hold in this instance.

According to the current-carrying capacity charts in Figures 11.5 and 11.6 of AC 43.13-1, a 6-gage aluminum electrical cable is rated at 83 amps in free air and 50 amps in a bundle or conduit, and an 8-gage copper electrical cable in free air is rated at only 73 amps and 46 amps in a bundle.

A 6-gage copper electrical cable which will carry 101 amps in free air, and 60 amps in a bundle will have to be used to replace a No. 6 aluminum electrical cable.

8872. In installations where the ammeter is in the generator or alternator lead, and the regulator system does not limit the maximum current that the generator or alternator can deliver, the ammeter can be redlined at what percent of the generator or alternator rating?

A—50.
B—75.
C—100.

According to AC 43.13-1, paragraph 426(c), in installations where the ammeter is in the generator or alternator lead and the regulator system does not limit the maximum current the generator or alternator can deliver, the ammeter can be redlined at 100 percent of the generator or alternator rating.

Answers

8866 [A] (041) AC 43.13-1	8867 [A] (041) AMT-SYS Ch 1	8868 [C] (015) AMT-SYS Ch 1	8869 [C] (042) AMT-G Ch 4
8870 [C] (042) AMT-SYS Ch 1	8871 [B] (042) AC 43.13-1	8872 [C] (042) AC 43.13-1	

8873. Which statement relating to electric wiring is true?

A—When attaching a terminal to the end of an electric cable, it should be determined that the strength of the cable-to-terminal joint is at least twice the tensile strength of the cable.
B—When attaching a terminal to the end of an electric cable, it should be determined that the strength of the cable-to-terminal joint is at least equal to the tensile strength of the cable itself.
C—All electric cable splices should be covered with soft insulating tubing (spaghetti) for mechanical protection against external abrasion.

The tensile strength of the wire-to-terminal joint should be at least equivalent to the tensile strength of the wire itself. The resistance of the joint should be negligible, relative to the normal resistance of the wire.

8874. Bonding connections should be tested for

A—resistance value.
B—amperage value.
C—reactance.

A bonding connection must be installed in such a manner that the resistance of each connection does not exceed 0.003 ohm.

8875. What kind of switch should you install in a single wire circuit that required the switch to be manually held in the ON position?

A—Single-pole, single-throw (SPST), two-position normally open (NO).
B—Single-pole, single-throw (SPST), single-position.
C—Single-pole, double-throw (SPDT), single-position normally open (NO).

A switch used in a single-wire circuit that requires the switch to be manually held in the closed, or ON, position is a single-pole, single-throw, normally open switch.

8876. A circuit breaker is installed in an aircraft electrical system primarily to protect the

A—circuit and should be located as close to the source as possible.
B—circuit and should be located as close to the unit as possible.
C—electrical unit in the circuit and should be located as close to the source as possible.

A circuit breaker is installed in an aircraft electrical system primarily to protect the circuit. It is installed as close to the source as is possible.

Circuit breakers are usually mounted directly on the main bus.

8877. How should a voltmeter be connected?

A—In series with the source.
B—In parallel with the load.
C—In series with the load.

In order for a voltmeter to read the voltage drop across the load, it must be connected in parallel with the load.

8878. A circuit protection device called a current limiter is essentially a slow-blow fuse and is designed to be used in

A—400 cycle AC circuits.
B—heavy power circuits.
C—starter-generator circuits.

A current limiter, such as is used in the armature circuit of a high-current DC generator, is a form of slow-blow fuse that will accept a surge of current greater than the generator rating. But if there is a continual flow of current in excess of the generator rating, it will open the armature circuit and remove the generator from the system. These current limiters cannot normally be replaced in flight.

The current limiter for a small, low-current generator is a variable resistor in the field circuit that decreases the output voltage when the current exceeds the generator rating.

8879. If it is necessary to use an electrical connector where it may be exposed to moisture, the mechanic should

A—coat the connector with grease.
B—use a special moisture-proof type.
C—spray the connector with varnish or zinc-chromate.

When electrical connectors are exposed to moisture, a special moisture-proof-type connector should be used.

8880. Which of the following are considered circuit-protective devices that are used in aircraft electrical systems?

A—Circuit breakers, relays, and current limiters.
B—Circuit breakers, fuses, and current limiters.
C—Circuit breakers, capacitors, and current limiters.

The three most commonly used circuit-protection devices are circuit breakers, fuses, and current limiters.

Circuit breakers and fuses protect the wiring in the load circuits of the aircraft and are accessible to the pilot in flight. Current limiters, a form of slow-blow fuse in the generator output circuit, are not available for replacement in flight.

Answers

8873 [B] (042) AC 43.13-1	8874 [A] (042) AC 43.13-1	8875 [A] (042) AMT-G Ch 4	8876 [A] (042) AMT-SYS Ch 1
8877 [B] (043) AMT-G Ch 4	8878 [B] (041) AC 43.13-1	8879 [B] (041) AMT-SYS Ch 1	8880 [B] (042) AMT-G Ch 4

8881. If a wire is installed so that it comes in contact with some moving parts, what protection should be given the wire?

A—Wrap with soft wire solder into a shield.
B—Wrap with friction tape.
C—Pass through conduit.

Anytime an electrical cable, a wire bundle, or an individual wire comes into contact with some moving part of the aircraft, the wire must be protected by passing it through conduit.

8882. In the American Wire Gauge (AWG) system of numbers used to designate electrical wire sizes, the number assigned to a size is related to its

A—combined resistance and current-carrying capacity.
B—current-carrying capacity.
C—cross-sectional area.

The AWG system is used to indicate the size of electrical wire. The AWG number relates to the diameter of the wire, and therefore to its cross-sectional area.

There is no direct correlation between the AWG number of a wire and its area, but the larger the number, the smaller the wire size.

8883. What is the voltage drop for a No. 18 copper wire 50 feet long to carry 12.5 amperes, continuous operation?

Use the formula VD = RLA

VD = Voltage drop
R = Resistance per ft = .00644
L = Length of wire
A = Amperes

A—1/2V.
B—1V.
C—4V.

Using the formula given with this question, the voltage drop in an 18-gauge copper wire, 50 feet long, carrying 12.5 amps, is 4.025 volts.

$$\begin{aligned} VD &= RLA \\ &= 0.00644 \times 50 \times 12.5 \\ &= 4.025 \text{ volts} \end{aligned}$$

8884. What is the purpose of the selection of derated switches for known continuous load current applications?

A—To calculate the voltage drop across the circuit.
B—To prevent short circuits in the motor field windings.
C—To obtain reasonable switch efficiency and service life.

Electrical switches must be derated when they are used with certain types of electrical loads.

These loads either have an abnormally high current inflow when the switch is first closed, or else they have extremely high voltage from an induced load when the switch is opened.

The use of derated switches is important to obtain reasonable switch efficiency and service life.

8885. What is the advantage of a circuit breaker when compared to a fuse?

A—It is easily replaced.
B—It controls current flow.
C—It is resettable and reusable.

A circuit breaker is resettable and reusable, whereas a fuse, once it is blown, must be replaced with a new one.

8886. What is the advantage of a current limiter?

A—It breaks circuit quickly.
B—It can be reset easily.
C—It will take overload for a short period.

A current limiter is a type of slow-blow fuse that will take a momentarily high overload of current but will open the circuit under a sustained overload in excess of its rating.

8887. What should be used to protect wires from chafing when they must pass through bulkheads, firewalls, ribs, etc.?

A—Aerodynamic duct tape.
B—Suitable grommet.
C—Plastic spiral wrap.

When an electrical cable must pass through a hole in a metal structure, the edges of the hole are covered with a rubber grommet to keep the metal from cutting or chafing the wire.

The cable should be attached to the structure with a clamp that holds it centered in the hole.

8888. In aircraft electrical systems, automatic reset circuit breakers

A—should not be used as circuit protective devices.
B—are useful where only temporary overloads are normally encountered.
C—must be used in all circuits essential to safe operation of the aircraft.

14 CFR Part 23 states that each resettable circuit protective device must be so designed that a manual operation is required to restore service after tripping.

Answers

8881 [C] (041) AC 43.13-1	8882 [C] (041) AC 43.13-1	8883 [C] (042) AC 43.13-1	8884 [C] (041) AMT-SYS Ch 1
8885 [C] (042) AC 43.13-1	8886 [C] (041) AMT-G Ch 4	8887 [B] (041) AC 43.13-1	8888 [A] (041) AMT-SYS Ch 1

8889. A certain switch is described as a single-pole, double-throw (SPDT) switch. The throw of a switch indicates the number of

A—circuits each pole can complete through the switch.
B—terminals at which current can enter or leave the switch.
C—places at which the operating device (toggle, plunger, etc.) will come to rest and at the same time open or close a circuit.

The throws of a switch indicate the number of circuits, or paths for current, the switch can select for each of its poles.

An SPDT switch can select either of two paths.

8890. When considering an alteration, the criteria upon which the selection of electric cable size should be based are

A—applied voltage and allowable voltage drop.
B—current-carrying capacity and allowable voltage drop.
C—current-carrying capacity and applied voltage.

When wire size is selected for an alteration of an aircraft electrical system, both the current-carrying capacity of the wire and the allowable voltage drop for the length of the wire must be considered.

8891. What is an important factor in selecting aircraft fuses?

A—The current exceeds a predetermined value.
B—The voltage rating should be lower than the maximum circuit voltage.
C—Capacity matches the needs of the circuit.

It is important when aircraft fuses are selected that all the current ratings are appropriate for the circuit protection required.

The aircraft service manual specifies the current ratings to be used.

8892. The circuit breaker in the instrument lighting system protects the

A—lights from too much current.
B—wiring from too much current.
C—wiring from too much voltage.

A circuit breaker is installed in an aircraft electrical system primarily to protect the wiring from too much current.

Circuit breakers are installed as close to the source of electrical power as is practical, usually on the main bus.

8893. One advantage of using AC electrical power in aircraft is

A—that AC electrical motors can be reversed while DC motors cannot.
B—greater ease in stepping the voltage up or down.
C—that the effective voltage is 1.41 times the maximum instantaneous voltage; therefore, less power input is required.

One advantage of using AC electrical power in aircraft is the ease with which the voltage may be increased or decreased.

Passing alternating current through a transformer changes its voltage.

8894. Why are the iron cores of most induction coils laminated?

A—To reduce the core reluctance.
B—To increase the core permeability.
C—To reduce the effects of eddy currents.

The iron cores used in most induction coils, transformers, and motors are made of laminated soft iron.

The thin laminations reduce the losses caused by eddy currents flowing in the iron.

8895. Certain transport aircraft use AC electrical power for all normal operation and battery furnished DC electrical power for standby emergency use. In aircraft of this type that operate no DC generators, the batteries are kept charged by

A—inverters which use the aircraft's AC generators as a source of power.
B—alternators which use the aircraft's generators as a source of power.
C—rectifiers which use the aircraft's AC generators as a source of power.

Large aircraft that use AC for normal electrical operation often use battery furnished DC for standby use.

These systems use transformers to reduce the voltage and rectifiers to change the alternating current into direct current to keep the batteries charged.

Answers

8889 [A] (041) AMT-G Ch 4	8890 [B] (042) AMT-SYS Ch 1	8891 [C] (042) AMT-G Ch 4	8892 [B] (015) AMT-G Ch 4
8893 [B] (041) AMT-G Ch 4	8894 [C] (041) AMT-SYS	8895 [C] (041) AMT-G Ch 4	

8896. The voltage in an AC transformer secondary that contains twice as many loops as the primary will be

A—greater and the amperage less than in the primary.
B—greater and the amperage greater than in the primary.
C—less and the amperage greater than in the primary.

A transformer that contains twice as many turns (loops) in the secondary winding as there are turns in the primary winding will have a secondary voltage that is twice the voltage in the primary.

The current in the secondary will be only one-half the current in the primary.

8897. If the positive field lead between a generator and a generator control panel breaks and is shorted while the engine is running, a voltmeter connected to generator out-put would indicate

A—zero voltage.
B—residual voltage.
C—normal voltage.

If the positive field lead between a generator and its control panel or voltage regulator breaks and shorts to ground while the engine is running, the generator can produce only residual voltage.

With both ends of the field at ground potential there can be no field current. The only magnetic field for the armature windings to cut is that caused by the permanent magnetism in the generator field frame.

Permanent magnetism in the field frame produces residual voltage, which is somewhere between one and two volts.

8898. What is a method used for restoring generator field residual magnetism?

A—Flash the fields.
B—Reseat the brushes.
C—Energize the armature.

Residual magnetism may be restored to a generator by flashing its field.

To flash the field, momentarily pass direct current from the battery through the generator field coils in the normal direction of current flow.

8899. The major advantages of alternating current (AC) over direct current (DC) is the fact that its current and voltage can easily be increased or decreased

A—by means of a inverter.
B—by means of a rectifier.
C—by means of a transformer.

Alternating current may have its voltage changed to any other value of AC by the use of a transformer.

A transformer does not change the power of the AC, but when the voltage is increased, the current will correspondingly decrease.

8900. Which of the following must be accomplished when installing an anticollision light?

A—Install a switch independent of the position light switch.
B—Use shielded electrical cable to assure fail-safe operation.
C—Connect the anticollision light to the aircraft position light switch.

When installing an anticollision light, you must use a switch that is independent of the position light switch.

8901. The inductor-type inverter output voltage is controlled by the

A—number of poles and the speed of the motor.
B—voltage regulator.
C—DC stator field current.

An inductor-type inverter uses a rotor made of soft iron laminations. Grooves are cut laterally across the surface of the rotor to provide poles that correspond to the stator poles.

The voltage produced by an inductor-type inverter is controlled by the DC stator-field current.

8902. When using an ohmmeter to check the continuity of a generator field coil, the coil should

A—be removed from the generator housing.
B—show high resistance when the meter prods are connected to the terminals of the coil.
C—show very low resistance if it is a series field coil.

Series field coils are wound of relatively few turns of heavy wire and have a very low resistance. All of the generator output current flows through them.

Answers

8896 [A] (041) AMT-G Ch 4	8897 [B] (041) AMT-SYS Ch 1	8898 [A] (054) AMT-G	8899 [C] (041) AMT-G Ch 4
8900 [A] (015) AC 43.13-2	8901 [C] (041) AMT-G	8902 [C] (042) AMT-G Ch 4	

8903. The strength of the core of an electromagnet depends upon the material from which it is constructed and which of the following?

A—The number of turns of wire in the coil and the applied voltage.
B—The number of turns of wire in the coil and the amount of current (amperes) passing through the coil.
C—The size (cross section) and the number of turns of wire in the coil and the applied voltage.

The strength of an electromagnet depends upon the material used for the core, the number of turns of wire in the coil, and the amount of current flowing through the coil.

8904. A voltage regulator controls generator voltage by changing the

A—resistance in the generator output circuit.
B—current in the generator output circuit.
C—resistance of the generator field circuit.

A voltage regulator controls generator output voltage by varying the resistance of the generator field circuit.

This may be done by using a carbon-pile voltage regulator, a vibrator-type voltage regulator, or a transistor voltage regulator.

The resistance in the field circuit determines the amount of field current allowed to flow.

8905. The overvoltage control automatically protects the generator system when excessive voltage is present by

A—opening the shunt field circuit.
B—opening and resetting the field control relay.
C—breaking a circuit to the trip coil of the field control relay.

An overvoltage control protects a generator system when there is excessive voltage in the system.

The overvoltage control opens the generator shunt field circuit to reduce the output voltage.

8906. When DC generators are operated in parallel to supply power for a single load, their controls include an equalizer circuit to assure that all generators share the load equally. The equalizer circuit operates by

A—increasing the output of the low generator to equal the output of the high generator.
B—decreasing the output of the high generator to equal the output of the low generator.
C—increasing the output of the low generator and decreasing the output of the high generator until they are equal.

An equalizer circuit in a multiengine DC generator system maintains an equal sharing of the load between all of the generators.

When the load is shared unequally, the output voltage of the low generator is increased, and the output voltage of the high generator is decreased.

8907. What is the maximum amount of time a circuit can be in operation and still be an intermittent duty circuit?

A—Three minutes.
B—Two minutes.
C—One minute.

An intermittent duty circuit is one that is in operation for a maximum of two minutes.

8908. The most common method of regulating the voltage output of a compound DC generator is to vary the

A—current flowing through the shunt field coils.
B—total effective field strength by changing the reluctance of the magnetic circuit.
C—resistance of the series field circuit.

The most common method of regulating the output voltage of a compound DC generator is by varying the current flow through the shunt field coils.

Answers

8903 [B] (041) AMT-G Ch 4
8904 [C] (041) AMT-SYS Ch 1
8905 [A] (041) AMT-G
8906 [C] (054) AMT-SYS Ch 4
8907 [B] (041) AC 43.13-1
8908 [A] (054) AMT-G Ch 4

8909. (Refer to Figure 18.) Which of the batteries are connected together incorrectly?

A—1.
B—2.
C—3.

The batteries in 1 are connected correctly in a series circuit.

The batteries in 2 are connected correctly in a parallel circuit.

The batteries in 3 are connected incorrectly in a parallel circuit. The polarity of the center battery is reversed and it will act as a short circuit across the other two batteries.

8910. (Refer to Figure 19.) Upon completion of the landing gear extension cycle, the green light illuminated and the red light remained lit. What is the probable cause?

A—Short in the down limit switch.
B—Short in the gear safety switch.
C—Short in the up limit switch.

In order for the red light to remain on when the landing gear is down and locked, there must be a short in the up-limit switch that keeps wire 19 electrically connected to wire 8. This keeps power supplied to the red light.

8911. If any one generator in a 24-volt DC system shows low voltage, the most likely cause is

A—an out-of-adjustment voltage regulator.
B—shorted or grounded wiring.
C—a defective reverse current cutout relay.

If one generator in a 24-volt DC system produces too low a voltage, the most logical cause would be an out-of-adjustment voltage regulator.

8912. How can the direction of rotation of a DC electric motor be changed?

A—Interchange the wires which connect the motor to the external power source.
B—Reverse the electrical connections to either the field or armature windings.
C—Rotate the positive brush one commutator segment.

The direction of rotation of a DC motor may be changed by reversing the connection to either the field or the armature winding, but not to both of them.

8912-2. Static inverters are electronic devices that change DC to AC with the

A—use of an oscillator.
B—properties of an exclusive OR gate.
C—input from an amplifier control by integrated circuits.

A static inverter is an electronic device that changes DC into AC. It incorporates an oscillator that changes DC into AC with the proper frequency and waveform. Then an amplifier changes the voltage to the value needed.

8913. Aircraft which operate only AC generators (alternators) as a primary source of electrical power normally provide current suitable for battery charging through the use of

A—a stepdown transformer and a rectifier.
B—an inverter and a voltage-dropping resistor.
C—a dynamotor with a half-wave DC output.

Aircraft that use AC generators as the primary source of electrical power usually have a transformer-rectifier unit to provide direct current where it is needed.

8914. During inspection of an anticollision light installation for condition and proper operation, it should be determined that

A—electrical or mechanical interconnections are provided so that the anticollision light will operate at all times that the position light switch is in the ON position.
B—an appropriately rated fuse is in position at the light to protect the connecting wiring against electrical faults.
C—the anticollision light can be operated independently of the position lights.

An anticollision light must be installed so that it can be operated independently of the position lights.

8915. Major adjustments on equipment such as regulators, contactors, and inverters are best accomplished outside the airplane on test benches with necessary instruments and equipment. Adjustment procedure should be as outlined by

A—the equipment manufacturer.
B—the FAA.
C—aircraft technical orders.

Any major adjustments on electrical equipment must be done in direct compliance with the equipment manufacturer's maintenance recommendations.

Answers

8909 [C] (030) AMT-SYS	8910 [C] (068) AMT-G Ch 4	8911 [A] (054) AMT-G Ch 4	8912 [B] (039) AMT-G Ch 4
8912-2 [A] (041) AMT-G Ch 4	8913 [A] (041) AC 43.13-2	8914 [C] (015) AMT-G	8915 [A] (070) AMT-G Ch 11

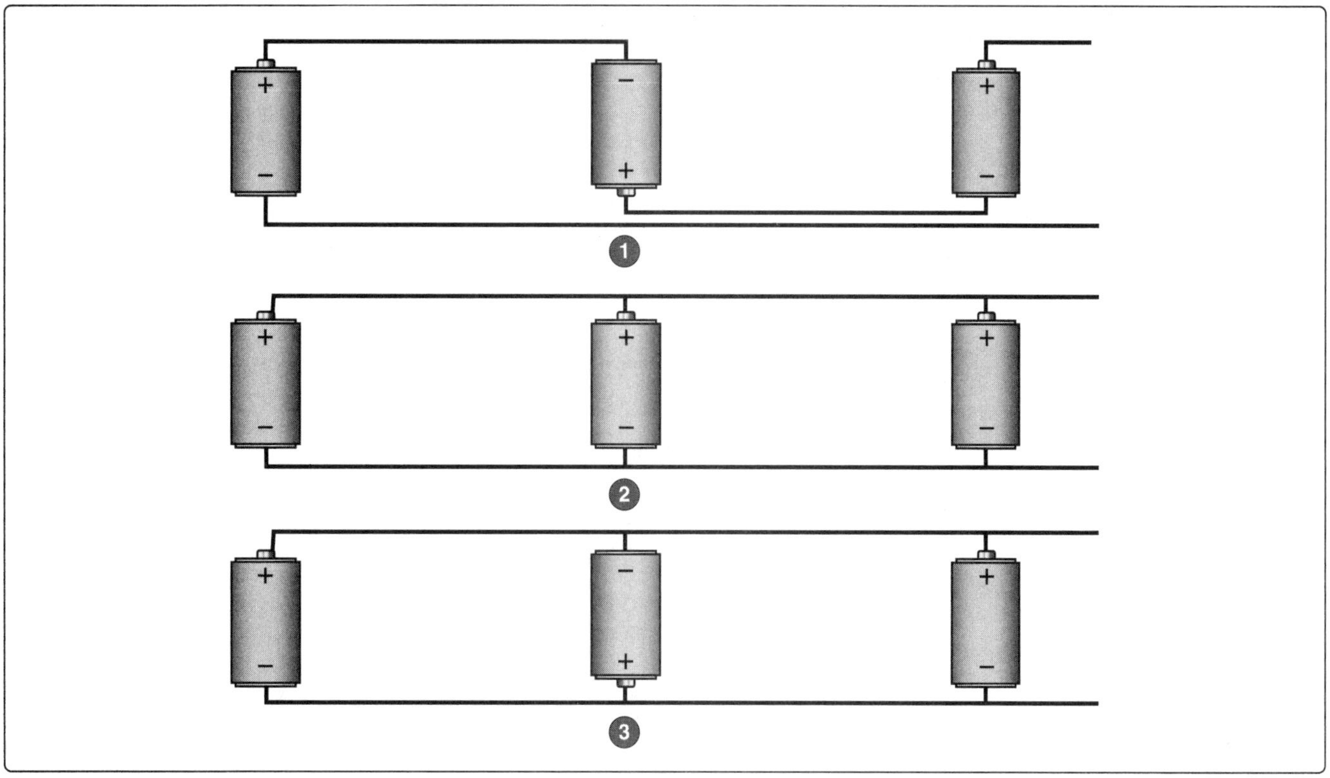

Figure 18. Battery connections

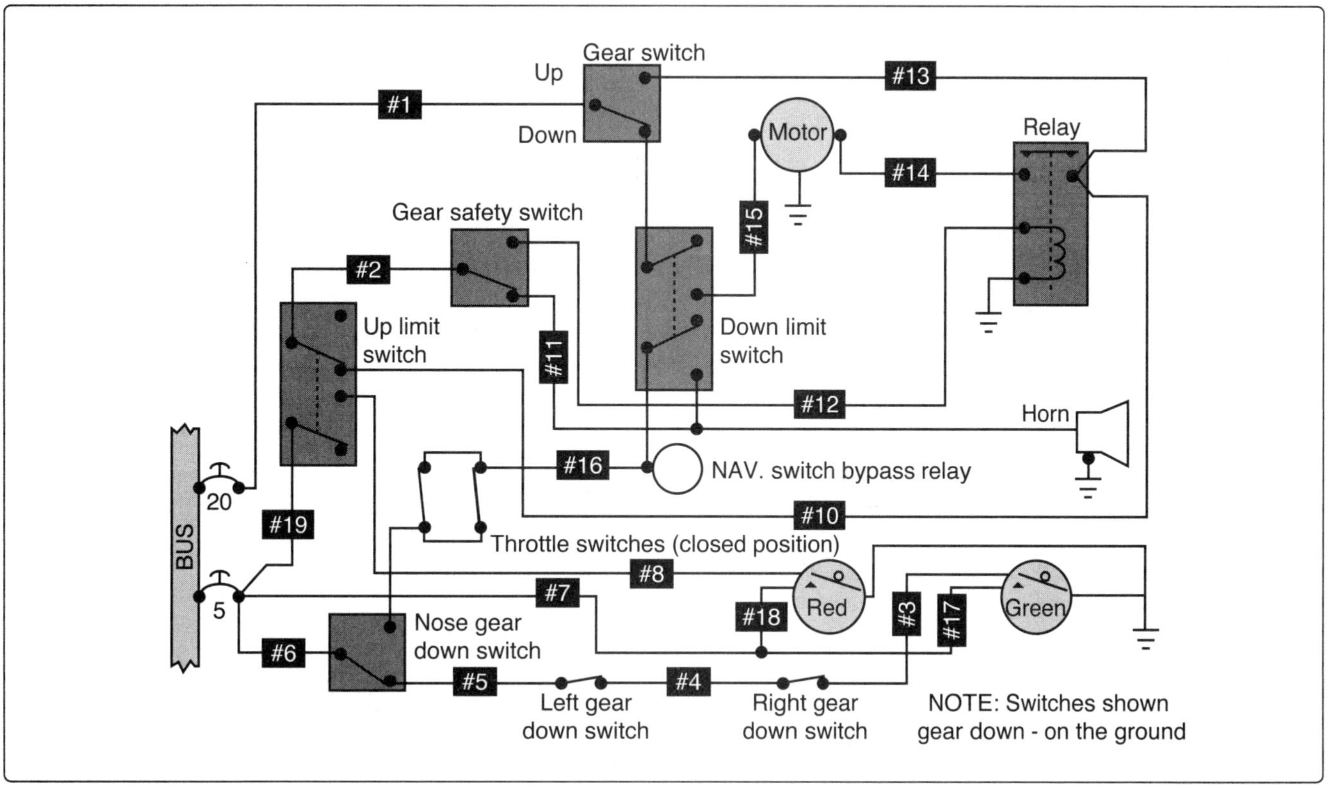

Figure 19. Landing gear circuit

8916. A battery-generator system provides direct current. On installations requiring alternating current from the battery-generator system, it is necessary to have

A—a transformer.
B—an inverter.
C—a variable resistor between the battery and generator.

An inverter is a device that converts direct current into alternating current.

8917. An aircraft electrical circuit control relay is

A—an electrically operated switch.
B—a device which converts electrical energy to kinetic energy.
C—any conductor which receives electrical energy and passes it on with little or no resistance.

A relay is a magnetically operated electrical switch.

8918. The purpose of a rectifier in an electrical system is to change

A—the frequency of alternating current.
B—direct current to alternating current.
C—alternating current to direct current.

A rectifier is an electrical check valve that allows electrons to flow in one direction only.

A rectifier is used to change alternating current into direct current.

8919. What is the ratio of turns between the primary coil winding and the secondary coil winding of a transformer designed to triple its input voltage?

A—Primary will have one-third as many turns as its secondary.
B—Primary will have twice as many turns as its secondary.
C—Primary will have three times as many turns as its secondary.

If a transformer has a three-to-one step-up ratio, the secondary winding will have three times as many turns as the primary winding.

The secondary voltage will be three times the primary voltage.

8920. In an AC circuit with no phase lead or lag, which is true?

A—Real power is zero.
B—Real power is greater than apparent power.
C—Real power equals apparent power.

In an AC circuit that has no phase lead or lag, the power factor is one (100 percent). All of the current is in phase with the voltage.

The real power is equal to the apparent power.

8921. How are generators rated?

A—Watts at rated voltage.
B—Amperes at rated voltage.
C—The impedance at rated voltage.

Generators are rated according to the current they can produce at their rated voltage.

8922. How is a shunt-wound DC generator connected?

A—One field is shunted across the other.
B—Both fields are shunted across the armature.
C—The field and armature are shunted with a capacitor.

This question assumes the generator has two field poles and two field coils.

The two field coils are connected together in series, and the two coils are shunted across (connected in parallel with) the armature.

8923. The poles of a generator are laminated to

A—reduce flux losses.
B—increase flux concentration.
C—reduce eddy current losses.

The pole shoes of a generator are usually made of laminated soft iron to reduce the eddy current losses.

Eddy currents produce heat and are a source of power loss in the generator.

8924. What is the frequency of an alternator dependent upon?

A—Voltage.
B—RPM.
C—Current.

The frequency of the alternating current produced by an aircraft alternator is dependent upon the speed (RPM) of the alternator.

Answers

8916 [B] (042) AMT-G Ch 4	8917 [A] (041) AMT-G Ch 4	8918 [C] (041) AMT-G Ch 4	8919 [A] (041) AMT-G Ch 4
8920 [C] (041) AMT-G Ch 4	8921 [B] (054) AMT-G Ch 4	8922 [B] (041) AMT-G Ch 4	8923 [C] (054) AMT-G
			8924 [B] (022) AMT-G Ch 4

8925. Where is the generator rating and performance data located?

A—In the pilot operating handbook.
B—Stamped on the generator data plate.
C—In the aircraft maintenance manual.

The current rating of a generator is usually stamped on the generator data plate.

If the rating is not on the data plate, it may be found in the generator specifications by referring to the part number of the generator, which is stamped on the data plate.

8926. Residual voltage is a result of magnetism in the

A—field windings.
B—field shoes.
C—armature.

Residual voltage produced by a generator when no current is flowing through the field coils is produced by the permanent magnetism in the field shoes of the generator.

8927. In troubleshooting an electrical circuit, if an ohmmeter is properly connected across a circuit component and some value of resistance is read,

A—the component has continuity and is open.
B—either the component or the circuit is shorted.
C—the component has continuity and is not open.

If the ohmmeter is connected correctly and indicates some value of resistance, current is flowing through the component and it has continuity. It is not open.

8928. CSD generators are usually cooled by

A—oil spray.
B—an integral fan.
C—both ram air and an integral fan.

An AC generator that is built integral with the constant-speed drive is cooled by an oil spray delivered by the CSD section. The oil used in cooling is held in a reservoir in the CSD.

8929. A CSD unit drives a generator through the use of

A—a synchronous electric motor.
B—an infinitely variable mechanical gearing system.
C—a variable hydraulic pump and hydraulic motor.

AC generator speed is held constant as the engine speed varies by a CSD unit. A variable-delivery hydraulic pump supplies fluid to a hydraulic motor. The ratio of the speed between the input and output of the CSD is varied to maintain a constant generator speed by controlling the pressure of the fluid that is delivered to the motor.

8930. Integrated drive generators (IDG) employ a type of high output AC generator that utilizes

A—brushes and slip rings to carry generated DC exciter current to the rotating field.
B—battery current to excite the field.
C—a brushless system to produce current.

An IDG is a high-output brushless alternator built into a single unit with a constant-speed drive. A permanent-magnet generator produces three-phase AC, which is sent to the voltage regulator section of the GCU. The output of the GCU supplies current to the exciter field coil which controls the output voltage of the generator.

8931. If the Integrated Drive Generator (IDG) scavenge oil filter is contaminated with metal, you should

A—do an oil analysis to diagnose the problem.
B—remove and replace the IDG.
C—replace the oil and filter at 25 hour intervals.

An IDG has its own integral lubrication system. Contamination of the IDG scavenge oil filter with chunks or pieces of metal indicates a mechanical failure in the IDG, and the IDG must be removed and replaced.

8932. When necessary during operation, CSD disconnect is usually accomplished by

A—a switch in the cockpit.
B—circuit breaker activation.
C—a shear section in the input shaft.

Constant speed drive units are equipped with an electrically actuated disconnect that is controlled manually by a switch in the cockpit or automatically by the generator control unit. The disconnect is actuated in the event of certain types of generator malfunctions.

8933. A CSD unit that is disconnected in flight, due to a malfunction such as overtemperature, may be reconnected

A—automatically if the temperature falls back into the normal operating range.
B—manually by the flightcrew.
C—only on the ground by maintenance personnel.

Some jet transport aircraft that use AC as the primary electrical power have a switch on the flight engineer's panel that allows the CSD unit to be disconnected in flight if there is a malfunction, such as an excessively high generator-drive oil temperature.

The CSD unit can be reconnected only by maintenance personnel when the aircraft is on the ground.

Answers

8925 [B] (054) AMT-G	8926 [B] (041) AMT-P Ch 17	8927 [C] (042) AMT-G Ch 4	8928 [A] (041) AMT-SYS
8929 [C] (041) AMT-P Ch 17	8930 [C] (041) AMT-P Ch 17	8931 [B] (054) AMT-SYS	8932 [A] (041) AMT-SYS
8933 [C] (041) AMT-SYS			

Position and Warning Systems

8934. An antiskid system is designed to

A—solely sense the deceleration rate of every main landing gear wheel.
B—release then reapply pressure at a slightly lower value when a skid is detected only.
C—sense the deceleration rate of every main landing gear wheel and release then reapply pressure at a slightly lower value when a skid is detected.

Antiskid generators are mounted in the wheel hubs, and they produce a signal whose frequency is proportional to the wheel rotational speed.

This signal is sent into a computer where its rate of frequency change is compared with an allowable rate of change. If the rate is too fast, it signals that a skid is impending.

8935. In a brake antiskid system, when an approaching skid is sensed, an electrical signal is sent to the skid control valve which

A—acts as a bypass for the debooster cylinders.
B—relieves the hydraulic pressure on the brake.
C—equalizes the hydraulic pressure in adjacent brakes.

If the antiskid computer senses that one wheel is decelerating fast enough to indicate an impending skid, it sends a signal to the skid control valve for that wheel. The skid control valve relieves hydraulic pressure from that brake until the rate of deceleration for its wheel is no longer excessive.

8936. An antiskid system is

A—a hydraulic system.
B—an electrohydraulic system.
C—an electrical system.

An antiskid system is an electrohydraulic system. It uses an electrical signal to actuate a hydraulic valve in the brake system.

8937. Antiskid braking systems are generally armed by

A—the application of brakes.
B—a switch in the cockpit.
C—the rotation of the wheels above a certain speed.

A brake antiskid system is armed by placing the arming switch in the ARMED position. This releases the brakes and initiates the locked-wheel protection circuit. The armed antiskid system will not allow the brakes to be applied until the weight of the aircraft is on the wheels and the wheels have reached a rotational speed of more than 15 to 20 mph.

This same switch allows the pilot to deactivate the system.

8938. A typical takeoff warning indication system, in addition to throttle setting, monitors the position of which of the following?

A—Ailerons, elevators, speed brake, and steerable fuselage landing gear.
B—Elevators, speed brake, flaps, and stabilizer trim.
C—Aerodynamically actuated slats, elevators, flaps, and speed brake.

A takeoff warning indicator system senses a number of items, and if any of them are not in the correct configuration for takeoff when the throttle for engine No. 3 is advanced for takeoff, an aural warning will sound to inform the pilot of the problem.

The items sensed are:

- *elevator or stabilizer trim in the takeoff range*
- *speed brake (spoilers) handle in the 0° position*
- *steerable fuselage landing gear is centered*
- *wing flaps are at 10°*
- *leading-edge flaps are extended*

8939. The primary purpose of a takeoff warning system is to alert the crew that a monitored flight control is not properly set prior to takeoff. The system is activated by

A—an 80 knot airspeed sensor.
B—an ignition system switch not set for takeoff.
C—a thrust lever.

The takeoff warning system is actuated by a switch on the power lever (thrust lever).

If any of the monitored flight controls are not properly set for takeoff, when the thrust lever is advanced, a warning will sound.

Answers

8934 [C] (031) AMT-SYS Ch 1	8935 [B] (031) AMT-SYS Ch 1	8936 [B] (031) AMT-SYS Ch 1	8937 [B] (032) AMT-SYS Ch 1
8938 [B] (018) AMT-SYS	8939 [C] (018) AMT-SYS		

8940. An airspeed indicator measures the differential between

A—pressure and temperature.
B—pitot and cabin air pressure.
C—pitot and static air pressure.

An airspeed indicator is a differential pressure gauge that measures the difference between ram (pitot) pressure and the static pressure surrounding the aircraft at any moment of the flight.

8941. The angle-of-attack detector operates from differential pressure when the airstream

A—is parallel to the longitudinal axis of the aircraft.
B—is not parallel to the true angle of attack of the aircraft.
C—is parallel to the angle of attack of the aircraft.

The angle-of-attack indicating system consists of an airstream-direction detector mounted on the side of the fuselage and an indicator mounted in the instrument panel.

The airstream-direction detector contains a sensing element that measures the direction of the local airflow relative to the true angle of attack.

It makes this measurement by finding the angular difference between the direction of the local airflow and the fuselage reference plane.

8942. (1) When an airplane is slowed below approximately 20 mph, the antiskid system automatically deactivates to give the pilot full control of the brakes for maneuvering and parking.

(2) An antiskid system consists basically of three components; wheel speed sensors, control box, and control valves.

Regarding the above statements,

A—only 1 is true.
B—only 2 is true.
C—both 1 and 2 are true.

Statement 1 is true. When all of the wheels are turning at less than 20 mph, the locked-wheel arming circuit becomes inoperative, giving the pilot full braking action for low-speed taxiing and parking.

Statement 2 is also true. An antiskid system consists basically of three components: the wheel speed sensors, the control box, and the control valves.

8943. In an antiskid system, wheel skid is detected by

A—an electrical sensor.
B—a discriminator.
C—a sudden rise in brake pressure.

A wheel skid is detected by the electrical wheel-speed sensor in the wheel hub. If the wheel slows down faster than it should, the sensor sends a signal to the control box, and the hydraulic pressure on the brake in that wheel is released.

8944. Which of the following functions does a skid control system perform?

A—Normal skid control, normal braking, fail safe protection, locked wheel skid control.
B—Normal skid control, fail safe protection, locked wheel skid control, touchdown protection.
C—Normal skid control, normal braking, touchdown protection, takeoff protection.

The skid control system performs four functions: normal skid control, locked wheel skid control, touchdown protection, and fail safe protection.

8945. In the air with the antiskid armed, current cannot flow to the antiskid control box because landing gear

A—squat switch is open.
B—down and lock switch is open.
C—antiskid valves are open.

An aircraft with an antiskid system cannot land with the brakes applied even if the brake pedals are depressed.

When the aircraft is airborne, the landing gear squat switch causes the antiskid control box to prevent fluid reaching the brakes.

8946. At what point in the landing operation does normal skid control perform its function?

A—When wheel rotation deceleration indicates an impending skid.
B—When wheel rotation indicates hydroplaning condition.
C—Anytime the wheel is rotating.

Normal skid control comes into play when any wheel decelerates at a rate that indicates an impending skid.

Answers

8940 [C] (076) 14 CFR Part 23	8941 [B] (010) AMT-SYS Ch 4	8942 [C] (031) AMT-SYS Ch 1	8943 [A] (041) AMT-SYS Ch 1
8944 [B] (031) AMT-SYS Ch 1	8945 [A] (068) AMT-SYS Ch 1	8946 [A] (031) AMT-SYS Ch 1	

8947. (1) An antiskid system is designed to apply enough force to operate just below the skid point.

(2) A warning lamp lights in the cockpit when the antiskid system is turned off or if there is a system failure.

Regarding the above statements,

A—only 1 is true.
B—only 2 is true.
C—both 1 and No. 2 are true.

Statement 1 is true. An antiskid system is designed to apply the correct amount of force to operate the wheel just below the skid point. This gives the most effective braking.

Statement 2 is also true. A warning lamp lights when the system is turned off or when there is a system failure.

8948. When an airplane's primary flight control surfaces are set for a particular phase of flight, such as landing or takeoff, the corresponding control-surface indicating system will show

A—flap/slat position.
B—speed break position.
C—trim position.

The control surface indicating system used in some aircraft notes the position of the primary flight control surface, and shows whether or not the trim tab is set properly for the existing flight condition.

8949. The pneumatic (reed) type stall warning system installed in some light aircraft is activated by

A—static air pressure.
B—positive air pressure.
C—negative air pressure.

Reed-type stall warning indicators used in some of the small general aviation aircraft are actuated when the angle of attack is increased to the position at which there is a negative pressure at the pickup hole in the leading edge of the wing.

8950. Stall warning systems are generally designed to begin warning the pilot when a stall

A—is imminent.
B—is starting to occur.
C—first affects the outboard portions of the wings.

A stall warning system warns the pilot when a stall is imminent. It senses the angle of attack, and when the aircraft is approaching a stall it warns the pilot, providing ample time to take corrective action before the stall actually occurs.

8951. (Refer to Figure 19.) What is the indication of the red landing gear position light under the following conditions?

Aircraft on jacks.
Landing gear in transit.
Warning horn sounding.

A—extinguished.
B—flashing.
C—illuminated.

When the aircraft is on jacks, the gear safety switch is changed from that in Figure 19.

The landing gear is in transit, causing the position of the nose-gear-down switch and the down-limit switch to be changed.

The warning horn is sounding. Current is flowing from the 5-amp circuit breaker, through wire #6, the changed position of the nose-gear-down switch, one or both of the throttle switches, and the changed down-limit switch to the horn.

The landing gear has not yet reached its up-and-locked position, so the up-limit switch is in the position shown. Until the gear reaches its up-and-locked position, there is no power to the red landing gear position light, and the light remains extinguished.

8952. (Refer to Figure 19). Which repair should be made if the gear switch was placed in UP position and the gear does not retract?

A—Replace electrical wire No. 15.
B—Replace the down limit switch.
C—Replace electrical wire No. 12.

If the landing gear does not retract when the weight is off the landing gear and the gear switch is placed in the UP position, wire 12 could be faulty and need to be replaced.

Current flows from the bus through the 20-amp circuit breaker, through wire 1 to the gear switch in the UP position, through wires 13 and 10 to the up-limit switch in the position shown, through the gear safety (squat) switch whose position is changed, through wire 12 to the relay coil. When the relay is energized, current flows through its contacts and wire 14 to the gear motor to retract the landing gear.

8953. Which of the following conditions is most likely to cause the landing gear warning signal to sound?

A—Landing gear locked down and throttle advanced.
B—Landing gear locked down and throttle retarded.
C—Landing gear not locked down and throttle retarded.

The landing gear warning horn will sound if the landing gears are not all down and locked, and the throttle is retarded to reduce power for landing.

Answers

8947 [C] (031) AMT-SYS Ch 1
8948 [C] (010) AMT-SYS
8949 [C] (018) AMT-SYS Ch 4
8950 [A] (018) AMT-SYS Ch 4
8951 [A] (068) AMT-SYS Ch 1
8952 [C] (068) AMT-SYS Ch 1
8953 [C] (068) AMT-SYS Ch 1

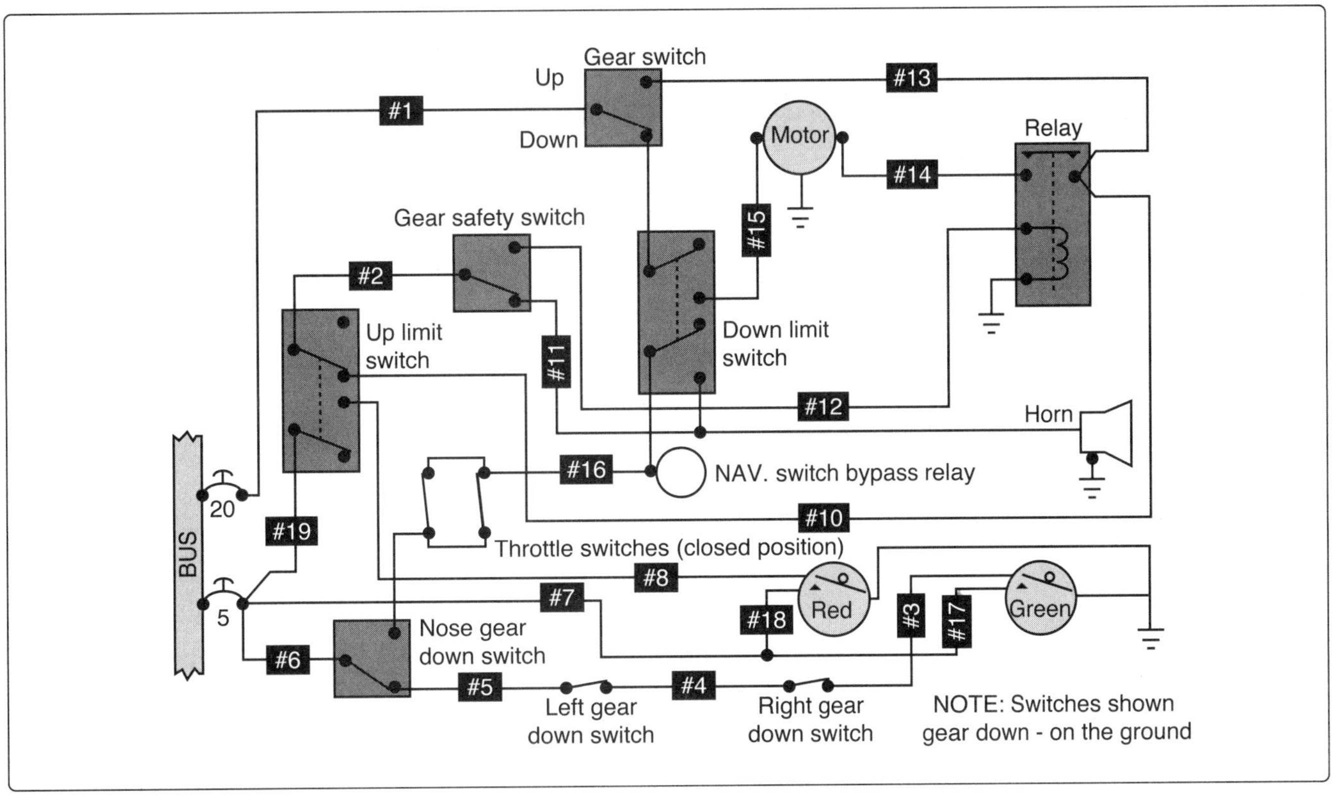

Figure 19. Landing gear circuit

8954. (Refer to Figure 20.) What will illuminate the amber indicator light?

A—Closing the nosewheel gear full retract switch.
B—Retarding one throttle and closing the left wheel gear locked down switch.
C—Closing the nose, left and right wheel gear full retract switches.

In order for the amber indicator light to illuminate, all three of the landing gears must be in their up-and-locked position.

The full retracted switches for the nosewheel, left wheel, and right wheel must all be closed.

8955. (Refer to Figure 20.) What is the minimum circumstance that will cause the landing gear warning horn to indicate an unsafe condition?

A—All gears up and one throttle retarded.
B—Any gear up and both throttles retarded.
C—Any gear not down and locked, and one throttle retarded.

The landing gear warning horn (aural warning) will sound anytime either throttle is retarded and any one of the landing gears is not down and locked.

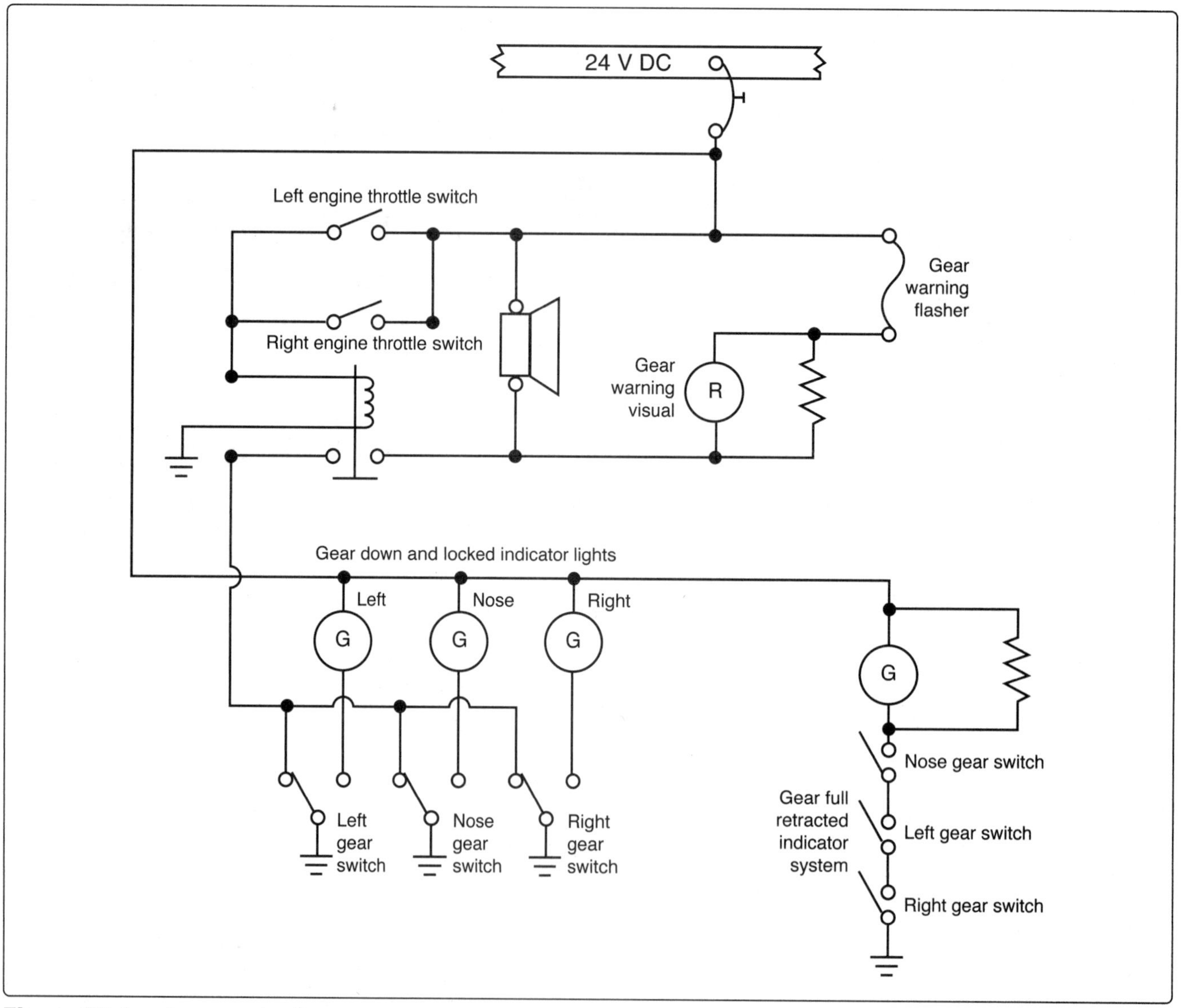

Figure 20. Landing gear circuit

Answers
8954 [C] (069) AMT-SYS Ch 1
8955 [C] (068) AMT-SYS Ch 1

8956. Where is the landing gear safety switch usually located?

A—On the main gear shock strut.
B—On the landing gear drag brace.
C—On the pilot's control pedestal.

The landing gear safety switch, or squat switch, is usually located on one of the main landing-gear shock struts.

8957. What safety device is actuated by the compression and extension of a landing gear strut?

A—Uplock switch.
B—Downlock switch.
C—Ground safety switch.

The ground safety switch (squat switch), is actuated by the compression of the landing gear oleo strut.

The ground safety switch prevents the landing gear from retracting when the weight of the aircraft is on the landing gear.

8958. Which repair would require a landing gear retraction test?

A—Landing gear safety switch.
B—Red warning light bulb.
C—Gear downlock microswitch.

The replacement of a landing gear downlock microswitch would require a retraction test in which the airplane is put on jacks and the landing gear is retracted and extended.

This type of test is required anytime any change or adjustment is made that could affect the operation of the retracting mechanism.

8959. Landing gear warning systems usually provide which of the following indications?

A—Red light for unsafe gear; green light for gear up.
B—Green light for gear up and down; red light for unsafe gear.
C—Red light for unsafe gear; green light for gear down; no light for gear up.

Some landing gear systems indicate in the manner shown here.

A red light shows an unsafe condition and a green light shows when each gear is down and locked. There is no light to show when the landing gear is up and locked.

8960. In most modern hydraulically actuated landing gear systems, the order of gear and fairing door operation is controlled by

A—sequence valves.
B—shuttle valves.
C—microswitches.

Hydraulically actuated landing gear systems that have hydraulically actuated wheel-well doors, control the operating sequence of the doors and the landing gear by the use of sequence valves.

These valves prevent the landing gear from retracting while the doors are closed.

8961. What landing gear warning device(s) is/are incorporated on retractable landing gear aircraft?

A—A visual indicator showing gear position.
B—A light which comes on when the gear is fully down and locked.
C—A horn or other aural device and a red warning light.

All retractable-landing-gear aircraft must have some type of device to warn the pilot if the landing gear is not down and locked when the throttles are retarded for landing.

All of the devices listed in the alternatives for this question are indicators except the horn or other aural device and a red warning light.

8962. When a landing gear safety switch on a main gear strut closes at liftoff, which system is deactivated?

A—Landing gear position system.
B—Antiskid system.
C—Aural warning system.

When the landing gear strut indicates that the weight is off of the landing gear, the safety switch deactivates the antiskid system.

An antiskid system has a provision that prevents the brakes from being applied, regardless of the position of the brake pedal, until weight is on the landing gear.

8963. The rotor in an Autosyn remote indicating system uses

A—an electromagnet.
B—a permanent magnet.
C—neither an electromagnet nor a permanent magnet.

The Autosyn remote indicating system uses an electromagnet as its rotor.

Answers

8956 [A] (068) AMT-SYS Ch 1	8957 [C] (068) AC 43.13-1	8958 [C] (069) AMT-SYS Ch 1	8959 [C] (068) AMT-SYS Ch 1
8960 [A] (068) AMT-SYS Ch 1	8961 [C] (068) AMT-SYS Ch 1	8962 [B] (068) AMT-SYS Ch 1	8963 [A] (010) AMT-SYS Ch 4

8964. The basic difference between an autosyn and a magnesyn indicating system is the

A—rotor.
B—transmitter.
C—receiver.

A basic difference between the Autosyn and Magnesyn remote indicating systems is the type of rotor used by each system. The Magnesyn system uses a permanent magnet and the Autosyn system uses an electromagnet.

8965. The rotor in a Magnesyn remote indicating system uses

A—a permanent magnet.
B—an electromagnet.
C—an electromagnet and a permanent magnet.

The Magnesyn remote indicating system uses a permanent magnet as its rotor.

8966. Microswitches are used primarily as limit switches to

A—limit generator output.
B—control electrical units automatically.
C—prevent overcharging of a battery.

Microswitches are used primarily as limit switches to provide automatic control of such electrical units as flap and landing gear actuator motors.

8967. Which of the following are some uses for a DC selsyn system?

A—Indicate the position of retractable landing gear, cowl flaps position, cooler door position, fuel quantity, and position of wing flaps.
B—Indicate the position of retractable landing gear, angle of incidence, and altitude.
C—Indicate the fuel quantity, rate of climb, and position of wing flaps.

DC selsyn systems are a widely used electrical method of indicating remote mechanical condition. They are used to show the movement and position of retractable landing gear, wing flaps, cowl flaps, oil cooler doors, and other movable parts of an aircraft. They are also used for measuring fuel quantity.

8968. (1) A DC selsyn system is a widely used electrical method of indicating a remote mechanical movement or position.

(2) A synchro-type indicating system is an electrical system used for transmitting information from one point to another.

Regarding the above statements,

A—only 1 is true.
B—only 2 is true.
C—both 1 and 2 are true.

Statement 1 is true. A DC selsyn system is a widely used electrical method of indicating a remote mechanical movement or position.

Statement 2 is also true. A synchro-type indicating system is an electrical system used for transmitting information from one point to another.

Ice and Rain Control Systems

8969. Prior to installation of a pneumatic surface-bonded type deicer boots, on the leading edge of the wing, you should

A—remove all paint from the area to be covered by the deicer boot.
B—clean the surface with MEK and apply adhesive to the back of the deicer boot and leading edge of the wing.
C—rough the surface with a mild abrasive.

When installing a surface-bonded deicer boot on an aircraft wing, remove all the paint from the area to which the boot is to be bonded.

The metal must be perfectly clean and the bonding material must be applied in strict accordance with the instructions furnished by the maker of the deicer boots.

Answers

8964 [A] (010) AMT-SYS Ch 4
8965 [A] (010) AMT-SYS Ch 4
8966 [B] (041) AMT-SYS Ch 1
8967 [A] (010) AMT-SYS Ch 4
8968 [C] (010) AMT-SYS Ch 4
8969 [A] (020) AMT-SYS Ch 6

8970. Which of the following are found in a laminated integral electrically heated windshield system?

A—Autotransformer, heat control relay, heat control toggle switch, and indicating light.
B—Heat control relay, heat control toggle switch, 24V DC power supply, and indicating light.
C—Autotransformer, head control relay, heat control toggle switch, and indicating light.

An aircraft windshield that has an integral heater laminated into the panel uses a 115-volt AC power supply, an autotransformer, a heat-control toggle switch, a heat control relay and indicating lights, but no DC power supply.

8971. What is one check for proper operation of a pitot-static tube heater after replacement?

A—Ammeter reading.
B—Voltmeter reading.
C—Continuity check of system.

A visual inspection should naturally be made of all of the connections.

A check of the ammeter reading when the pitot-static tube heater is operating is a final check of the proper installation of the heater.

8972. What controls the inflation sequence in a pneumatic deicer boot system?

A—Shuttle valve.
B—Vacuum pump.
C—Distributor valve.

A distributor valve controls the inflation sequence in a pneumatic deicer boot system.

8973. What is the source of pressure for inflating deicer boots on reciprocating engine aircraft?

A—Vane-type pump.
B—Gear-type pump.
C—Piston-type pump.

Normally the air pump used on a reciprocating engine for the inflation of deicer boots is a vane-type pump.

8974. Which of the following regulates the vacuum of the air pump to hold the deicing boots deflated when the pneumatic deicing system is off?

A—Distributor valve.
B—Pressure regulator.
C—Suction relief valve.

A suction-relief valve regulates the vacuum supplied by the air pump to hold the deicer boots deflated when the pneumatic deicing system is off.

8975. What may be used to clean deicer boots?

A—Unleaded gasoline or Jet A fuel.
B—Naphtha.
C—Soap and water.

Since deicer boots are normally made of rubber, they should be cleaned with mild soap and water.

8976. Some aircraft are protected against airframe icing by heating the leading edges of the airfoils and intake ducts. When is this type of anti-ice system usually operated during flight?

A—Continuously while the aircraft is in flight.
B—In symmetric cycles during icing conditions to remove ice as it accumulates.
C—Whenever icing conditions are first encountered or expected to occur.

An anti-icing system is operated in flight when icing conditions are first encountered or when they are expected to occur.

The leading edge of the wing is kept warm by a continuous supply of heated air.

When the system is designed to deice the leading edge, much hotter air is supplied to the inside of the wing, but for shorter periods of time and in a cyclic sequence.

A deicer system allows the ice to accumulate and then breaks it off.

8977. Which of the following indications occur during a normal operational check of a pneumatic deicer system?

A—Relatively steady readings on the pressure gauge and fluctuating readings on the vacuum gauge.
B—Fluctuating readings on the pressure gauge and relatively steady readings on the vacuum gauge.
C—Pressure and vacuum gauges will fluctuate as the deicer boots inflate and deflate.

A pneumatic deicer system is operating normally when the pressure gauge fluctuates as the various tubes inflate, and the vacuum gauge shows a relatively steady reading as all of the tubes are held deflated.

Answers

8970 [C] (024) AMT-SYS Ch 6
8971 [A] (076) AC 43.13-1
8972 [C] (024) AMT-SYS Ch 6
8973 [A] (024) AMT-SYS Ch 6
8974 [C] (024) AMT-SYS Ch 6
8975 [C] (024) AMT-SYS Ch 6
8976 [C] (024) AMT-SYS Ch 6
8977 [B] (024) AMT-SYS Ch 6

8978. What method is usually employed to control the temperature of an anti-icing system using surface combustion heaters?

A—Thermo-cycling switches.
B—Thermostats in the cockpit.
C—Heater fuel shutoff valves.

Thermo-cycling switches control the temperature of an anti-icing system that uses combustion heaters.

These switches shut off the fuel to the heater when the temperature is high enough.

8979. What is the purpose of the distributor valve in a deicing system utilizing deicer boots?

A—To equalize the air pressure to the left and right wings.
B—To sequence the deicer boots inflations symmetrically.
C—To distribute anti-icing fluid to the deicer boots.

The distributor valve in a deicer system sequences the deicer boot inflation and deflation cycle so the ice will be removed symmetrically from the aircraft.

8980. What is the purpose of the oil separator in the pneumatic deicing system?

A—To protect the deicer boots from oil deterioration.
B—To remove oil from air exhausted from the deicer boots.
C—To prevent an accumulation of oil in the vacuum system.

The oil separator in a pneumatic deicing system is located in the exhaust of a wet-type vacuum pump.

Oil from the engine is used to lubricate and seal the pump. After passing through the pump, this oil is discharged with the exhaust air.

The oil separator removes the oil from the air and returns it to the engine crankcase.

Getting rid of this oil, before the air reaches the deicer boots, helps prevent their deterioration.

8981. Where are the heating elements located on most aircraft with electrically heated windshields?

A—Laminated in the glass.
B—Attached to the glass.
C—Inside the windshield frame.

The thermistor-type heat sensors in an electrically heated windshield are laminated into the glass panels.

8982. Two possible sources of heat for the operation of a wing thermal anti-icing system are

A—first stage of the aircycle turbine and turbo compressor.
B—compressor bleed air and aircraft electrical system.
C—combustion heater and exhaust gases.

Wing thermal anti-icing systems usually use heated bleed air from the turbine-engine compressor, but electrically heated elements are also used in some installations.

8983. What maintains normal windshield temperature control in an electrically heated windshield system?

A—Thermal overheat switches.
B—Thermistors.
C—Manually-controlled rheostat.

Thermistors (a special form of electrical resistor whose resistance is a function of its temperature) are used to control the amount of current used in an electrically heated windshield.

8984. Arcing in an electrically heated windshield panel usually indicates a breakdown in the

A—temperature-sensing elements.
B—autotransformers.
C—conductive coating.

Arcing inside an electrically heated windshield panel usually indicates a breakdown of the conductive coating through which the current passes.

8985. Which of the following connects vacuum to the deicer boots when the system is not in operation, to hold the boots tightly against the leading edges in flight?

A—Vacuum relief valve.
B—Ejector.
C—Distributor valve.

A distributor valve in the deicer system directs vacuum to the deicer boots to hold them tightly against the leading edges in flight when they are not needed.

8986. How do deicer boots help remove ice accumulations?

A—By preventing the formation of ice.
B—By breaking up ice formations.
C—By allowing only a thin layer of ice to build up.

Deicer boots inflate and deflate to break up ice that has formed on the leading edges of the wing and the tail surfaces.

Answers

8978 [A] (024) AMT-SYS Ch 6
8982 [B] (024) AMT-SYS Ch 6
8979 [B] (024) AMT-SYS Ch 6
8983 [B] (041) AMT-SYS Ch 6
8980 [A] (024) AMT-SYS Ch 6
8984 [C] (024) AMT-SYS Ch 6
8981 [A] (041) AMT-SYS Ch 6
8985 [C] (079) AMT-SYS Ch 6
8986 [B] (024) AMT-SYS Ch 6

8987. Why are the tubes in deicer boots alternately inflated?

A—Alternate inflation of deicer boot tubes keeps disturbance of the airflow to a minimum.
B—Alternate inflation of deicer boot tubes does not disturb airflow.
C—Alternate inflation of deicer boot tubes relieves the load on the air pump.

Pneumatic deicer boots are inflated alternately to keep the disturbance of the air over the airfoil to a minimum.

8988. What system component aids in the prevention of carburetor icing?

A—Alcohol injection nozzle.
B—Bleed air valve.
C—Air diverter butterfly.

Carburetor icing can be minimized by spraying isopropyl alcohol into the throat of the carburetor and by using heated induction air.

8989. Why should a chemical rain repellant not be used on a dry windshield?

A—It will etch the glass.
B—It will restrict visibility.
C—It will cause glass crazing.

If a syrupy, chemical rain repellant is sprayed on the windshield of an airplane without a heavy rain striking it, it will smear and restrict visibility through the windshield.

8990. What is the principle characteristic of a windshield pneumatic rain removal system?

A—An air blast spreads a liquid rain repellant evenly over the windshield that prevents raindrops from clinging to the glass surface.
B—An air blast forms a barrier that prevents raindrops from striking the windshield surface.
C—A pneumatic rain removal system is simply a mechanical windshield wiper system that is powered by pneumatic system pressure.

A windshield pneumatic rain removal system blows the rain from the windshield with a blast of compressor bleed air.

A blast of high-velocity air, directed against the outside surface of the windshield, forms a barrier that keeps raindrops from hitting the surface of the windshield.

8991. What mixture may be used as a deicing fluid to remove frost from an aircraft surface?

A—Ethylene glycol and isopropyl alcohol.
B—Methyl ethyl ketone and ethylene glycol.
C—Naphtha and isopropyl alcohol.

Frost may be removed from an aircraft by spraying it with a deicing fluid which normally contains ethylene glycol and isopropyl alcohol.

8992. Which of the following is the best means to use when removing wet snow from an aircraft?

A—A brush or a squeegee.
B—Hot air.
C—Warm water.

Wet snow deposits should be removed from an aircraft with a brush or squeegee.

8993. What are three methods of anti-icing aircraft windshields?

A—An electric heating element in the windshield, a heated air circulating system, and windshield wipers and anti-icing fluid.
B—A blanket-type heating system, an electric heating element in the windshield, and a ribbon-type heating system.
C—An electric heating element in the windshield, a heated air circulating system, and a hot water system..

Some aircraft prevent ice formation on the windshield by using a double-panel windshield with warm air blown through the space between the panels. Others use windshield wipers with anti-icing fluid sprayed on. Most modern airplanes use an electrical heater element in the windshield.

8994. What icing condition may occur when there is no visible moisture present?

A—Injector ice.
B—Inlet ice.
C—Carburetor ice.

Carburetor ice can form when the outside air temperature is well above freezing and when there is no visible moisture present.

Much of the temperature drop that causes carburetor ice comes from the evaporation of the fuel.

Answers

8987 [A] (024) AMT-SYS Ch 6	8988 [A] (033) AMT-SYS Ch 6	8989 [B] (034) AMT-SYS Ch 6	8990 [B] (079) AMT-SYS Ch 6
8991 [A] (024) AMT-SYS Ch 6	8992 [A] (024) AMT-SYS Ch 6	8993 [A] (024) AMT-SYS Ch 6	8994 [C] (033) AMT-SYS Ch 6

8995. What should be used to melt the ice in a turbine engine if the compressor is immobile because of ice?

A—Deicing fluid.
B—Anti-icing fluid.
C—Hot air.

Ice should be melted from the inside of a turbine engine by flowing warm air through the engine until all of the rotating parts move freely.

8996. What is used as a temperature-sensing element in an electrically heated windshield?

A—Thermocouple.
B—Thermistor.
C—Thermometer.

Thermistors (a special form of electrical resistor whose resistance is a function of its temperature) are used as temperature sensors in an electrically heated windshield.

Fire Protection Systems

8997. In what areas of aircraft would you find a carbon monoxide detector?

A—Cargo and baggage compartment.
B—Cabin and cockpit.
C—Lavatory and engine nacelle.

Carbon monoxide detectors are installed in the cabin and in the cockpit of an aircraft to inform the occupants of the presence of this deadly gas.

8998. What occurs when a visual smoke detector is activated?

A—A warning bell within the indicator alarms automatically.
B—A lamp within the indicator illuminates automatically.
C—The test lamp illuminates and an alarm is provided automatically.

When a visual smoke detector is activated, a lamp inside the indicator is automatically turned on.

The light is scattered by the smoke so the smoke is visible against the black background inside the window of the indicator.

8999. The types of fire-extinguishing agents for aircraft interior fires are

A—water, carbon dioxide, dry chemical, and halogenated hydrocarbons.
B—water, dry chemical, methyl bromide, and chlorobromomethane.
C—water, carbon tetrachloride, carbon dioxide, and dry chemical.

Fire-extinguishing agents that are suitable for aircraft interior fires are water, carbon dioxide, dry chemical, and Halon 1301 or 1211, which are both forms of halogenated hydrocarbons.

9000. When air samples contain carbon monoxide, portable carbon monoxide detectors containing yellow silica gel will turn which color?

A—Blue.
B—Green.
C—Red.

When an air sample containing carbon monoxide passes over silica-gel crystals that have been dyed with a yellow indicator dye, the crystals turn to a shade of green.

The intensity of the green color is proportional to the concentration of carbon monoxide in the sample of air.

9001. Smoke detection instruments are classified by their method of

A—construction.
B—maintenance.
C—detection.

Smoke detection instruments are classified according to the method they use for detecting the presence of smoke.

9002. Smoke detectors that use a measurement of light transmissibility in the air are called

A—thermocouple devices.
B—photoelectrical devices.
C—ultraviolet optical devices.

Smoke detectors that measure the light transmissibility of the air (the ability of the air to allow light to pass through it) are called photoelectrical devices.

Answers

8995 [C] (024) AMT-SYS Ch 6	8996 [B] (041) AMT-SYS Ch 6	8997 [B] (046) AMT-SYS Ch 7	8998 [B] (095) AMT-SYS Ch 7
8999 [A] (048) AMT-SYS Ch 7	9000 [B] (095) AMT-SYS Ch 7	9001 [C] (095) AMT-SYS Ch 7	9002 [B] (095) AMT-SYS Ch 7

9003. A contaminated carbon monoxide portable test unit may be returned to service by

A—cleaning the indicating element with soap and water.
B—removing the indicating element and installing a new indicating element.
C—removing the indicating element from the exposed area for 24 hours.

A contaminated carbon monoxide test unit should be serviced by installing a new indicating element.

9004. Which fire-detection system measures temperature rise compared to a reference temperature?

A—Fenwal continuous loop.
B—Lindberg continuous element.
C—Thermocouple.

The thermocouple-type fire-detection system is activated by an abnormal rate of temperature rise.

9005. A carbon dioxide (CO_2) hand-held fire extinguisher may be used on an electrical fire if the

A—horn is nonmetallic.
B—handle is insulated.
C—horn is nonmagnetic.

A carbon-dioxide fire extinguisher should not be used on an electrical fire unless the horn is made of a nonmetallic material.

Most of the horns are made of pressed fiber.

9006. The proper fire-extinguishing agent to use on an aircraft brake fire is

A—water.
B—carbon dioxide.
C—dry powder chemical.

Aircraft brake fires are properly extinguished by the use of a dry-powder chemical fire extinguisher.

9007. Smoke in the cargo and/or baggage compartment of an aircraft is commonly detected by which instrument?

A—Chemical reactor.
B—Photoelectric cell.
C—Sniffer.

Smoke detectors used in the cargo and/or baggage compartments of aircraft are usually of the photoelectric-cell type, which measures the amount of light that can pass through the air.

If there is smoke in the area being protected, the amount of light passing through the smoke is decreased and the system warns the flight crew of the presence of smoke in the compartment.

9008. Light refraction smoke detectors are activated when the detector

A—measures a reduction in the amount of visible or infrared light in the surrounding area.
B—senses light reflected from smoke particles passing through a chamber.
C—uses radiation induced ionization to detect the presence of smoke.

Light refraction-type smoke detectors detect the presence of smoke by sensing the light that is reflected from smoke particles passing through a chamber.

9009. Why does the Fenwal fire-detection system use spot detectors wired parallel between two separate circuits?

A—A control unit is used to isolate the bad system in case of malfunction.
B—This installation is equal to two systems: a main system and a reserve system.
C—A short may exist in either circuit without causing a false fire warning.

The Fenwal fire-detection system is wired between two parallel circuits so that a short can exist in either circuit without causing a false fire warning.

9010. A fire extinguisher container can be checked to determine its charge by

A—attaching a remote pressure gauge.
B—weighing the container and its contents.
C—a hydrostatic test.

Fire extinguishers containing carbon dioxide are weighed to determine their state of charge.

Containers of freon and nitrogen, and containers of dry powder, have the condition of their charge measured by the use of pressure gauges that are part of the container.

Answers

9003 [B] (046) AMT-SYS Ch 7	9004 [C] (046) AMT-SYS Ch 7	9005 [A] (095) AMT-SYS Ch 7	9006 [C] (048) AMT-G Ch 10
9007 [B] (095) AMT-SYS Ch 7	9008 [B] (095) AMT-SYS Ch 7	9009 [C] (046) AMT-SYS	9010 [B] (046) AMT-SYS Ch 7

9011. What is the color code for fire extinguisher lines?

A—Brown.
B—Yellow.
C—Red and green.

Aircraft plumbing that contains fire-extinguishing agents is color coded with a stripe of brown tape and a series of diamonds.

9012. The most common cause of false fire warnings in continuous-loop fire-detection systems is

A—improper routing or clamping of loops.
B—moisture.
C—dents, kinks, or crushed sensor sections.

Dented, kinked, or crushed sensor sections are a common cause of false fire warnings in the continuous-loop fire-detection system.

9013. A thermocouple in a fire-detection system causes the warning system to operate because

A—it generates a small current when heated.
B—heat decreases its electrical resistance.
C—it expands when heated and forms a ground for the warning system.

A thermocouple in a fire-detection system generates its warning signal by producing a small current when it is heated.

This small current activates a sensitive relay which in turn causes the slave relay to indicate the presence of a fire.

9014. The thermocouple fire-warning system is activated by a

A—certain temperature.
B—core resistance drop.
C—rate-of-temperature rise.

The thermocouple-type fire-warning system is activated by an abnormal rate of temperature rise rather than by a specific temperature.

9015. When used in fire-detection systems having a single indicator light, thermal switches are wired in

A—parallel with each other and in series with the light.
B—series with each other and the light.
C—series with each other and parallel with the light.

In fire-detection systems using a single indicator light, the thermal switches are wired in parallel with each other, and the entire combination of switches is in series with the indicator light.

9016. Built-in aircraft fire-extinguishing systems are ordinarily charged with

A—carbon dioxide and nitrogen.
B—halogenated hydrocarbons and nitrogen
C—sodium bicarbonate and nitrogen.

Most of the modern aircraft built-in fire-extinguishing systems are charged with a halogenated hydrocarbon agent, such as Halon 1211 or Halon 1301, pressurized with nitrogen.

9017. In reference to aircraft fire-extinguishing systems,

(1) during removal or installation, the terminals of discharge cartridges should be grounded or shorted.

(2) before connecting cartridge terminals to the electrical system, the system should be checked with a voltmeter to see that no voltage exists at the terminal connections.

Regarding the above statements,

A—only 2 is true.
B—both 1 and 2 are true.
C—neither 1 nor 2 is true.

Statement 1 is true. The discharge cartridges for a fire-extinguishing system contain explosive charges called squibs. These squibs are ignited with an electrical current when the fire extinguisher agent discharge switch is closed. When removing or installing a discharge cartridge, ground or short the terminals to prevent an accidental firing.

Statement 2 is also true. Before connecting the cartridge terminals to the electrical system, the system should be checked with a voltmeter to be sure that there is no voltage at the terminal connections.

9018. What method is used to detect the thermal discharge of a built-in fire-extinguisher system?

A—A discoloring of the yellow plastic disk in the thermal discharge line.
B—A rupture of the red plastic disk in the thermal discharge line.
C—The thermal plug missing from the side of the bottle.

If a built-in fire-extinguishing system is discharged because of a thermal (overheat) condition, the red indicator disk is blown out.

Answers

9011 [A] (048) AMT-SYS Ch 7	9012 [C] (047) AMT-SYS Ch 7	9013 [A] (047) AMT-SYS Ch 7	9014 [C] (046) AMT-SYS Ch 7
9015 [A] (046) AMT-SYS Ch 7	9016 [B] (048) AMT-SYS Ch 7	9017 [B] (048) AMT-P Ch 18	9018 [B] (048) AMT-SYS Ch 7

9019. The thermal switches of a bimetallic thermal-switch type fire-detection (single-loop) system are heat-sensitive units that complete circuits at a certain temperature. They are connected in

A—parallel with each other, and in parallel with the indicator lights.
B—parallel with each other, but in series with the indicator lights.
C—series with each other, but in parallel with the indicator lights.

The thermal switches in a bimetallic thermal-switch type of fire-detection system are connected in parallel with each other. The entire combination of switches is connected in series with the indicator light.

If any switch completes a circuit to ground, the indicator light will turn on.

9020. (Refer to Figure 21.) Using the chart, determine the temperature range for a fire-extinguishing agent storage container with a pressure of 330 psig. (Consider 330 psig for both minimum and maximum pressure.)

A—47 to 73°F.
B—47 to 71°F.
C—45 to 73°F.

For this problem, we must interpolate.

330 psig is 0.3 of the way between 319 and 356, and 73° is 0.3 of the way between 70° and 80°.

330 psig is 0.52 of the way between 317 and 342, and 45.2 is 0.52 of the way between 40° and 50°.

The fire extinguisher could have a pressure of 330 psig over a temperature range of 45° to 73°F.

Container Pressure Versus Temperature		
Temperature °F	Container Pressure (PSIG)	
	Minimum	Maximum
-40	60	145
-30	83	165
-20	105	188
-10	125	210
0	145	230
10	167	252
20	188	275
30	209	295
40	230	317
50	255	342
60	284	370
70	319	405
80	356	443
90	395	483
100	438	523

Figure 21. Fire extinguisher chart

9021. (Refer to Figure 21.) Determine what pressure is acceptable for a fire extinguisher when the surrounding area temperature is 33°F. (Rounded to the nearest whole number.)

A—215 to 302 psig.
B—214 to 301 psig.
C—215 to 301 psig.

For this problem, we must interpolate.

33°F is 0.3 of the way between 30° and 40°.

215 psig is 0.3 of the way between 209 and 230 psig, and 302 psig is 0.3 of the way between 295 and 317 psig.

At 33°F the acceptable pressure range is between 215 and 302 psig.

9022. On a periodic check of fire extinguisher containers, the pressure was not between minimum and maximum limits. What procedure should be followed?

A—Release pressure if above limits.
B—Replace the extinguisher container.
C—Increase pressure if below limits.

On a periodic check of fire extinguisher containers, if the pressure, when corrected for ambient temperature, was not between the minimum and maximum limits, the fire extinguisher container must be replaced.

9023. In some fire-extinguishing systems, evidence that the system has been intentionally discharged is indicated by the absence of a

A—red disk on the side of the fuselage.
B—green disk on the side of the fuselage.
C—yellow disk on the side of the fuselage.

If a fire extinguisher system has been intentionally discharged, the yellow disk on the side of the fuselage is blown out.

If the fire extinguisher system has been discharged because of an overtemperature condition, the red disk is blown out.

Answers
9019 [B] (047) AMT-SYS Ch 7
9020 [C] (048) AMT-SYS Ch 7
9021 [A] (048) AMT-SYS Ch 7
9022 [B] (048) AMT-SYS Ch 7
9023 [C] (048) AMT-SYS Ch 7

9024. If a fire extinguisher cartridge is removed from a discharge valve, it should be

A—pressure checked.
B—used only on the original discharge valve assembly.
C—replaced with a new cartridge.

The fire extinguisher cartridge discussed here is the type used in a high-rate-discharge (HRD) freon container.

If a cartridge is removed from a discharge valve for any reason, it should not be used in another discharge valve assembly. The distance the contact point protrudes may vary with each unit.

Continuity might not exist if a used plug that has been indented with a long contact point were installed in a discharge valve that has a short contact point.

9025. Which of the following are fire precautions which must be observed when working on an oxygen system?

A—Display "No Smoking" placards and keep all tools and oxygen servicing equipment free from oil or grease.
B—Display "No Smoking" placards and provide adequate fire-fighting equipment.
C—Display "No Smoking" placards, provide adequate fire-fighting equipment, keep all tools and oxygen servicing equipment free from oil or grease, and avoid checking aircraft radio or electrical systems.

All four items listed here are safety precautions to be followed when working with an oxygen system.

9026. Which fire-extinguishing agent is considered to be the least toxic?

A—Carbon dioxide.
B—Bromotrifluoromethane (Halon 1301).
C—Bromochloromethane (Halon 1011).

Halon 1301 is a popular fire extinguishing agent that is suitable for use in aircraft cabin fires because it is the least toxic of the commonly used extinguishing agents.

9027. Maintenance of fire-detection systems includes the

A—repair of damaged sensing elements.
B—servicing of the pressure type responder system.
C—replacement of damaged sensing elements.

Of the maintenance functions listed here, the only allowable maintenance for a fire-detection system is the replacement of a damaged sensing element.

9028. A squib, as used in a fire-protection system, is a

A—temperature-sensing device.
B—device for causing the fire-extinguishing agent to be released.
C—probe used for installing frangible disks in extinguisher bottles.

A squib is an electrically actuated explosive device used to break the seal on a high-rate-discharge fire extinguisher bottle in order to release the agent.

Answers
9024 [B] (048) AMT-SYS Ch 7
9025 [C] (072) AMT-SYS Ch 7
9026 [B] (048) AMT-SYS Ch 7
9027 [C] (047) AMT-SYS Ch 7
9028 [B] (048) AMT-SYS Ch 7

Airframe Oral & Practical Study Guide

The Oral and Practical Tests

Prerequisites

All applicants must have met the prescribed experience requirements as stated in 14 CFR §65.77. In addition, all applicants must provide:

1. Proof of having unexpired passing credit for the Aviation Mechanic General (AMG) knowledge test by presenting an Airman Computer Test Report (except when properly authorized under the provisions of 14 CFR §65.80 to take the practical tests before the airman knowledge tests).
2. Identification with a photograph and signature.

Test Standards

The examiner will download an oral and practical examination that is generated at random for each applicant that reflects all the knowledge and skill "Areas of Operation."

"Areas of Operation" are subject areas in which aviation mechanic applicants must have knowledge or demonstrate skill.

"Tasks" are the items that should be performed according to standards acceptable to the examiner.

"Reference" identifies the publication(s) that describe the task. Information contained in manufacturer and/or FAA approved data always takes precedence over textbook referenced data.

The objective of each Task lists the elements that must be satisfactorily performed to demon-strate competency in the Task.

The objective includes:

1. Specifically what the applicant will be able to do.
2. Conditions under which the Task is to be performed.
3. Acceptable standards of performance.

These terms apply to each Task:

- "Inspect" means to examine by sight and touch.
- "Check" means to verify proper operation.
- "Troubleshoot" means to analyze and identify malfunctions.
- "Service" means to perform functions that ensure continued operation.
- "Repair" means to correct a defective condition.
- "Overhaul" means to disassemble, inspect, repair as necessary, and check.

The applicant should be well prepared in all knowledge and skill areas included in the standards.

Satisfactory performance to meet the requirements for certification is based on the applicant's ability to:

1. Show basic knowledge.
2. Demonstrate basic mechanic skills.
3. Perform the Tasks within the standards of the reference materials.

The practical test is passed if, in the judgment of the examiner, the applicant demonstrates the prescribed level of proficiency on the assigned Tasks in each Area of Operation. Each practical examination item must be performed, at a minimum, to the performance level in the practical test standards. For mechanic testing, there are three practical performance levels:

- Level 1: You must know basic facts and principles and be able to locate information and reference materials. You do not have to interpret information or demonstrate a physical skill.
- Level 2: Know and understand principles, theories, operations, and concepts. You must be able to find, interpret, and apply maintenance data and information. You must be able to select and utilize the appropriate tools and equipment. While you need to demonstrate adequate performance skills, you do not need to demonstrate skill at a high or return-to-service quality level.
- Level 3: Know and understand principles, theories, operations, and concepts. You must be able to find, interpret, and apply maintenance data and information, select and utilize the appropriate tools and equipment to the overall operation and maintenance of an aircraft. You must be able to demonstrate the ability to work independently and make accurate judgments of airworthiness. You must demonstrate skills at a high level which includes the ability to perform return-to-service levels of work.

If, in the judgment of the examiner, the applicant does not meet the standards of any Task performed, the associated Area of Operation is failed and therefore, the practical test is failed.

Typical areas of unsatisfactory performance and grounds for disqualification are:

1. Any action or lack of action by the applicant that requires corrective intervention by the examiner for reasons of safety.
2. Failure to follow recommended maintenance practices and/or reference material while performing projects.
3. Exceeding tolerances stated in the reference material.
4. Failure to recognize improper procedures.
5. The inability to perform to a return-to-service standard, where applicable.
6. Inadequate knowledge in any of the subject areas.

When an applicant fails a test the examiner will record the applicant's unsatisfactory performance and Tasks not completed in terms of Areas of Operation appropriate to the practical test conducted.

Wood Structures

Study Materials

Aviation Mechanic Series: Airframe Structures textbook .... ASA .... Chapter 3

Aviation Maintenance Technician Handbook—Airframe FAA-H-8083-31 Vol. 1...... FAA .... Chapter 6

Advisory Circular 43.13-1B........ FAA ....Pages 1-1–1-37

Typical Oral Questions

1. Which species of wood is considered to be the standard when comparing other woods for use in aircraft structure?

   Sitka spruce.

2. What is the basic difference between plywood and laminated wood?

   The grain in each layer of laminated wood runs in the same direction. The grain in the layers of plywood runs at 90 degrees or 45 degrees to each other.

3. What kind of glue is recommended for making a repair to a wooden aircraft structure?

   Synthetic resin glue.

4. How is aircraft plywood prepared for making a compound bend?

   The wood is soaked in hot water until it is pliable.

5. How is pressure applied to the glued joint when splicing a wooden aircraft wing spar?

   With cabinetmakers parallel clamps.

6. How much pressure must be applied to a glue joint in a piece of softwood to produce a strong joint?

   125 to 150 pounds per square inch.

7. What is the correct repair to a wooden aircraft wing spar if the wing-attach bolt holes in the spar are elongated?

   Splice in a new section of the spar and drill new holes.

8. What kind of repair is recommended for a hole in the plywood skin of an aircraft wing?

   A scarf patch.

9. What is the recommended taper for a splayed patch in a plywood aircraft skin?

   5 to 1.

10. What is the recommended taper for a scarf patch in a plywood aircraft skin?

    12 to 1.

11. Why should sandpaper never be used when preparing a scarf joint in a wing spar for splicing?

    The dust caused by sanding will plug the pores of the wood so the glue cannot get in to form a good bond.

12. What is the largest hole in a plywood wing skin that can be repaired with a fabric patch?

    One inch in diameter.

13. Why are light steel bushings often used in bolt holes in a wooden wing spar?

    The bushing keeps the spar from being crushed when the nut on the attachment bolt is tightened.

14. How long should a glue joint be kept under pressure when splicing a wooden aircraft wing spar?

    For at least seven hours.

15. Are mineral streaks in a piece of structural aircraft wood reason for rejecting the wood?

    No, if there is no evidence of decay in the wood.

16. Which area of a wooden aircraft wing spar must not contain any splice?

    There must be no splice under wing-attach fittings, landing gear fittings, engine mount fittings, or lift and interplane strut fittings.

17. How is compression wood identified?

    It has a high specific gravity, it appears to have an excessive growth of summer wood, and little contrast between the spring wood and the summer wood.

18. What is done to a splice in a wooden aircraft wing spar to strengthen the splice?

    Reinforcing plates are glued to both sides of the splice.

19. Why must abrupt changes in the cross-sectional area of a wooden structural member be avoided?

    Abrupt changes in the cross-sectional area of a structural member concentrate stresses and can cause failure.

Typical Practical Projects

1. Explain to the examiner the correct way to repair a wing spar that has an elongated bolt hole in its root end.

2. Install a scarf patch in a damaged piece of aircraft plywood.

3. Inspect a piece of wood for evidence of dry rot. Explain to the examiner what should be done if dry rot is found.

4. Make a scarf splice to a piece of wing rib cap strip material. Reinforce the splice to get maximum strength.

5. Inspect a piece of wing spar material to determine if the grain deviation is within the limits allowed for aircraft wood.

6. Properly mix a batch of resin glue and explain to the examiner the correct way to apply this glue to the wood when making a repair to aircraft wood structure.

7. Given several pieces of wood, examine them for condition and for meeting the specifications for aircraft structural wood.

8. Inspect a wooden aircraft structure to determine whether or not it is in an airworthy condition.

9. Inspect a plywood aircraft structure for evidence of delamination of the plywood or for the failure of the glue joint between the skin and the underlying structure.

10. Explain to the examiner the correct way of repairing a piece of aircraft structure that has been glued with casein glue, when the glue has deteriorated.

Aircraft Covering

Study Materials

Aviation Mechanic Series: Airframe Structures textbook	ASA	Chapter 3
Aviation Maintenance Technician Handbook—Airframe FAA-H-8083-31 Vol. 1	FAA	Chapter 3
Advisory Circular 43.13-1B	FAA	Pages 2-1–2-40

Typical Oral Questions

1. What are three types of fabric that can be used to cover an aircraft?

   Cotton fabric, synthetic fabric, and glass fabric.

2. What paperwork must be completed if an aircraft that was originally covered with Grade-A cotton fabric is re-covered using a synthetic fabric?

   The covering must be done according to an STC, and a Form 337 must be executed, stating that all materials and processes complied with the requirements of the STC.

3. What type of rib lacing cord is recommended for attaching cotton fabric to an aircraft structure?

   Waxed linen cord.

4. How wide should the surface tape be that is used to cover the trailing edge of an aircraft wing?

   Three inches wide

5. Why is the surface tape used on the trailing edge of the control surfaces of some airplanes notched?

   Since the edges of this tape face into the wind, it is possible that it could start to lift and form a very effective spoiler. If the tape is notched, it will tear off at a notch.

6. What is the purpose of the reinforcing tape that is used between the fabric and the rib lacing on an aircraft wing?

   The reinforcing tape keeps the rib lacing cord from pulling through the fabric.

7. Should a sewed seam in the fabric used to cover an aircraft wing run spanwise or chordwise?

   Both spanwise and chordwise seams are permissible, but chordwise seams are preferred.

8. What is the preferred seam used for machine-sewing pieces of aircraft fabric together?

   The French fell seam.

9. What type of material is used for inter-rib bracing in a fabric-covered aircraft wing?

   Cotton reinforcing tape.

10. What type of knot is used for locking the stitches that are used for rib lacing on a fabric-covered aircraft wing?

    A modified seine knot.

11. What determines the spacing of the rib lacing stitches on a fabric-covered aircraft wing?

    The never-exceed speed of the aircraft.

12. When is the finishing tape applied to a fabric-covered wing when it is being recovered?

    After the second coat of dope has dried and the nap of the fabric has been sanded off.

13. What is the recommended type of repair to a fabric-covered aircraft surface when it has an L-shaped tear with each of the legs of the tear more than 14 inches long?

    If the never-exceed speed of the aircraft is less than 150 mph, a doped-on repair can be made.

14. What type of hand-sewing stitch is used when sewing in a panel of new fabric on an aircraft fabric-covered wing?

    A baseball stitch, locked every eight to ten stitches.

15. What is the minimum strength to which aircraft fabric is allowed to deteriorate before it is considered to be unairworthy?

    Fabric can deteriorate to 70 percent of the strength of the fabric that is required for the aircraft.

16. What is an antitear strip, and when are they required on a fabric-covered aircraft?

    An antitear strip is a strip of the same type of fabric as is used for covering the wings. It is laid over the rib between the reinforcing tape and the fabric. An antitear strip is required for aircraft that have a never-exceed speed in excess of 250 mph.

17. When are drainage grommets applied when an aircraft is being re-covered?

    They are laid into the third coat of dope, at the same time the surface tape is applied.

18. Where are drainage grommets located on a fabric-covered aircraft wing?

    At the lowest point in each bay. It is customary to install a grommet on each side of a wing rib, on the underside of the wing, at the trailing edge.

19. How is the strength of the fabric on an aircraft structure determined?

    An approximate strength test can be made with an FAA-approved fabric punch tester, but the only way to know for sure that the fabric has sufficient strength is by pull-testing a one-inch-wide sample of the fabric.

20. Why are some portions of the structure of an aircraft dope proofed before they are covered with fabric?

    Dope proofing keeps the fabric from sticking to the structure when the first coat of dope is applied. The fabric normally sags enough to touch the structure before it begins to pull taut.

21. What is done to cotton and linen fabric to protect it from mildew?

    The first coat of dope that is used on cotton and linen fabric has a mildewcide mixed in it.

22. How is polyester synthetic fabric shrunk on an aircraft structure?

    It is shrunk with heat from an iron or from a heated blower.

Typical Practical Projects

1. Demonstrate to the examiner the proper way to stitch fabric to an aircraft wing.
2. Test the fabric on an aircraft structure to determine if it is airworthy.
3. Make a doped-on patch to a damaged area in a fabric-covered aircraft structure.
4. Demonstrate to the examiner the proper way to sew a piece of new fabric to a piece of damaged fabric on an aircraft structure.
5. Install a drainage grommet on the trailing edge of a fabric-covered aircraft wing. Demonstrate the correct way of opening the hole in the grommet.
6. Explain to the examiner the correct procedure for covering an aircraft wing with polyester synthetic fabric.
7. Demonstrate the proper splice knot to use when joining pieces of waxed rib lacing cord.
8. Determine the correct spacing to use for rib lacing on an aircraft that is specified by the examiner.
9. Test the strength of a piece of aircraft fabric using the pull test.
10. Explain to the examiner the correct way of removing wrinkles from cotton fabric that is installed on an aircraft structure before the dope is applied.

Aircraft Finishes

Study Materials

Aviation Mechanic Series: Airframe Structures textbook .... ASA .... Chapter 3
Aviation Maintenance Technician Handbook—Airframe FAA-H-8083-31 Vol. 1 ...... FAA .... Chapter 8

Typical Oral Questions

1. Why should wooden wing spars be finished with a transparent varnish?

   The transparent finish allows any decay or rot that develops in the wood to be detected.

2. Why is retarder used in dope when the dope is being sprayed in humid conditions?

   The retarder slows the drying of the dope and keeps it from blushing.

3. What is used as a protective finish for the inside of steel tubing?

   Hot linseed oil.

4. How thick should a coat of wash primer be that is used on an aluminum alloy aircraft structure?

   It should be thin enough that it does not hide the surface of the metal.

5. What happens to an enamel finish when paint remover is applied to it?

   The enamel softens and swells so that it pulls away from the surface of the metal.

6. What should be done to an aircraft surface that is covered with paint remover to give the remover the maximum amount of time to soak into the old finish?

   The surface should be covered with a piece of polyethylene sheeting such as a paint drop cloth. This will keep the solvents from evaporating before they have time to penetrate the paint film.

7. When mixing epoxy paint, should the converter be added to the resin or the resin to the converter?

   The converter should always be added to the resin, never the resin to the converter.

8. What is the general reason for runs and sags in a finish that is being sprayed onto a flat surface?

   Too much paint is being applied. The film is too thick.

9. What can be done to remedy blushing that has formed on a doped surface that has just been sprayed?

   Spray a very light mist coat of a mixture of one part retarder to two parts of thinner over the blushed area. Allow it to dry and spray on another coat. If this does not remove the blush, the blushed dope will have to be sanded off and new dope applied.

10. How can a vinyl film decal be removed from an aluminum alloy surface?

    Place a cloth saturated with cyclohexanone or MEK over the decal until it is softened, and scrape it off of the surface with a plastic scraper.

11. What safety precaution must be observed when sweeping a paint room that has dried dope or lacquer overspray on the floor?

    The floor must be wet down with water before it is swept. Static electricity from dry sweeping can cause a fire.

12. When an aircraft is being re-covered, when is fungicidal dope applied to the fabric?

    With the first coat of dope that is brushed into the fabric.

13. What will happen if dope is sprayed over an enameled surface?

    The thinner in the dope will penetrate the enamel surface and cause it to swell.

14. What are three types of primer that may be used when painting an aircraft?

    Zinc chromate primer, wash primer, and epoxy primer.

15. How is the finish removed from a fiberglass aircraft component that is being repaired?

    The finish must be sanded off. Paint remover can soften the resin of which the component is made.

16. What are the two basic types of dope that are used on fabric-covered aircraft?

    Nitrate dope and butyrate (CAB) dope.

17. What kind of dope is used on polyester synthetic fabric that has been heat-shrunk on an aircraft structure?

    Nontautening butyrate dope.

18. What type of thinner is used with zinc chromate primer?

    Toluol or toluene.

Typical Practical Projects

1. Mix dope and the correct thinner to get the proper viscosity for spraying. Demonstrate to the examiner the correct way to spray the dope on an aircraft surface.

2. Properly clean a piece of aluminum alloy and apply the correct amount of primer for best adherence of the topcoat material.

3. Determine whether the dope that is on a piece of fabric-covered structure is nitrate or butyrate.

4. Demonstrate to the examiner the correct way of applying the first coat of dope to the fabric that is being installed on an aircraft structure.

5. Demonstrate to the examiner the correct way of dry sanding a fabric-covered aircraft wing.

6. Demonstrate to the examiner the correct way to spray a surface with a polyurethane enamel.

7. Identify the correct thinner to use with a list of finishing materials that is furnished by the examiner.

8. Properly adjust the pressure of the air on a spray gun and pressure pot for spraying aircraft dope.

9. Explain to the examiner the correct size and location for the identification numbers that are required on an aircraft.

10. Properly remove the finish from a piece of fiberglass-reinforced aircraft structure so the structure can be repaired.

11. Explain to the examiner the reason for using aluminum-pigmented dope on a fabric-covered aircraft structure. Explain why it is important to not use too much aluminum dope.

Sheet Metal Structures

Study Materials

Aviation Mechanic Series: Airframe Structures textbook .... ASA .... Chapter 2

Aviation Maintenance Technician Handbook—Airframe FAA-H-8083-31 Vol. 1 ...... FAA .... Chapter 4

Advisory Circular 43.13-1B .... FAA .... Pages 4-11–4-51

Typical Oral Questions

1. What are three requirements for a repair to a piece of sheet metal aircraft structure?

   The repair must restore the lost strength and rigidity, and it must not change the aerodynamic shape of the part.

2. When making a riveted repair to an aircraft sheet metal structure, which should be the stronger, the shear strength of the rivet, or the bearing strength of the metal sheet?

   The two strengths should be close to each other, but the bearing strength of the sheet should be the greater.

3. What kind of stress is in the upper skin of an aircraft wing in flight?

   Compression.

4. What type of device is a Cleco fastener?

   A patented fastener that is inserted in the rivet holes and is used to hold two pieces of sheet metal together until they can be riveted.

5. What is the main function of throatless shears in an aircraft sheet metal shop?

   Throatless shears are used to cut mild carbon steel up to 10-gage, and stainless steel up to 12-gage. They can be used to cut irregular curves in the metal.

6. What is the purpose of a sight line when laying out sheet metal to be bent in a cornice brake?

   The sight line allows the jaws of a cornice brake to be positioned so the bend made by the brake will start at the bend tangent line.

7. What kind of metal forming is done by a slip roll former?

   Simple curves with a large radius.

8. What kind of metal forming is done by bumping?

   Compound curves in sheet metal.

9. What must be done to the flanges of an angle for it to be curved?

   The flanges must be stretched for a convex curve and shrunk for a concave curve.

10. What is meant by the bend allowance used in making a bend in a piece of sheet metal?

    The bend allowance is the amount of metal that is actually used in making the bend in a piece of sheet metal.

11. What determines the minimum bend radius that can be used with a piece of sheet metal?

    The thickness of the material and its hardness.

12. What is meant by setback when bending a piece of sheet metal in a cornice brake?

    Setback is the distance the jaws of the brake must be set back from the mold line to form the bend.

13. Why are the lightening holes in a sheet metal wing rib flanged?

    Flanging the lightening holes gives the rib rigidity.

14. When hand-forming a piece of sheet metal that has a concave curve, should the forming be started in the center of the curve, or at its edges?

    Start at the edges and work toward the center.

15. What is meant by a joggle in a piece of sheet metal?

    A joggle is a small offset near the edge of a piece of sheet metal that allows the sheet to overlap another piece of metal.

16. When drilling stainless steel, should the drill be turned fast or slow?

    It should be turned slowly.

17. What is the minimum edge distance allowed when installing rivets in a piece of aircraft sheet metal structure?

    Two times the diameter of the rivet.

18. What is the recommended transverse pitch to use when making a riveted two-row splice in a piece of sheet metal?

    Three-fourths of the pitch of the rivets in the rows.

19. Why should aluminum alloy rivets be driven with as few blows as is practical?

    Excessive hammering will work-harden the rivets and make them difficult to drive.

20. What determines whether a piece of sheet metal should be dimpled or countersunk when installing flush rivets?

    The thickness of the sheet. Countersinking should be done only when the thickness of the sheet is greater than the thickness of the rivet head.

21. What type of metal should be hot-dimpled?

    7075-T6, 2024-T81 aluminum alloys, and magnesium alloys should be hot-dimpled.

22. What kind of repair can be made to a small damage of the core material and one face sheet of a piece of aluminum alloy honeycomb structure?

    A potted compound repair.

23. What special precautions must be taken when repairing a radome?

    Nothing must be done to the radome that will affect its electrical transparency or its aerodynamic strength.

24. How is the point of a twist drill ground that is to be used for drilling transparent acrylic material?

    The cutting edge should be dubbed off to a zero rake angle, and the included angle of the tip should be ground to 140 degrees.

25. What causes crazing in a piece of transparent acrylic material?

    Uneven stresses in the material, usually caused by heat.

26. What is the purpose of anodizing a piece of aluminum alloy, and how is it applied?

    Anodizing is a protective oxide film that is de-posited on the surface of aluminum alloy by an electrolytic process.

Typical Practical Projects

1. Lay out and form a channel of specified dimensions from a piece of aluminum alloy sheet. Use the minimum bend radius allowed for the material.
2. Select the correct length and diameter of special rivets furnished by the examiner, and properly install them to join two pieces of aluminum alloy sheet.
3. Make a flush patch repair to a hole in a sheet metal aircraft structure.
4. Select the proper twist drill and demonstrate to the examiner the correct way to drill stainless steel.
5. Select the proper twist drill and demonstrate to the examiner the correct way to drill transparent acrylic plastic.
6. Lay out an octagonal patch that will restore the strength lost by a crack in a piece of stressed fuselage skin.
7. Distinguish between a piece of acrylic plastic and a piece of cellulose acetate plastic.
8. Form a compound curved channel to reinforce a damage in a fuselage frame specified by the examiner.
9. Given an assortment of aircraft rivets, identify each by their proper part number and the type of material.
10. Demonstrate to the examiner the correct way to set up and use a squeeze riveter.
11. Properly remove a series of rivets from a piece of aircraft structure.
12. Repair a small damage to a piece of honeycomb structure.
13. Demonstrate to the examiner the correct way to check a bonded honeycomb structure for indication of internal delamination.
14. Repair a shallow scratch in a piece of transparent acrylic material.

Welding

Study Materials

Aviation Mechanic Series: Airframe Structures textbook....................................... ASA.............................. Chapter 2
Aviation Maintenance Technician Handbook—Airframe FAA-H-8083-31 Vol. 1...... FAA .... Chapter 5
Advisory Circular 43.13-1B... FAA ....Pages 4-53–4-80

Typical Oral Questions

1. Why is TIG (GTA) welding preferred over oxyacetylene welding for building and repairing welded steel tube aircraft structure?

   The heat is concentrated in the weld and does not cause as much distortion as gas welding.

2. What are two types of electric resistance welding used in aircraft construction?

   Spot welding and seam welding.

3. Why is it important that the pressure of the gas in an acetylene cylinder be kept low?

   Acetylene gas becomes unstable when it is kept under pressure of more than about 15 psi.

4. What determines the amount of heat that is put into a weld by an oxy-acetylene torch?

   The size of the orifice in the torch tip.

5. What is the difference in the appearance of an oxidizing flame, a neutral flame, and a reducing flame produced by an oxy-acetylene torch?

   An oxidizing flame has a pointed inner cone, and the torch makes a hissing noise. A neutral flame has a rounded inner cone, and there is no feather around the inner cone. A reducing flame has a definite feather around the inner cone.

6. What is meant by tack welding?

   Tack welding is the use of small welded spots to hold the material together until the final bead is run.

7. Why must thick plates of metal be preheated before they are welded?

   Preheating is a method of controlling the expansion and contraction of the metal that is being welded. Preheating minimizes the stresses that are caused when welding thick metal.

8. Why is it important that all traces of the welding flux be removed after a piece of aluminum or magnesium is welded?

   Welding flux is corrosive and it must be removed to keep the metal from corroding.

9. What is the function of the inert gas that is used in TIG (GTA) and MIG (GMA) welding?

   The inert gas forms a shield to keep oxygen away from the weld puddle so oxides cannot form and weaken the weld.

10. What is the difference between brazing and welding?

    In brazing, the base metal is not melted, but is covered with a low-melting-point alloy. In welding, the base metal is melted.

11. What is used as the electrode in TIG (GTA) welding?

    A small-diameter tungsten wire.

12. Is a heat-treated steel part normally repairable by welding?

    No, welding destroys the heat treatment.

13. What is the function of the flux in brazing and soldering?

    Flux covers the cleaned and heated metal to keep oxygen away from it. Oxides keep the solder or brazing material from adhering to the surface of the metal.

14. What kind of solder is recommended for soldering electrical wires?

    60/40 resin-core solder.

15. What kind of flame should be used when gas welding aluminum?

    A soft, neutral oxy-hydrogen flame is recommended.

16. What is an acceptable acetylene line pressure to use when welding with an oxyacetylene rig?

    About 5 psi.

17. What kind of flame should be used when gas welding stainless steel?

    A slightly carburizing flame.

18. How much should the bead penetrate the material when welding two pieces of steel with a butt weld?

    The joint should have 100 percent penetration.

19. What is meant by a soft flame?

    A soft flame is one that is made when the pressures of the gases are low enough that the flame does not make a noise and does not blow the puddle.

20. What must be done to an aircraft fuel tank before it can be repaired by welding?

    The gas fumes must all be purged from the tank by running live steam through it for at least 30 minutes, by soaking it in hot water, or by filling it with nitrogen or carbon dioxide.

Typical Practical Projects

1. Demonstrate to the examiner the correct way to set up an oxy-acetylene welding rig, to light the torch, to adjust it to get a neutral flame, and to shut down the rig.

2. Demonstrate to the examiner the correct way to install, light, and adjust an oxy-acetylene cutting torch. Demonstrate the correct way to cut across a piece of steel.

3. Prepare two pieces of steel tubing, and weld them together to form a T.

4. Using examples of welds furnished by the examiner, select the ones that are not airworthy, and explain the reasons the welds are not acceptable.

5. Correctly set up a TIG (GTA) welding rig, and make a proper bead across a piece of steel.

6. Correctly prepare and join two pieces of steel by brazing.

7. Correctly prepare and solder a stranded copper wire into an electrical connector.

8. Demonstrate the correct use of tack welds and skip welding to prevent thin sheets of metal warping when they are being butt welded.

9. Demonstrate forehand and backhand welding and explain to the examiner the reason each type of welding is used.

10. Demonstrate the correct way to remove flux from a piece of aluminum that has been welded.

11. Make a paper template of a reinforcing patch that would be properly used to repair a longeron in a steel tube fuselage that has been dented at a cluster weld.

Assembly and Rigging

Study Materials

Aviation Mechanic Series: Airframe Structures textbook..ASA.................. Chapters 1 and 4
Aviation Maintenance Technician Handbook—Airframe FAA-H-8083-31 Vol. 1...... FAA .... Chapter 2

Typical Oral Questions

1. Why is it specially important that the leading edge of a wing and the upper surface of the forward half of the wing be kept free of dents and any dirt or contamination?

   The air flowing over this portion of the wing must be smooth to produce the maximum amount of lift. If the surface is rough or dirty, the air flow will be distorted and lift will be lost.

2. What is meant by the angle of attack of an airplane wing?

   The acute angle that is formed between the chord line of an airfoil and the direction of the air that strikes it.

3. What are the four basic forces that act on an aircraft in flight?

   Lift, drag, thrust, and gravity.

4. What is meant by the angle of incidence of an airplane wing?

   The acute angle that is formed between the chord line of an airfoil and the longitudinal axis of the aircraft on which it is mounted.

5. What causes parasite drag on an airplane?

   The friction of the air flowing over the surface.

6. Name the three axes of an airplane and the control that rotates the airplane about each of its three axes.

   Longitudinal axis—ailerons
   Lateral axis—elevators
   Vertical axis—rudder

7. Does the lift that is produced by the horizontal tail surfaces of an airplane act upward or downward in normal flight?

   Downward.

8. What is the function of lateral dihedral in the wings of an airplane?

   Lateral dihedral gives the aircraft roll stability, or stability about the longitudinal axis.

9. What is the purpose of a stall strip on an airplane wing?

   Stall strips distort the air flowing over the top of the wing in the root area at high angles of attack. They cause the root of the wing to stall out at a lower angle of attack than the portion of the wing ahead of the ailerons.

10. What is the function of a servo tab on an aircraft control surface?

    A servo tab produces an aerodynamic force on a control surface that aids the pilot in moving the surface.

11. Why do most high-performance aircraft use slotted flaps?

    Slotted flaps can be deflected to a greater angle than other types of flaps before the airflow over their surface breaks away.

12. What is the purpose of a movable slat in the leading edge of some airplane wings?

    The movable slat remains flush with the leading edge of the wing during all low-angle-of-attack flight conditions. When the angle of attack becomes high, the slat automatically moves out of the wing and forms a duct which forces the air back over the upper surface of the wing. This delays the stall.

13. What causes dissymmetry of lift produced by the rotor of a helicopter?

    The forward speed of the helicopter produces dissymmetry of lift. The rotor blade which is traveling forward as the helicopter is flying produces more lift than the blade that is traveling rearward.

14. Why do single-rotor helicopters use an auxiliary rotor on their tail?

    The thrust from the auxiliary rotor on the tail of the helicopter counteracts the torque produced by the main rotor.

15. Why is it important that the leading edge of a supersonic airplane wing be kept free from dents and damage?

    A sharp leading edge allows an oblique shock wave to attach to the airfoil in supersonic flight. If the leading edge is dented or blunt, a normal shock wave will form and slow the air immediately behind it to a subsonic velocity.

16. What is the purpose of vortex generators on the wing of a high-speed airplane?

    Vortex generators pull high-energy air down to the surface of the wing and keep shock-induced separation from occurring.

17. Why are the control cables of large airplanes normally equipped with automatic tension regulators?

    The large amount of aluminum in the aircraft structure contracts so much as its temperature drops in flight that the control cables could become dangerously loose. The automatic tension regulators keep the cable tension constant as the dimensions of the aircraft change.

18. Why is it important that the blades of a helicopter rotor system be in track?

    If the blades are not in track, vertical vibration can develop.

19. Why is it important that any repairs to the control surfaces of an airplane not change their original condition of balance about their hinge line?

    A control surface that is out of static balance can flutter in certain flight conditions. Flutter normally tears the surface off the aircraft.

20. In what FAA publication could you find correct control surface movement for a particular airplane?

    In the Type Certificate Data Sheet for the airplane.

Typical Practical Projects

1. Locate in the appropriate document the control surface movement for an airplane specified by the examiner. Measure this movement and determine whether or not it is correct.

2. Adjust the tension of an aircraft control cable and properly safety wire the turnbuckle.

3. Properly install a swaged-on terminal on an aircraft control cable. Demonstrate to the examiner the correct way to check the terminal for proper swaging.

4. Check the flight controls of an airplane, including all of the secondary controls for the correct direction of movement when the cockpit controls are moved.

5. Demonstrate to the examiner the correct way to inspect a piece of aircraft control cable for indication of internal corrosion.

6. Check a primary flight control surface for its condition of static balance.

7. Using the appropriate document, locate the jacking points of an airplane. Explain to the examiner the precautions that should be taken when jacking the aircraft.

8. Check an aircraft landing gear for the proper amount of toe-in or toe-out and for the proper amount of camber.

9. Explain to the examiner the correct way to check the track of a helicopter rotor system. Explain the correct way to adjust the blades to bring them into the proper condition of track.

10. Demonstrate to the examiner the correct way to determine whether or not a rod-end bearing is screwed into a push-pull tube to the proper depth.

11. Demonstrate to the examiner the correct way to attach a rod-end bearing to a control horn.

12. Explain to the examiner the proper way to correct a specified airplane for a wing-heavy condition.

13. Connect a control cable to a control horn with a clevis bolt. Demonstrate to the examiner the correct way to adjust the tightness of the nut, and the proper way to safety the nut to the bolt.

Airframe Inspection

Study Materials

Aviation Mechanic Series: Airframe Systems textbook .... ASA .... Chapter 8
Title 14 of the Code of Federal Regulations, Part 43 .... FAA
Title 14 of the Code of Federal Regulations, Part 91 .... FAA

Typical Oral Questions

1. What must the mechanic furnish the owner or operator of an aircraft if the aircraft he is giving a 100-hour inspection to proves to be unairworthy?

   A signed and dated list of all of the discrepancies that keep the aircraft from being airworthy.

2. Where can you find the recommended statement to use for recording the approval or disapproval of an aircraft for return to service after a 100-hour inspection?

   In 14 CFR §43.11.

3. Under what conditions can an aircraft be operated with a 100-hour inspection overdue?

   The aircraft can be operated for no more than 10 hours after an inspection is due for the purpose of flying it to a place where the inspection can be performed.

4. For how long can an aircraft be operated if a 100-hour inspection is overdue?

   For no more than 10 hours. This time beyond the 100 hours allowed must be subtracted from the time before the next inspection is due.

5. Under what conditions can an aircraft that is due an annual inspection be operated?

   It can only be flown when a special flight permit is issued.

6. What certification is required for a mechanic to be able to approve an aircraft for return to service after a 100-hour inspection?

   A mechanic certificate with Airframe and Powerplant ratings.

7. What determines whether or not an aircraft must be given a 100-hour inspection?

   Aircraft that carry persons for hire and aircraft that are used for flight instruction for hire must be given 100-hour inspections.

8. What is the difference between an annual inspection and a 100-hour inspection?

   The inspections themselves are identical. An annual inspection can be performed only by an A&P mechanic who holds an Inspection Authorization, while a 100-hour inspection can be performed by an A&P mechanic without an IA.

9. What certification is required for a mechanic to conduct an annual inspection and approve the aircraft for return to service after the inspection?

   A mechanic certificate with Airframe and Powerplant ratings and an Inspection Authorization.

10. Does the FAA require that a checklist be used when conducting an annual or a 100-hour inspection?

    Yes, according to 14 CFR §43.15(c)(1).

11. What certification is required for a mechanic to conduct a progressive inspection?

    A mechanic certificate with an Airframe and Powerplant ratings and an Inspection Authorization.

12. Where can you find the requirements for inspecting the altimeter and static system of aircraft that are operated under Instrument Flight Rules?

    In 14 CFR Part 43, Appendix E.

13. Where can you find the requirements for inspecting the ATC transponder that is installed in an aircraft?

    In 14 CFR Part 43, Appendix F.

Typical Practical Projects

1. Determine from the aircraft records furnished by the examiner whether or not any repetitive Airworthiness Directives must be complied with on a 100-hour inspection.

2. Using the aircraft model and serial number specified by the examiner, determine what Airworthiness Directives apply to the aircraft. Examine the aircraft maintenance records to determine if all of the applicable ADs have been complied with.

3. Determine from the aircraft records furnished by the examiner when the next 100-hour inspection is due and when the next annual inspection is due.

4. Prepare an aircraft for a 100-hour inspection. Perform the inspection. Make the correct maintenance record entries to show that the inspection has been conducted.

5. Describe to the examiner the record entry that must be made when an altimeter system has been inspected in accordance with 14 CFR §91.171.

Landing Gear Systems

Study Materials

Aviation Mechanic Series: Airframe Structures textbook.. FAA .... Chapter 6

Aviation Maintenance Technician Handbook—Airframe FAA-H-8083-31 Vol. 2...... FAA .... Chapter 13

Typical Oral Questions

1. What takes up the shock of the landing impact in an oleo shock strut?

   The metered transfer of oil from one compartment to another inside the shock strut.

2. What takes up the taxi shocks in an oleo shock strut?

   Compressed air.

3. How much oil should be put into an oleo shock strut?

   Deflate the strut completely, remove the filler plug and fill the strut with oil to the level of the filler plug.

4. What is the purpose of the centering cam in a nosewheel shock strut?

   The centering cam forces the nosewheel straight back with the strut before it is retracted into the nose wheel well.

5. How does a shimmy damper keep a nosewheel from shimmying?

   It acts as a small hydraulic shock absorber between the piston and the cylinder of the nosewheel shock strut.

6. What is the purpose of the debooster in a hydraulic power brake system?

   The debooster decreases the pressure and increases the volume of fluid going to the brakes. This gives the pilot better control of the brakes.

7. What should be done to hydraulic brakes when the pedal has a spongy feel?

   The spongy feel is caused by air in the brake. The brakes should be bled of this air.

8. What is used in a split wheel to keep air from leaking between the two wheel halves?

   An O-ring seal.

9. What causes an aircraft tire to wear more on the shoulders than in the center of the tread?

   Operating the tire in an underinflated condition.

10. What causes an aircraft tire to wear more in the center of the tread than on the shoulders?

    Operating the tire in an overinflated condition.

11. What should be done to an aircraft tire if the sidewalls are weather checked enough to expose the cord?

    The tire should be scrapped.

12. Why is it important that some aircraft with retractable landing gear be given a retraction test after new or retreaded tires are installed?

    It is possible in some aircraft that a new or retreaded tire can be different enough in size from the previous tire that it could lock up in the wheel well when the landing gear is retracted.

13. How is the correct amount of air in an oleo shock strut determined?

    By the amount the strut extends out of the cylinder when the weight of the aircraft is on it.

14. What should be done with a tire that was on a wheel which was overheated enough to melt the fusible plug in the wheel?

    The tire should be scrapped.

15. Where can you find the correct inflation pressure for the tires on an aircraft?

    In the aircraft service manual.

16. What is the purpose of the compensator port in the master cylinder of aircraft brakes?

    The compensator port in the master cylinder opens the brake reservoir to the wheel cylinders when the brakes are off. This prevents pressure from building up in the brake lines and causing the brakes to drag.

17. What is the purpose of the shuttle valve in the brake system of an aircraft using hydraulic power brakes?

    The shuttle valve is an automatic transfer valve. It allows the brakes to be operated by hydraulic system pressure under all normal conditions, but if this pressure is lost, it allows the brakes to be operated by the emergency backup system.

18. How does an antiskid brake system keep the wheels of an aircraft from skidding on a wet runway?

    The antiskid system monitors the rate of deceleration of the wheels. If any wheel slows down faster than it should (as it would at the beginning of a skid), the pressure on the brake in that wheel is released until the wheel stops decelerating, then the pressure is reapplied.

Typical Practical Projects

1. Demount a tire from an aircraft wheel, inspect the tire for wear, and the wheel and tire for damage. Reinstall the tire on the wheel.

2. Check an aircraft brake for the condition of the lining and the disks.

3. Check the fluid level in an aircraft brake master cylinder.

4. Bleed an aircraft brake.

5. Check the fluid level in an aircraft oleo strut. Inflate the strut with the correct amount of air or nitrogen.

6. Inspect a nosewheel shimmy damper, and service it with fluid if it is needed.

7. Check the main wheels of an aircraft for the proper amount of camber, and toe-in or toe-out.

8. Inspect an aircraft tire and explain to the examiner the conditions that could cause a tire to be unairworthy.

9. Replace the seals in the wheel cylinder of a single-disk brake.

10. Explain to the examiner the correct way to jack an aircraft so a landing gear retraction check can be performed.

11. Explain to the examiner the correct way to store aircraft tires.

12. Explain to the examiner the way a particular retractable landing gear is prevented from retracting when the weight of the aircraft is on it.

Hydraulic and Pneumatic Power Systems

Study Materials

Aviation Mechanic Series: Airframe Structures textbook .... ASA .... Chapter 5
Aviation Maintenance Technician Handbook—Airframe FAA-H-8083-31 Vol 2 ...... FAA .... Chapter 12

Typical Oral Questions

1. What are the two basic types of hydraulic fluid that are used in modern aircraft?
   Mineral base fluid and phosphate ester base fluid.

2. What kind of filter is a micronic filter?
   A filter with a special paper element.

3. Does the main hydraulic pump take its fluid from the bottom of the reservoir, or from a standpipe?
   The main pump normally takes its fluid from a standpipe, while the emergency pump takes its fluid from the bottom of the reservoir. If a break in the system should allow the main pump to pump all of its fluid overboard, there will still be enough fluid in the reservoir to allow the emergency system to extend the landing gear and actuate the brakes.

4. Why are some hydraulic reservoirs pressurized?
   Pressurization ensures that fluid will be supplied to the inlet of the pumps at high altitude where there is not enough atmospheric pressure to do this.

5. What is a double-action pump?
   A pump that delivers fluid with the movement of the pump handle in both directions.

6. Why do most engine-driven hydraulic pumps have a shear section in their drive couplings?
   If the pump should seize, the shear section will break, disconnecting the pump from the engine and preventing further damage.

7. What does an unloading valve do in a hydraulic system?
   The unloading valve, or pressure regulator, controls system pressure by shifting the pump outlet fluid from the pressurized system back into the reservoir when the system pressure is high enough. The fluid circulates with very little load on the pump until the system pressure drops to the regulator kick-in value. The pump then forces fluid into the system until the pressure builds back up to the regulator kick-out value.

8. What is the purpose of an accumulator in an aircraft hydraulic system?
   The accumulator holds pressure on the hydraulic fluid in the system. The pressure is held by compressed air or nitrogen acting on the fluid through a bladder, a diaphragm, or a piston.

9. What is the purpose of an orifice check valve in an aircraft hydraulic system?
   An orifice check valve allows full flow of fluid in one direction through the valve, but restricts the flow in the opposite direction.

10. Where are line-disconnect fittings normally located in an aircraft hydraulic system?
    Normally in the lines that connect the engine-driven pump to the aircraft hydraulic system.

11. What is meant by a single-action hydraulic actuating cylinder?
    A linear actuating cylinder that uses hydraulic fluid under pressure to move the piston in only one direction. The piston is returned by a spring.

12. What is the source of the compressed air that is used in a medium-pressure pneumatic system on a turbine-engine powered aircraft?
    This air is normally bled from one of the stages of the engine compressor.

13. What kind of device is used to control the speed of movement of the piston in a pneumatic actuator?
    A variable orifice.

14. Why do most high-pressure pneumatic systems include a moisture separator?
    When the pressure of the stored air is reduced to the value that is needed in the system, the temperature drops enough to freeze any water that is in the air. The moisture separators remove this water before it can freeze and block the system.

15. What is the difference between an open-center selector valve and a closed-center selector valve?

    Open-center selector valves are installed in series with each other, and the hydraulic fluid flows through their center when no component is being actuated. The valves act as a pump unloading valve. Closed-center selector valves are installed in parallel with each other. They direct fluid under pressure to one side of the actuator, and fluid from the other side of the actuator to the system return manifold. In their off position, they trap fluid in the lines between the valve and the actuator.

16. What is used to flush a hydraulic system that uses Skydrol hydraulic fluid?

    Trichlorethylene.

17. What is used to flush a hydraulic system that uses mineral base hydraulic fluid?

    Naphtha, varsol or Stoddard solvent.

18. Where can you find the type of hydraulic fluid that is required for a particular aircraft?

    In the maintenance manual for the aircraft. This information is also on a placard on the system reservoir.

19. What is used to remove phosphate-ester base hydraulic fluid from aircraft tires?

    Soap and water.

20. What must be done to the lines that are disconnected when servicing an aircraft hydraulic system?

    They must be capped with the correct fluid line cap or plug. Masking tape or other types of adhesive tape should never be used.

21. What are two ways aircraft hydraulic reservoirs may be pressurized?

    By an aspirator in the fluid return line or by bleed air from one of the engine compressors.

22. Why do some hydraulic pressure gages have a snubber installed between them and the hydraulic pump?

    The snubber keeps the gage from fluctuating.

Typical Practical Projects

1. Measure the air preload in an accumulator.
2. Charge an accumulator with the correct amount of air or nitrogen.
3. Determine the correct type of hydraulic fluid that is required by a particular aircraft and check the system for the correct amount of fluid.
4. Explain to the examiner the correct sequence for adjusting the pressure relief valves in an aircraft hydraulic system.
5. Inspect a hydraulic system filter and service it according to the instructions of the aircraft manufacturer.
6. Identify the type of hydraulic fluid by its color. Explain to the examiner the appearance of contaminated fluid.
7. Using a selection of seals furnished by the examiner, identify the seals that are one-way and those that seal in both directions.
8. Properly install an O-ring seal and backup ring in the cylinder of a hydraulic or pneumatic actuator.
9. Service the emergency air bottle in an aircraft brake system with the correct amount of air or nitrogen.
10. Remove and replace an actuating cylinder in an aircraft system. Purge the air from the system after the cylinder is reinstalled.
11. Explain to the examiner the action of an aircraft hydraulic system when the accumulator has no air preload.
12. Explain to the examiner the correct way to stop a leak at an MS flareless fitting.
13. Adjust the pressure at which a hydraulic pressure relief valve relieves pressure.

Cabin Atmosphere Control Systems

Study Materials

Aviation Mechanic Series: Airframe Systems textbook.. ASA.............................. Chapter 3

Aviation Maintenance Technician Handbook—Airframe FAA-H-8083-31 Vol. 2...... FAA .... Chapter 16

Typical Oral Questions

1. What are the two main gases that make up our atmosphere?

   Nitrogen and oxygen.

2. Why are the cabins of most turbine-powered aircraft pressurized?

   These aircraft fly at such high altitudes that supplemental oxygen would be needed for the occupants if the cabins were not pressurized.

3. Where does the pressurizing air come from on most turbine-powered aircraft?

   From air bled from one of the engine compressors.

4. Where does the pressurizing air come from on most of the smaller reciprocating-engine-powered aircraft?

   From the engine turbocharger.

5. What determines the amount of pressurization that an aircraft can use?

   The structural strength of the aircraft cabin.

6. How is cabin pressure controlled in a pressurized aircraft?

   More pressure than is needed is pumped into the aircraft cabin, and the pressure controller modulates the outflow valve to maintain the correct pressure in the cabin.

7. What is meant by the isobaric mode of cabin pressurization?

   The isobaric mode of cabin pressurization is the mode that keeps the cabin altitude constant as the aircraft changes its flight altitude.

8. What is meant by the constant differential mode of cabin pressurization?

   After the pressure in the aircraft cabin reaches the maximum value that is allowed by structural considerations, the constant differential mode of operation is the mode that holds the pressure inside the cabin a constant amount above the outside air pressure.

9. What is the function of the cabin outflow valve on a pressurized aircraft?

   The cabin outflow valve, which is controlled by the pressure controller, maintains the correct amount of pressure inside the cabin.

10. What is the function of the cabin pressure safety valve on a pressurized aircraft?

    The cabin pressure safety valve prevents cabin pressure from exceeding the maximum allowable differential pressure.

11. Why must pressurized aircraft have a negative pressure relief valve?

    The structure of an aircraft cabin is not designed to tolerate the inside pressure being lower than the outside pressure.

12. What keeps the cabin of a pressurized aircraft from being pressurized when the aircraft is on the ground?

    A squat switch on the landing gear holds the safety valve open when the aircraft is on the ground.

13. What are two types of air conditioning systems that may be installed on an aircraft?

    Air cycle systems and vapor cycle systems.

14. Where does the warm air come from that is used to heat the cabin of a large jet transport aircraft?

    Warm engine compressor bleed air is used.

15. Where does the warm air come from that is used to heat the cabin of most small single engine reciprocating-engine-powered aircraft?

    From a shroud around the engine muffler.

16. Where does the fuel come from that is used in an aircraft combustion heater?

    From the aircraft fuel tanks.

17. What happens to a combustion heater if the flow of ventilating air is restricted?

    If the ventilating air is restricted and the temperature reaches a preset value, the limit switch will cause the fuel to be shut off to the heater.

18. How is the heat removed from an aircraft cabin with a vapor-cycle air conditioning system?

    The cabin heat is absorbed by the refrigerant in the evaporator, and it is carried outside the aircraft where it is given up to the outside air in the condenser.

19. What produces the cool air in a vapor-cycle air conditioning system?

    Warm cabin air is blown across the evaporator where its heat is transferred into the refrigerant. The air that leaves the evaporator is cool.

20. Why must air cycle air conditioning systems incorporate a water separator?

    The rapid cooling of the air in the expansion turbine causes moisture to condense in the form of fog. This moisture is trapped in the moisture separator before the air is released into the cabin.

21. What is used as the refrigerant in a vapor-cycle air conditioning system?

    A Freon liquid refrigerant known as Refrigerant 12, or the more environmentally friendly R-134a.

22. What are three ways supplemental oxygen can be carried in an aircraft?

    As a high-pressure gas, in its liquid form, and as a solid in the form of a chemical candle.

23. What kind of gaseous oxygen must be used to service an aircraft oxygen system?

    Only aviators' breathing oxygen. Hospital oxygen and welding oxygen contain too much moisture to be used.

24. What is used to check an oxygen system for leaks?

    A special leak detector liquid that is a form of non-oily soap.

25. What is a continuous-flow oxygen system?

    An oxygen system that continuously flows a metered amount of oxygen into the mask.

26. What is a pressure-demand oxygen system?

    An oxygen system that flows oxygen to the mask only when the wearer of the mask inhales. Above a specified altitude, the regulator meters oxygen under pressure into the mask when the wearer inhales.

27. What identification must be stamped on an oxygen bottle that is carried in an aircraft?

    The identification DOT 3AA or DOT 3HT, the date of manufacture, and the date of all of the hydrostatic tests.

Typical Practical Projects

1. On an aircraft specified by the examiner, locate and identify the compressor, the condenser, the evaporator, and the service valves of a vapor-cycle air conditioning system.

2. On a pressurized aircraft specified by the examiner, locate and identify the source of pressurizing air, the cabin outflow valve, the cabin pressure safety valve, and the cabin pressure controller.

3. Explain to the examiner the correct way to service a vapor-cycle air conditioning system with refrigerant.

4. Explain to the examiner the correct way to check a vapor-cycle air conditioning system for leaks.

5. Demonstrate to the examiner the correct way to check an oxygen system for leaks.

6. Purge an oxygen system to remove all traces of air from the lines.

7. Service an oxygen system with the proper type and amount of oxygen.

8. Check the oxygen bottles in an aircraft for the required identification marks and for the status of their hydrostatic tests.

9. On an aircraft specified by the examiner, locate and identify the combustion heater, the fuel strainer, the fuel valve, and the thermostat.

10. Inspect for leaks in the portion of the engine exhaust system that supplies heat for the aircraft cabin heater.

Instrument Systems

Study Materials

Aviation Mechanic Series: Airframe Systems textbook.. ASA.............................. Chapter 4
Aviation Maintenance Technician Handbook—Airframe FAA-H-8083-31 Vol. 2...... FAA .... Chapter 10

Typical Oral Questions

1. What instruments in an aircraft are connected to the static system?

   The airspeed indicator, the vertical speed indicator, and the altimeter.

2. What types of repairs or alterations can a certificated A&P mechanic make to aircraft instruments?

   None. All repairs and alterations must be made by the instrument manufacturer or by an FAA-approved repair station certificated for the particular instrument.

3. What is the significance of a red radial line on the dial of an aircraft instrument?

   A red radial line marks a never-exceed condition.

4. What is the significance of a yellow arc on the dial of an aircraft instrument?

   A yellow arc marks a caution range of operation.

5. What is the significance of a green arc on the dial of an aircraft instrument?

   A green arc indicates the normal range of operation.

6. What is the significance of a white arc on the dial of an airspeed indicator?

   A white arc on an airspeed indicator indicates the airspeeds at which the flaps may be lowered.

7. What is used to warn a mechanic that the glass on an aircraft instrument that contains the range marks has slipped?

   A white slippage mark that extends across the lower part of the instrument cover glass and the instrument case bezel shows whether or not the glass has slipped. A slipped glass would put the range marks over the incorrect numbers.

8. Where can a mechanic find the range markings that are required on the instruments in a particular aircraft?

   In the Type Certificate Data Sheets for the aircraft.

9. What check must be made if a mechanic replaces any instrument that is connected to the instrument static system?

   The static system must be checked for leaks.

10. Why are many of the electrical instruments mounted in steel cases?

    A steel case concentrates the flux produced by magnets in the instrument and keeps it from affecting other nearby instruments.

11. Why must an aircraft instrument panel be electrically bonded to the primary aircraft structure?

    The bonding straps carry the return current from the instruments into the aircraft structure.

12. What error is corrected when an aircraft compass is swung?

    Deviation error.

13. What fluid is used in an aircraft magnetic compass?

    A special water-clear fluid that is similar to kerosine.

14. What is the maximum amount of deviation error that is allowed when a magnetic compass is installed in an aircraft?

    10 degrees.

15. What is the maximum amount of leakage that is allowed when checking the static system of an aircraft that is operated under Instrument Flight Rules?

    For an unpressurized aircraft, the system is checked with a 1,000-foot indication on the altimeter. It must not leak more than 100 feet in one minute. For a pressurized aircraft, the system is checked at the maximum certificated pressure differential of the cabin. It must not leak, in one minute, more than 2 percent of the equivalent altitude of the maximum differential pressure or 100 feet, whichever is greater.

16. Why must the length of the thermocouple leads not be altered when installing a cylinder head temperature indicator?

    An instrument operated by a thermocouple is a current-measuring device. The resistance of the thermocouple and its leads must be kept at the value specified for the indicator.

17. What should a manifold pressure gage read when the engine is not operating?

    It should read the existing barometric pressure.

18. What is the difference between a two-minute and a four-minute turn and slip indicator?

A two-minute turn indicator gives a one-needle-width deflection for a standard rate of turn (three degrees per second). A four-minute turn indicator gives a one-needle-width deflection for a half-standard rate of turn (1-1/2 degrees per second). A four-minute turn indicator has doghouse shaped marks located two needle widths away from the center mark. When the needle is lined up with a doghouse, the aircraft is making a standard rate turn.

19. What is the difference between a turn and slip indicator and a turn coordinator?

A turn and slip indicator is sensitive about only the yaw (vertical) axis of the aircraft. A turn coordinator uses a canted gyro which makes it sensitive about both the roll and yaw axes.

20. What is used as the sensor in the fuel tank for an electronic-type fuel quantity indicating system?

Tubular capacitors which extend across the fuel tank from top to bottom.

21. Why is a dual tachometer used on a single-engine helicopter?

One needle indicates the speed of the engine, and the other indicates the speed of the main rotor. When the needles are married, the clutch is not slipping and the rotor is solidly engaged to the engine.

22. In what units is the tachometer used on a turbine engine calibrated?

In percentage of the takeoff RPM.

23. What kind of system is used to measure the exhaust gas temperature of a turbine engine?

An averaging system made up of a series of thermocouples arranged around the inside of the exhaust duct of the engine.

24. What would likely cause the needle of an electrical oil temperature gage to peg on the high side of the instrument dial?

There is probably an open in the bulb circuit that is causing the instrument to see an infinite resistance. The higher the resistance of the bulb circuit, the further the needle moves across the dial.

25. What is used as a flowmeter for most of the small horizontally opposed fuel injected aircraft engines?

A pressure gage that measures the pressure drop across the injector nozzles.

26. What two sources of power are used to operate the gyro instruments in an aircraft?

They may be air operated, either by suction or pressure, or they may be electrically operated.

Typical Practical Projects

1. Determine from the proper source what range markings are required on the instruments of an aircraft specified by the examiner. Determine whether or not the instruments are properly marked.
2. Remove and properly reinstall an instrument from the panel of an aircraft.
3. Perform a static system check on an aircraft specified by the examiner. Determine from the proper source if the system meets the requirements for flight under Instrument Flight Rules.
4. Swing an aircraft compass. Properly prepare and install a compass correction card.
5. Install the proper range marks on glass of an aircraft instrument.
6. Using an altimeter to find the existing barometric pressure, check a manifold pressure gage to determine whether or not its pointers are set correctly.
7. Prepare a gyro instrument for shipping.
8. Check the pitot heater to determine whether or not it is functioning properly.
9. Locate and identify the components in an exhaust gas temperature indicating system.
10. Explain to the examiner the proper precautions that should be taken when removing a thermocouple-type cylinder head temperature indicator from an instrument panel.

Communication and Navigation Systems

Study Materials

Aviation Mechanic Series: Airframe Systems textbook.. ASA.............................. Chapter 5
Aviation Maintenance Technician Handbook—Airframe FAA-H-8083-31 Vol. 2...... FAA .... Chapter 11

Typical Oral Questions

1. Is a certificated airframe mechanic allowed to adjust a communications transmitter?

   No, this requires a license issued by the Federal Communications Commission.

2. Which frequency band is used for most aircraft communications?

   The VHF band, between 30 and 300 megahertz.

3. In which frequency band does the VOR equipment operate?

   In the VHF band, between 108.0 and 117.95 megahertz.

4. What is the preferred location for a VOR antenna on an airplane?

   On top of the aircraft, along the center line of the fuselage.

5. Which component of the Instrument Landing System shares the antenna with the VOR?

   The ILS localizer.

6. In what frequency band does the DME equipment operate?

   In the UHF band, between 962 and 1,024 megahertz and between 1,151 and 1,213 megahertz.

7. What is the preferred location for a DME antenna?

   Along the center line of the belly of the aircraft as far from any other antenna as is practical.

8. On what frequency is the marker beacon signal transmitted?

   75 megahertz.

9. What do the three marker beacon lights indicate to the pilot?

   The blue light indicates passage over the outer marker in an ILS approach, the amber light indicates passage over the middle marker, and the white light indicates passage over any other location specified on the instrument approach.

10. What precautions should be observed when working around aircraft radar?

    The pulses of electrical energy transmitted from a radar antenna are strong enough that they can seriously injure a person struck by them. They can be reflected from nearby buildings and return with enough power to destroy the receiver circuitry. For this reason, aircraft radar should never be operated when there are people or buildings within 100 yards of the antenna sweep, and it must not be operated when the aircraft is being fueled or defueled.

11. Which frequency band is used for long range communications from an aircraft?

    The high frequency band (2 to 25 megahertz).

12. What is meant by a transceiver?

    A piece of radio communications equipment in which all of the circuits for the receiver and the transmitter are contained in one housing.

13. On what two frequencies does the Emergency Locator Transmitter operate?

    121.5 and 243.0 megahertz.

14. Where is the ELT transmitter normally located on an aircraft?

    In the tail of the aircraft or as far aft as possible, so it will be least likely to be damaged in a crash.

15. What three components of an Instrument Landing System are installed in an aircraft?

The receivers for the localizer, the glide slope, and the marker beacons.

16. What kind of antenna is used for VHF communications?

    A vertically polarized whip antenna.

17. What kind of antenna is used for the ATC transponder?

    A UHF stub antenna.

18. What is the preferred location for the ATC transponder antenna?

    On the center line of the belly of the aircraft as far from any other antenna as is practical.

19. What kind of conductor is used to connect a VHF or UHF antenna to its receiver or transmitter?

    Coaxial cable.

20. What two types of antenna are used with most ADF receivers?

    A directional loop antenna and a nondirectional sense antenna.

21. Why is it important that all shock-mounted electronic equipment be connected to the aircraft structure with a bonding braid?

    The bonding braid is used to carry the return current from the equipment into the aircraft structure.

22. Why is it necessary to install a doubler on the inside of the aircraft skin when antenna is mounted on the skin?

    The doubler reinforces the skin so wind loads on the antenna will not cause the skin to flex and crack.

Typical Practical Projects

1. Locate and identify the antenna for the VOR, the DME, the ATC transponder, the ADF, and the Glide Slope, and the VHF communications equipment.

2. Locate the static discharge wicks on an aircraft and explain their function to the examiner.

3. Inspect the battery of the ELT and determine when it must be replaced.

4. Demonstrate to the examiner the way to determine that the ELT is not transmitting.

5. Demonstrate to the examiner the correct way to check the ELT for operation.

6. Locate and check the condition of the bonding braid that is used to provide a ground for some piece of electronic equipment.

7. Demonstrate to the examiner the correct way to check the accuracy of VOR equipment using a VOT signal.

8. Demonstrate to the examiner the way to determine the functioning of the ADF system.

9. Check all of the antenna on an aircraft for security of mounting.

10. Properly install a BNC connector on a piece of coax cable.

11. Locate and identify to the examiner the servos that are used in an autopilot system.

12. Check the installation of the avionics equipment in an aircraft to determine the condition of its mounting, the electrical connections, the antenna, and the ventilation and cooling provisions.

13. Check the shock mounts on a piece of avionics equipment to determine their condition and whether or not they allow the equipment to strike any adjacent component or structure.

Fuel Systems

Study Materials

Aviation Mechanic Series: Airframe Systems textbook... ASA .... Chapter 2
Aviation Maintenance Technician Handbook—Airframe FAA-H-8083-31 Vol. 2...... FAA .... Chapter 14
Title 14 of the Code of Federal Regulations, Part 23... FAA

Typical Oral Questions

1. What are two reasons Prist is added to the fuel that is used in a turbojet aircraft?

   Prist is a biocidal agent that (1) kills the scum-forming bacteria in the fuel tank, and (2) acts as an antifreeze agent, lowering the freezing point of the entrained water that is released from the fuel.

2. What are two types of fuel cells that are used in modern aircraft?

   Integral fuel cells (cells that are a sealed-off portion of the structure) and bladder-type cells.

3. Why are fuel tanks divided into compartments or have baffles installed in them?

   The compartments or baffles keep the fuel from surging back and forth as the aircraft changes its attitude in flight.

4. What is meant by an integral fuel cell?

   A part of the structure in which all of the seams and joints are sealed so they will be fuel tight. The structure itself then becomes the fuel tank.

5. Where are fuel system strainers located?

   One strainer is located in the outlet to the tank, and the main strainer is located in the fuel line between the outlet of the fuel tank and the inlet to the fuel metering device.

6. What are three uses of a centrifugal booster pump that is installed in an aircraft fuel tank?

   Booster pumps are used to produce fuel pressure for starting the engine, to keep the fuel from vapor locking at high altitude, and to transfer fuel from one tank to another.

7. What is meant by a compensated engine-driven fuel pump?

   An engine-driven fuel pump whose pressure relief valve is acted upon by the pressure of the atmosphere. A compensated pump varies its outlet fuel pressure so it will stay a constant amount higher than the pressure of the air that is entering the carburetor.

8. Why do engine-driven fuel pumps have a bypass valve in them?

   The bypass valve allows fuel from the booster pump to flow around the engine-driven pump mechanism for starting the engine and to supply the engine with fuel if the engine-driven pump should fail.

9. Why must an aircraft fuel valve have a detent in its operating mechanism?

   The detent gives the pilot a positive indication by feel when the selector valve is in the full ON and full OFF position.

10. What characteristic of the fuel is measured with the mass-flow fuel flowmeter that is used with turbine engine aircraft?

    The density of the fuel.

11. What is used as a flowmeter for a fuel-injected, horizontally opposed aircraft engine?

    A pressure gage that measures the pressure drop across the injector nozzles in the engine.

12. What is meant by a cross-feed system in an aircraft fuel system?

    A cross-feed system allows fuel from any tank to flow to any engine.

13. Why do some aircraft have provisions for jettisoning fuel in flight?

    Aircraft that are certificated with a higher takeoff weight than their allowable landing weight must have provision for jettisoning fuel. This allows enough fuel to be dumped to bring the weight down to that allowed for landing in case an emergency occurs before this amount of fuel can be burned off.

14. What must be done to a welded fuel tank before it can be repaired by welding?

    All of the fuel vapors must be purged by flowing live steam through the tank, by soaking it in boiling water, or by chemically neutralizing the fumes.

15. What safety precautions must be taken before a person enters the fuel cell of a large aircraft?

The cell must be thoroughly purged of all fumes, the person entering the cell must wear proper safety equipment, and there must be a person standing by on the outside of the cell.

16. What is meant by a single-point fueling system?

A pressure fueling system in which the fuel is pumped into the aircraft through an underwing fueling port. The fuel flows into a manifold, and then into the correct fuel tank as selected at the fueling station.

17. What gas is used to purge a fuel tank of all fuel vapors?

Carbon dioxide or nitrogen.

18. Why do turbojet aircraft normally have fuel temperature indicators?

Because of the low temperatures at which these aircraft operate, it is possible for water to precipitate out of the fuel and freeze on the filters, shutting off fuel to the engines. The temperature can be kept above freezing by directing it through a fuel heater as is needed.

19. How is a fuel leak indicated on a reciprocating-engine-powered aircraft?

The dye that is in the gasoline stains the area around the leak.

20. What is the purpose of a drip gage in the fuel tank of a large aircraft?

The drip gage allows a mechanic to check the fuel level in a tank from the bottom of the tank.

21. What safety precautions should be taken before an aircraft is defueled?

Be sure that the fuel truck is properly located, the truck and the aircraft are electrically grounded, all electrical power except that needed for the defueling operation is turned off, and the fuel is returned to the proper truck or other container.

22. What markings must appear near the filler opening of the fuel tanks on reciprocating-engine-powered aircraft, and on a turbine-powered aircraft?

On a reciprocating engine powered-aircraft: the word FUEL and the minimum grade of fuel.

On a turbine engine powered aircraft: the word FUEL, the permissible fuel designations, the maximum permissible fueling supply pressure, and the maximum permissible defueling pressure.

Typical Practical Projects

1. Properly identify the fuel in the tank of a reciprocating-engine-powered aircraft by its color.
2. Drain all of the sumps of an aircraft fuel system and check for the presence of water.
3. Remove and clean the fuel strainers in an aircraft fuel system. Reinstall the strainers and check them for leakage.
4. Locate and identify the fuel tank probes, the amplifier, and the indicator of an electronic fuel quantity system. Explain to the examiner the correct way to calibrate such a system.
5. Inspect the fuel selector valves of an aircraft and determine whether or not there is positive indication of the valve being fully on and fully off.
6. Locate in the proper documentation, the correct grade of fuel to be used in an aircraft specified by the examiner.
7. Demonstrate to the examiner the correct way to adjust the fuel pressure that is produced by an engine-driven fuel pump.
8. Explain to the examiner the correct way of repairing a leak in an integral fuel tank.
9. Explain to the examiner the correct way to check a bladder-type fuel cell for leakage and the correct way to repair this leakage.
10. Demonstrate to the examiner the correct way to use a fuel drip gage to measure fuel quantity.
11. Explain to the examiner the correct procedure to follow if a reciprocating engine-powered aircraft has been fueled with turbine fuel, and the engine has been run.

Electrical Systems

Study Materials

Aviation Mechanic Series: Airframe Systems textbook.. ASA.............................. Chapter 1
Aviation Maintenance Technician Handbook—Airframe FAA-H-8083-31 Vol. 1...... FAA .... Chapter 9
Advisory Circular 43.13-1B.. FAA ....Pages 11-1–11-118

Typical Oral Questions

1. What two things must you take into consideration when selecting the wire size to use in an aircraft electrical system installation?

   The current carrying capability of the wire and the voltage drop caused by the current flowing through the wire.

2. What is the maximum number of wires that should be connected to any single stud in a terminal strip?

   Four.

3. How is a wire bundle protected from chafing where the bundle goes through a hole in a fuselage frame or bulkhead?

   The edges of the hole are covered with a flexible grommet, and the bundle is secured to the structure with a cushioned clamp.

4. What kind of clamp is used to secure a wire bundle to the aircraft structure?

   A cushioned clamp.

5. Why are solderless splices usually better than soldered splices in the wiring of an aircraft electrical system?

   Soldered joints are usually stiff, and vibration can harden the wire and cause it to break. Solderless splices are designed to keep the joint flexible so vibration cannot cause the wire to break.

6. What size generator must be used in an aircraft electrical system if the connected electrical load is 30 amps, and there is no way of monitoring the generator output?

   When monitoring is not practical, the total continuously connected electrical load must be no more than 80 percent of the rated generator output. This would require a generator with a rating of 37.5 amps. Practically, a 40-amp generator would be installed.

7. Why must a switch be derated if it is used in a circuit that supplies incandescent lamps?

   The high inrush current caused by the low resistance of the cold filaments requires that the switches be derated.

8. On which wing is the red navigation light?

   On the left wing.

9. What kind of fault can be found in a generator armature with a growler?

   Shorted coils.

10. Does an aircraft engine electric starter use a series or a parallel motor?

    A series-wound motor.

11. What is the main disadvantage of aluminum wire over copper wire for use in an aircraft electrical system?

    Aluminum wire is more brittle than copper. It is more subject to breakage when it is nicked or when it is subjected to vibration.

12. What kind of rectifier is used in the small DC alternators installed in most light aircraft?

    Six silicon diodes arranged in a three-phase, full-wave rectifier.

13. What kind of instrument would you use to measure very high resistance?

    A megohmmeter. Megger is the registered trade name of such an instrument.

14. When is it important that aircraft electrical system wire bundles be enclosed in some type of conduit?

    Any time a wire bundle is routed in an area where it is subject to abrasion or rough handling, it should be enclosed in a conduit.

15. What size aluminum wire would be proper to replace a piece of four-gage copper wire?

    Two-gage. When you substitute aluminum wire for copper wire, use a wire that is two gage numbers larger.

16. What is the smallest size aluminum wire that is approved for use in aircraft electrical systems?

    Six-gage.

17. What three things must be synchronized before an aircraft AC generator is placed on the same bus with another AC generator?

    The voltage, the frequency, and the phase rotation.

18. How can the direction of rotation of the armature of a DC shunt-wound electric motor be reversed?

    By reversing the connections to the shunt field coil with reference to the armature.

19. What is meant by flashing the field of a generator?

    Restoring the residual magnetism to the frame of the generator. This is done by passing battery current through the field coils in the direction it normally flows when the generator is operating.

Typical Practical Projects

1. Using a wiring diagram of an aircraft electrical system, identify the switches, circuit breakers, wire splices, lamps, and motors.
2. Given the current requirements and the length of the wire, select the smallest size wire that will carry the current without overheating or producing more than the allowable voltage drop.
3. Install a solderless terminal on a piece of electrical wire.
4. Given the specifications of an aircraft generator, find its rated current output.
5. Check the diodes in a DC alternator for opens or shorts.
6. Using an ohmmeter, determine whether or not the filament in a light bulb is good.
7. Using a voltmeter, measure the output voltage of an aircraft generator.
8. Explain to the examiner the correct way to flash the field of an aircraft generator.
9. Using a voltmeter and an ohmmeter, demonstrate to the examiner the correct way to troubleshoot an aircraft electrical circuit.
10. Inspect the ground cable of the battery installed in an aircraft for condition, tightness of connections, and for evidence of corrosion.
11. Explain to the examiner the correct way to adjust the voltage controlled by a vibrator-type voltage regulator.
12. Using a growler and continuity light, check the armature of an aircraft generator for shorted or open coils.
13. Secure an electrical wire bundle to an aircraft structure using the proper clamps and grommets.
14. Using the illustrated parts list for a particular aircraft, inspect an anticollision light installation to see whether or not it conforms with the aircraft manufacturer's installation drawings.
15. Using the correct test instruments, measure the current that flows through an electrical load specified by the examiner.
16. Demonstrate to the examiner the correct way to tie an electrical wire bundle with spot ties.
17. Given the specifications of a shock-mounted electrical component, describe to the examiner the correct choice of a bonding strap.
18. Splice an electrical wire, using the correct type of splice and the correct insulation.
19. Correctly attach wires to the terminals of a quick-disconnect connector.

Position and Warning Systems

Study Materials

Aviation Mechanic Series: Airframe Structures textbook .... ASA .... Chapter 6
Aviation Mechanic Series: Airframe Systems textbook .... ASA .... Chapters 1 and 4

Typical Oral Questions

1. What is an annunciator panel in an aircraft?

   A single location that contains all of the warning and condition lights for the aircraft. This makes it easy for the pilot to monitor all of the systems at a glance.

2. Which device in an antiskid brake system would likely cause the brakes to fail to release when a skid developed?

   A malfunctioning antiskid valve.

3. Where are the skid detectors located in an antiskid brake system?

   In the center of the wheel hub.

4. What condition could cause a takeoff warning system to actuate?

   The takeoff warning system gives an aural warning when the power lever is advanced for takeoff if the flight controls for the stabilizer, the flaps, and the speed brakes are in an unsafe condition for takeoff.

5. What would cause the warning horn to sound when the throttles are pulled back, reducing the engine power for landing?

   The warning horn will sound if any of the landing gears are not down and locked.

6. What is indicated by a red light in the landing gear position indication portion of the annunciator panel.

   The red light indicates that the landing gear is not in a safe condition for landing.

7. Where is the landing gear safety switch normally located?

   On one of the landing gear shock struts so the switch is actuated when the weight of the aircraft is on the landing gear.

8. What information is given to a pilot to indicate that all of the landing gears are down and locked?

   Three green lights are used on most aircraft to indicate that all three landing gears are down and locked.

Typical Practical Projects

1. Locate and identify for the examiner: the down-limit switches, the up-limit switches, and the landing gear safety switch on an aircraft with retractable landing gear.

2. Locate and identify for the examiner: the wheel speed sensors, the antiskid valves, and the antiskid control box in an aircraft equipped with an antiskid brake system.

3. Using a wiring diagram of the landing gear warning system of an aircraft, explain to the examiner the malfunctions that could cause the warning horn to fail to sound when the throttles are retarded and the landing gear is not down and locked.

4. Demonstrate to the examiner the correct way to check the wheel speed sensors of an antiskid brake system for operation.

5. Demonstrate to the examiner the correct way to check for a malfunction in a cabin door warning light circuit.

6. Using the correct circuit diagram, indicate to the examiner the items you would check if a takeoff warning system failed to warn the pilot that the flaps were not in the takeoff position.

Ice and Rain Control Systems

Study Materials

Aviation Mechanic Series: Airframe Systems textbook... ASA.............................. Chapter 6

Aviation Maintenance Technician Handbook—Airframe FAA-H-8083-31 Vol. 2...... FAA .... Chapter 15

Typical Oral Questions

1. Why is it important that ice not be allowed to build up on airplane wings in flight?

   Ice distorts the shape of the airfoil and destroys the aerodynamic lift. The weight of the ice loads the aircraft down.

2. Are pneumatic deicer boots operated before ice forms or after it has formed?

   Pneumatic deicer boots are not operated until ice has formed over them. When the boot inflates, it breaks the ice, and the air flowing over the airfoil blows it away.

3. Where does the air come from to operate the pneumatic deicer boots on a reciprocating-engine powered airplane?

   From the discharge side of the air pump that is used to operate the gyro instruments.

4. What is meant by a wet vacuum pump?

   A vacuum pump that uses engine oil to lubricate its steel vanes. A dry vacuum pump uses carbon vanes, and it does not require any oil for lubrication.

5. What is the purpose of the oil separator in a deicer system?

   Oil separators are used with wet vacuum pumps to remove the lubricating oil from the discharge air before this air is used in the deicer boots.

6. How are rubber deicer boots cleaned?

   By washing them with mild soap and water

7. How does a thermal anti-icing system operate?

   Hot compressor bleed air is ducted into a special chamber between a double skin in the leading edge of the wing. This hot air is controlled by a timer so ice is allowed to build up, and then the hot air breaks its bond to the skin. Air gets under the ice and blows it away.

8. What is used to remove frost from an aircraft before flight?

   A mixture of isopropyl alcohol and ethylene glycol.

9. How is ice prevented from forming on the windshield of modern jet transport airplanes?

   The windshield has a heater element embedded in it. Electric current heats the windshield and keeps ice from forming on it.

10. How is ice kept from forming on the pitot tube of an airplane?

    Pitot tubes are heated by electric current flowing through heater elements that are built into them.

11. What are two ways rain can be kept from obstructing the pilot's vision through the windshield of an airplane?

    The rain can be blown away by a high velocity blast of compressor bleed air, or it can be wiped away with electrically or hydraulically operated windshield wipers.

12. When should rain repellent be used on an airplane windshield?

    Only when the windshield is wet with rain.

13. How is carburetor ice prevented in the engines of the smaller aircraft?

    Heated air is directed into the carburetor. This heat comes from a muff around a part of the engine exhaust system.

14. How are rubber deicer boots attached to the leading edges of aircraft wings and tail surfaces?

    Some of them are attached with machine screws and Rivnuts; others are bonded to the surface with an adhesive.

15. What keeps an electrically heated windshield from overheating?

    Heat sensors built into the windshield control the current that is used to heat the windshield.

Typical Practical Projects

1. Demonstrate the correct way to inspect and clean rubber deicer boots.

2. Actuate a pitot heater and check it for proper operation.

3. Explain to the examiner the way electrical propeller deicers operate.

4. Locate and identify the components in a pneumatic deicer system.

5. Locate and identify the components in an electrically heated windshield system.

6. Examine the blades of a windshield wiper system, and check them for the correct tension and for the correct parking position.

7. Locate and identify the containers of chemical rain repellent.

Fire Protection Systems

Study Materials

Aviation Mechanic Series: Airframe Systems textbook.. ASA .... Chapter 7

Aviation Maintenance Technician Handbook—Airframe FAA-H-8083-31 Vol. 2...... FAA .... Chapter 17

Typical Oral Questions

1. Does a thermocouple fire detection system warn the pilot of a general overheat condition?

   No, it operates on the rate of temperature rise, and it identifies only a fire.

2. Does a thermal switch fire detection warn the pilot of a general overheat condition?

   No, it only actuates when there is a fire.

3. What type of fire extinguishing agent is best for both cabin fires and engine fires?

   Halon 1301.

4. What is a major disadvantage of "CB" fire extinguishing agent for extinguishing aircraft fires?

   It is corrosive to aluminum and magnesium.

5. Why is carbon tetrachloride not recommended as a fire extinguishing agent?

   Carbon tetrachloride produces phosgene, a deadly gas, when it is exposed to flames.

6. What is used as a fire extinguishing agent in most of the high-rate discharge systems installed in aircraft?

   One of the halogenated hydrocarbons, such as Halon 1301, pressurized with nitrogen.

7. What happens when the Fire-Pull T-handle is pulled in a jet transport aircraft?

   The bottle discharge switch is uncovered and armed, the generator field relay is tripped, fuel is shut off to the engine, and hydraulic fluid is shut off to the pump. The engine bleed air is shut off and the hydraulic pump low-pressure lights are deactivated.

8. What releases the fire extinguishing agent in a high-rate discharge bottle?

   An electrically ignited powder charge blows a knife through a seal in the HRD bottle.

9. What three types of fire extinguishers are recommended for extinguishing cabin fires in an aircraft?

   Water, Halon 1301, and carbon dioxide.

10. How does a carbon monoxide detector warn the occupant of an aircraft of an excess of carbon monoxide?

    The detector crystals in the indicator change color.

11. What are two types of smoke detectors that are used in an aircraft?

    Photoelectric and visual smoke detectors.

12. Where are smoke detectors normally located in an aircraft?

    Smoke detectors are located in baggage compartments and cargo areas.

13. What type of fire extinguisher is recommended for extinguishing a brake fire?

    A dry-powder type extinguisher.

14. How is a CO_2 fire extinguisher checked for the amount of charge it contains?

    By its weight.

15. How can you determine whether or not a built-in fire extinguishing system has been discharged?

    By checking the blowout plugs on the outside of the aircraft near the extinguisher agent bottles.

16. What precaution must you observe when checking the electrical squib of an HRD fire extinguisher bottle for electrical continuity?

    It takes only a small amount of current to ignite the powder charge, and the method of testing must not send this amount of current through it.

17. What is indicated if the red disk in a built-in fire extinguishing system is blown out?

    The agent bottle has been discharged because of an overheat condition.

Typical Practical Projects

1. Inspect a hand held CO_2 fire extinguisher and determine if it contains a full charge.

2. Examine a carbon monoxide detector and explain to the examiner the way it would change if it were exposed to an excess of CO.

3. Explain to the examiner the correct way to check a continuous loop fire detector system for its condition.

4. Locate and identify the components in a thermocouple-type fire detection system.

5. Check a fire detection system specified by the examiner for its condition.

6. Inspect an HRD fire extinguishing system for security of its components and for the state of charge of its bottles.

7. Explain to the examiner the way the electrical circuit for an HRD fire extinguishing system should be checked.

8. Locate and identify the blow-out plugs that indicate the status of the fire extinguisher system in an aircraft.

9. Demonstrate to the examiner the correct way to use a CO_2 fire extinguisher to extinguish a fire in fuel that has spilled on the ground.

10. Demonstrate to the examiner the correct way to use a CO_2 fire extinguisher to extinguish an induction system fire in a reciprocating-engine-powered airplane.